JOURNAL FOR THE STUDY OF THE NEW TESTAMENT
SUPPLEMENT SERIES

267

Editor
Mark Goodacre

Editorial Board
John M.G. Barclay, Craig Blomberg, Elizabeth A. Castelli, Kathleen E. Corley,
R. Alan Culpepper, James D.G. Dunn, Craig A. Evans, Stephen Fowl, Robert Fowler,
Simon J. Gathercole, Michael Labahn, Robert Wall, Robert L. Webb

The Original Language of the Lukan Infancy Narrative

Chang-Wook Jung

T & T CLARK INTERNATIONAL
A Continuum imprint
LONDON • NEW YORK

BS
2589
.J86
2004

Copyright © 2004 T&T Clark International
A Continuum imprint

Published by T&T Clark International
an imprint of Continuum

The Tower Building, 15 East 26th Street,
11 York Road, Suite 1703,
London SE1 7NX New York, NY 10010

www.tandtclark.com

All rights reserved. No part of this publication may be reproduced or transmitted in any form or by any means, electronic or mechanical, including photocopying, recording or any information storage or retrieval system, without permission in writing from the publishers.

British Library Cataloguing-in-Publication Data
A catalogue record for this book is available from the British Library

Typeset by Tradespools, Frome, Somerset
Printed on acid-free paper in Great Britain by Antony Rowe Ltd, Chippenham, Wilts

ISBN 0-567-08205-9 (hardback)

Contents

Acknowledgments	vii
Abbreviations and Main Text Editions	ix
INTRODUCTION	1

Chapter 1
THE GREEK OF THE LUKAN INFANCY NARRATIVE IN THE HISTORY
OF SCHOLARSHIP 5
    A. A Historical Survey on the Greek of the Gospel of
        Luke chs 3–24 5
    B. A Survey of Scholarly Views on the Greek of the
        Infancy Narrative 22
        I. The Translation Theory 23
        II. The Imitation Theory 33

Chapter 2
DEFINITIONS OF SEMITISMS AND SEPTUAGINTALISMS, LUKANISMS
AND NON-LUKANISMS 45
    A. Semitisms and Septuagintalisms 45
        I. Various Views on the Definition of Semitisms
           and Septuagintalisms 45
        II. The Definition of Septuagintalisms and
           Semitisms 54
    B. Lukanisms and non-Lukanisms 58
        I. The Definition of Lukanisms 58
        II. The Definition of non-Lukanisms 59

Chapter 3
A CLOSE EXAMINATION OF THE GREEK OF THE INFANCY
NARRATIVE 62
    A. Quotations 62
        I. The Quotation in Luke 2.23 68
        II. The Quotation in Luke 2.24 85
        III. The Quotation in Luke 1.15 92

B.	Allusions	103
	I. The Allusion in Luke 1.17	103
	II. The Allusion in Luke 1.37	112
	III. The Allusion in Luke 1.31	121
C.	Phraseology	132
	I. Constructions in Luke 1.5	135
	II. πλῆθος στρατιᾶς οὐρανίου 'A Multitude of the Heavenly Army' in Luke 2.13	160
	III. The Usage of the Passive Form of the Verb πίμπλημι with ἡμέρα or χρόνος	170
	IV. The Construction προβαίνω + ἐν (ταῖς) ἡμέραις (εἰμι)	179
	V. Words and Phrases in Luke 1.13b	193

Chapter 4
CONCLUSION 208
  A. Summary 208
  B. The Implication of This Study for the Quest of Source(s) for the Infancy Narrative 212

Bibliography
Index of References 217
Index of Authors 235
247

Acknowledgments

The writing of a PhD dissertation is a daunting task, full of uncertainty, frustration, even fear, and loneliness, especially for someone who, like me, must write his dissertation in a foreign country. I could not have completed the work without the spiritual, academic and emotional support of others. I want to express, therefore, my thanks to those who have helped me to complete this research project.

First and foremost, I give thanks to God for answering my prayers and providing me with the insight, perseverance, and even financial support needed to complete my work.

Second, I want to acknowledge the help of my supervisor, Professor M.C. de Boer, whose academic guidance and warm care made it possible for me not only to complete the thesis but also to greatly improve its quality. Due thanks have to be given also to my co-supervisor, Professor Tj. Baarda, and to the members of the reading committee of my dissertation, Professors T. Muraoka, M.J.J. Menken, P.W. van der Horst, and E. Talstra. Their comments and suggestions were useful in improving the quality of the thesis. I am grateful also to my friend William Manus for careful proofreading.

Third, I would like to thank churches and people who have supported me financially; Jong-Chun Choi, the senior pastor of Bundang Central Church, Choong-Hyun Church, and my brother Chang-Yong Jung. I also wish to give my thanks to the Faculty of Theology at the Free University for providing me with some financial aid. Special thanks have to be given to Dr Montsma, registrar of the theology department of the University. He has worked hard to find financial resources for my study.

Finally, it is my privilege to express my deep thanks to my dear wife, Myung-Ae Kim. In an eight and half year span of marriage that involved the birth of two children in Holland, she was and continues to be a source of constant encouragement and love. It is to her that this work is dedicated.

ABBREVIATIONS AND MAIN TEXT EDITIONS

1. Abbreviations

AJT	American Journal of Theology
ANRW	H. Temporini and W. Haase (eds.), *Aufstieg und Niedergang der römischen Welt*
ASTI	Annual of the Swedish Theological Institute
ATR	Anglican Theological Review
BAGD	W. Bauer, *A Greek-English Lexicon of the New Testament and Other Early Christian Literature*, ET, (eds.) W.F. Arndt, F.W. Gingrich, and F. Danker
BDF	F. Blass, A. Debrunner, and R.W. Funk, *A Greek Grammar of the New Testament*
BDR	F. Blass, A. Debrunner, and F. Rehkopf, *Grammatik des neutestamentlichen Griechisch*
BHS	Biblia Hebraica Stuttgartensia
Bib	Biblica
BibNot	Biblische Notizen
BibTrans	The Bible Translator
BJRL	Bulletin of the John Rylands University Library of Manchester
BZ	Biblische Zeitschrift
CBQ	Biblical Catholic Quarterly
EKKNT	Evangelisch-katholischer Kommentar zum Neuen Testament
EvQ	Evangelical Quarterly
ExpTim	Expository Times
FilNeo	Filologia Neotestamentaria
GL	Geist und Leben
IBS	Irish Biblical Studies
ICC	International Critical Commentary
Int	Interpretation
JBL	Journal of Biblical Literature

JBR	*Journal of Bible and Religion*
JBT	*Jahrbuch für biblische Theologie*
JNES	*Journal of Near Eastern Studies*
JQR	*Jewish Quarterly Review*
JSemSt	*Journal of Semitic Studies*
JSNT	*Journal for the Study of the New Testament*
JSNTSS	*Journal for the Study of the New Testament*, Supplement Series
JSOTSS	*Journal for the Study of the Old Testament*, Supplement Series
JTS	*Journal of Theological Studies*
HTR	*Harvard Theological Review*
LCL	Loeb Classical Library
NA	Nestle (ed.), *Novum Testamentum Graece*, rev. by K. and B. Aland *et al.*
NICNT	New International Commentary on the New Testament
NIGTC	The New International Greek Testament Commentary
NCBC	New Century Bible Commentary
NovT	*Novum Testamentum*
NT	*New Testament*
NTS	*New Testament Studies*
OT	Old Testament
OTS	*Oudtestamentische Studien*
PTR	*Princeton Theological Review*
RevQ	*Revue de Qumrân*
SBLDS	SBL Dissertation Series
SeB	*Sémiotique et Bible*
ST	*Studia theologica*
TDNT	G. Kittel and G. Friedrich (eds.), *Theological Dictionary of the New Testament*
TynNTC	Tyndale New Testament Commentaries
TLG	Thesaurus Linguae Graecae
TZ	*Theologische Zeitschrift*
VT	*Vetus Testamentum*
WBC	Word Biblical Commentary
WUNT	Wissenschaftliche Untersuchungen zum Neuen Testament
ZAW	*Zeitschrift für die alttestamentliche Wissenschaft*
ZNW	*Zeitschrift für die neutestamentliche Wissenschaft*

2. Main Text Editions

Greek OT passages are cited from A. Rahlf's edition (1935); the Göttingen edition (1931–) and the Greek text edited by H.B. Swete (1909) have been consulted when textual variants needed to be compared. Passages from the Hebrew OT are quoted in accordance with BHS (1967–77), and passages from the NT in accordance with NA^{27}.

For statistical research into the occurrence of an expression in classical and Hellenistic Greek literature including the papyri, this study has used TLG. Passages cited from classical and Hellenistic authors usually derive from LCL; when other editions have been used, they are cited in the footnotes.

INTRODUCTION

It has long been recognized that the Greek of the Lukan infancy narrative (Luke 1–2) displays numerous Semitic features compared with that of the remainder of the Gospel (Luke 3–24) and Acts. This phenomenon has been interpreted in one of two major ways:

(1) the Greek of the Lukan infancy narrative is a translation of a Semitic (i.e., Hebrew) source (or sources), and (2) this Greek imitates the Greek of the Septuagint (LXX). The former position is known as 'the translation theory' and the latter one 'the imitation theory' (also known as 'the pastiche theory'). Recent scholarship tends to accept the view that the Greek of the infancy narrative was influenced by the style of the Septuagint. Other scholars, however, still believe that the narrative was at some stage (if not by the author of the Gospel of Luke himself then by someone prior to him) translated from a Hebrew source or sources. More importantly, many recent proponents of the imitation theory simply assume rather than prove the theory to be correct. They either rely on the claims of other scholars without investigating the matter further for themselves, or simply presuppose that since the Evangelist (= the author of the Gospel of Luke) probably did not speak or write a Semitic language (Hebrew and/or Aramaic), he could not have used or translated a version of the infancy narrative in Hebrew. Furthermore, some important instances of possible translation from Hebrew into Greek in the Lukan infancy narrative proposed by the advocates of the translation theory remain unanswered by the proponents of the imitation theory. There is also the fact that many commentaries on the Lukan infancy narrative confusingly follow the translation theory in some places and the imitation theory in others.[1] This situation indicates that a fresh investigation into the question of the origin and the character of the language of the infancy narrative is necessary. The primary purpose of this study is to determine whether the Semitic features of the Greek of the Lukan infancy narrative can best be explained as the result of a

---

1. For documentation of these claims, see Chapter 1.

translation from Semitic (Hebrew) source material or as the result of the imitation of the Greek of the LXX.

As the comments in the previous paragraph indicate, an investigation into the original language of the infancy narrative is closely related to the issue of the possible source(s) the Evangelist may have used in composing the infancy narrative. The translation theory claims that the Evangelist had access to a source or sources written in Hebrew. A variation of this theory holds that if the Lukan infancy narrative, or portions thereof, can be traced back to an originally Semitic source, the author of Luke's Gospel only had access to this source in Greek translation. The imitation theory, while claiming that the Evangelist composed the infancy narrative under the influence of the Greek of the LXX, does not necessarily exclude the possibility that the Evangelist had access to source material written in Greek (i.e., in addition to, or apart from, the LXX itself). A secondary aim of this study, therefore, is to draw out the implication of this investigation into the Greek of the infancy narrative for the source issue. Did the author rely on a source or sources and in what language was this source material written?

This study is also related, though indirectly, to the interpretation of the infancy narrative. A follower of the translation theory will tend to resolve an exegetical difficulty, whether this be serious or trivial, by pointing to an underlying Semitic original. A follower of the imitation theory will tend to do the same by pointing to the influence of the language of the LXX. The different solutions to the problem of Luke's Greek in the infancy narrative can thus influence the interpretation of the text. This investigation of the Greek of the infancy narrative promises to give greater clarity about the possible use of sources by the Evangelist and as a result more certainty about the meaning the Evangelist intended to convey with the text (and *mutatis mutandis* with the story the text tells). It lies beyond the scope of the present work, however, to enter into the full implication of the investigation into the Greek of Luke 1–2 for the interpretation of the infancy narrative, though some suggestions along this line will be made in the course of the analysis undertaken in Chapter 3.

The study is organized as follows. Chapter 1, consisting of two main sections, provides a history of scholarship on the Greek of the infancy narrative. The first section begins by tracing the development of various scholarly views on the nature of the Greek of the New Testament in order to provide a context within which to locate the discussion of Lukan Greek in general and of the infancy narrative in particular. This first section also contains the historical survey of scholarship on the Greek of Luke 3–24. The second section is devoted to a survey of scholarly views on the Greek of the infancy story in Luke 1–2 and on the source(s) the Evangelist may have used in composing the infancy narrative.

From these surveys of scholarship, it will become evident how important it is to define Semitisms and Septuagintalisms as precisely as possible in order to be able to decide whether the infancy narrative was translated from a Hebrew source (or sources) or composed in imitation of Septuagint style. Confusion primarily arises from the absence of accurate definitions of the Septuagintalism and the Semitism. For this reason, Chapter 2 will deal with various views on the definition of the Semitism and the Septuagintalism and delineate these two concepts. In addition, Lukanisms and non-Lukanisms are defined in order to be able to distinguish the Evangelist's own style from that of any possible source material written in Greek and thus to be able to determine the possible influence of such a Greek source (or sources) on the Greek of the infancy story.

With these definitions in hand, the Greek of the Lukan infancy narrative will be investigated in Chapter 3. This chapter, which constitutes the heart of the investigation, consists of three sections: (1) quotations, (2) allusions, and (3) phraseology. The first section will seek to determine whether quotations from the Old Testament (OT) in the infancy narrative rely on the LXX or on the Hebrew text. The study of these quotations is critical for the issue of the original language of the source material used by the Evangelist: if an OT quotation in the infancy narrative clearly depends on the LXX, the possibility that the source material used by the Evangelist was originally composed in Hebrew is significantly *decreased*. By contrast, if the wording of the quotation is demonstrably dependant on the Hebrew text and not on the LXX, the possibility that the source material was originally composed in Hebrew is significantly *increased*. A fundamental problem is how to define a quotation and thus how to distinguish a quotation from an allusion. For this reason, the definition of a quotation will be discussed first. The manner in which a quotation is introduced or 'marked' (e.g., with the use of an introductory formula) is an important dimension of this problem. Not only the quoted text but also the manner in which the quotation is introduced or 'marked' will be examined to decide whether the quotation originates from a source or from Luke's own hand.

The study of allusions to the OT is also a critical test for our investigation and for the same reason that the study of quotations is. Some allusions come close to being quotations and the two are not always easy to distinguish clearly, as already noted above. The Lukan infancy narrative contains many allusions (especially in the Magnificat and the Benedictus), and it will not be possible within the scope of this dissertation to treat all the instances that have been proposed. We must confine our analysis to those allusions which proponents of the translation theory have regarded as strong support for their case. Such instances will be scrutinized afresh to determine whether they depend on the LXX or on the Hebrew text.

Along with quotations and allusions, phraseology, i.e., Greek words and phrases which seem to be Semitic to one degree or another, also requires investigation, since such phraseology has been used to support the translation theory. Here again, because such phraseology may involve an allusion to one or more passages in the Old Testament, it is not always possible to draw a clear line between the study of allusions and the study of seemingly Semitic phraseology. However, a distinction between allusions and phraseology will be proposed. Furthermore, only clear instances which have been used to support the translation theory will be treated.

The final chapter will summarize what has been examined in the preceding chapter with an eye on the primary aim of this study, i.e., to decide whether the Semitizing Greek of Luke's infancy narrative can best be explained in terms of (a) the Evangelist's reliance on source material originally written in Hebrew (and translated into Greek by him or a predecessor, (b) imitation of the Greek of the LXX. As indicated above, an investigation into the Greek of the Lukan infancy narrative is closely related to the issue of a source (or sources) which the Evangelist may have used in composing the infancy narrative; for this reason, the final chapter will also address the issue of source material which the Evangelist had at his disposal and the influence of its language on the Greek of the infancy narrative.

Chapter 1

THE GREEK OF THE LUKAN INFANCY NARRATIVE IN THE HISTORY OF SCHOLARSHIP

This chapter will describe scholarly views on the Greek of the Gospel of Luke chs 3–24, followed by a detailed examination of the Greek of Luke's opening two chapters. The first section, 'A Historical Survey on the Greek of the Gospel of Luke chs 3–24' will serve as a preface. It will initially trace the development of various scholarly positions on the nature of NT Greek. The purpose is to provide a context within which to locate discussion of Lukan Greek in general and of the infancy narrative in particular.

A. *A Historical Survey on the Greek of the Gospel of Luke chs 3–24*

The Gospel has traditionally been attributed to Luke,[1] probably a

---

1. The oldest extant copy of the Gospel, P75 (A.D. 175–225), includes 'εὐαγγέλιον κατὰ Λουκᾶν'. *Papyrus Bodmer XIV–XV: Evangiles de Luc et Jean*. Tome I (eds. R. Kasser and V. Martin; Cologny Geneva: Bibliotheque Bodmer, 1961), pl. 61, 150. See M. Hengel, *Die Evangelienüberschriften* (Heidelberg: Carl Winter/Universitaetsverlag, 1984), p. 11. See also J. Nolland, *Luke 1–9:20* (Word Biblical Commentary, 35a; Dallas: Word Books, 1989), Introduction, pp. xxxiv–xxxv. The Muratorian canon (A.D. 170–180) ascribes the Gospel to Luke, and the so called anti-Marcionite prologue (A.D. 175), attributing the Gospel to Luke, describes Luke as composing it moved by the Holy Spirit. Church fathers also confirm Luke's authorship. Irenaeus certainly contends that Luke composed the Gospel (*Adversus haereses*, 3.1,1). Tertullian assigns the Gospel to Luke (*Adversus Marcionem*, 4.2,2) and Clement of Alexandria also attributes it to Luke (cited in Eusebius, *Historia ecclesiastica*, 6.25,6). For these references, see A. Plummer, *A Critical and Exegetical Commentary on the Gospel according to St. Luke* (ICC; Edinburgh: T. & T. Clark, 4th edn, 1953), Introduction, pp. xvi–xvii; E.E. Ellis, *The Gospel of Luke* (London: Oliphants, 2nd edn, 1974), pp. 40–41; C.F. Evans, *Saint Luke* (TPI New Testament Commentaries; London: SCM Press, 1990), pp. 5–7. See also F.F. Bruce, *The Acts of the Apostles: Greek Text with Introduction and Commentary* (London: Tyndale Press, 1951; 3rd edn. Grand Rapids: Eerdmans, 1990), pp. 1–2. For more detailed information and argument on the references, see Fitzmyer, *The Gospel According to*

gentile,[2] although it is actually anonymous. From the earliest Christian centuries, Luke has been described as a physician[3] and a well-educated

---

Luke, I–IX. Anchor Bible 28 (New York/London/Toronto/Sydney/Auckland: Doubleday, 1981), pp. 37–40; see also his book, *Luke the Theologian: Aspects of his Teaching* (London: Geoffrey Chapman, 1989), pp. 7–11. The large majority of scholars believe that the traditional view is essentially correct. D.L. Bock, *Luke 1.1–9.50* (BECNT; Grand Rapids: Baker, 1994), pp. 4–6; Fitzmyer, *Luke I–IX*, p. 41. Ellis, *Luke*, p. 42. See also Plummer, *St. Luke*, Introduction, xvii and Nolland, *Luke 1–9.20*, Introduction, p. xxxvii. One may raise a question about the validity of the traditional view by pointing out that it was inferred solely from some NT texts: Phil 24; Col. 4.14; 2 Tim. 4.11; Acts 16.11f (a so-called 'we' section). However, it must be remembered that the tradition concerning the Gospel of Luke is uncontested and unambiguous, different from that concerning Matthew. As I.H. Marshall notes, 'there is never any suggestion of a rival candidate for the honour of writing the Gospel.' *The Gospel of Luke: A Commentary on the Greek Text* (NIGTC; Exeter: Paternoster, 1978), pp. 33–34. To assume that the clear and unanimous tradition stemmed solely from the NT texts presumes too much. It is also remarkable that the Gospel is attributed to a relatively insignificant figure who is not an 'apostle' or a 'man of apostolic times'. For details, see Ellis, *Luke*, p. 41 and Fitzmyer, *Luke I–IX*, p. 41. 'A combination of external and internal evidence suggests,' as Bock claims, 'that Luke was the author of both works (*Luke-Acts*)' (*Luke 1.1–9.50*, p. 5).

2. As to Luke's ethnic background, most scholars agree that Luke was a gentile (see Evans, *Luke*, p. 12 and Ellis, *Luke*, p. 52, both of whom point out the general tendency, though they do not follow it), but the evidence is not strong as in the case of Luke's authorship (see Plummer, Fitzmyer, Bock, etc. See also F. Bovon, *Das Evangelium nach Lukas: Lk 1.1–9.50* [Zürich: Benziger/Neukirchener Verlag, 1989], p. 22). They base their argument on the following elements: 'the superior quality of the Greek language, the avoidance of Semitic words (except *Amen*), the omission of gospel traditions about Jesus' controversies with the Pharisaic understanding of the Law and about what is clean or unclean, the transformation of Palestinian local colour and details into Hellenistic counterparts' (Fitzmyer, *Luke I–IX*, pp. 41–42). They also make Col. 4.10f. and 14 reliable sources for their argument. According to these verses, Luke did not belong to those of 'the circumcision'. Ellis, pointing out that most scholars believe Luke was a gentile, attempts to refute this argument by arguing that it is not clear to whom the phrase refers. He argues that Luke was a Hellenistic Jewish Christian (*Luke*, pp. 52–53). See also Evans who is cautious to accept the view of the majority (*Luke*, p. 13). Bock rejects Ellis' assertion by positing that all Jews were circumcised and Luke was not included in the circumcised (Col. 4.14) [*Luke 1.1–9.50*, p. 6; see also Plummer, *Luke*, Introduction, pp. xviii–xix]. Fitzmyer argues that Luke is a gentile Christian, not as a Greek, as most scholars assume, but as a Semite (*Luke I–IX*, pp. 42–47). It is hard to decide whether he had a Semitic cultural background. While following the view of the majority that Luke is a gentile Christian, this study will also try to confirm its validity.

3. Col. 4.14 records that Luke was a physician. Upon this reference alone church tradition describes Luke as a physician, and thus as a well-educated man. Both the Muratorian canon and the so-called anti-Marcionite prologue describe him as a physician. D.L. Bock, 'Luke, Gospel of', in *Dictionary of Jesus and the Gospels* (eds. J.B. Green, S. McKnight, and I.H. Marshall; Downers Grove, Leicester: Intervarsity, 1992), p. 496. See also A.R.C. Leaney, *The Commentary on the Gospel According to St. Luke* (London: Adam & Charles Black, 1958), p. 1. The Muratorian canon and anti-Marcionite prologue appear to have relied on the reference in Col. 4.14. Scholars thus are cautious to confirm the tradition that Luke was a physician. For the problem of this reference, see R. Maddox, *The Purpose of Luke-Acts* (Göttingen:

man. Jerome, for example, comments that Luke, a medical doctor, made use of the most versatile Greek among all the Evangelists.[4] Many modern scholars follow Jerome's description of Lukan Greek by insisting that the Gospel of Luke was written in the most polished Greek or in the most literary Greek compared with the Greek of other NT authors.[5] Although Jerome's statement is correct in a sense, there is another side to the coin. As H.F.D. Sparks notes, even the casual reader of the Gospel of Luke is confronted with a problem: 'After an author's preface of four verses,' he notes, 'written in good idiomatic Greek, he is presented with a narrative of twenty-four chapters, of which the background, the ideas, and much of the phraseology, are unquestionably Semitic.'[6] As a result, scholars began to offer various views about Lukan Greek.[7]

Before discussion of Lukan Greek in the last century begins, academic tendencies concerning NT Greek in the eighteenth and nineteenth century need to be highlighted. Prior to A. Deissmann's published work in the last part of the nineteenth century and the beginning of the

---

Vandenhoeck & Ruprecht, 1982), pp. 6–7. Scholars like W.K. Hobart attempt to authenticate this reference by proving the presence of medical elements in the language of Luke-Acts. W.K. Hobart, *The Medical Language of St. Luke: A Proof from Internal Evidence that 'The Gospel of according to St. Luke' and 'The Acts of the Apostles' Were Written by the Same Person, and that the Writer was a Medical Man* (Dublin: Hodges, Figgis, 1882; reprinted Grand Rapids: Baker, 1954). For a brief survey on the topic, see Bruce, *The Acts of the Apostles*, p. 7. See also Fitzmyer, *Luke I–IX*, pp. 51–53. Though this position is not appreciated any more, it is not necessary to assume the information in Col. 4.14 to be incorrect.

4. *Epistle* XX. 4. Jerome does not treat Lukan Greek with special interest, but inserts his ideas about the Greek of the Evangelists while commenting upon the hymn of the Jewish people on Jesus' entrance into Jerusalem in Mt 21. 9 (Par. Mk 11. 9, Jn 12. 13, and Lk. 19. 38). After mentioning that 'hosanna', which Luke intentionally omitted in 19.38, is a Hebrew word like 'alleluia' and 'Amen', he writes, 'Lucas igitur, *qui inter omnes evangelistas Graeci sermonis eruditissimus fuit*, quippe ut medicus et qui in Graecis evangelium scripserit, -qui a se iudicavit proprietatem sermonis transferre non posse, melius arbitratus est tacere, quam id ponere, quod legenti faceret quaestionem.' The literal translation of the italicized sentence is 'who was the most learned (one) of Greek language among all the Evangelists.' The text revised by Isidorus Hiberg is used here. '*Sancti Eusebii Hieronymi Epistulae*,' p. 108.

5. Plummer notes that Luke is the most versatile of all the NT writers (*St. Luke*, Introduction, p. 49). M. Gilmour, *The Gospel according to St. Luke and St. John* (The Interpreter's Bible, vol. 8; Nashville: Abingdon, 1952), p. 3, states that Luke's Greek was the most polished one in the NT except for the Greek of the author of the Epistles to the Hebrews. According to Bruce, the Gospel of Luke alongside Acts is 'the most literary part of the NT' (*The Acts of the Apostles*, p. 66). D. Guthrie writes that Luke used a good literary Koine Greek, though he accepts the presence of some Semitisms. *New Testament Introduction* (Downers Grove: Intervarsity, 1990), p. 131.

6. H.F.D. Sparks, 'The Semitisms of St. Luke's Gospel', *JTS*, 44 (1943), p. 129.

7. One could infer that if Luke, the most literary of NT authors, contains many Semitisms, other Evangelists probably utilize more Semitisms. This inference is misleading, for Semitisms occur more frequently in Luke than in the other Gospels. For details, see below.

twentieth century,[8] many scholars had taken the 'Holy Ghost Greek' theory, also known as the 'sacred Greek' theory, and the 'Jewish Greek' theory for granted.[9] A sacred Greek theory arose from the notion that the Bible was mechanically inspired by the Holy Spirit. NT Greek as well as the content of the NT obtained its inspired peculiarity as distinguished from the Greek of secular literatures. Scholars bound both the Greek of the LXX and that of the NT together and named it 'sacred Greek'.[10] The idea of mechanical inspiration saturated the field of text and language. As the Holy Spirit inspired the content of the Bible, the language of the NT was also inspired. The Greek of Luke, according to this theory, does not require special treatment, since Luke wrote his Gospel in a sacred Greek as the other Evangelists did. The sacred Greek theory is closely connected with the Jewish Greek theory. Both theories emphasize the peculiarity of Biblical Greek, although each explains the origin of the peculiarity differently. While the sacred Greek theory considers the peculiarity as stemming from divine inspiration, the Jewish Greek theory finds its origin in 'racial idioms' of the NT writers. The sacred Greek theory was dismissed gradually as the mechanical inspiration theory for the NT collapsed.[11] Nevertheless, the Jewish Greek theory dealt with later in detail survived the severe criticisms of both theories.[12]

---

8. For Deissmann's publications, see below.

9. Richard Rothe calls NT Greek 'Holy Ghost Greek' (*Zur Dogmatik* [Gotha, 1863], p. 238). H.J. Cadbury notes that NT students in the eighteenth century assumed NT Greek as a distinct dialect of Greek. *The Making of Luke-Acts* (London: SPCK, 1927. 2nd edn, 1958), pp. 115–16.

10. Christian teachers and writers assumed that the LXX translation was inspired, and was not inferior to the Hebrew original. Cf. H.B. Swete, *Introduction to the Old Testament in Greek* (rev. R.R. Ottly; Cambridge: The University Press, 1914), p. 462. Even some ancient Jewish scholars like Philo also did so for the Pentateuch. For details, see M. Müller, *The First Bible of the Church: A Plea for the Septuagint* (JSOTSS, 206; Sheffield: Sheffield Academic Press, 1996), especially pp. 66–78.

11. To distinguish the form from the content is necessary in order to keep the Bible a sacred book, since the language of the NT may include some deficiencies because of the errors of copyists or their lack of language skill. Conservative scholars accordingly have to admit that NT Greek language itself is not holy, if they want to claim the divine inspiration of the Bible.

12. A few recent commentaries hold that the translation of the LXX produced a peculiar Greek shaped by Semitisms. For example, C.F. Evans notes that the Greek of the LXX was 'strongly moulded by the idiom of Hebrew original and would overlap, and itself be a source of, written or spoken Jewish Greek.' 'It was, however,' he continues, 'more self-consciously religious, and established itself as a style proper to religious narrative and speech.' C.F. Evans, *Saint Luke* (TPI New Testament Commentaries; London: SCM Press, Philadelphia: Trinity Press International, 1990), pp. 40–41. He also assumes Palestinian Greek to be a dialect impregnated with Semitic idioms which Luke took over (Evans, p. 40).

Dissenting voices against both the sacred Greek theory and the Jewish Greek theory, whether claiming that NT Greek was a language for the whole Jewish people or only for Jewish Christians, have their origin in the German scholar Deissmann.[13] 'The notion of the canon,' according to him, 'is transferred to the language and there is fabricated a "sacred Greek" of Primitive Christianity.'[14] He acknowledges that the early Christians adopted many religious terms peculiar to their language. He adds, however, that such a phenomenon may not be restricted to Christianity, as it was widespread throughout all religions. In order to undertake a precise investigation for NT Greek, a reader must be free 'first of all from such a methodological notion as the sacred exclusiveness of its texts'. Deissmann develops his argumentation in light of the discovery of the papyri in Egypt. The Greek of the papyri, written in contemporary Hellenistic Greek, is substantially the same as the Greek of the NT. Most of the alleged Semitisms in NT Greek, Deissmann contends, can be found in the vernacular Greek of the market place. Deissmann concedes, however, that LXX Greek, a translation Greek, is different from NT Greek, which is mainly non-translation Greek, and thus that the Septuagint was written in 'Semitic Greek' (*Bible Studies*, 67, pp. 69–70).[15]

Deissmann suggests that the Greek of Luke's Gospel and the *Wisdom of Jesus Ben Sira* produces striking evidence against the advocates of the Jewish Greek theory. Both of them include a prologue which could never be labelled 'Jewish Greek' or even Hebraic.[16] The remainders of both books, however, contain Semitic Greek. The supporters of the Jewish Greek hypothesis, Deissmann claims, must answer the question of why the authors of these two writings did not employ so-called 'Jewish Greek' for their prologues. He posits that in the preface the authors adopted their spoken Greek, while afterwards they depended directly or indirectly on

---

13. His argument needs to be scrutinized to prevent confusion. While most scholars consider Deissmann a representative of the vernacular Greek theory, some recent scholars point out his logical weakness and argue that he must be included in a group advocating that Semitic Greek exercised influence on NT Greek. S.E. Porter, 'The Language of the Apocalypse in Recent Discussion', *NTS*, 35 (1989), p. 593. This confusion arises from the complexity of his statements. Porter's criticism of Deissmann will be evaluated in note 48.

14. A. Deissmann, *Bible Studies* (2nd edn., trans. A. Grieve; Edinburgh: T. & T. Clark, 1903), p. 65.

15. Porter complains that most scholars ignore his concession. See note 13. For further argument, see Porter's article, 'The Language of the Apocalypse in Recent Discussion', p. 594.

16. A. Deissmann, 'Hellenistic Greek with special Consideration of the Greek Bible', in *The Language of the New Testament: Classic Essays* (JSNTSS, 60; ed. S.E. Porter; Sheffield: Sheffield Academic Press, 1991. Trans. of 'Hellenistisches Griechisch', in *Realencyklopaedie für protestantische Theologie und Kirche*, vol. 7; ed. A. Hauck; Leipzig: Hinrichs, 1899), p. 56.

Semitic source material (or *Vorlage*) ('Hellenistic Greek', p. 57).[17] Deissmann's argument begs clarification. He concedes that LXX Greek was a Semitic Greek. However, he claims that the NT was written in vernacular Greek, and that most of the alleged Semitic idioms do not represent real Semitisms, but vulgarisms. Although Semitisms exist in the NT, especially in the Gospel of Luke, they stem from Semitic sources, not from the influence of the LXX. Therefore Deissmann denies or at least minimizes the influence of the LXX on the NT, especially with respect to the Gospel of Luke. In order to gain more support, Deissmann's argument must await further discoveries or the arrival of help from linguistic scholars and computer aids.

While it is not necessary to evaluate his entire position about NT Greek, the following points concerning Deissmann's argument on Lukan Greek need to be mentioned. He overlooks the possibility that Luke imitated Attic Greek style in the prologue and the LXX in the remainder. This is the simplest answer to the question of why Luke preferred to write his Gospel in semitized Greek rather than in polished Greek. In addition, the prologue of the Gospel is too short to confirm with certainty that Luke here made use of spoken Greek.[18]

---

17. Some scholars, recognizing the peculiarities of Lukan Greek, argue that the Gospel of Luke obtained Semitisms from Semitic sources on which the Evangelist depended, or attribute them to the 'subject matter'. According to the latter explanation, the authors of the Greek Bible adopted Semitic expressions because the topics which they dealt with were accompanied by 'Semitic' circumstances. However, some of them can not be explained in this way, nor by positing a source. Luke's Gospel uses Semitic expressions like 'καὶ ἐγένετο' more frequently than other NT books. Luke apparently inserted the construction 'καὶ ἐγένετο' in the parts or places where Luke appears to have depended on Mark (cf. Lk. 19.29 – Καὶ ἐγένετο ὡς ἤγγισεν; Mk 11.1 – Καὶ ὅτε ἐγγίζουσιν). The subject matter explanation must face the same criticism. Some episodes with settings in Palestine, of course, show an abundant influence of Semitisms (e.g., the visits of the angel Gabriel [1.11–20; 26–38; cf. 2.9–14]; the priestly service at the temple etc.). However, all the episodes in the Gospel of Luke happened in Palestine (for details, see H.F.D. Sparks, 'The Semitisms of the Acts', *JTS*, ns. 1 [1950] pp. 27–28). Therefore an explanation on the basis of sources and subject matter must be surrendered as an insufficient answer to our present problem, although they play a role in shaping semitized parts. It is impossible to deny the influence of sources on Lukan Greek, when we compare the Greek of the Gospel with that of Acts. For example, the use of the participle in the Gospel of Luke is very different from that in the Acts of the Apostles. While the frequency of the participle in Acts reaches seven percent, the highest occurrence in the NT, it remains just about five percent in Luke, which, though higher than the Gospel of John, is similar to Matthew and Mark. These data indicate that even Luke relied on some semitized sources and was influenced by Semitisms. Nonetheless this analysis does not necessarily demonstrate that all of Luke's Semitisms originated from the sources.

18. Deissmann also does not recognize the apparent difference between the Greek of chs 1–2 and that of chs 3–24. The Greek of the Lukan infancy story is different from that of the remaining chapters. For details, see next section of this chapter.

Although following Deissmann in major issues, J.H. Moulton betrays a different position concerning Lukan Greek.[19] He agrees with Deissmann in refuting the theory of 'Jewish Greek'. Moulton also stands in the same line with Deissmann when he declares that 'the Greek of the Pentateuch is the pure vernacular of daily life with a very small admixture of abnormal phrases due to literal translation.'[20] He departs from Deissmann, however, by arguing that Luke made use of deliberate archaism proper to literature as distinguished from ordinary educated speech ('New Testament Greek', p. 68). Whereas Deissmann assumes that Luke depended on a Semitic original except in the prologue, Moulton claims that Luke imitated the Greek of the LXX 'consciously'.

H.J. Cadbury, who agrees with Moulton, disputes the existence of a 'language of the Holy Ghost' or a special dialect of Greek (*Making of Luke-Acts*, p. 116). In the eighteenth century, according to Cadbury, scholars assumed that the Greek of the LXX and other Jewish writings reflected a distinct Greek dialect. Thus, they argued that biblical authors including Luke composed books in their own special style, and called it sometimes 'the language of the Holy Ghost', or at other times 'a special Jewish dialect of Greek'. Cadbury declares with certainty that no spoken Greek by the Jews existed which 'differed extensively and uniformly from the language of other nationals'. He concedes that there are some characteristics which are to be explained by the influence of the translation of Semitic originals, of Aramaic, or of the Septuagint itself. Many biblical

---

19. The first resistance to Deissmann's proposal, in fact, comes from LXX scholars. F.C. Conybeare and G. Stock propose that the Greek of the LXX influenced the Greek of the NT. They refute Deissmann's assertion that the Greek Bible does not present a linguistic unity when compared with contemporary 'profane Greek', but only when compared with classical Greek. F.C. Conybeare and G. Stock, *Grammar of Septuagint Greek: with Selected Reading from the Septuagint According to the Text of Swete* (repr. of 1905 edition, Peabody: Hendrickson, 1988), p. 22. They claim that the linguistic unity of Biblical Greek exists, which is different from the current Alexandrian of the papyri or from the language of first-century authors. No one can understand the Greek of the NT, they continue, without comparing it to the OT, since NT Greek was influenced by the phraseology of the Old Testament (*Grammar of Septuagint Greek*, p. 21). New Testament writings could not have been produced without the LXX. NT Greek, then, is not a literary Greek but a colloquial Greek 'of men whose original language and way of thinking were Semitic.' Thus, it is 'so deeply affected by Semitic influence', that the original language of NT authors, which was a Semitic language, influenced their colloquial language in which the NT was written. Unfortunately, Conybeare and Stock misunderstand the situation of NT authors. Only the author of Revelation may actually fit their description. It is speculative to think that Luke, probably a gentile Christian, thought in a Semitic way to the effect that the way of thinking affected his language.

20. J.H. Moulton, 'New Testament Greek in the Light of Modern Discovery', in *The Language of the New Testament: Classic Essays* (repr. of the article in *Essays on Some Biblical Questions of the Day: By Members of the University of Cambridge*, ed. H.B. Swete; London: Macmillan, 1909), p. 72.

writers show genuine Semitic characteristics, while others exhibit the influence of Aramaic, or of the Septuagint (*Making of Luke-Acts*, p. 117). However, the majority of such characteristics did not stem from Semitic or religious antecedents, but from the vernacular speech of their time. Not only the Hellenistic Jews but also contemporary Egyptians, Macedonians, Anatolians and Italians could understand NT Greek.

Cadbury makes use of Deissmann's research into Lukan Greek, but like Moulton he claims that Luke, imitating the LXX without depending on Semitic sources, composed the Gospel in a Hellenistic Greek different from either classical or modern Greek (*Making of Luke-Acts*, p. 114). Depending on the new discoveries of his time in Egypt, he argues that NT Greek was understood not only by Hellenistic Jews but by the contemporary Greek-speaking world. As the result of these discoveries, many words, which scholars formerly regarded as peculiar to Luke's style, fell into the category of a common vocabulary which his contemporaries employed. While Cadbury, following Deissmann, denies the possibility of a 'Jewish Greek' or 'Holy Ghost Greek', claiming that Luke wrote his books, the Gospel and Acts, in vernacular Greek, he concludes, unlike Deissmann, that the Greek of the LXX affected Lukan Greek style by virtue of Luke's imitation of the LXX. Although he notes that he can not decide whether such imitation is conscious or unconscious (contrast Moulton above), he is receptive to the possibility of conscious imitation by mentioning that imitation was not unusual at that time (*Making of Luke-Acts*, p. 132). Lukan Greek, according to him, 'is not of the lowest cultural grade on the one hand, nor on the other does he belong with the Atticists of the time.'[21] Luke's style betrays Semitisms, whether they originate from conscious imitation or unconscious imitation (*Making of Luke-Acts*, p. 122). However, it also betrays a literary tendency, according to Cadbury, in its avoidance of Semitic words like 'hosanna', 'Gethsemane', or 'Golgotha'.

Although Deissmann continued his publications and added more evidence from new discoveries in Egypt, and many confidently argued for 'the LXX pastiche theory',[22] they could not prevent other scholars from suggesting theories based on alleged Semitisms. This result was inevitable since many parts of the NT seemed difficult to interpret correctly without studying Semitic originals. Moreover, new discoveries were not sufficient to satisfy other scholars. C.C. Torrey, having found that the NT involves many difficult passages and while not confining himself to the Gospel of Luke, claims that the Gospels and Acts were the translation of an Aramaic

---

21. Atticists tried to imitate the style of the classical masters of Greek prose by rigid rules. See Cadbury, *The Making of Luke-Acts*, pp. 114–15.

22. The term 'pastiche' is synonymous with 'imitation' in this study.

original.²³ He remarks that a gospel intended for the Palestine Jews could not have been written in any language other than Aramaic, since Hebrew had not been the language of popular literature for centuries. He notes further that the national sentiment of the Jews in Palestine could not allow a Greek gospel. Torrey argues that many mistranslations in the NT Greek Bible can be explained only by assuming Aramaic originals. With his great knowledge of Hebrew and Aramaic as well as Greek, he investigates some problematic verses and tries to clarify the meanings of some dubious passages by suggesting Aramaic originals. Concerning the Gospel of Luke, he admits that it was published in Greek, but posits that the gospel is composed entirely from Semitic documents 'assembled and translated by Luke himself', while Mark, Matthew, and John were written and published in Aramaic.²⁴ Torrey expresses his surprise at A.T. Olmstead's assertion²⁵ that the gentile author did not have any knowledge of Semitic languages,²⁶ and he details his own argument on the problem of Lukan Greek in his book, *Our Translated Gospels*. After refuting the LXX pastiche theory and restricting Luke's imitation to the opening phrase for a new paragraph 'and it came to pass (καὶ ἐγένετο or ἐγένετο δέ),' he notes that 'all the other Semitic idioms, "Biblical" only in the sense that they are translation Greek, are Luke's faithful and skilful reproduction of the text which lay before him.'²⁷ Luke substituted 'a less literary use' in order to render his original exactly (*Our Translated Gospels*, p. 58).²⁸

Torrey's presuppositions are open to criticisms. His critical weakness lies in his extreme view. The robust debate against an Aramaic original is summarized by F.L. Horton, Jr. Horton criticizes the Aramaic original theory by pointing out some questionable assumptions, for example, 1) that Jesus taught *only* in Aramaic, 2) that the language of the earliest

---

23. C.C. Torrey, *Our Translated Gospels: Some of the Evidence* (London: Hodder and Stoughton, n.d), Preface, p. ix. Torrey has predecessors like A. Meyer, J. Wellhausen, E. Nestle, G. Dalman, and F. Blass. For their publications and the weakness of their views, see S.E. Porter, 'The Greek of the New Testament As a Disputed Area of Research', in *The Language of the New Testament: Classic Essays*, p. 18. Torrey is followed by scholars like C.F. Burney, J.A. Montgomery, R.B.Y. Scott, and M. Burrows. For their arguments, see E.C. Maloney, *Semitic Interference in Marcan Syntax* (SBL Dissertation Series, 51; Chico: Scholars, 1981), pp. 12–13.

24. Interestingly, Torrey, a representative dissident of the vernacular Greek theory, assents to Deissmann's proposal that Luke depended on Semitic sources, although Deissmann does not argue explicitly that the Gospel was translated from Aramaic.

25. A.T. Olmstead, 'Could an Aramaic Gospel be Written?', *JNES*, 1 (1942), pp. 41–75.

26. C.C. Torrey, 'The Aramaic of the Gospels', *SBL*, 61 (1942), p. 84.

27. *Our Translated Gospels*, Introduction, p. lvii. Torrey asserts that Luke 'gives by far the plainest and most constant evidence of being a translation' of all the Gospels (Torrey, p. lix).

28. Although Torrey's book caused a sensation at first, his thesis could not withstand the counter arguments from other scholars, and finally most found his argument unconvincing.

14   *The Original Language of the Lukan Infancy Narrative*

Christians was Aramaic, and 3) that there was an early Christian Aramaic literature.[29] The majority of scholars believe that Jews in first-century Palestine spoke three languages – Aramaic, Hebrew, and Greek – or at least that Aramaic was not the only spoken language in Palestine.[30] Moreover, most literary writings in Palestine were written in Hebrew rather than in Aramaic, which was confined to so-called vulgar or folk genres, not the religious genres.[31] Furthermore, it is not plausible that Luke, who was probably a gentile author, and who depended on several sources for his composition (Lk. 1.1), translated Aramaic originals to compose his Gospel for a gentile audience.[32] No one today maintains the

---

29. F.L. Horton Jr., 'Reflections on the Semitisms of Luke-Acts', in *Perspectives on Luke-Acts* (ed. C.H. Talbert; Edinburgh: T. & T. Clark, 1978), p. 5.

30. For the multilingual situation in first-century Palestine, see J. Fitzmyer, 'The Languages of Palestine in the First Century A.D.', *CBQ*, 99 (1980), pp. 501–31. See also S.E. Porter, *Verbal Aspect in the Greek of the New Testament with Reference to Tense and Mood* (New York/Bern/Frankfurt/Paris: Peter Lang, 1989), pp. 154–56; Porter, 'Jesus and the Use of Greek in Palestine', in *Studying the Historical Jesus: Evaluations of the State of Current Research* (New Testament Tools and Studies, XIX; eds. B. Chilton and C.A. Evans; Leiden: Brill, 1994), pp. 123–54. Porter notes that the multilingual environment in first-century Palestine differed slightly from that in Alexandria, where the LXX was translated. The 'prestige language' was still Greek in Palestine as in Alexandria, but Aramaic was the prestige language for some NT authors. He concludes that '1st-cent. Palestine was almost certainly a bilingual (Greek and Aramaic) if not trilingual (plus Hebrew) environment for most inhabitants, including Jesus' (*Verbal Aspect*, p. 156). For the use of Greek in first-century Palestine, see A.W. Argyle, 'Did Jesus Speak Greek?', *ExpTim*, 67 (1955–56), pp. 92–93, 383; Argyle, 'Greek among the Jews of Palestine in NT Times', *NTS*, 20 (1974), pp. 87–89. He argues that Greek as well as Aramaic was spoken by Jesus and his disciples. See also G. Mussies, 'Greek in Palestine and the Diaspora', in *The Jewish People in the First Century* (eds. S. Safrai and M. Stern; Compendia Rerum Judaicarum ad Novum Testamentum, Section I, vol. 2; Assen, the Netherlands: Van Gorcum, 1976), pp. 1040–64. Mussies accepts the importance of Greek in first-century Palestine, though he emphasizes that Greek was not a prestige language but only a second one. For the rebuttal of the thesis that Hebrew was not spoken in first-century Palestine, see J. M. Grintz, 'Hebrew as the Spoken and Written Language in the Last Days of the Second Temple', *JBL*, 79 (1960), pp. 32–47. For a more cautious attitude, see J.A. Emerton, 'The Problem of Vernacular Hebrew in the First Century A.D. and the Language of Jesus', *JTS*, n.s. 24 (1954), pp. 1–23. Emerton admits that it is probable that Hebrew was spoken as a vernacular by some Jews in the first century A.D., while it is certain that Aramaic was widely used in Judaea.

31. Aramaic was used to compose some writings, but these were usually intended for the Diaspora and limited to certain genres. For detailed description, see M.O. Wise, 'Language of Palestine', in *Dictionary of Jesus and the Gospels*, pp. 437–39.

32. Mainstream scholarship suggests that the Gospel of Luke was written for a gentile audience. See Sparks, 'The Semitisms of St. Luke's Gospel', p. 132. Fitzmyer also notes that 'it is widely held today that Luke has written his Gospel for a Gentile Christian audience, or at least one that was predominantly Gentile Christian' (*Luke I–IX*, pp. 57–58). These Gentile Christians, according to him, were not 'in a predominantly Jewish setting,' but 'in a

theory of translated Aramaic originals, even though several troublesome passages may lend themselves to that theory.

Criticizing the Aramaic original theory, Sparks, a New Testament scholar, suggests a more logical and comprehensive view concerning the influence of the LXX on NT Greek. Concentrating on the Greek of Luke, he claims that although some Semitisms stemmed from sources, Luke himself added others by semitizing consciously ('The Semitisms of St. Luke's Gospel', p. 131). In other words, Luke was 'a deliberate semitizer'. He criticizes the Aramaic original theory by arguing that no scholar can demonstrate an Aramaic original for Lukan Greek ('The Semitisms of St. Luke's Gospel', p. 132). Some of Luke's Semitisms, Sparks continues, derived from Biblical Hebrew rather than Aramaic. Does this mean that Luke learned Hebrew to write his Gospel? Sparks' answer is 'no'. A gentile author has no reason to learn Biblical Hebrew in order to compose his Gospel for gentile audiences. How can we, then, account for Semitisms in Luke? There remains, Sparks argues, only one alternative, the Septuagintal pastiche theory. He strengthens his position by offering five pieces of evidence: 1) Luke normally quoted from the LXX; 2) The forms of OT names recur in the almost same way in Luke; 3) Most of Luke's characteristic vocabulary could have been drawn from the LXX; 4) Many of Luke's striking phrases have either exact, or a very close parallel in the LXX; 5) Luke rephrased many expressions of Mark following LXX usage. Sparks concludes that Luke, depending on his sources, i.e., Mark and Q, composed his Gospel as a whole, while imitating the LXX without using another written source special to Luke (L) ('The Semitisms of St. Luke's Gospel', p. 135, 138).

In spite of their brilliant efforts, Deissmann and Cadbury as well as Sparks failed to persuade other scholars to discard the theory of Jewish Greek, although they succeeded in dismissing the Holy Ghost Greek theory. The advocates of the Jewish Greek theory share the view of the Septuagintal pastiche theory that the NT authors imitated LXX Greek. They go further, however, by postulating that LXX Greek represents a Jewish Greek, whether it was used by all Jews or by only some Jews for cultic purposes. While many scholars are hesitant to stake out definite positions, a German scholar, H.S. Gehman, having investigated LXX Greek, sought to revive the 'Jewish Greek' theory. Although it does not treat Lukan Greek in detail, his study is relevant to our investigation. Gehman claims uniqueness for NT Greek and builds his foundation on the study of LXX Greek instead of NT Greek. He argues in his article 'The

---

predominantly Gentile setting' (Fitzmyer, p. 59). L.T. Johnson follows the majority, asserting that 'everything about Luke's narrative confirms that it was directed to Gentile Christians.' *The Gospel of Luke* (Sacra Pagina, Series 3; Collegeville: The Liturgical Press, 1990), p. 9.

Hebraic Character of LXX Greek' that the concept of a Jewish Greek must be reintroduced into the study of LXX Greek.[33] Hebrew had such an influence on LXX Greek that it is undeniable that the Greek of the LXX is acquainted with Hebrew psychology. Greek-speaking Jews could understand the language of the LXX. In the transitional period, in which public language passed from Semitic languages to Greek, Hebrew and Aramaic influenced their speech. This implies a semitized Jewish Greek 'used and understood in religious circles,'[34] even if the theory of a 'Jewish Greek jargon' can not be sustained. Gehman has been criticized by those scholars[35] who observe that although contending that a Jewish Greek jargon did not exist, Gehman in reality subscribes to the theory by inferring the presence of 'a semitized Greek'. In addition, it is dubious that a language can exercise influence on another language to the effect that a peculiar language is formed in a so-called 'transitional period'.[36]

The most famous scholar for the theory of Jewish Greek, N. Turner, supports Gehman's argument. He goes further than Gehman by positing that biblical Greek was moulded as a 'Jewish Greek' or 'Holy Ghost Greek' under the influence of Septuagintal Greek.[37] Turner is the strongest and most tireless defender of the hypothesis that biblical Greek was 'peculiar Greek', namely, 'Jewish Greek' for peculiar people, the Jews of Palestine.[38] In the first part of his article 'The Language of Jesus and His Disciples', Turner seems to agree with the theory of an Aramaic original or Aramaic sources. He concedes that 'as a matter of fact, in the four Gospels there are enough traces of Semitic construction to attract scholars to the conclusion either that the authors of the Gospels wrote their original drafts in Aramaic, or that they used Aramaic written sources.' He goes on, however, to propose his 'Jewish Greek' theory ('The Language', pp. 174-75). There existed a 'Jewish Greek' which was different from Koine Greek which Jewish people utilized together with Jesus. The Jewish Greek dialect influenced other Greek dialects and the Greek of other regions including Egyptian. Turner claims, as distinct from Gehman, the possibility of Jewish Greek not as a transitional dialect, but as a settled language. NT

---

33. H.S. Gehman, 'The Hebraic Character of Septuagint Greek', *VT*, 1 (1951), p. 81.
34. 'The Hebraic Character', p. 90.
35. M. Silva criticizes Gehman in his article, 'Bilingualism and the Character of Palestinian Greek', in *the Language of the New Testament: Classic Essays* (repr. of the article in *Bib*, 61 [1980]), pp. 217-19.
36. Porter, 'The Language of the Apocalypse in Recent Discussion', p. 602. He asserts that there is no such language as that which Gehman describes.
37. Silva asserts that Turner's position does not move substantially from Moulton's position that New Testament Greek is not sharply distinguished from non-biblical Greek. 'Bilingualism and the Character of Palestinian Greek', p. 208.
38. N. Turner, 'The Language of Jesus and His Disciples', in *The Language of the New Testament: Classical Essays*, p. 184.

Greek authors composed their books in this Greek using a sacred means for Christian doctrine to express its sacred ideas ('The Language', p. 187). Although Turner acknowledges that some Egyptian papyri contain seemingly Semitic expressions, he concludes that Jewish Greek influenced Egyptian Greek through the Diaspora.

Turner's position may suggest a solution to the question of why Luke wrote his Gospel in semitized Greek for the Gentiles. Even the Gentiles, according to Turner's thesis, could understand Jewish Greek. He concedes in his article 'The Quality of the Greek of Luke-Acts', following Plummer, that 'some of the Semitisms occur most frequently in those parts of Luke-Acts where Semitic sources are most likely, that is, Luke 1 and 2 and Acts 1–15.'[39] However, 'St. Luke owes little of his Semitic style to his sources and more to the peculiar language of Biblical or Jewish Greek which he shared with the LXX' ('The Quality', p. 387). Luke imitated the Greek of the LXX, but, Turner argues, Luke needed no effort to imitate LXX Greek style, since LXX Greek was a Jewish Greek which was 'his natural speech, and he was expert enough to make it sound quite classical at times' ('The Quality', p. 400). Turner has written many articles in defence of his argument. Even though his argument on Lukan Greek appears to be correct when he maintains that Luke imitated the LXX, his assertion that LXX Greek was a Jewish Greek seems to be dubious.

A recent scholar, F.L. Horton Jr. augments Turner's thesis by introducing 'synagogue Greek'. He argues that Biblical Greek had been ignored until scholars recognized the presence of 'a robust, common Greek which demonstrated a remarkable unity and coherence in texts from Macedonia to Egypt.'[40] He admits that some expressions formerly regarded as exposing Hebraic influence were common in Hellenistic Greek and some of them are found in the Septuagint. However, he continues to claim, suggesting some inevitable Semitisms in the book of Luke-Acts, that research into the Koine and the Septuagint cannot account for all of the Semitisms in the NT. After accepting C. Rabin's argument that the Jewish people of the first century retained classical Hebrew for cultic purposes while they spoke Mishnaic Hebrew in ordinary life, Horton applies the argument to the Greek of the LXX. This Greek was not a spoken language for the public but a representative of synagogue Greek. Since the Hebrew language carried over its sense and feeling into Greek only for religious purposes, he continues, biblical Greek was a cultic language limited to religious purposes. Horton concludes that the NT Bible was designed to be

---

39. N. Turner, 'The Quality of the Greek of Luke-Acts', in *Studies in New Testament Language and text* (Supplements to Novum Testamentum, 44; ed. J.K. Elliott; Leiden: E.J. Brill, 1976), p. 399.

40. F.L. Horton Jr., 'Reflections on the Semitisms of Luke-Acts', in *Perspectives on Luke-Acts* (ed. C.H. Talbert; Edinburgh: T. & T. Clark, 1978), p. 3.

read in religious groups of Hellenistic Jews and 'the language of the Septuagint would be a "synagogue Greek".' 'The second class of Septuagintalisms,' i.e., expressions which 'have only an appearance of being septuagintal in character' appear in Luke-Acts and they clearly suggest the presence of 'synagogue Greek' ('Reflections', p. 19). He thus resurrects a 'Jewish Greek' theory in a different form from his predecessors.

The advocates of the vernacular Greek theory and the proponents of the translation theory remained silent until S.E. Porter and W.G. Most refreshed these two theories respectively. W.G. Most tries to resurrect the translation theory for the Gospel of Luke.[41] He poses a question in his article: 'Did St. Luke Imitate the LXX?',[42] and his answer is 'no'. Most argues that Luke failed to imitate the LXX style with consistency if he had intended to do so. He suggests, for example, that the use of apodotic καί, which is employed to introduce the apodosis, clearly militates against the imitation theory ('Did St. Luke Imitate', pp. 32–37). The LXX frequently adopted the apodotic καί to connect the main clause to the preceding subordinate clause. In contrast, the apodotic καί is not frequent in Luke's Gospel; its percentage in the Gospel is very low compared to that of the LXX. If Luke had intended to imitate the Septuagint, Most avers, he should have employed the apodotic καί more frequently. Whence then did the Semitic flavour of Luke's Greek originate? Most argues that Luke slavishly translated his Hebrew sources. Luke's sources, according to Most, were not in Aramaic, since apodotic 'w' was very rare in Aramaic ('Did St. Luke Imitate', p. 32). The following question arises: why did Luke omit the apodotic καί in most cases if he translated Hebrew sources, while Biblical Hebrew kept it in most cases? The Hebrew of the first century, according to Most, was in two forms: a neoclassical form and a more conservative form. In the new Hebrew, the apodotic ו had almost disappeared ('Did St. Luke Imitate', p. 36), while in the conservative Hebrew, it had been retained. Luke translated these two kinds of Hebrew documents. Most explains the presence of Lukanisms by pointing out that Luke was a meticulous author who could impose his Greek style in the process of his translation.

Parallel to Most's work with the 'translation theory', Porter reinvigorates the vernacular Greek theory on the basis of computer aids.[43] In order

---

41. F. Zimmerman recently tried to revive the Aramaic original theory for the Gospels. See his book, *The Aramaic Origin of the Four Gospels* (New York: Ktav, 1979). His argument on the Greek of the infancy narrative will be dealt with in the next section.

42. W.G. Most, 'Did St. Luke Imitate the LXX?', *JSNT*, 15 (1982), pp. 30–41.

43. Silva may be included as an advocate of vernacular Greek theory of Deissmann-Moulton. He claims linguistic distinction is essential in order to understand NT Greek properly. See his article, 'Bilingualism and the Character of Palestinian Greek', pp. 205–26.

to understand a language, Porter argues, 'the natural process of linguistic development' must be recognized, since Biblical Greek was not formed in a vacuum separated from the stream of Hellenistic Greek. NT Greek contains, he acknowledges, 'resistant strangeness'. To construe this phenomenon Porter recognizes the distinction between code and test, or grammar and style.[44] The different style of each writer creates varieties, but grammar is the same for all. Porter holds to another distinction: language and dialect. In his view, there was no New Testament Greek as a language, but only a dialect used in first-century Palestine by the Jews. In order to understand NT Greek properly, he continues, we must investigate it in a natural process of linguistic development ('The Language of the Apocalypse', p. 593).

Porter declares it impossible to find 'sizable and significant' instances which prove Semitic influence on NT Greek,[45] although he concedes the possibility of some Semitic vocabulary entering into NT Greek.[46] Having defined his analysis as based upon the principles of modern linguistics, he posits that 'I have taken a synchronic approach to the NT, treating it as consisting of representative Greek texts produced by actual language users of the first century AD' (*Idioms*, p. 13). He agrees with Deissmann's claim that NT Greek is vernacular Greek.[47] He goes further than Deissmann, however, by postulating that 'Semitic Greek' did not exist at all even for the LXX, and LXX Greek did not influence NT Greek.[48] Rather some

---

44. Porter is not the first NT Greek scholar to introduce such a distinction. Silva calls attention to 'the well-known Saussarean distinction between language and parole'. 'The former,' he explains, 'refers to the (abstracted) linguistic system in the consciousness of a community, whereas the latter designates the actual utterances of individual speakers.' 'Bilingualism and the Character of Palestine Greek', p. 215.

45. In his study on the Semitic influence concerning verbal structure, he claims that no clear instance appears for the Semitic influence on verbal aspect of the NT. See below.

46. S.E. Porter, *Idioms of the Greek New Testament* (Sheffield: Sheffield Academic Press, 2nd ed, 1994), p. 13.

47. Deissmann and Porter play a similar role in their respective historical context. Deissmann, depending on new discoveries, disputed the dominant hypothesis, i.e., 'Holy Ghost Greek', of contemporary NT Greek study. His suggestion that NT books were written in vulgar Greek was revolutionary at that time. Moulton defines Deissmann as 'the leader in a very real revolution' ('NT Greek in the Light of Modern Discovery', in *The Language of the New Testament: Classic Essays*, p. 60). In the same manner, Porter criticizes a dominant trend of his time, 'a Jewish Greek'. He also depends on modern linguistic discoveries and theories (*Idioms*, p. 15).

48. Porter complains, following M. Silva, of the exaggeration of scholars' assessments concerning Deissmann's contribution by indicating that scholars often ignore his assertion that LXX Greek was a 'Semitic Greek' and the Hebraisms of the LXX exercised influence on the Greek of early Christianity. Porter himself seems to misunderstand Deissmann's argument or at least to exaggerate its weakness. Deissmann certainly employs the term 'Semitic Greek' to describe LXX Greek (*Bible Studies*, p. 67). He chooses the term, however, to denote a

awkward expressions may have gained currency only for a short period. However, says Porter, if an expression endured for a long period in the LXX, it may not be deemed clumsy since only correct expressions could survive and remain. Some seemingly clumsy expressions indicate only that Hellenistic Greek involved a 'standard variety'. In other words, they indicate that Hellenistic Greek, which was spread by various users, formed a 'standard variety' or 'common dialect' by being mingled with other dialects ('The Language of the Apocalypse', p. 596). Because of this variety, the Greek style of NT authors varies from one to another. Porter concludes that Semitisms in the NT 'are seen as not affecting the essential grammatical structure or code of the language' ('The Language of the Apocalypse', p. 599).

Concerning the Greek of Luke, Porter notes that Luke often contains a literary quality.[49] A sizable work, *Verbal Aspect in the Greek of the New Testament, with Reference to Tense and Mood*, discloses his view on Lukan Greek in detail. After scrutinizing possible instances of Semitic influence upon the Greek of NT concerning verbal aspect, which appears mainly in Luke's writings, Porter concludes that no Semitic interference, which refers by his definition to the occurrence of non-Greek constructions solely because of the influence of Semitic constructions (*Verbal Aspect*, p. 118), is

---

different language from what Porter supposes. He defines the translation Greek of the LXX as 'Semitic Greek' in the sense that the Greek was not really spoken by the Jewish people but arose in the process of translating the Hebrew Bible in Greek. Although the translators of the LXX, Deissmann argues, utilized vernacular Greek, the entrance of some disparate Semitic expressions, usually Hebraisms, was inevitable, because of the difference between Semitic and Greek vocabulary and syntax (p. 69). In addition, he notes that 'many alleged Hebraisms of the LXX are really a phenomenon of Egyptian or of popular Greek' (p. 70). Therefore, doubtless, he mentions 'Semitic Greek' not because he thought there was a 'Semitic Greek', but because Semitic Greek arose as a result of translating Hebrew into Greek. Deissmann regards the influence of LXX language on the Greek of the next period, including that of the early Christians, as a separate phenomenon from the influence of an alleged 'Jewish Greek' upon LXX Greek. Although his argumentation may have some flaws, its main point is valid. He dissents from the 'Jewish Greek' theory and refutes the assertion that the LXX was translated into 'Jewish Greek'. He accepts only the rise of Semitic Greek as a consequence of a process of translation. Even though no serious difference exists between LXX Greek and the popular Greek of Alexandria, LXX Greek must not have been the same as popular Greek, since a translation is different from a writing in the same language which is not a translation. Deissmann's emphasis is only on the 'translation', not on the translation into 'Semitic Greek'.

49. 'The Language of the Apocalypse', p. 599. Porter cites some examples only from the Gospel of Luke, though mentioning both of Luke's books. He ignores Luke's choice of many essentially 'Semitic expressions', especially ἐγένετο δέ, in comparison with the authors of other Gospels. Attic expressions also occur much more frequently in Acts than in the Gospel of Luke. The parable of the prodigal son which Porter thinks was written in a good Greek, is filled with Semitisms, as Turner has demonstrated. The use of the participle in Luke also affirms that the Gospel of Luke does not always attain a 'literary quality'. Cf. above note 17.

found in NT Greek, at least in the verbal structure.⁵⁰ Rejecting the argument for Semitic intervention upon the verbal aspect of NT Greek, Porter argues that only some examples of enhancement (which, according to Porter, points to the frequent occurrence of a construction that is rare in Greek, but increasingly used under the influence of Semitic literature) occur in Luke's writings. There is no room accordingly for Semitic intervention even in Luke-Acts.⁵¹ He admits only 'several cases of enhancement' (*Verbal Aspect*, p. 141). These enhancements are restricted mainly to Luke and derive from Luke's conscious imitation of the Greek of the LXX. He acknowledges Luke's imitation of the LXX in order to minimize the Semitic influence on the Gospel of Luke.⁵² He does not forget to recognize, however, that awkward Greek usages in Luke-Acts are attested in Greek literature. Porter tries to establish that Luke adopted such usages because they were allowed in the Greek language. He thus places the emphasis on the Greek language to explain Luke's own language.

Like Porter, David Mealand focuses on the Greek of Luke-Acts by means of computer aids, and also emphasizes the verbal aspect of Greek. His argument concerning the Greek style of Acts is balanced. First he insists that the Greek of Acts is not especially close to Attic prose, although Acts shares some affinities with classical Greek.⁵³ Second, Acts reveals more similarities with major Hellenistic writers – Polybius, Diodorus Siculus, Dionysius of Halicarnassus and Strabo – than has sometimes been recognized ('Hellenistic Historians', p. 43). Nevertheless Mealand considers the argument that 'Acts is most closely related to the LXX' as indispensable. He tries to maintain balance by stating that 'once again I am not doubting that Acts has a very great deal in common with

---

50. Porter, *Verbal Aspect*, pp. 111–62. For the examples in the infancy narrative which he details to prove his thesis that there is no clear Semitic intervention in the verbal structure of the Greek NT, see Porter, pp. 131–33.

51. Although he concedes that the hymns in Luke 1–2 are the most probable place to find Semitic influence on verbal aspect, he adds that Luke imitated the style of the LXX consciously to enhance his final product (*Verbal Aspect*, p. 133). For the detailed argument with regard to Luke's first two chapters, see the next section of this chapter.

52. His main point lies in the assertion that Greek tense does not denote time sequence even in the indicative mood, a position which includes some advantages. First, his argument is based upon the principles of modern linguistics, utilizing a more advanced method, and promising new insights for NT Greek. Second, his position has logical consistency, since he sustains his principles. Although his argument on verbal aspect seems to be convincing, he must accept that in Greek the tense of the indicative mood has a temporal meaning. For the problem of Greek tense, see C.W. Jung, *The Use of the Participle in Luke-Acts* (Th.M Thesis; Grand Rapids: Calvin Seminary, 1996), especially the section 12, 'General Meaning of the Tense in the Greek Language', pp. 75–87.

53. D. Mealand, 'Hellenistic Historians and the Style of Acts', *ZNW*, 82 (1991), p. 42.

the LXX, I am trying to demonstrate that the style of Acts also has much in common with major non-Jewish Hellenistic writings' ('Hellenistic Historians', p. 43). His thesis emerges clearly in another article published in 1996. After comparing non-Attic verb forms in Luke-Acts with those in Dionysius of Halicarnassus and his predecessors, Mealand concludes that most of the forms 'have precedents somewhere in a range of writers from Herodotus through Polybius and Diodorus to Dionysius.'[54] He opposes the view of those who overstress the elements of the LXX as well as Semitic languages ('Luke-Acts', pp. 66–67). He emphasizes the affinity of Lukan Greek with Higher Koine, or good Hellenistic Greek style. He supports Porter's proposal that NT writings are collections of Hellenistic Greek literature by noting that Luke is no Atticist, that his writings do not contain many Semitisms, and that Luke's writings have much in common with Hellenistic writers. The Greek of the author of Luke-Acts, according to Mealand, is close to that of the major Hellenistic writers. Septuagintal elements, of course, exist in Luke-Acts, but they must not be over-emphasized. He is interested in proving that Lukan Greek is a good Hellenistic Greek rather than Septuagintalized Greek.

The above historical survey has shown that recent scholarship tends to emphasize the Greek side of NT Greek. Scholars recognize more and more that NT Greek must be understood from the perspective of the Greek language. Nonetheless, the majority of scholars acknowledge that the Gospel of Luke reflects the influence of one or more Semitic languages. Even Deissmann and Porter, the representatives of the vernacular Greek theory, admit the existence of Semitic elements in Luke. Most scholars, apart from the advocates of the translation theory, which seems no longer convincing, agree that Luke's Semitic colourings resulted from Luke's imitation of LXX style, whether or not they assume the Greek of the LXX to have formed a distinct 'Jewish Greek language'. Does the same judgement hold for the Greek of Luke's first two chapters? Or does a different explanation emerge due to the peculiarity of the language of the infancy story? The next section will address this issue.

B. *A Survey of Scholarly Views on the Greek of the Infancy Narrative*

Since the argumentation on the Greek of the Lukan infancy narrative is more complicated than that concerning other parts of the NT, many scholars have attempted to contribute to the study of the topic and

---

54. D. Mealand, 'Luke-Acts and the Verbs of Dionysius', *JSNT*, 63 (1996), p. 86.

discussion will certainly continue.⁵⁵ In order to clarify the problem raised by the infancy narrative this section will summarize some of the theories that have been critiqued by others and treat recent contributions in considerable detail.⁵⁶

I. *The Translation Theory*

(1) *The Hebrew Original Theory*

The advocates of translation theories for the Gospels and Acts assume that the infancy story has been translated from a Semitic original. One defendant of this view, C.C. Torrey, interestingly contends that the infancy narrative was translated from Hebrew while arguing for an Aramaic original for the rest of the Gospel and Acts. He points out some mistranslations that in his view reflect Luke's misunderstanding of a Hebrew original. A representative example is found in 1.39: Ἀναστᾶσα δὲ Μαριὰμ ἐν ταῖς ἡμέραις ταύταις ἐπορεύθη εἰς τὴν ὀρεινὴν μετὰ σπουδῆς εἰς πόλιν Ἰούδα. The phrase εἰς πόλιν Ἰούδα has been the source of much confusion.⁵⁷ The heart of the problem, Torrey argues, lies in the fact that no 'city of Judah' existed and the last word seems definitely to echo a Hebrew original.⁵⁸ The phrase 'πόλιν Ἰούδα', he claims, is grammatically impossible, since the correct locution must include the genitive case of the proper name, i.e., Ἰουδαίας, as in Lk. 1.65 and Jn 4.5. The indeclinable noun without the article may refer to a translation from Hebrew. Torrey suggests that the phrase is a mistranslation of the Hebrew אל מדינת יהודה. The word מדינת means 'province' in Hebrew and Jewish Aramaic writings, whereas in non-Jewish usage it always means 'city' ('Medina', p. 84). According to Torrey, Luke had an Aramaic or most likely a Hebrew source containing the noun מדינת. This Gentile author who lived outside Palestine translated it as 'city' in accordance with non-Jewish usage ('Medina', p. 89). Torrey concludes that Luke should have translated the

---

55. As disclosed by the historical survey of the Greek of the Gospel of Luke, the discussion on the nature of New Testament Greek, including Lukan Greek, continues. Porter correctly raises the question of the possibility of any final word on the topic ('The Language of the New Testament as a Disputed Area of Research', p. 34). 'Discussion of this topic,' he continues in the same page, 'will almost certainly continue if for no other reason than its outcome has serious consequences in several areas.'

56. For a condensed summary of the language and sources of the infancy narrative, see H.H. Oliver, 'The Lukan Birth Stories and the Purpose of Luke-Acts', *NTS*, 10 (1963–64), pp. 205–15. For a detailed historical survey of the Greek of the infancy narrative, see S. Farris, *The Hymns of Luke's Infancy Narrative: Their Origin, Meaning, and Significance* (JSNTSS, 9; Sheffield: JSOT, 1985), pp. 31–50.

57. For the detailed argument for this phrase, see C.C. Torrey, 'Medina and Πόλις and Luke 1:39', *HTR*, 17 (1924), pp. 83–89.

58. Torrey summarizes his own argument in his book *Our Translated Gospels*, pp. 85–86.

Hebrew phrase as εἰς τὴν χώραν τῆς Ἰουδαίας and therefore the meaning of the phrase must be 'into the province of Judea'.

Torrey's solution has generated much discussion. Whereas M. Black labels his suggestion 'brilliant',[59] some scholars doubt its credibility.[60] Torrey's solution concerning the phrase in 1.39 may raise more problems than it answers. If it is evident that there was no 'city of Judah', it is also evident, as Fitzmyer notes, that there was no 'province of Judah' in the reign of Herod the Great. Torrey constructs his argument starting from a contextual difficulty and advances to the study of the abnormality of Greek expressions. He argues first that the 'city of Judah' did not exist. It is noteworthy to point out that the locution itself does not deviate from the Greek of the LXX, whose influence Torrey does not consider. He overlooks the possibility that the phrase was derived from the usage of the LXX where the indeclinable form of 'Judah' modifies nouns, including the noun πόλις, with or without the article (2 Sam. 2.1: εἰς μίαν τῶν πόλεων Ἰούδα, 'into any of the cities of Judah'; 2 Chron. 35.19: ἐν γῇ Ἰούδα, 'in the land of Judah'; *1 Macc.* 1.51: ταῖς πόλεσιν Ἰούδα, 'the cities of Judah', etc.). It is accepted that an inappropriate starting point of Torrey does not necessarily mean that all the instances of mistranslation from Hebrew suggested by him (1.66; 2.1; 2.11; 2.21, 27) do not have some value.[61] These instances, however, need not concern us, because none of them causes serious problems.[62]

Like Torrey, H. Sahlin claims that Luke translated a Hebrew source for the infancy narrative (chs 1–2, and including 3.1-7a), and an Aramaic original for the rest of the Gospel and Acts 1–15.[63] He suggests that the Aramaic part starts from 3.7b because John the Baptist must have spoken Aramaic, not Hebrew (*Der Messias*, p. 57). The composition of a book in two languages, he continues, is well attested in Daniel and Ezra-Baruch,

---

59. M. Black, *An Aramaic Approach to the Gospel and Acts* (Oxford: Clarendon, 1967), p. 12.

60. Fitzmyer points out the weaknesses of Torrey's argument. For details, see Fitzmyer, *Luke I–IX*, p. 363.

61. Torrey, *Our Translated Gospels*. For 1.66 and 2.11, see pp. 26–27, for 2.1, see p. 84, and for 2.21, 27, see pp. 71–73.

62. All these instances have been well explained in other ways. For the use of the tense in 1.66, see Porter, *Verbal Aspect*, p. 209; for the words πᾶσαν τὴν οἰκουμένην to designate the Palestine in 2.1, see Marshall, *Luke*, p. 98, Brown, *The Birth of the Messiah*, p. 395, and Fitzmyer, *Luke I–IX*, p. 400. Marshall provides a rather long explanation concerning the phrase Χριστὸς κύριος in 2.11 (see also Brown, *The Birth of the Messiah*, pp. 402–3 and Fitzmyer, *Luke I–IX*, pp. 409–10). The use of the redundant conjunction καί in the apodosis after a temporal subordinate clause in 2.21, 27 is found in Homer (Porter, *Verbal Aspect*, p. 123; see also BDF 442.[7]).

63. H. Sahlin, *Der Messias und das Gottesvolk: Studien zur Protolukanischen Theologie* (Uppsala: Almqvist & Wiksells, 1945), p. 9.

which start with 'sacred language', i.e. Hebrew, and then switch to Aramaic. Luke's source had been so composed. Luke then translated and expanded his Semitic source, composed in Hebrew for the first two chapters and in Aramaic for the rest of the Gospel and the first part of Acts. Having recognized that the Greek of Luke's writings and especially the pre-Lukan source are both heavily semitized (*Der Messias*, p. 312), Sahlin proceeds to ask how this phenomenon can be explained. He denies that Luke himself composed the pre-Lukan source in imitation of the LXX. Sahlin contends that Lk. 1–2 is a translation of a written Hebrew *Vorlage*.[64]

It is undeniable that his exegetical notes are very informative about the language of the infancy narrative. However, Sahlin ignores the possibility that most alleged Semitisms can be explained as the influence of the LXX. Sahlin argues, for example, that the sentence in 2.16, καὶ ἦλθαν σπεύσαντες, is a translation of a Hebrew original וימהרו ויבאו (*Messias*, pp. 233–34). He correctly recognizes that the Greek participle must represent the finite verb in Hebrew as all the examples in the OT show: Gen. 24.46; 45.9; Exod. 34.8; Josh. 8.19; 1 Sam. 4.14, 16. He also observes correctly that the verb is used only in Luke-Acts, which could indicate that Luke translated a Semitic source. He ignores, however, the fact that the LXX usually adopted the participle to correspond to the finite verb in the Hebrew OT. The use of the Greek participle σπεύσαντες for the Hebrew finite verb ימהרו could thus be Septuagintalistic rather than Hebraistic. Sahlin fails to consider the possible influence of the LXX. Sahlin's main purpose is not to prove the translation theory but to trace the theology of proto-Lukan sources by reconstructing the proto-Lukan text of Lk. 1–2 in Hebrew. He clearly presupposes rather than demonstrates Luke's translation.

Joining the discussion, P. Winter suggests a clear-cut method for proving the influence of the Hebrew language. He attempts to argue in favour of a Hebrew original for the infancy narrative, and tries to refute the LXX imitation theory by demonstrating that OT phrases or verses reflect the MT rather than the LXX.[65] Among the canonical Gospels the compiler of the Gospel of Luke is, for Winter, the most well educated in the Greek language. Winter also assumes that Luke wrote his Gospel for 'an educated Greek public' ('Some Observations', p. 112). The Greek of

---

64. Sahlin accepts Harnack's analysis that Luke's double corpus has very strong linguistic and stylistic unity. However, he criticizes Harnack's argument that Lukanisms support Luke's direct composition. The Lukanisms, according to Sahlin, may have derived from Luke's sources, i.e., proto-Lukan sources (*Der Messias*, p. 313). In other words, 'Lukanisms' become 'proto-Lukanisms'.

65. P. Winter, 'Some Observations on the Language in the Birth and Infancy Stories of the Third Gospel', *NTS*, n.s. 1 (1954), pp. 111–21.

the infancy narrative is, however, full of Hebraisms.[66] Did Luke intend, Winter asks, to commit 'an unforgivable sin' against the language as a writer by employing un-Greek expressions? With the presumption of Luke's direct composition for the infancy story, Winter continues, no reasonable explanation can be given concerning the frequent occurrence of Hebraisms in it. The only probable answer, he concludes, is that the compiler depended on a source written primarily in Hebrew. Some verses and expressions in the infancy narrative can be correctly interpreted only by retranslating Greek into Hebrew.

Separating Luke's original sources from his immediate ones, Winter suggests that Luke depended on Greek sources which were anonymously and previously translated from Hebrew originals.[67] This Greek source was not related to any other sources available to Luke during his composition of the Gospel ('On Luke', p. 218). Winter does not suppose that Luke himself translated or composed the infancy narrative, though Luke provided its present location. Winter assumes that Luke's knowledge of Hebrew was not sufficient to translate Semitic sources for the infancy story. The separation of the original Semitic source from an immediate Greek one provides the answer to the question of why Luke, who was capable of writing excellent Greek, employed barbarous Greek in the infancy story.

To support his case, Winter discusses some clear examples, including the phrase προβεβηκότες ἐν ταῖς ἡμέραις in 1.7. Neither the LXX nor other Greek literature uses the verb προβαίνω with the preposition ἐν.[68] In contrast, the Hebrew text does use the preposition ב: באים בימים (Gen. 18.11). The LXX translators followed classical Greek by employing the genitive or dative of time indicator without ἐν, though classical authors do not use ἡμέραι but ἡλικία as a time indicator. The presence of the preposition, according to Winter, is critical evidence for the dependence of Luke's text on the MT. Winter's article instigated a debate with N. Turner.[69]

---

66. Winter argues that the lyrics and the narrative proper are 'Hebraic in character, in style and spirit'. He goes further by noting that 'these Hebraisms occur word after word, sentence after sentence, line after line in all but a handful of verses from the Lukan Infancy Story' ('Some Observations', p. 121).

67. P. Winter, 'On Luke and Lukan Sources', *ZNW*, 4 (1956), p. 238. See also his article 'The Proto-Source of Luke I', *Nov Test*, 1 (1956), pp. 184–99. The Lukan infancy narrative, he argues here, is 'based almost entirely on a literary record that was composed in Hebrew'. 'The Third Evangelist,' he continues, 'had at his disposal a Greek translation of that record which he took over with minor alternations and included in the Gospel' ('The Proto-Source of Luke I', p. 185).

68. Some examples in *2 Maccabees* use the accusative case of ἡλικία: *2 Macc* 4.40. προβεβηκότος τὴν ἡλικίαν; 6.18 – προβεβηκὼς τὴν ἡλικίαν. For details, see Chapter 3.

69. N. Turner, 'The Relation of Luke I and II to Hebraic Sources and the Rest of Luke-Acts', *NTS*, 2 (1955–56), pp. 100–9.

Because the examples suggested by Winter will be under intense scrutiny later, it is not necessary to treat them here. It will suffice to point out that Winter does not take into account Luke's method of quoting and alluding to the Old Testament. Most scholars observe that Luke relied on the Septuagint for his quotations, but did not hesitate to alter a part of the quoted verse or passage to suit his context.[70] And certainly Luke did change OT verses more readily in cases of allusion. Winter does not consider this at all. He argues, for example, that the Old Testament allusion in 1.37 (οὐκ ἀδυνατήσει παρὰ τοῦ θεοῦ πᾶν ῥῆμα) reflects the MT of Gen. 18.14 rather than the LXX (μὴ ἀδυνατεῖ παρὰ τῷ θεῷ ῥῆμα). He assumes that the retranslation of the sentence into Hebrew secures a correct interpretation.[71] One can object by pointing out that the sentence in Gen. 18.14 is a question whereas Luke has it an assertion in Lk. 1.37. This change may have facilitated altering other parts of the sentence. It is also noteworthy that the meaning of the sentence becomes clear when one interprets the sentence as it is.[72] Although Winter's argument betrays the chief weakness mentioned above, his approach is clearer than that of those other scholars who do not consider the possible influence of the LXX on Luke, and whose starting point is contextual difficulties and concentrate on this aspect.[73] Winter begins with linguistic observations and focuses on them. He also spends some time refuting the LXX pastiche theory (= the LXX imitation theory). Moreover, Turner's refutation of Winter's suggestion is not effective enough to convince others. The examples to which Winter points will require subsequent close examination.

Recently reviving the Hebrew original theory, S. Farris concentrates especially on the Magnificat and Benedictus (*The Hymns*, pp. 50–65). He is the latest scholar to investigate the language of the infancy narrative in order to demonstrate the presence of a Semitic original. Although he focuses on the hymns, Farris concludes that the infancy story as a whole had been composed in a Semitic language, either Aramaic or more probably Hebrew (*The Hymns*, p. 62) and that Luke absorbed Semitic features from the source(s) before him.[74] He first tries to prove that Luke did not compose the hymns as a whole by adapting the subtraction method

---

70. For scholars' views on quotations and allusions, see the sections 'Quotations' and 'Allusions' in Chapter 3.

71. This verse will be dealt with in detail in the sections 'Quotations' and 'Allusions'.

72. For the detailed argument on this verse, see the sections 'Quotations' and 'Allusions'.

73. This is why Winter found the phrase προβαίνω ἐν ταῖς ἡμέραις awkward, while Torrey did not.

74. His attitude toward Luke's source is ambiguous. He does not take up the question of whether Luke depended on translated Greek sources or translated Semitic sources himself. He simply states that 'Luke has once again absorbed some of the style of a source' (*The Hymns*, p. 62).

which A. von Harnack invented (*The Hymns*, pp. 22–30). Harnack subtracts Septuagintalistic expressions from the hymns.[75] Septuagintalisms cannot be regarded as critical evidence for Luke's direct composition, though they may indicate Luke's imitation of the LXX. According to Harnack, some of the leftovers, which remain after the subtraction, i.e., non-Septuagintalistic locutions, belong to Lukanisms that indicate Luke's direct composition. Farris, following Harnack, uses Lukanisms to judge whether Luke composed the hymns as a whole. By Lukanisms, Farris means 'those words and phrases which occur with some regularity in Luke-Acts and only rarely elsewhere in the New Testament' (*The Hymns*, p. 23). These Lukanisms may indicate Luke's direct composition. The Magnificat, according to Harnack, contains fourteen Lukanisms throughout the whole hymn, once Septuagintalistic locutions are excluded. Farris follows Harnack's subtraction method by applying it to the Magnificat, but deviates from Harnack by finding only three real Lukanisms in the Magnificat, all in v. 48. Harnack's other alleged Lukanisms Farris excludes by precise and strict examination. He concludes by this criterion that the Magnificat (1.46–55) as a whole was not composed by Luke, since real Lukanisms, which support Luke's direct composition, appear only in v. 48. This is also true for the Benedictus (1.67–79), where only vv. 76–77 include Lukanisms. It is certain, according to his judgement, that Luke did not compose the hymns out of nothing but relied on sources. If so, Farris asks, which language lies behind Luke's first two chapters?

Farris attempts to demonstrate Semitic originals behind the infancy story on the basis of R.A. Martin's methodology, which concentrates on syntactical features.[76] Martin establishes 17 criteria for judging whether some parts of the NT are Greek translations or were originally written in Greek. 'The difference between the style of Greek which is a translation of Semitic originals and original Greek style,' he argues, 'is often to be seen in the relative frequency or infrequency of an idiom, rather than in its mere occurrence or non-occurrence' (*Syntax Criticism of the Synoptic Gospels*, p. 5). For example, the frequency of the preposition ἐν, involved in the first eight of seventeen criteria, is compared with the relative infrequency of

---

75. For Harnack's method, see his article, 'Das Magnificat der Elisabeth (Lk. 1.46–55) nebst einigen Bemerkungen zu Luk 1 und 2', *Sitzungberichte der Koeniglichen Preussischen Akademie der Wissenschaften zu Berlin*, 27 (1900), pp. 538–66.

76. R.A. Martin, *Syntactical Evidence of Semitic Sources in Greek Documents* (Septuagint and Cognate Studies; Missoula: Scholar's Press, 1974), p. 1f. See also his book, *Syntax Criticism of the Synoptic Gospels* (Studies in the Bible and Early Christianity, 10; Lewiston: Edwin Mellen, 1987), p. 6f.

other prepositions like διά, εἰς, κατά, περί, πρός, and ὑπό.[77] The preposition ἐν reflects ב which occurs frequently in Hebrew and Aramaic, while the other prepositions do not have common equivalents in Semitic languages. Their infrequency in comparison with the frequency of ἐν, according to Martin, indicates a Greek translation; by contrast, their relatively frequent occurrence suggests original composition. He points out that 'the degree of consistency in distributions of Semitisms throughout the document' is 'a very important aspect to be kept in mind in the study of this problem concerning the nature and origin of Semitisms in the Gospels and Acts' (*Syntax Criticism of the Synoptic Gospels*, p. 4). A more or less consistent distribution of Semitic features, he continues, can be explained by the translation theory of the whole document or by the theory that an author composed the document while thinking in Hebrew or Aramaic. The theory of the use of some Semitic sources or the LXX imitation theory is proven correct only when the distribution is inconsistent and erratic. Concerning the first two chapters of the Gospel of Luke, Martin argues that Luke himself translated Semitic sources for most of the first chapter and parts of chapter two.[78] Only the translation theory, in his view, provides the appropriate explanation for the consistent distribution of Semitic features throughout the first chapter and parts of the second chapter. He rules out the possibility of Luke's dependence on a Greek source translated from a Semitic original for the first two chapters on the ground that Luke 'generally makes a Semitic Greek text which he is using less Semitic' in dealing with his primary sources of Mk. 1–10.[79] In other words, the frequency of the Semitic features is so high in the infancy story, being

---

77. Although the number of the prepositions is only six, two prepositions, κατά and διά, involve two criteria, since they are construed with more than one case. κατά is construed with the accusative and another case and διά with the genitive and another case.

78. *Syntax Criticism of the Synoptic Gospels*, p. 110. He includes also 4.16–30, 12.13–21, 13.10–17, 19.39–44, 24.13–35 in this category.

79. Martin has written an article entitled 'Syntactical Evidence of Aramaic Sources in Acts I–XV', *NTS*, 10 (1964/65), pp. 38–59. He applies three criteria for examining the language of underlying sources for the first part of Acts: 1) the relative frequency of καί and δέ; 2) the relative frequency of ἐν compared with other prepositions; 3) separation of the Greek article from its substantive. (Cf. In his book, *Syntactical Evidence of Semitic Sources in Greek Documents*, he inflates the second category to eight criteria.) He contends that the language of underlying sources for Acts I–XV was Aramaic, while Hebrew sources were translated for Lk. 1–2. Martin compares the statistics for the Aramaic section of Daniel with that for the Hebrew section of Daniel and suggests that there is a difference between the sections. He applies this result to the comparison between the syntactical features in Acts 1–15 and those in Lk. 1–2. He concludes that the original language of the infancy story was Hebrew ('Syntactical evidence', p. 59). Martin does not seem to sustain this theory in his book *Syntactical Evidence of the Synoptic Gospels*.

distributed throughout the whole story, that one may not suppose Luke's use of any Greek source.

On the basis of Martin's criteria, Farris asserts that the Greek of the first two chapters of Luke's Gospel displays significant differences from a Greek original. Martin's achievement increases the probability of the translation theory. However, Farris does not adopt Martin's argument without criticism. He keeps an ambiguous attitude about the question of who translated Semitic sources for the infancy story while Martin asserts that Luke translated them. Luke, according to Farris, may have either translated Semitic sources or been dependent on translated Greek sources. He does not forget to discuss the question of the credibility of Martin's method. It seems unreasonable to him, for example, that the first eight criteria, all of which are related to the frequency of the preposition ἐν, carry the same weight as the remaining nine. A more serious problem, Farris continues, is that Martin's method does not provide criteria which help to distinguish between 'Greek translated from a Semitic source and Greek written by one influenced by Semitic idiom' (*The Hymns*, p. 59). Despite these problems, he avers, Martin's method appears reliable concerning the infancy story for two reasons: 1) the frequency of translation Greek in Lk. 1–2 is the most prominent of the whole NT; 2) Luke composed the second half of Acts in a non-Semitized and polished Greek, and thus he was not influenced by Semitic idiom.

Farris's approach is more reliable than the approach of other scholars, since it is not based upon contextual difficulties or upon one or two awkward expressions. He understands both aspects of the Greek of the infancy narrative: on the one hand, it is embedded with Hebraisms, and on the other hand, Luke's intervention is clear (*The Hymns*, p. 32). He also recognizes a possible role of Lukanisms by showing that they may decide the issue of Luke's direct composition. In addition, Farris modifies and complements Martin's criteria to make them more credible, especially concerning the infancy story. He also avoids, differently from Martin, a possible criticism by omitting a direct judgement about whether Luke himself or someone else translated Semitic sources; he simply notes that the original language of the infancy story was Hebrew.

However, it needs to be pointed out that Martin's method is not convincing for refuting the argument that the conscious imitation of the LXX by the author could be a source for the so-called translation Greek frequencies in the first two chapters of the Gospel of Luke, at least for some of its subsections.[80] A more serious problem is that the application of

---

80. Farris counters the argument that translation Greek frequencies could occur because of Luke's conscious imitation by saying that adopting some characteristic locutions like καὶ

the criteria produces inconsistent results.⁸¹ These elements demonstrate that Martin's methodology does not provide a reliable solution to the question of the original language of the Lukan infancy narrative, as Farris believes. In short, Farris's argument for a Semitic original is unconvincing.

(2) The Aramaic Original Theory

It is remarkable that many proponents for the existence of an Aramaic original for the Gospels and Acts do not propose the same for the infancy story (e.g. Torrey and Sahlin above and Burney below). However, F. Zimmerman attempts to prove that the theory holds for the infancy narrative as well. In agreement with Torrey that the four Gospels were translated from Aramaic into Greek,⁸² he nonetheless disagrees with him on the question of the infancy narrative. In his view, the latter contains no examples of the mistranslation from a putative Hebrew except for the Magnificat and the prayer of Zechariah (*The Aramaic Original*, p. 97). The underlying source must have been Aramaic. Zimmerman lists five examples to support the thesis of an Aramaic original (1.17; 1.24–25; 1.35; 1.39; 1.78). The phrase περιέκρυβεν ἑαυτὴν in 1.24, according to him, represents a clear instance of an Aramaic original: Μετὰ δὲ ταύτας τὰς ἡμέρας συνέλαβεν Ἐλισάβετ ἡ γυνὴ αὐτοῦ καὶ περιέκρυβεν ἑαυτὴν μῆνας πέντε λέγουσα...; 'After those days his wife Elizabeth conceived, and she remained in seclusion for five months, saying...' (*The Aramaic Original*, p. 99). It is hard to explain Elizabeth's motivation for hiding her pregnancy, for Elizabeth must have been proud of conceiving a baby at her age. Zimmerman suggests that Luke misunderstood the Aramaic word אתבסית, the reflexive *Etpe'el* form which must mean 'she adorned herself'. He concludes that Elizabeth adorned herself in order to let others know of her pregnancy.

Zimmerman's starting point and main focus are context. Thus, to solve the problem of the meaning of the sentence, he turns quickly to the supposition of an Aramaic original. Elizabeth's motivation does in fact need elucidation, but this is a theological rather than a philological

---

ἐγένετο is totally different from adapting some 'obscure characteristics which do not depend on subject matter or vocabulary' (*The Infancy Narrative*, pp. 55–56). His argument is not convincing, since Luke may have consulted the LXX very carefully in the infancy narrative.

81. Specific statistics prove that his argument is not reliable. The most prominent example, according to Porter, is found in Josephus's *Jewish War* which Josephus himself claims to have been translated from Aramaic into Greek. The result of the application of Martin's criteria to this book shows that the book was written directly in Greek, which is improbable. Porter tries to refute Martin's methodology by applying it also to other authors. For his argument and statistics see his *Verbal Aspect*, pp. 160–61.

82. F. Zimmerman, *The Aramaic Origin of the Four Gospels* (New York: Ktav, 1979), p. 5.

matter.[83] As Fitzmyer suggests, the seclusion may be a preparation for 1.36 which describes Elizabeth's pregnancy as being told to Maria by the angel first. In addition, the following verse may indicate the motivation. Elizabeth's seclusion, 'like Zechariah's muteness, preserved the secret until the plan of salvation-history reaches the point at which it is to be made known'.[84] The issue is certainly theological and exegetical.[85] It is true, of course, that this problem cannot completely nullify Zimmerman's claim that Luke translated an Aramaic original. Nevertheless, the Aramaic original theory for the infancy story need not concern us here as all recent scholars assume the theory to be improbable.[86] In fact, all the Semitisms in chs 1–2 of the Gospel of Luke, at least those which still raise a question, belong to Hebraisms, not Aramaisms, as we shall see in Chapter 3 below.[87]

---

83. Although the Greek locution περιέκρυβεν ἑαυτήν seems unusual, since the Greek verb can mean 'to hide oneself' by itself and the reflexive pronoun ἑαυτήν is unnecessary, the Greek construction is acceptable; only the middle voice means 'hide oneself' (BAGD, p. 648). Zimmerman's thesis of an Aramaic original is thus unnecessary for this example.

84. Fitzmyer, *Luke I–IX*, p. 329.

85. Evans, *Luke*, p. 153. For the summary of possible solutions, see Bock, *Luke 1.1–9.50*, pp. 97–98.

86. See Nolland, *Luke 1–9.20*, p. 21, who notes that 'little recent support has been found for the Aramaic sources suspected by some earlier scholars'. 'The field,' he continues, 'remains fairly equally divided between those who stress Luke's ability to write Jewish (Septuagintal) Greek... and those who insist on a Hebrew substratum.' See also Guthrie, *New Testament Introduction*, p. 196. For the list of more scholars, see Chapter 3. Noteworthy is that some scholars, who argue for the Aramaic original theory for the remainder of the Gospel and Acts or other Gospels, argue for the Hebrew original theory for the infancy narrative (e.g., Torrey, Sahlin [for their argument, see above], Burney [for his argument see below]).

87. Fitzmyer argues that possible Aramaic interference can be recognized in Lk. 1.32–35 whose parallel appears in 4Q246; there are several parallels of language between these two passages (Fitzmyer, *Luke I–IX*, p. 117) and it is striking that the two titles for Jesus in Lk. 1.32 (Son of the Most High) and 35 (Son of God) are found in 4Q246 1.7 and 2.1 respectively (cf. Nolland, *Luke 1–9:20*, pp. 51–52). His argument is not convincing, however. As Marshall notes, these parallels of the language only confirm that the language of Lk. 1.32–35 originated from Palestine and it is thus unnecessary to assume that it is from a specific Aramaic source (*Luke*, p. 67). Also noteworthy is that scholars interpret some features in Lk. 1.32–35 as indicating the influence of Hebrew, not Aramaic: e.g., Sahlin (*Der Messias*, pp. 113–36), who argues for the Hebrew original of expressions in this passage like γεννώμενον in Lk. 1.35; Nolland (*Luke 1–9:20*, pp. 51–56), who suggests some instances which point to the influence of the Hebrew OT. In addition, the Greek of this part can best be explained as affected by the LXX; even the two titles are attested in the LXX (for detailed remarks of the LXX influence on words and phrases, see Marshall, *Luke*, pp. 67–71). These considerations indicate that no clear example of Aramaisms is found in the infancy narrative.

II. *The Imitation Theory*

(1) Earlier Contributions

The LXX pastiche theory (= the LXX imitation theory) for the infancy story has been suggested mainly by those scholars who deny or at least minimize the influence of Semitic languages on the NT. The classic and standard argument for the imitation theory is presented by the German scholar A. von Harnack, who tries to prove that Luke directly composed the first two chapters in affinity with the Septuagint. He also classifies 'Lukanisms' on the belief that they support Luke's direct composition. Harnack disposes of an underlying source for the infancy story, since its style is identical to Luke's.[88] If Luke had used sources, he must have revised them sentence by sentence in line with his style. Even the Magnificat and the Benedictus are Luke's own compositions. Harnack also distinguishes himself from others by suggesting a positive approach to the issue. Other scholars refute the translation theory mainly by pointing out that alleged Semitisms can be explained as the influence of the LXX. In contrast, Harnack subtracts Septuagintalisms from the hymns and identifies some of the non-Septuagintal characteristics as Lukan ones. These Lukanisms, according to him, prove Luke's direct composition. Harnack succeeds in forcing scholars to pay attention to Lukanisms in the infancy narrative. But the problem persists because even the advocates of the translation theory admit the intervention of Luke's hand in the process of the translation. In addition, Harnack's criteria for subtracting Lukanisms are not precise.[89]

Presenting an intriguing view, Burney postulates that John translated an Aramaic original for his Gospel, whereas the author of the Gospel of Luke derived his Hebraisms from the LXX. Thus, Luke did not have sources for the infancy narrative. He goes on to argue that Hebraisms appear in the Apocalypse and attributes their origin to a 'first-hand imitation of Biblical Hebrew'.[90] Luke also engaged in this direct imitation even in the infancy narrative. Burney correctly recognizes that Luke's Gospel, in contrast to John's Gospel, includes many Septuagintalisms, though he names them Hebraisms, and interprets them to be the result of Luke's imitation of the LXX.

Refuting Winter's view that Luke used a Hebrew source for the infancy narrative, Turner argues that the examples suggested by Winter to support

---

88. A. von Harnack, *Lukas der Arzt* (Leipzig: J.C Hinrichs'sche Buchhandlung, 1906), p. 150. For the treatment of 1.5–15 see pp. 69–72.
89. For Farris's criticism and evaluation of Harnack's method, see above.
90. C.F. Burney, *The Aramaic Origin of the Fourth Gospel* (Oxford: Clarendon, 1922), p. 16.

his case indicate the influence of the LXX rather than the MT.[91] Luke's adoption of some Greek locutions, which Winter regards as the result of translating Semitic sources, was not inevitable. In other words, Luke could have used other words or locutions which do not occur in the LXX. For example, Turner argues that Luke could have avoided the Septuagintal verb προβαίνειν in 1.7 for בוא. The adoption of ἡμέραι for ימים also indicates the influence of the LXX. The difference between locutions in Luke and those in the Septuagint may have resulted from a different Septuagint version available to Luke. Turner argues for Luke's direct composition, at least for most of the infancy narrative on the ground that Lukan Greek style is consistently found in it. The presence of alleged Semitisms in the infancy narrative need not indicate Semitic originals but only Luke's imitation of the LXX here as in the rest of the Gospel.[92] Turner postulates that the first two chapters of Luke's Gospel are especially embedded with Septuagintalisms, not with Semitisms ('The Relation', p. 100).

Turner succeeds in making it clear that scholars must investigate and focus on the Greek language of the Lukan infancy story. He also correctly points out that the Lukan style prevails in the story and that the influence of the LXX must be taken into account. Nonetheless, some scholars, such as Farris, are critical of Turner's approach, regarding it as inconsistent. On the one hand, Turner posits that Luke's LXX is different from ours so that he can refute Winter's argument. On the other hand, he relies on the present LXX version to support his argument. In addition, it may be argued that Turner does not deal with Winter's examples in detail, which would be necessary for an effective refutation of Winter's argument. Turner's main argument is to show that the Greek of the infancy narrative is virtually identical to the rest of the Gospel, but this cannot, by itself, be sufficient as an argument for direct composition by Luke. It is evident that he needs to examine the examples in depth before pointing to the difference between Luke's LXX and ours, and to the identity between the Greek of the infancy narrative and that of 3–24. The presence of Lukan style in the infancy narrative may demonstrate both Luke's direct composition and Luke's translation of a possible source (or sources).

---

91. Turner, 'The Relation of Luke I and II to Hebraic Sources and the Rest of Luke-Acts', pp. 100–9. For Winter's argument, see above, section I.

92. Luke's conscious imitation of the LXX, Turner argues, 'would adequately account for the Hebraisms of Luke 1 and 2'. 'In the Appendix of *the Grammar*, vol. II,' he continues, 'W.F. Howard quoted with approval Harnack's view that Luke 1–2 shows such intrinsic unity with the rest of Luke-Acts as to eliminate the probability of Luke's use of sources.' 'That judgement,' he concludes, 'still stands.' *A Grammar of New Testament Greek*, vol. IV: *Style* (Edinburgh: T. & T. Clark, 1976), p. 56.

(2) Recent Contributions

Many recent scholars as well as earlier ones seem unclear about Semitisms. R. Brown in *The Birth of the Messiah*, for example, announces that he gave up trying to determine the original language of the infancy narrative through philological and linguistic criteria.[93] However, he does list Semitisms in the 'Notes' section.[94] Brown calls Greek locutions which reflect Hebrew constructions Semitisms. He does not forget to mention the 'good LXX style' or that some locutions echo the LXX (*The Birth*, pp. 258–59). His method in the 'Notes' is problematic, however, when using the term 'Semitisms' and avoiding the term 'Septuagintalisms'. The presence or absence of the terms may or may not be significant, but the importance of establishing criteria for determining whether the Greek constructions are Semitisms or echo the LXX cannot be denied. For example, he notes that the Greek construction in v. 5 τὸ ὄνομα αὐτῆς Ἐλισάβετ; 'her name was Elizabeth' occurs in the LXX Gen. 17.5,15.[95] He does not call this construction a Semitism, even though the locution reflects the Hebrew construction in Gen. 17.5 ([היה] שמד אברהם). He also argues that the sentence in v. 13, καλέσεις τὸ ὄνομα αὐτοῦ Ἰωάννην; 'you will call his name John', is a Semitism. This expression echoes the Hebrew construction in Gen. 16.11: וקאדת שמו ישמעאל. Why does Brown include only the latter among the Semitisms? The answer is not clear. Again, in v. 15, ἐκ κοιλίας μητρὸς αὐτοῦ; 'from his mother's womb' must be a Semitism according to Brown, but the Greek locution appears six times in the Greek OT. It is thus arguably a Septuagintalism, rather than a Semitism, as is the construction in v. 5. Brown, in short, does not sufficiently distinguish between Semitisms and Septuagintalisms (see Chapter 2).

Brown denies the possibility that one can reach any conclusion on the source problem of the infancy narrative through language or style. For him, the debate between the advocates of the translation theory and those of the imitation theory is inconclusive. The decisive answer, he contends, could only emerge from a study of the content and theme. Nevertheless, an approach on the basis of content and theme is also limited and cannot yield a final solution. Any decision must also include the linguistic aspect. New investigation may produce a result that breaks the stalemate.

In his new edition of *The Birth of the Messiah* in 1993, Brown understands the heart of the problem:

---

93. R. Brown, *The Birth of the Messiah: A Commentary on the Infancy Narrative in Matthew and Luke* (London: Geoffrey Chapman, 1977), p. 246.
94. This statement does not negate his accomplishment in his study for the infancy story. It is simply intended to point out a weakness in his approach towards the Greek of the story.
95. The 'be' verb is implied in Luke, while the Hebrew text contains it.

Where there are Hebraisms and Aramaisms, we do not know whether they represent a direct translation from Hebrew or Aramaic or the influence of a Septuagint where the Greek was translated from Hebrew or Aramaic. (p. 623)

Despite this difficulty, he argues, following Fitzmyer, that most Semitisms can be explained as Septuagintalisms. Brown also points out that ninety percent of Luke's vocabulary appears in the Septuagint.[96] Abandoning the view of the debate as inconclusive, he leans toward the imitation theory. This may present a positive development. However, Brown does not elaborate on the Notes where he lists possible Semitisms. His view, moreover, is not based on detailed investigation, but on the work of other scholars like that of Fitzmyer. Although Fitzmyer is for Brown one of the foremost Aramaists in the world, this does not guarantee the correctness of his view.[97]

Concerning the source of the infancy story, Brown believes that Luke freely composed most of the infancy narrative on the basis of pre-Lukan information (not written sources). It is unnecessary thus for him to assume that Luke depended on written sources except for the canticles (*The Birth* [2nd edn], p. 622).

Fitzmyer believes that there are no Hebraisms in the Gospel of Luke – only Aramaisms derived from Luke's mother tongue, Aramaic. Concerning the infancy story, he believes that the passage in 1.32-35 has a parallel in the Aramaic text of 4Q246 and that Aramaic intervention may be discernable in this section (*Luke I–IX*, pp. 116–17). He also claims that the infancy narrative is heavily Semitized, standing in contrast to the rest of the Gospel and Acts. However, Fitzmyer regards the vast majority of Semitisms in the nativity story as Septuagintalisms (*Luke I–IX*, p. 312). He interprets the abundant presence of Septuagintalisms as indicating Luke's imitation of the Septuagintal style. Fitzmyer's judgement should be held in high esteem, since he is a New Testament scholar who has also specialized in the study of Aramaic. His treatment of the language of the infancy narrative is solid and consistent compared with other scholars. It is also problematic, however, because he does not define the terms Semitisms and Septuagintalisms concretely.[98] He simply considers any Greek locution a

---

96. For the discussion of the use of statistics for the authorship issue of the NT, see M. O'Donnell, 'Linguistic Fingerprint or Style by Numbers? The Use of Statistics in the Discussion of Authorship of New Testament Documents', in *Linguistics and the New Testament: Critical Junctures*, eds. S.E. Porter and D.A. Carson (JSNTSS, 168; Sheffield: Sheffield Academic Press, 1999), pp. 206–7.

97. He also refers to O'Fearghail as arguing strongly for the imitation theory, although the latter does not prove but mainly assumes Luke's imitation. For the detailed argument and evaluation of O'Fearghail's views, see below.

98. Here again, this problem does not nullify his achievement. His commentary is a rich one and we are only pointing to one weakness.

Septuagintalism if it occurs in the LXX. This ambiguous attitude results in inconsistent and inappropriate comments on the specific locutions. On the one hand, Fitzmyer overlooks some problematic locutions due to his presupposition that Luke did not know any Hebrew. He is not interested in refuting even prominent examples of alleged Semitisms. A representative instance is found in v. 7: προβεβηκότες ἐν ταῖς ἡμέραις. The preposition is problematic, but Fitzmyer appears to overlook it. He comments that the LXX translators frequently used the expression (*Luke I–IX*, p. 323) but he does not note that Luke's construction is in some way closer to the Hebrew than the LXX since the Hebrew uses ב and the LXX does not use ἐν. On the other hand, Fitzmyer classifies some Greek locutions as Semitisms, although they do appear in the LXX. He betrays confusion in his note on the phrase ἄγγελος κυρίου in 1.11.[99] The absence of the article indicates, he notes, that it is a Semitism (*Luke I–IX*, p. 324). This phrase reflects 'the Hebrew construct chain, מלאך יהוה', but he ignores its occurrence in the LXX: Exod. 3.2; Judg. 13.3; Judg. (A) 6.12; *Tob.* (s) 12.22. The first reference contains exactly the same phrase as Luke: ὤφθη δὲ αὐτῷ ἄγγελος κυρίου.[100] It is also remarkable that the LXX does not once use the phrase ἄγγελος τοῦ κυρίου, while the phrase ἄγγελος κυρίου occurs more than 69 times. These factors call into question Fitzmyer's assertion that the phrase is a Semitism, according to his own argument that 'the Semitisms of Lukan Greek which are found in the LXX should be frankly labelled as "Septuagintalisms"' (*Luke I–IX*, p. 114).[101] These two examples demonstrate that the lack of the precise criteria for distinguishing between Septuagintalisms and Semitisms leads Fitzmyer to an inconsistent result. In addition to this inconsistency, Fitzmyer does not offer an appropriate explanation of why Luke imitated the LXX, if he did, in the infancy story so strongly.

Although Fitzmyer emphasizes Luke's imitation of the LXX and argues that Luke composed most of the infancy narrative, he admits that Luke relied on two sources for the narrative (*Luke I–IX*, p. 309). One is 'a Jewish-Christian source', which consisted of the hymns (the Magnificat, the Benedictus, and probably Nunc Dimittis) and probably the episode in Jerusalem of ch. 2 (vv. 41–50). Another one is 'an earlier Baptist source', which contained the annunciation of John's birth (1.5–25), and his birth, circumcision, and manifestation (1.57–66b). Luke seems to have directly

---

99. Exactly the same phrase occurs again in Lk. 2.9.

100. The phrase occurs three times in Acts (8.26; 12.7, 23). The example in Acts 27.23 shows the modifying word 'τοῦ θεοῦ'. For the detailed argument see Chapter 3.

101. According to his logic, the phrase ὄνομα αὐτοῦ in 1.63 must be a Semitism because of the absence of the article. This is a better example than the phrase ἄγγελος κυρίου, since it occurs only five times without the article in the LXX, while there are about 125 examples with the article in the LXX. Fitzmyer says nothing about the phrase in 1.63.

composed the remaining parts. Fitzmyer resolves the problem of the presence of Lukanisms in the sections in which Luke depended on sources by saying that Luke reworked his sources in his own style.

Differing with Fitzmyer, M.D. Goulder and M.L. Sanderson present an extreme view when they posit that Luke composed the nativity story without any source on the basis of his historical knowledge of the OT (LXX), partly using Matthaean material.[102] The co-authors insist that 'the main strand of Lk. I–II consists of the theme of the fulfilment of Abraham-Isaac-Jacob in Jesus and his forerunner' ('St. Luke's', p. 13). Luke did not need to depend on sources. Consulting the LXX, Luke expanded Matthew's birth story whose basic historical data are the same as Luke's: Jesus was described as the son of Joseph and Mary, and was from Nazareth. Zechariah and Elizabeth appear as the new Abraham and new Sarah to indicate the beginning of the history of the new Israel, as Abraham and Sarah represented the beginning of the history of the old Israel. The infancy narrative, according to Goulder and Sanderson, did not stem from an independent tradition, but from Luke's direct composition via 'pious meditation'. The co-authors seem to argue that the Greek in the infancy narrative is Lukan Greek influenced by the LXX.

Additionally, Goulder details his view of the Greek of the infancy story in his book published in 1989.[103] He argues that the Greek of the infancy narrative is Septuagintalistic and that its language as well as theology is substantially identical to that in the remaining chapters of the Gospel (*A New Paradigm*, p. 215). According to him, there are no underlying sources except for Matthew and Mark. Luke depended on Matthew, Mark, and the LXX for the narrative part while relying only on the LXX for the canticles, specifically Hannah's song in 1 Samuel for the Magnificat and the song of David for the Benedictus (*A New Paradigm*, p. 243). Goulder claims that Harnack's radical view that Luke directly composed the canticles must be accepted. Luke's imagination on the basis of Matthew, Mark, and the LXX played a major role in the composition of the nativity story. The Greek of the infancy story, according to him, is so embedded with Septuagintalisms that no one may argue for the translation theory. He denies the possibility of translation on the grounds that the language of the infancy narrative is the same as that of the rest of the Gospel and that it is Septuagintal.

Goulder finally has to acknowledge that the Greek of chs 1–2 is strongly coloured by apparent Semitisms, which may exclude its substantial identity with that of chs 3–24. Even if the language of the infancy narrative is identical to that of 3–24, this observation may support either Luke's direct

---

102. M.D. Goulder and M.L. Sanderson, 'St. Luke's Genesis', *JTS*, ns. 8 (1957), p. 12.
103. M.D. Goulder, *Luke: A New Paradigm*, vol. 1 (JSNTSS, 20; Sheffield: JSOT, 1989).

composition or translation, as far as the language is not identified in detail. Concerning his argumentation for the Septuagintalistic character of the Greek in the infancy narrative, Goulder appears to oversimplify the problem. Since Septuagintalisms can overlap with Semitisms, it is not effective to point out that Septuagintalisms are so strong in order to argue for the imitation theory without examining alleged Semitisms carefully. He clearly assumes, but does not demonstrate, the imitation theory. In addition, he ignores the possible influence of Luke's sources. Before denying underlying sources, he needs to examine their possibility by investigating the Greek of the infancy story in detail. Here again, he simply presupposes that there is no underlying source behind the infancy narrative.

In his treatment on the last episode in 2.41–52, i.e., Jesus in Jerusalem at age twelve, Goulder clearly discloses how he explains Luke's composition procedure. He insists that Luke created the episode to show that Jesus knew his sonship of God before his baptism. Luke started to imagine with Mt. 3.15, 'Let (*it*) be now, for so it is proper to fulfill all righteousness,' which for Goulder means that Jesus knew he was God's son prior to his baptism. Goulder argues that Luke attempted to give his readers certainty about such an insight. As shown by this example, Goulder does not demonstrate but only assumes Luke's imitation and composition. He is interested in explaining Luke's composition procedure.

Also arguing that Luke did not use sources for the infancy narrative, F. O'Fearghail believes Luke purposely imitated the LXX. He defines the term 'Septuagintalisms' as vocabulary or phrases 'typical of the Septuagint'[104] while tracing the origin of such 'typical' expressions to Semitisms. Semitisms in the LXX deviated from normal Greek because of the influence of Semitic languages. This category includes not only intervention but also enhancement.[105] Septuagintalisms become Lukanisms when the latter are used exclusively by Luke. O'Fearghail claims that 'Septuagintalisms are features of language and style and should be distinguished from reminiscences of septuagintal text'. Luke composed the infancy story, according to him, not by adopting Septuagintalisms, but mainly by imitating the LXX style. This is why Luke appears to fail to imitate the LXX expressions precisely. O'Fearghail proposes the concept 'Septuagintal-type expression' which refers to a locution that 'is cast in the mould of a septuagintal expression but which does not have an exact

---

104. F. O'Fearghail, 'The Imitation of the Septuagint in Luke's Infancy Narrative', *Proceedings of the Irish Biblical Association*, No. 12 (ed. W. Harrington; Dublin: The Columbus Press, 1989), p. 59.

105. Enhancement means that Greek locutions which occur rarely in non-biblical Greek literature appear frequently in the NT due to their frequent occurrence in the LXX. For the definition of intervention, see 'Introduction' of this book.

parallel there, or represents an inaccurate or unsuccessful attempt at reproducing a septuagintal expression' ('Imitation', p. 59).

O'Fearghail suggests three factors which support Luke's imitation.[106] First, Luke was familiar with the Septuagint and used it frequently and variously. Luke did not follow, for example, the Hebrew original but the LXX in Acts 15.16–17, which is based on Amos 9.11–12. Second, Lukanisms prevail in the infancy story, though Luke imitated the LXX. Third, Luke lived in a literary setting where imitation was accepted and even recommended. Typical education of Luke's time centred on literary imitation. Therefore, alleged Semitisms, O'Fearghail concludes, must be considered as products of the imitation of the LXX.

But despite these factors, O'Fearghail believes that Luke was unable to sustain consistency in employing the Septuagintalisms in the first two chapters. Luke should have tried to maintain consistency if he had composed the story using Septuagintalisms. However, Luke, according to O'Fearghail, only *attempted* to imitate the LXX and as a result some apparent inconsistencies occurred. He resolves the problem of so-called 'failed Septuagintalisms' by distinguishing between Septuagintalisms and 'Septuagintal-type expressions'. The participial phrase in 1.6 (πορευόμενοι ἐν πάσαις ταῖς ἐντολαῖς καὶ δικαιώμασιν τοῦ κυρίου), for example, does not belong to Septuagintalisms but to the Septuagintal-type expression, since the phrase πάσαις ταῖς ἐντολαῖς καὶ δικαιώμασιν is construed in the LXX with the verb φυλάσσεσθαι and/or ποιεῖν, but never with the verb πορεύεσθαι ('Imitation', p. 62). O'Fearghail's study also helps resolve the question of why the Greek of the infancy story in particular is heavily Septuagint-alized.[107] O'Fearghail suggests the similarity of motifs and situations between the infancy story and the OT as the main reason for imitation. Luke also intended to point to God's intervention, a frequent occurrence in the OT. Luke composed the infancy narrative in affinity with the LXX in order to introduce the idea that God intervened anew in salvation history in the NT, fulfilling the promise of the OT ('Imitation', pp. 71–73).

Despite its positive aspects, O'Fearghail's argument is vulnerable to criticism. He displays a confusion about Septuagintalisms when he contends that Septuagintalisms which occur due to intervention of the Semitic language are Semitisms. His position is the direct opposite of those scholars who assume that all the Semitisms are Septuagintalisms. He holds that all the Septuagintalisms are Semitisms. He does not distinguish

---

106. He proposes four grounds for Luke's imitation. However, one of them is not connected with linguistic observations, but with thematic and structural ones. See his article, 'The Imitation', pp. 59–60.

107. As Farris notes, the critical weakness of the imitation theory is that its advocates have not offered a proper explanation as to the motivation for imitating the Septuagint (*The Hymns*, p. 36).

between Septuagintalisms and Semitisms. Instead, O'Fearghail introduces the rather vague term 'Septuagintal-type expression' to interpret non-Septuagintalistic expressions as a possible influence of the LXX. If a Greek locution in the infancy story does not follow the LXX style exactly, according to him, it should be regarded as a 'Septuagintal-type expression'. He seems to succeed in avoiding refutation by the introduction of this term. However, he does not recognize the necessity of comparing the usage of Septuagintal-type Greek locutions in the infancy story with those in the rest of the Gospel before claiming that they represent Septuagintal-type expressions by Luke's imitation activity. This step is necessary for proving whether they represent failed Septuagintal expressions or not. O'Fearghail suggests, for example, that the use of the verb πίμπλημι with the time indicator ἡμέρα in 1.23a (καὶ ἐγένετο ὡς ἐπλήσθησαν αἱ ἡμέραι τῆς λειτουργίας αὐτοῦ) is a Septuagintal-type expression, since the verb πληρόω, not πίμπλημι, is always used in the LXX for that purpose. The problem lies in the fact that Luke, following the LXX, adopted the verb πληρόω for this usage in the rest of his writings without exception (Lk. 21.24; Acts 7.23; 7.30; 9.23; 24.27). The use of the verb πίμπλημι with ἡμέρα is not a Septuagintal-type expression but rather a non-Septuagintal expression and a non-Lukanism, which may indicate Luke's dependence on immediate Greek sources. O'Fearghail ignores the possibility that the failed Septuagintalisms may have been derived from Luke's possible Greek sources.

O'Fearghail includes 'enhancement' among Septuagintalisms, i.e., Semitisms in his definition, and suggests two examples for enhancement: the use of ἐνώπιον as a preposition and parataxis. The first one, however, occurs frequently in other Hellenistic authors. He does not consider the possibility that Luke's Greek could have been influenced by Hellenistic writers for the use of this preposition. Before deciding whether or not a word or phrase represents a Septuagintalism, one must see if it occurs in other Hellenistic literature. O'Fearghail needs to explain more clearly why enhancement is to be included among Septuagintalisms.[108]

Another shortcoming is that O'Fearghail's study does not provide much information for determining whether Luke translated his Semitic sources. He claims, without examining them in detail, that some expressions fall into the category of the Septuagintal-type expressions. In fact, he concentrates in the latter part of his study on the question of why Luke imitated the LXX. The critical flaw in his argument lies in the fact that he,

---

108. He betrays his inadequate attitude about Septuagintalisms when he suggests the same instances both as Septuagintalisms and Lukanisms, for example, Luke's use of the preposition ἐνώπιον. This preposition also appears frequently in Hellenistic authors and may belong to Koine Greek. A better example would be unemphatic καὶ αὐτός which does not occur in Acts, rarely in the other Gospels, but frequently in the Gospel of Luke.

like Goulder, presupposes rather than demonstrates Luke's imitation of the LXX. For example, he notes that the opening section of the infancy story resembles passages in the Old Testament. Luke consulted Jeremiah, Amos and others for the first part of the sentence:

ἐν ταῖς ἡμέραις Ἡρῴδου βασιλέως τῆς Ἰουδαίας (Lk. 1.5);
ἐν ταῖς ἡμέραις Ἰωσια υἱοῦ Ἀμως βασιλέως Ἰούδα (Jer. 1.2). The rest recalls 1 Kgs 1. 1–2:

(Lk. 1.5) Ἐγένετο ἱερεύς τις ὀνόματι Ζαχαρίας ἐξ ἐφημερίας Ἀβιά, καὶ γυνὴ αὐτῷ ἐξ τῶν θυγατέρων Ἀρὼν καὶ τὸ ὄνομα αὐτῆς Ἐλισάβετ.

(1 Kgs 1.1–2) ἄνθρωπος ἦν ἐξ Ἀρμαθαιμ Σιφα ἐξ ὄρους Ἐφραιμ καὶ ὄνομα αὐτῷ Ἐλκανα υἱὸς Ἰερεμεηλ υἱοῦ Ἡλιου υἱοῦ Θοκε ἐν Νασιβ Ἐφραιμ καὶ τούτῳ δύο γυναῖκες ὄνομα τῇ μιᾷ Ἀννα καὶ ὄνομα τῇ δευτέρᾳ Φεννανα καὶ ἦν τῇ Φεννανα παιδία καὶ τῇ Ἀννα οὐκ ἦν παιδίον.

O'Fearghail adds that 'the Semitic style of the indication of Hannah's childlessness is recalled in the Lukan reference to the childlessness of Zechariah and Elizabeth in 1.7' ('Imitation', p. 61). What is 'Semitic style?' What is its origin? Why did Luke use ἐγένετο while 1 Kgs 1.1 of the LXX includes ἦν? O'Fearghail does not deal with these questions. His method does not help much in deciding whether Luke followed the LXX or the Hebrew OT, for he clearly assumes Luke's dependence on the LXX.[109]

Focusing on the verbal aspect of the Greek language, S.E. Porter locates the most probable examples of Semitic intervention in the Greek of the New Testament mainly in Luke's infancy narrative. The Magnificat and the Benedictus contain awkward tense usage: 1.46-47; 1.51-53; 1.68b, 70. He rejects, however, the argument that this usage is due to Semitic originals of the two hymns. Many alleged Semitic interventions with respect to verbal tense are attested even in the Greek language. For example, the shift from the present to the aorist tense in 1.46-47 also occurs in Greek poetry (*Verbal Aspect*, pp. 131–32). Since such apparent intervention can be explained on the basis of the Greek language, the question centres on where the emphasis lies. Porter concedes that the hymns in the infancy narrative betray 'Semitic poetic style in their

---

109. O'Fearghail's weakness is apparent in his argument for the locution in v. 7b: προβεβηκότες ἐν ταῖς ἡμέραις αὐτῶν ἦσαν ('Imitation', p. 62). He attempts to solve the problem by pointing out that ἐν ταῖς ἡμέραις αὐτῶν is typical of Luke, who always utilizes ταῖς ἡμέραις with the preposition ἐν except for 1.75. He classifies it as a 'Septuagintal-type phrase'. But O'Fearghail fails to consider one important element: προβεβηκότες ἐν ταῖς ἡμέραις is not attested in any Hellenistic or classical author nor in the LXX. It is a wrong expression. While other locutions like πορευόμενοι ἐν in v. 5 which never occur in other Greek writings are clearly attested in the LXX, the expression προβεβηκότες ἐν ταῖς ἡμέραις never occurs even in the LXX. This example demonstrates his misunderstanding of the complexity of the issue. The question of why Luke even adopted a wrong expression must be answered. Again, it becomes clear that O'Fearghail presupposes but does not prove Luke's imitation of the Septuagint.

structure and language'. However, he understands Luke's conscious imitation of the LXX as the origin of that style.

Porter's approach is correct in his emphasis on the importance of the Greek language rather than the Semitic languages. Nevertheless, the following observations weaken his argument on the infancy narrative. Although Porter assumes Luke's conscious, stylistic imitation of the LXX for the tense shift in Lk. 1.46-47, he omits giving concrete instances from the LXX to prove it. The example of tense shift in the Septuagint must be singled out as showing Luke's conscious imitation of it. Moreover, Porter's study is restricted to the verbal aspect. He finally does not explain why Luke heavily Septuagintalized the Greek of the infancy narrative.

The above survey has demonstrated that both the advocates of the translation theory and the proponents of the imitation theory, at least in recent debate, recognize two things: on the one hand, the Greek of the Lukan infancy story is embedded with Hebraistic characteristics, whether they are called 'Semitisms' or 'Septuagintalisms'; on the other hand, Luke's style prevails throughout the story. Concerning the first, the advocates of the imitation theory assume alleged Semitisms to be in reality Septuagintalisms, while the proponents of the translation theory believe that they represent real Semitisms derived from a Semitic (Hebrew) original.[110] This contradictory tendency indicates how difficult and important it is to set and apply criteria for distinguishing between Septuagintalisms and Semitisms. Concerning the function of Lukan style, the imitation theory interprets it as indicating Luke's direct composition, while the translation theory regards it as occurring in the process of translation or of Luke's editing activity of his immediate Greek sources translated from Hebrew. It is evident that the mere similarity of the Greek in the infancy narrative with the rest of the Gospel may prove either Luke's direct composition or Luke's translation. Lukanisms can not provide critical evidence for Luke's direct composition. However, they may give a hint regarding Luke's composition, especially when they do not reflect Semitic influence. In this sense, Lukanisms also require a correct definition.

The survey has also shown that the topic of the Greek of the infancy narrative is interwoven with the problem of sources, at least on the basic level. A linguistic examination alone is unable to provide a complete solution to the source problem. However, no one can deny that such an examination may offer an important contribution to solving the source problem. Scholars who argue for the translation theory assume that Luke possessed either Semitic sources translated into Greek by Luke or Greek

---

110. As we saw above, Luke's possible reliance on Aramaic source material has little or no support.

sources translated by an unknown person before Luke's access to them. In contrast, scholars who hold to the imitation theory believe that Luke, imitating the LXX style, himself composed the infancy narrative, either without or in part depending on sources. An examination of the Greek of the infancy narrative is closely connected with the search for Luke's sources for it.[111] The question as to whether Luke translated Semitic sources for the whole infancy story, or whether he depended on immediate Greek sources, either translated from Hebrew or composed in Greek, can be answered by the presence of non-Lukanisms, which excludes the possibility that Luke himself translated a putative (Hebrew or Aramaic) source as well as the possibility that he himself directly composed the infancy narrative without relying on source material. Non-Lukanisms may indicate that Luke depended on (probably written) Greek sources. This means that non-Lukanisms also need to be delineated correctly. The next chapter will thus discuss the definitions of Septuagintalisms and Semitisms, and Lukanisms and non-Lukanisms.

---

111. As scholars admit, the procedure of the composition of the Lukan infancy narrative is still wrapped in fog.

Chapter 2

DEFINITIONS OF SEMITISMS AND
SEPTUAGINTALISMS, LUKANISMS AND
NON-LUKANISMS

A. *Semitisms and Septuagintalisms*

I. *Various Views on the Definition of Semitisms and Septuagintalisms*

Many NT Greek scholars and students suppose a consensus exists about the definition of 'Semitisms' since they so frequently encounter the term, not only in specific articles but also in general commentaries. In spite of this perception, however, no such consensus does exist, a condition which produces disagreement about the term's definition.[1] This disagreement results, as demonstrated by the survey in the preceding chapter, in precisely two opposite conclusions on the issue of the influence of Semitic languages on New Testament Greek. While some scholars assert without doubt that Semitic languages exercised a great influence on NT Greek, others maintain with the same certainty that the influence was trivial. Concerning the infancy narrative, the lack of consensus on the definition of Semitisms plays an important role in yielding two opposite views, i.e., 1) the translation theory and 2) the direct composition theory in imitation of the LXX. This situation makes it necessary to precisely delineate 'Semitisms' in order to determine the characteristics of the Greek of the infancy narrative.

There is a consensus on the question what 'Semitic' means. The term indicates either Hebrew or Aramaic: the former represents the language of the OT and first-century Jews and the latter refers to the 'prestige' language in first-century Palestine. Although most scholars dealing with the topic of Semitic influence distinguish between Hebraisms and

---

1. Horton, 'Reflections on the Semitisms of Luke-Acts', p. 5.

Aramaisms, they also use the term 'Semitisms' for both of them.[2] More importantly, the distinction between Hebraisms and Aramaisms is of little practical importance for the study of the influence of Semitic languages on the Greek of the Lukan infancy story, since most Semitisms in the story are thought to be Hebraisms, not Aramaisms.[3]

Septuagintalisms indicate the influence of the Greek of the LXX, which was the translation of the OT Hebrew (or Aramaic in a few places) Bible, on the NT. The definition of Semitisms is closely connected to the definition of the Septuagintalisms. The evaluation of the influence of LXX Greek on the Greek of the NT is also closely related to the evaluation of the influence of Semitic languages on NT Greek. The following discussion will thus focus on determining the relationship between Semitisms and Septuagintalisms in order to make reliable definitions of these two concepts.

(1) *Views which emphasize the influence of Semitic languages*
Without sufficiently recognizing the position of the LXX and the importance of Hellenistic Greek for the New Testament authors, some scholars, especially those belonging to an older generation, do not clearly distinguish between 'Semitisms' and 'Septuagintalisms'. They assume, emphasizing the importance of Semitic languages, that a Greek locution in the NT must refer to the influence of Semitic languages if it seems to be abnormal and reflect Semitic syntax. Moulton, the representative of this group, defines Semitisms as 'a deviation from genuine Greek idiom due to too literal rendering of the language of a Semitic original.'[4] In other words, Semitisms refer to un-Greek expressions that occur because of the

---

2. See below for Porter, Maloney, Wilcox, and Fitzmyer. All of them use two terms 'Hebraisms' and 'Aramaisms', but they call them both 'Semitisms'. Especially Porter argues that the distinction between Hebraisms and Aramaisms, which is standard since Dalman, is not always essential (*Verbal Aspect*, p. 118). See also H. Koester, *Einführung in das Neue Testament* (Berlin/New York: de Gruyter, 1980), p. 114.

3. G. Dalman, *The Word of Jesus: Considered in the Light of Post-Biblical Jewish Writings and the Aramaic Language* (Trans. D.M. Kay; Edinburgh: T. & T. Clark, 1902), p. 39. M.-J. Lagrange, *Evangile selon Saint Luc* (Paris: Gabalda, 1921), p. lxxxvii. Torrey and Burney argue for Aramaic originals for other parts of the NT, but Hebrew originals for the infancy narrative. For their argument, see Chapter 1. See also Sparks, 'The Semitisms of St. Luke's Gospel', p. 135. Recent commentaries accept this assessment: Marshall, *Luke*, p. 46; Nolland, *Luke 1–9:20*, p. 21. Introductory books for the New Testament also betray this tendency: W.G. Kümmel, *Introduction to the NT* (London: SCM Press, 1975), p. 136; Guthrie, *New Testament Introduction*, p. 196. See also M. Wilcox, 'Semitisms in the New Testament', in *Aufstieg und Niedergang der römischen Welt*; II. 25. 2 (ed. W. Haase; Berlin: de Gruyter, 1984), p. 979.

4. *Accidence and Word-Formation*, vol. 2 of *A Grammar of New Testament Greek* (Edinburgh: T. & T. Clark, 1929), p. 14.

intervention of Semitic syntax. His definition in the introduction of *Accidence and Word-Formation* excludes renderings, resulting from Semitic syntax, which are 'perfectly idiomatic' in Greek. Moulton offers two possible origins of true Semitisms in the NT: 1) conscious or unconscious imitation of the LXX; 2) slavish renderings of Semitic sources, including a writer's native Semitic in which he devised the story in his mind which was translated into Greek when he wrote it down (*Accidence and Word-Formation*, p. 16).

Although he accepts, following R.H. Charles, that many awkward Greek expressions in the Apocalypse derived from a literal transference of Semitic idioms, Moulton recognizes that many alleged Semitic locutions are found in late vernacular Greek. Moulton, however, emphasizing the aspect of Semitic influence, includes some of these locutions in his definition of Semitisms by broadening the meaning of the term 'un-Greek' which now includes idiomatic Greek expressions if they stem from Semitic languages and occur more frequently in the New Testament (*Accidence and Word-Formation*, p. 414).[5] An overuse of a rare locution, according to his argument, indicates the direct influence of Semitisms. He accordingly separates 'pure Semitisms' from 'secondary Semitisms'.[6] The latter refer to the overuse of locutions which belong to good Koine Greek, but originate clearly from the writers' native tongue. In other words, even enhancement belongs to Semitisms.[7] These 'secondary Semitisms' are important, he continues, especially when one is 'seeking for evidences of Semitic birth in a writer whose Greek betrays deficient knowledge of the resources of the language.' Although Moulton succeeds in making a place for 'pure Semitisms', which are different from 'secondary Semitisms', he still emphasizes that 'secondary Semitisms' virtually belong to Semitisms. It is hardly possible, however, to determine whether an overuse of some locutions in the New Testament derived from native Semitic or native Greek. Thus, 'secondary Semitisms' cannot provide evidence for the Semitic origin of New Testament Greek. Moreover, Moulton does not consider the position of LXX Greek for the NT writers for whom the Greek of the LXX may have been regarded as normal Greek.

---

5. W.F. Howard notes in the Appendix of *Accidence and Word-Formation*, p. 413, that 'Dr. Moulton's attitude to the subject of Semitisms in the New Testament was slightly modified after the first edition of the *Prolegomena* appeared.'

6. Moulton simply distinguishes between two categories, i.e., Semitisms and secondary Semitisms. Howard names the former 'pure Semitisms' and describes the latter as 'those to which that title (Semitisms) can only be given in a secondary sense' (*Accidence and Word-Formation*, p. 414).

7. As we saw in Chapter 1, 'enhancement' conveys the idea that rare Greek locutions occur frequently because of the influence of Semitic language.

W.F. Howard points out that 'when once the LXX had become a standard of sacred speech for Hellenistic Jews and proselytes, its idioms would easily find their way into free composition' (*Accidence and Word-Formation*, p. 478). The language of the LXX was 'normal' Greek rather than a Semitized language for the NT authors. Therefore, Hebraisms in the NT, according to him, mainly originated from the influence of the LXX, which does not necessarily mean direct Semitic influence on the NT. Howard does not, however, adopt the term 'Septuagintalisms' and leaves the definition ambiguous, even though it is necessary to distinguish between 'Semitisms' and 'Septuagintalisms' to effectively examine the influence of Semitic languages on the NT.

The confusion around the terminology appears also in other scholars. C.F. Burney distinguishes between 'Hebraisms' and 'Aramaisms', and utilizes the term 'Hebraisms' while defining 'Septuagintalisms' by content. The term 'Hebraisms' stands for 'a construction or word usage' which the LXX translators used to render a Hebrew original and one which the NT authors employed through the influence of the LXX. Burney regards Semitisms other than Hebraisms as Aramaisms. He distinguishes Hebraisms from Aramaisms to argue that Aramaisms in the Gospel of John owe their origin to Aramaic originals. Semitisms in the Gospel of Luke, on the other hand, indicates 'Hebraisms' introduced by the author's imitation of the LXX. Burney does not recognize that the direct influence of the LXX on the NT could be called Septuagintalisms rather than Hebraisms.

With a cautious attitude, Maloney introduces, along with 'direct interference', 'indirect interference' of Semitic languages, which implies the influence of Semitic languages on the NT through the Greek Old Testament (*Semitic Interference*, p. 2). It is important, he argues, to clarify first whether a Greek locution is normal or abnormal. Some Greek locutions which are quite abnormal, or totally unattested in Hellenistic Greek 'whereas their appearance in Semitic is normal (sometimes only possible)', in Maloney's view, 'are true Semitisms' (*Semitic Interference*, p. 245). Accordingly, 'indirect interference' should mean for Maloney Greek locutions in the Greek Old Testament which are 'un-Greek' and echo the syntax of Semitic languages. Maloney's argument is on the right track because he compares NT Greek with Hellenistic Greek and emphasizes the abnormality of Greek locutions. However, he does not consider, like Moulton, the position of the LXX for the NT authors. While so-called 'indirect interference' in NT Greek texts may be interference for the LXX translators, because they translated Hebrew or Aramaic originals, it may not fall into the category of interference for the NT authors, who may have composed their writings imitating the Greek style of the Greek Old Testament. All the expressions in the LXX may have been quite normal for the NT authors, especially for Luke, who may have employed alleged Semitic locutions not to conform with normal idiomatic Semitic usage but to compose his books in affinity to the LXX. This element needs to be considered.

This brief survey has shown that scholars in this group hesitate to distinguish between Septuagintalisms and Semitisms. Emphasizing Semitic languages, they include Septuagintalisms in Semitisms without employing the term Septuagintalisms and deciding what constitutes them in detail. This ambiguous attitude makes it difficult to evaluate precisely the influence of Semitisms on NT Greek.

(2) *Views which emphasize or clearly recognize the important role of the LXX*

Recent scholarship tends to assume that every Greek locution attested in the LXX must be counted as a Septuagintalism. Fitzmyer argues, for example, that alleged Semitisms, if they occur in the LXX, must be regarded as Septuagintalisms and only those Semitisms which are not found in the LXX should be regarded as true Semitisms (*The Gospel According to Luke I–IX*, p. 114).[8] This means that alleged Semitic locutions in the NT indicate the influence of the LXX rather than Semitic languages. Even though some Semitisms in Luke are regarded as direct Semitic interference,[9] they belong, according to Fitzmyer, to Septuagintalisms rather than to Semitisms considering the important position of the LXX for the NT authors. The Greek OT, especially the LXX, he continues, influenced Lukan Greek so much that the majority of alleged Semitisms should fall into the category of Septuagintalisms. With this consideration, he concludes, it is better to assume that the author of the Gospel of Luke depended on the LXX rather than that he composed his work using Semitisms. In this sense, his argument is convincing. Nevertheless, Fitzmyer takes an ambiguous stance on Septuagintalisms by commenting on alleged Semitisms without defining Septuagintalisms in

---

8. Fitzmyer assumes the presence of Aramaisms in Luke because Luke's hometown, Antioch according to Fitzmyer, represents a place where people spoke Aramaic. He insists that there is Aramaic 'interference' in Luke. However, he adds that only a few possible Aramaisms exist in the Lukan Gospel (*Luke I–IX*, p. 116, 312). According to him, Lk 1.32-35 has a parallel in the Aramaic text of *4Q246*. This parallel is the only possible Aramaic interference in the infancy story for Fitzmyer. As pointed out in Chapter 1.B, however, it is not convincing that the Aramaic interference occurs in the infancy narrative. For details, see Chapter 1.B.

9. As pointed out in Chapter 1, interference conveys the idea that Semitic languages imposed awkward constructions upon Greek.

detail, resulting in inconsistency.[10] He fails to define the exact meaning of Septuagintalisms.

Recognizing this problem, other scholars have tried to clarify the meaning of 'Septuagintalisms.' However, additional confusion arises in their attempts to define the term. F. Rehkopf, having divided 'Semitisms' into 'translation Semitisms' and 'Septuagintalisms', suggests 'Hebraisms' and 'Aramaisms' as two subcategories of 'translation Semitisms' and names 'Septuagintalisms' 'secondary Hebraisms'.[11] He recognizes that not all the expressions that seem to be Semitisms are Semitisms. Rehkopf remarks that the intimacy of the NT authors with the LXX is the origin of Septuagintalisms. However, the overlap between Hebraisms and Septuagintalisms is confusing. Hebraisms, according to Rehkopf, are found in the New Testament in literal and free quotations of the LXX, furthermore also in the parts which are embedded with the style of the OT like hymns and doxologies ('Griechisch', pp. 232–33). 'Translation Hebraisms' in biblical citations, he continues, can be identified by comparison with the Hebrew text, while it is less possible to check Hebrew texts for reminiscence. Rehkopf divides Septuagintalisms into two types: those in the lexical area and those pertaining to syntax and style. He postulates that Septuagintalisms in the lexical area render words which appear more frequently in the LXX than in non-LXX Greek, like προσευχή or πειρασμός, or whose meaning deviates from normal Greek due to the influence of Hebrew, like ῥῆμα or εἰρήνη. The influence of the LXX appears to be clear in the vocabulary. Septuagintalisms in syntax and style, according to him, refer to locutions which do not occur in non-biblical Greek and reflect Semitic syntax by the imitation of LXX style. Rehkopf excludes from syntactical Septuagintalisms expressions which can be found in Greek, like the participle λέγων introducing direct discourse instead of ὅτι recitativum, and those which are only possible in Greek but occur frequently in the LXX through the influence of Hebrew, like the use of the preposition ἐν with the dative for an instrumental meaning. This means that 'Septuagintalisms' in syntax, i.e. 'secondary Hebraisms' in syntax, are to be virtually included in Hebraisms. He suggests, in fact, that translation Hebraisms, apart from those derived from citations, include secondary Hebraisms in syntax, which indicate Septuagintalisms by his definition. A possible flaw of his argument is that he does not clearly separate Septuagintalisms from Hebraisms. Although Septuagintalisms represent a kind of Hebraism in the sense that they reflect the influence of Hebrew syntax, Septuagintalisms

---

10. He does not offer criteria to distinguish between verbatim expressions found in the LXX and those which are cast in the mould of Septuagintal expressions but do not occur in the LXX. For details, see Chapter 1.

11. F. Rehkopf, 'Griechisch', in *Theologische Realenzyklopaedie, Studienausgabe*, Teil I (Berlin/New York: de Gruyter, 1993), p. 232.

should be regarded primarily as linguistic phenomena from the perspective of the Greek language in which they are written rather than from the perspective of the Semitic language (Hebrew) from which they originate. This distinction is imperative in order to investigate the influence of Semitic languages on the NT. Septuagintalisms may signify Semitisms, mainly Hebraisms, for the LXX translators. However, they were not Semitisms for the NT authors; LXX Greek may have been primarily (sacred) Greek for them.

D. Schmidt tries to delineate 'Septuagintalisms' as narrowly as possible. On the presumption that 'the less the two categories (Semitisms and Septuagintalisms) overlap, the more likely there can be consensus on possible instances of each', he insists that Septuagintalisms must point to Greek expressions 'that are not reflective of Semitic syntax', which he names 'un-Semitic', 'but used to render Semitic constructions into Greek in one of the translation styles in the Septuagint'.[12] In other words, Septuagintalisms are 'syntactical peculiarities that are not typical of Semitic syntax, but are stylistic features characteristic of one of the varieties of translation Greek within the LXX' ('Semitisms', p. 596). Schmidt contributes to the problem of ambiguous definition. His narrow definition is effective for the topic of his study of the Greek of Revelation, where allusions to Daniel occur frequently. The translation of Theodotion, according to Schmidt, provides examples of typical Semitisms, that is, peculiarities in Greek that reflect the syntax of a Hebrew/Aramaic text, whereas the Old Greek version offers some instances for 'un-Greek' characteristics 'that are also "un-Semitic" in a freer translation', and they 'represent distinctive stylistic features of that translation.' While his method may work effectively for the study of the Greek of the Apocalypse, it does not fit the study of other parts of the NT, including the Lukan infancy narrative. A broad definition is required to effectively trace the topic of Semitic influence in the infancy narrative.

Some scholars, adopting the term 'Septuagintalisms' and distinguishing between Semitisms and Septuagintalisms, present a more advanced view for the study of Semitic influence in the NT in general, by defining what constitutes Septuagintalisms. Following Moulton-Howard's definition of Semitisms, Wilcox expresses it in different words, and maintains the same content by delineating Semitisms as words and phrases 'whose use or construction departs from normal idiomatic Greek usage in such a way as to conform with normal idiomatic Semitic usage' (*The Semitisms of Acts*, p. 17). His definition, like Maloney's, focuses on the abnormality of Greek expressions. Wilcox also makes progress by recognizing the problem of distinguishing between 'Septuagintalisms' and 'Semitisms'. Accordingly,

---

12. 'Semitisms and Septuagintalisms in the Book of Revelation', *NTS*, 37 (1991), p. 594.

the imitation of the LXX, which Moulton considers the origin of NT Semitisms, cannot be for Wilcox a cause of Semitisms. He posits that one must exclude possible Septuagintalisms at the first stage to identify true Semitisms.[13] He suggests a broad definition of Septuagintalisms by dividing possible Septuagintalisms into three categories: 1) 'those "typical" of the LXX such as καὶ ἐγένετο' and 'ἐν τῷ followed by the infinitive'; 2) others which are non-typical of the LXX, but found both in the LXX and NT; 3) locutions which do not occur in the LXX at all but which are 'cast in the same mould' as that of the LXX.[14] Wilcox contends that only 'hard core' Semitisms are real ones,[15] and thus useful as a guide to the tracing of Semitic influence on the sources for Acts.[16] On the other hand, the last category, he continues, could be included either in Septuagintalisms or Semitisms. The constructions in the examples for this category, according to him, need to be examined to determine whether they indicate the influence of the Septuagint or of Semitic languages. Wilcox recognizes the important position of the LXX by defining Septuagintalisms as broadly as possible and his approach has an advantage in objectively estimating the influence of the LXX and Semitic languages.

Wilcox's definition of Septuagintalisms is adopted by Horton who accepts it on condition that his definition indicates only 'a possible Semitism'. Horton goes a step further by asking why alleged Semitisms depart from normal Greek usage. Only Semitic interference, according to him, can indicate a Semitism.[17] He accepts Weinreich's delineation of the term 'interference': 'the term interference implies the rearrangement of patterns that result from the introduction of foreign elements into the more highly structured domains of language.' Horton asserts that the over-use of Greek locutions in the NT which do not occur frequently in other Greek literature cannot be an instance of 'Semitisms' at all, though to consider their relation to Semitisms helps to understand what constitutes Semitisms. The tendency to regard all Hebraisms as Septuagintalisms and translations, he argues, must be corrected. Horton recognizes that Septuagintalisms cannot explain all the alleged Semitisms. 'Direct imitation of the Septuagint,' he notes, 'may indeed be fairly limited in Luke-Acts but the Septuagintal character of the books is pervasive.' Apart from the

---

13. 'Semitisms in the New Testament', p. 986.
14. M. Wilcox, *The Semitisms of Acts* (Oxford: University Press, 1965), p. 57 Wilcox 'Semitisms in the New Testament', p. 984.
15. 'Hard core Semitisms' point to Semitisms which are not included in Septuagintalisms ('Semitisms in the New Testament', pp. 985–86).
16. Wilcox rejects Luke's translation of a Semitic original for Acts but supposes that Luke may have depended on Greek sources translated from Semitic originals (*The Semitisms of Acts*, p. 182).
17. 'Reflections on the Semitisms', p. 7.

2. Definitions of Semitisms and Septuagintalisms

replications of the LXX language, 'unsuccessful attempts to imitate that language' are able to explain many alleged Hebraisms in Luke-Acts. However, some Hebraisms still remain unanswered even with these two categories. Horton introduces 'synagogue Greek' to resolve the problem of the remaining Hebraisms.[18] The third category of Septuagintalisms in Wilcox, i.e., 'those which have only an appearance of being Septuagintal in character', he continues, 'are vitally important as indicating the operation of the synagogue Greek' ('Reflections on the Semitisms', p. 19).[19] Some alleged Hebraisms, he concludes, originated from a Jewish dialect which was used only for religious purposes in the synagogue. While Horton acknowledges the importance of Septuagintalisms, he omits a precise definition of the term Septuagintalism by leaving ambiguous the distinction between 'unsuccessful Septuagintalisms' and 'remaining Hebraisms'.

Acknowledging the important position of the LXX, Porter defines a Septuagintalism as 'a construction in the LXX of prominence disproportionate to other Hellenistic Greek usage' and adds that it does not necessarily constitute a Semitism. He argues for a possible independent influence of the LXX on the NT Greek apart from Semitic languages 'on the basis of the place of the LXX in 1st cent. Judaism and Christianity, its relation to the Hebrew OT, and its being a translation document' (*Verbal Aspect*, p. 118). Porter suggests three levels of Semitic influence by distinguishing between direct translation,[20] intervention, and enhancement.[21] He excludes enhancement from real Semitisms, since it could be explained through the possible influence of Greek. Enhancements cannot prove direct Semitic influence. He defines a Hebraism as 'a Semitism that can be fairly confidently attributed to Biblical or Mishnaic Hebrew', while describing an Aramaism as 'a Semitism that can be attributed to Aramaic'.

Scholars treated above emphasize the Greek aspect of the OT Greek and its influence on NT Greek. They thereby appropriately evaluate the importance of Septuagintalisms for the NT writings, although their definitions need to be more precisely refined.

---

18. 'Reflections on the Semitisms of Luke-Acts', p. 23. For his argument, see Chapter 1.
19. Horton notes that Wilcox classifies Septuagintalisms into two categories: 'those which have an exact parallel in the Septuagint, and those which have only an appearance of being Septuagintal in character.' Horton includes those typical of the LXX, which Wilcox classifies separately, in the first category ('Reflection on the Semitisms'), p. 19.
20. Direct translation does not mean that the Evangelists translated Semitic originals but simply indicates their translation of some words like Ελωι ελωι λεμα σαβαχθανι in Mk 15.34 (Mt. 27.46). See Porter's article 'The Language of the Apocalypse in Recent Discussion', *NTS*, 35 (1989), p. 587.
21. For his definitions of intervention and enhancement, see footnote 7 and 9 of this chapter.

II. *The Definition of Septuagintalisms and Semitisms*

The above discussion has shown that the terminology chosen by scholars illustrates their personal views on the topic of the influence of Semitic languages on the NT. Scholars who lay their emphasis on Semitic languages tend to avoid the term 'Septuagintalisms' and add adjectives like 'secondary' or 'indirect' to 'Semitisms'. By contrast, those who emphasize or recognize the influence of the LXX employ the term 'Septuagintalisms'.

The survey above has also indicated that recent scholars who argue that Septuagintalisms ought to be investigated from the perspective of Greek take seriously the prominent role of the LXX in first-century Jewish and Christian communities. The LXX was the OT Bible for Greek-speaking Jews and gentiles who may have been attracted to Judaism for one reason or another. It also became the OT for the early Christian communities outside Palestine, as the Pauline letters alone attest. The Greek of the LXX was thus probably regarded as acceptable, understandable Greek by those who read and used it. It is clear that awkward expressions in the LXX could not have survived, apart perhaps from only a few in syntax[22] and from some in vocabulary, unless this was the case.[23] Moreover, such surviving awkward expressions became normal locutions to those who used the LXX.

More importantly, Luke, who was probably a Greek-speaking gentile author,[24] clearly depended on the LXX for quotations in Lk. 3–24 and Acts.[25] Luke consulted the LXX in the composition of Luke-Acts because the LXX was the only version of the OT his intended audience could read and understand.[26] It is certain that the language of the LXX influenced

---

22. The representative example is the construction, καὶ ἐγένετο or ἐγένετο δέ + (καὶ) finite verb.
23. For Porter's argument of this aspect, see Chapter 1.A.
24. For the identity of the author and audiences of the Gospel of Luke, see Chapter 1.
25. Quotations in Luke, ch.4 (4.4, 8, 10, 11, 12, 18-19), for example, are from the LXX (see Marshall, *Luke*, pp. 171–84 and Nolland, *Luke 1–9:20*, pp. 179–93). It is remarkable that even in Acts 15.16-18 where James speaks as the leader of the Aramaic-speaking Jerusalem church, the quoted text is from the LXX. For this quotation, see F.F. Bruce who notes that the quotation in these verses 'comes substantially from Amos 9:11f. LXX' (*The Acts of the Apostles*, p. 340). For the quotations which are found in the speeches of Peter and Paul in Acts, see G.F. Steyn, *Septuagint Quotations in the Context of the Petrine and Pauline Speeches of the Acta Apostolorum* (Contributions to Biblical Exegesis and Theology, 12; Kampen: Kok Pharos, 1995), p. 232, who concludes that 'the textform which Luke used was probably a Greek one, but one which greatly resembles our known LXX manuscripts.'
26. Wilcox, *The Semitisms of Acts*, p. 56. See also M. Müller, *The First Bible of the Church: A Plea for the Septuagint* (JSOTSS, 206; Sheffield: Sheffield Academic Press, 1996).

2. Definitions of Semitisms and Septuagintalisms

Lukan Greek in general[27] (for example, Luke frequently uses LXX expressions like ἐγένετο δέ). The circumstances in which Luke wrote his two-volume work were thus not at all like those in which the LXX translators did their work. The translators of the Septuagint no doubt held Semitic originals before them and for this reason were directly influenced by the Semitic languages (Hebrew and, to a much lesser extent, Aramaic) of the OT. In contrast, Luke had the LXX as his *Vorlage* in Lk. 3–24 and in Acts. For the Gospel, he also probably relied on the Greek Gospel of Mark. It is thus certain that Luke had Greek *Vorlagen* for these portions of his work. By contrast, it is not at all certain that Luke used a Semitic *Vorlage* (one or more) for the composition of his two-volume work, *including the infancy narrative of Lk. 1–2*, since no such *Vorlage* (if there was one) has survived.

These considerations make it reasonable to give Septuagintalisms a decidedly prominent place in the present study of the Greek of the Lukan infancy narrative and to define them as precisely and comprehensively as possible. To that end, this study introduces the distinction between 'hard core Septuagintalisms' and 'secondary Septuagintalisms', instead of that between 'pure Semitisms' and 'secondary Semitisms' to examine the Greek of the infancy story.

What are, then, 'hard core Septuagintalisms'? They represent syntactical peculiarities in the LXX which do not render *exactly* the Hebrew/Aramaic originals. The phrase 'syntactical peculiarities' indicates that they originated from the translation of the underlying Hebrew/Aramaic text. This does not necessarily mean, however, that those words or phrases completely deviate from normal Greek usage or do not occur in non-biblical Greek at all. Except for a few examples like the construction of ἐγένετο δέ followed by a finite verb,[28] in fact, the LXX translators employ normal or at least possible Greek locutions in Hellenistic or classical Greek.[29] Thus, words or phrases peculiar to the LXX mainly

---

27. See Sparks's two articles, 'The Semitisms of St. Luke's Gospel' and 'The Semitisms of the Acts'. He notes that 'St. Luke is to be regarded... as a habitual, conscious, and deliberate "septuagintalizer"' ('The Semitisms of the Acts', p. 16).

28. Porter attempts to prove that even this construction does not belong to direct Semitic interference. For more details, see his book *Verbal Aspect*, pp. 120–26.

29. J. Barr notes that 'in the main parts of the LXX this practice (literal rendition of the Semitic idiom) was not carried beyond the point where it led to serious and densely concentrated difficulties of understanding in Greek.' 'Hebrew, Aramaic, and Greek in the Hellenistic Age', in *The Cambridge History of Judaism* (eds., W.D. Davies and L. Finkelstein; Cambridge: University Press, 1989), p. 106. 'The expressions in Greek, though strange when first seen,' he continues, 'are often statistically peculiar rather than quite unintelligible or impossible.' 'Often an expression that in *koine* is strange but possible,' he concludes, 'is made more common and normal in LXX and New Testament, that is, the difference is a statistical one.'

include only those which are the result of translation from the Hebrew/ Aramaic syntax of the OT, even if they may occasionally occur in non-Biblical Greek or represent possibly acceptable Greek. A clear example is the use of the preposition ἐν with the articular infinitive to denote temporal meaning as in 1.8: Ἐγένετο δὲ ἐν τῷ ἱερατεύειν αὐτόν. Some scholars regard this construction as a clear Hebraism because it is found in Hebrew while it does not occur in classical Greek.[30] It is true that the locution reflects Hebrew usage. However, the construction ἐν τῷ followed by the infinitive to convey temporal meaning is used in classical Greek, rare though it is.[31] The use of this locution in a temporal sense is pre-Septuagintal in Greek.[32] Another example of peculiarities in the LXX is ἐν ταῖς ἡμέραις to indicate 'in the days (time) [of].' ἡμέρα could mean 'time' or 'the state or time of life' (Liddell and Scott, p. 770), though this meaning is not common in general Greek usage.[33] The noun, however, is never used with the preposition to indicate 'in the time [of]' outside of the LXX. However, ἐν is widely used to clarify duration of time in the classical language (BDF 200). The preposition refers to both point and duration of time, while the dative alone indicates point of time. This phrase in the LXX resulted from translation, and thus it belongs to the syntactical peculiarities of the LXX, though it is possible in Greek. Needless to say, the abnormality of a Greek word or phrase must be determined by comparing it not only with classical Greek usage but also with Hellenistic Greek usage. It is evident that 'hard core Septuagintalisms' indicate the effect of LXX Greek on the NT.

'Secondary Septuagintalisms' denote syntactical peculiarities in the LXX which *exactly* reflect Semitic syntax. Secondary Septuagintalisms may not clearly support the direct influence of LXX Greek on NT Greek as much as hard core Septuagintalisms do; secondary Septuagintalisms may actually represent direct translations from a Semitic source whereby the syntax of the translation happens to match the wording used by the LXX translators to render a similar underlying Hebrew (or Aramaic) expression. Secondary Septuagintalisms, however, can also indicate precisely the

---

30. Beyer, *Syntax*, pp. 32–52. BDR (404.1) claim that this construction is not used in this way in Greek, while Hebrew uses the preposition ב for a temporal meaning, which the LXX translated ἐν τῷ with the infinitive. This implies that the locution is not allowed in Greek. BDR also cite Dalman's proposal that the construction is not found in Aramaic (Cf. Dalman, *The Words of Jesus*, p. 32).

31. Classical Greek authors usually utilize the participial phrase or subordinate clause to express temporal meaning (BDR 404.1).

32. This expression occurs also in Hellenistic authors like Polybius. For detailed argument, see Mealand, 'Hellenistic Historians and the Style of Acts', pp. 57–61 and Porter, *Verbal Aspect*, p. 124.

33. G. Delling, *TDNT*, vol. 2, p. 947.

2. Definitions of Semitisms and Septuagintalisms 57

opposite, namely, that an NT author relied directly on the LXX instead of a Semitic *Vorlage*. Secondary Septuagintalisms assume an important role in refuting the claim of Semitic intervention in the NT. If a locution is found in the LXX, it could indicate the influence of the LXX rather than direct Semitic influence (direct translation of a Semitic original). They can provide evidence which militates against the translation theory and indicates the influence of the LXX instead.

Another critical problem persists with 'unsuccessful or failed Septuagintalisms', or 'Septuagintal-type expressions'. The issue centres on the question of where the line must be drawn to distinguish between non-Septuagintalisms and unsuccessful Septuagintalisms. It must be decided whether Septuagintalisms include unsuccessful Septuagintalisms or not, and what constitutes unsuccessful Septuagintalisms. The so-called 'unsuccessful Septuagintalisms' or 'Septuagintal-type expressions', which *seem to be cast in the mould of LXX style, but whose exactly identical locutions are not found in the LXX*, can be *included in Septuagintalisms*. However, they must be excluded from the category of Septuagintalisms unless it can be shown that their usages occur due to the influence of LXX style. For example, the use of the verb πίμπλημι with the time indicator (Lk. 1.23a, 57; 2.6, 21, 22), as shown in Chapter 1, does not belong to Septuagintal-type expressions, though a very similar construction occurs in the LXX, since the verb πληρόω, not πίμπλημι, appears without exception in the LXX parallels. The Lukan construction is thus a non-Septuagintalism.[34] Another example is found in 1.31: συλλήμψῃ ἐν γαστρί. This phrase could belong to unsuccessful Septuagintalisms because a very similar one appears in the LXX.[35] However, a different verb (ἔχω) is used for this idiomatic phrase in the LXX; the Lukan construction thus has only a superficial similarity to the LXX idiom, and that needs an explanation. Before deciding whether a word or phrase belongs to Septuagintal-type expressions, its usage must be carefully examined to confirm that it reflects LXX style. The reason why the word or phrase deviates from LXX style needs to be carefully investigated.

The meaning of 'Semitisms' emerges as 'Septuagintalisms' are defined. 'Semitisms' refer to Greek locutions in the NT which are *un-Greek expressions and non-Septuagintalisms, and contain characteristics typical of Semitic languages*. 'Un-Greek' means *abnormal Greek compared with Hellenistic Greek as well as classical Greek*. Un-Greek locutions include those which are possible in classical Greek and Hellenistic Greek, but do not occur in either one. This definition of the Semitism is virtually identical

---

34. For more detailed argument on the use of this verb, see Chapter 3.
35. This construction, according to Liddell and Scott, is used in classical Greek. See further, Chapter 3.

to that of the 'hard core Semitism' which is the 'pure-Semitism' in Howard, 'direct interference' in Maloney, and comes under the category of 'interference or intervention' in Horton and Porter. These could provide evidence for the presence or the use of Semitic originals by Luke.

B. *Lukanisms and non-Lukanisms*

It has been pointed out in Chapter 1 that Lukanisms in the infancy narrative may indicate either Luke's own translation of a source or his own free composition of the material. Lukanisms indicate Luke's hand in either case. In contrast, non-Lukanisms could point to Luke's dependence on a Greek source or sources. Thus, it is useful to define Lukanisms and non-Lukanisms in order to examine the Greek of the infancy narrative.

I. *The Definition of Lukanisms*

The definition of a Lukanism is found in J.C. Hawkins. For him, a Lukanism is a word or a phrase 'characteristic of Luke': 'characteristic of Luke' means 'the words and phrases which occur at least four times in this Gospel, and which either (a) are not found at all in Matthew or Mark, or (b) are found in Luke at least twice as often as in Matthew and Mark together.'[36] Farris, having criticized Hawkins' definition by saying that his definition is too strict and needs to be relaxed, describes Lukanisms as 'those words and phrases which occur with some regularity in Luke-Acts and only rarely elsewhere in the New Testament' (*The Hymns*, p. 23). Following the lead of Farris, and applying his definition to the examination of the Greek of the infancy narrative, we shall define Lukanisms as *phrases and words in the infancy narrative of Luke which occur with regularity in the remainder of the Gospel and in Acts, regardless of whether or not they occur outside of Luke-Acts in the NT.*

It is useful to distinguish between 'hard core Lukanisms' and 'secondary Lukanisms'. Hard core Lukanisms refer to *words and phrases in the first two chapters of Luke which appear with some regularity in chs 3–24 of the Gospel and in Acts, and do not occur at all or appear less than twice in the other NT books*. Secondary Lukanisms stand for *the locutions in the Lukan infancy narrative which occur in Lk. 3–24 and in Acts with regularity and also appear three or more times in the other NT books*. While secondary Lukanisms only point to the possibility of Luke's translation or composition of the material, hard core Lukanisms more clearly point to

---

36. J.C. Hawkins, *Horae Synopticae: Contribution to the Study of the Synoptic Problem* (Oxford: Clarendon, 1899), p. 13.

Luke's participation in either translation or direct composition. A locution can be both a Lukanism and a Septuagintalism if it is typical of both Luke and the LXX. This 'Lukan-Septuagintalism' can thus indicate Luke's hand or the influence of the LXX, or perhaps both.

II. *The Definition of non-Lukanisms*

The meaning of 'non-Lukanisms' in the infancy narrative is rather straightforward. They refer to *words and phrases in the infancy narrative*

a. *which are not found in the rest of the Gospel (chs 3–24) and Acts, and for which corresponding Lukan expressions appear in the remainder of the Gospel or in Acts*

or

b. *which are found in the rest of the Gospel and/or Acts, but the usage deviates syntactically or lexically from that of the infancy narrative.*

The mere absence of a locution in Lk. 3–24 and Acts, does not indicate that it belongs to non-Lukanisms; another expression for the same meaning has to be found in them. This category also includes *words and phrases in the first two chapters which occur elsewhere in the Gospel, but whose parallels in Matthew and/or Mark contain them*, since these probably were Luke's sources in the writing of his Gospel. The examples which seem to reflect Mark or a common source for Matthew and Luke (so-called 'Q')[37] must be excluded since they cannot be critical evidence for non-Lukanisms, at least to scholars who believe Marcan priority or the presence of a common source for Matthew and Luke to be correct and they, in fact, are the majority.[38] This category also excludes *the words and*

---

37. Every scholar admits that the identity of Q is ambiguous and uncertain. The term could cause a confusion. For details, see G.N. Stanton, 'Q', in *Dictionary of Jesus and the Gospels* (eds. J.B. Green, S. McKnight, I.H. Marshall; Downers Grove: Intervarsity Press, 1992), pp. 644–50. Recognizing such ambiguity and uncertainty, this study avoids the term 'Q' and adopts the term 'a common source for Matthew and Luke', which simply points to a source (sources) possibly used both by Matthew and Luke.

38. This does not necessarily mean that this study adopts Marcan priority or the presence of Q, but it simply indicates the necessity of following a theory which most scholars believe to be correct. For detailed discussion on the Synoptic problem, see Kümmel, *Introduction to the New Testament*, pp. 35–80. After arguing for Marcan priority over Matthew and Luke and refuting the hypothesis of an Urmarkus he concludes that 'by far the most probable conclusion is that in the form handed down to us Mk served as a source for Mt and Lk' (*Introduction to the New Testament*, p. 63). Concerning the topic on a common source for Matthew and Luke, he denies the hypothesis of Luke's dependence on Matthew which has been suggested by many scholars repeatedly. He also rejects the written source Q and suggests an oral tradition of Q. However, Kümmel asserts that 'the indications of the use of a common written source are so clear that the majority of scholars consider this position to be

phrases in the Lukan infancy narrative whose corresponding expressions are found in Lk. 3–24 and Acts, but are proved to have depended on Luke's source. In this case, clear evidence has to be suggested. A probable non-Lukanism could be also explained as deriving from Luke's intentional change if there is a probable explanation about the change. Such instances cannot be included in non-Lukanisms. Non-Lukanisms may prove Luke's dependence on immediate Greek sources, probably written ones including the LXX. This is true especially when they are at the same time non-Septuagintalisms and there is no compelling reason for their use, like the influence of a Semitic language. They clearly point to the influence of immediate Greek sources other than the LXX. This study will thus introduce the term 'hard core non-Lukanisms', which refer to *words and phrases that are non-Lukanisms and non-Septuagintalisms and do not exactly reflect Semitic constructions.* 'Hard core non-Lukanisms' clearly call into question both the theory that Luke himself directly translated a Semitic source or sources and the theory that the infancy narrative is solely his own composition. In fact, they demonstrate that Luke had Greek source(s) before him and that he was influenced, directly or indirectly, by the source(s).[39] The terms 'non-Lukan Septuagintalisms' or 'non-Lukan, non-Septuagintalisms' need not to be defined, since their meanings are clear enough. 'Non-Lukan Septuagintalisms' do not directly stem from Luke's hand, but ultimately from the LXX. They do not make probable the theory that Luke translated the Hebrew original; they just indicate the influence of the LXX.

With these definitions, the Greek of the Lukan infancy narrative will be investigated in the next chapter. The primary purpose of this study is to investigate whether the Greek of the Lukan infancy narrative ultimately resulted from the translation of a Semitic source or from the imitation of the LXX. The first section of Chapter 3 will inquire into quotations in the infancy story in order to decide whether the quotations in the story depend

---

inescapable' (*Introduction to the New Testament*, pp. 63–67). It is impossible to enumerate the names of scholars who accept Marcan priority and the presence of a common source. For the list of those scholars, see Kümmel, *Introduction to the New Testament*, p. 48, nt. 8 and 65, nt. 55. See also W. Marxsen, *Einleitung in das neue Testament: Einführung in ihre Probleme* (Gütersloh: Gütersloher Verlagshaus, 1978), p. 156. Marxsen begins the section 'Zum Inhalt und Aufbaus des Lucas Werkes' with the statement that 'der Verfasser des Lk hat als Quellen das Mk und Q benutzt.' See also Guthrie who notes that 'among continental scholars the two-source theory which regards Matthew and Luke as using Mark and Q has remained dominant' (*New Testament Introduction*, p. 179). For recent argument, see R.H. Stein, 'Synoptic Problem', in *Dictionary of Jesus and the Gospels* (eds. J.B. Green, S. McKnight, and I.H. Marshall; Downers Grove: Intervarsity, 1992), pp. 787–92.

39. Whether the influence of the source(s) is direct or indirect will be investigated. 'Indirect' influence of the source(s) means that the Greek of the source compelled Luke to avoid or to create some proto-Lukan expressions. For details, see Chapter 3.

2. Definitions of Semitisms and Septuagintalisms

on the LXX or the Hebrew text. Not only the quoted text but also the manner of the quotation (e.g., the use of introductory formulas) will be examined. In the second section, allusions will be treated, mainly those which some scholars still believe reflect the direct influence of the Hebrew OT. The final section, 'Phraseology', will examine phrases and words that have been suggested as supporting the translation theory. While it is possible to undertake a thorough study of quotations in the infancy narrative, it is impossible and unnecessary to investigate all the instances of allusions and phraseology. Thus, only the instances that are still used to defend the translation theory will be treated for these topics.

This study is related to the source issue of the infancy narrative and the issue will be discussed in the final chapter, i.e., Chapter 4, on the basis of the results yielded by the study in Chapter 3.

Chapter 3

A CLOSE EXAMINATION OF THE GREEK
OF THE INFANCY NARRATIVE

A. *Quotations*

One needs to study quotations to understand the sources of the Gospels. This issue is connected with the problem of the original language of the sources. If the Gospels rely on the LXX for quotations, the probability that the Evangelists translated Semitic sources is decreased. In contrast, if the Gospels depend on the Hebrew OT for quotations, it becomes more probable that the Evangelists translated Semitic sources. Quotations might provide one of the critical tests for the issue of the original language of the Gospels.[1] The same principle also applies to the Lukan infancy narrative.

Concerning the study of quotations, a key problem is the definition of the term 'quotation'. 'Complete agreement', as Z.C. Hodges and A.L. Farstad note, 'as to what constitutes an Old Testament quotation is impossible, since many of the quotations are not word for word, and others are from a translation of the Old Testament.'[2] Most difficult is to distinguish between quotation and allusion,[3] but without defining

---

1. K. Stendahl, *The School of St. Matthew and its Use of the Old Testament* (Acta Seminarii Neotestamentici Upsaliensis, XX; Lund: C.W.K.Gleerup, 1954), p. 42.
2. Z.C. Hodges and A.L. Farstad, *The Greek New Testament: According to the Majority Text* (Nashville/Camden/New York: Thomas Nelson, 1982), Introduction, p. xlii.
3. Every scholar who deals with the problem of quotation expresses this difficulty. B.F. Westcott and F.J.A. Hort, conceding that it is hardly possible to distinguish between clear quotations and implied quotations, remark that 'the line has been extremely difficult to draw, and may perhaps have wavered occasionally' (B.F. Westcott and F.J.A. Hort, *The New Testament in the Original Greek: Introduction and Appendix* [London: Macmillan, 1907], p. 316). R. Longenecker expresses the difficulty of distinguishing between 'quotation' and 'allusion' by stating that 'some arbitrariness of classification is, of course, inevitable in any listing of biblical quotations apart from allusions' (R. Longenecker, *Biblical Exegesis in the Apostolic Period* [Grand Rapids: Eerdmans, 1975], p. 134). Stendahl also remarks that 'the question of where to draw the line between quotations and allusions is a problem in itself' (*The School of St. Matthew*, p. 45). It is intriguing to observe that one scholar includes a verse in quotations which another omits. M. Rese, for example, noting the difficulty of distinguishing between 'quotation' and 'allusion' in Stephen's speech in Acts 7, excludes Acts

'quotation' precisely, we cannot proceed to examine quotations as well as allusions in the Lukan infancy narrative, which will be treated in the next section.

Scholars have presented various views on how to define 'quotation,'[4] and different definitions result in different decisions about specific cases.[5] Westcott and Hort, accepting the difficulty of distinguishing between clear quotations and implied quotations, suggest broad criteria by regarding even one or two words from the OT as a quotation (*Introduction*, pp. 315–16).[6] The phrase οἱ πτωχοὶ in Mt. 5.3a (Μακάριοι οἱ πτωχοὶ τῷ πνεύματι), for example, is deemed to be a quotation from Isa. 61.1a where the noun appears (πνεῦμα κυρίου ἐπ' ἐμέ, οὗ εἵνεκεν ἔχρισέν με εὐαγγελίσασθαι πτωχοῖς). Both οἱ πενθοῦντες and παρακληθήσονται in Mt. 5.4 (μακάριοι οἱ πενθοῦντες, ὅτι αὐτοὶ παρακληθήσονται) are also included in their list of quotations, since both occur in Isa. 61.2 (καλέσαι ἐνιαυτὸν κυρίου δεκτὸν καὶ ἡμέραν ἀνταποδόσεως παρακαλέσαι πάντας τοὺς πενθοῦντας). Having recognized that the list by Westcott and Hort cannot make it possible to distinguish between 'direct quotations' and 'mere allusions and reminiscences', Swete tries to narrow down the definition of quotation by considering an introductory formula[7] a sufficient indicator for a citation (*The Old*

7.40 from quotations, which H.B. Swete regards as a citation. Swete, on the other hand, does not include Acts 7.32, which Rese counts as a quotation. See M. Rese, 'Die Funktion der alttestamentlichen Zitate und Anspielungen in den Reden der Apostelgeschichte', in *Les Actes des Apôtres: Traditions, Rédaction, Théologie* (ed. J. Kremer; Leuven: University Press, 1979), p. 69, nt. 31 and H.B. Swete *An Introduction to the Old Testament in Greek* (rev. R. R. Ottley; Cambridge: University Press, 1902; repr. New York: Ktav, 1968), p. 388. These illustrations demonstrate the difficulty of distinguishing between 'quotation' and 'allusion'.

4. For a brief survey on the topic of quotation before 1878, see E. Böhl, *Die alttestamentlichen Citate im Neuen Testament* (Wien: Wilhelm Braumüller, 1878), Einleitung, pp. xix–xxviii. The survey of the topic between the beginning of this century and recent years was presented by G.J. Steyn, whose study concentrates on matters of the explicit quotation, especially from the LXX. See his book, *Septuagint Quotations in the Context of the Petrine and Pauline Speeches of the Acta Apostolorum* (Contributions to Biblical Exegesis and Theology, 12; Kampen: Kok Pharos, 1995), pp. 4–21.

5. For instance, while NA regards the sentence in Lk. 1.15 (καὶ οἶνον καὶ σίκερα οὐ μὴ πίῃ) as a quotation, Hodges and Farstad do not count it (*The Greek New Testament*, p. 78). See above nt. 3.

6. Westcott and Hort include the sentence in Lk. 1.17 (Ἠλίου, ἐπιστρέψαι καρδίας πατέρων ἐπὶ τέκνα) as well as the sentence in 1.15 as a quotation (B.F. Westcott and F.J.A. Hort, *The New Testament in the Original Greek: Text* [London: Macmillan, 1898], p. 115, 584). In a similar way, F. Johnson interprets allusions as included in quotations when dividing a quotation into six sub-categories. He includes fragmentary quotations in the category of quotations (F. Johnson, *The Quotations of the New Testament from the Old Considered in the Light of General Literature* [Philadelphia: American Baptist, 1896]). Cited from Steyn, *Septuagint Quotations*, p. 14.

7. The first scholar who pays explicit attention to the formulas is E. Hühn in his book *Die alttestamentlichen Citate und Reminiscenzen im Neuen Testamente* (Tübingen: Mohr, 1900),

Testament in Greek, pp. 381-82). He broadens the definition, however, by adding that some instances which do not contain the formula can be quotations when their context seems to be intended for quotations or 'their wordings agree with some context in the OT' as in Mt. 11.4f and Mk 12.29 (*The Old Testament in Greek*, pp. 382, 384).[8] This rather ambiguous approach leads him to include allusions under the rubric of 'quotation'. The example in Mt. 19.4 (ὁ δὲ ἀποκριθεὶς εἶπεν, Οὐκ ἀνέγνωτε ὅτι ὁ κτίσας ἀπο ἀρχῆς ἄρσεν καὶ θῆλυ ἐποίησεν αὐτούς), according to Swete, can be a quotation, although it has no introductory formula, because the wording of the underlined part is identical to Gen. 1.27 of the OT (καὶ ἐποίησεν ὁ θεὸς τὸν ἄνθρωπον κατ' εἰκόνα θεοῦ ἐποίησεν αὐτὸν ἄρσεν καὶ θῆλυ ἐποίησεν αὐτούς). On the other hand, Mt. 5.31 (Ἐρρέθη δέ, "Ὃς ἂν ἀπολύσῃ τὴν γυναῖκα αὐτοῦ, δότω αὐτῇ ἀποστάσιον) is also included in quotations, though its wording is very different from a possible reference in Deut. 24.1 (ἐὰν δέ τις λάβῃ γυναῖκα καὶ συνοικήσῃ αὐτῇ καὶ ἔσται ἐὰν μὴ εὕρῃ χάριν ἐναντίον αὐτοῦ ὅτι εὗρεν ἐν αὐτῇ ἄσχημον πρᾶγμα καὶ γράψει αὐτῇ βιβλίον ἀποστασίου καὶ δώσει εἰς τὰς χεῖρας αὐτῆς καὶ ἐξαποστελεῖ αὐτὴν ἐκ τῆς οἰκίας αὐτοῦ), simply because Mt. 5.31 begins with an introductory formula, Ἐρρέθη.[9] He also argues that the wording of some verses may have occurred due to 'loose citation' as in Mt. 2.18 and Mt. 21.4f (*The Old Testament in Greek*, p. 394). Swete's definition of quotation is broad and confusing.[10]

---

p. 269. He distinguishes between quotations with 'Citerformel' and quotations without it. He also admits the difficulty of separating the citation without the introductory formula from mere reminiscence. M. Wilcox defines 'explicit quotations' as those with the introductory formula and names them 'formula quotations'. He adds that recent scholarship tends to concentrate on the study of these 'formula quotations', which is not surprising. See his article, 'Text Form' in *It is Written: Scripture Citing Scripture: Essays in Honour of Barnabas Lindars* (eds. D.A. Carson and H.G.M. Williamson; Cambridge: University Press, 1988), p. 194. Cf. B. Lindars, *New Testament Apologetic: The Doctrinal Significance of the Old Testament Quotations* (London: SCM Press, 1961), p. 259, where he uses the term 'formula-quotations'. Steyn states that only the presence of the explicit introductory formulae indicates 'explicit quotations' (*Septuagint Quotations*, p. 26). It is remarkable that Böhl treats only quotations with introductory formulas with few exceptions already in 1878, though he does not clarify the role of the formulas.

8. W.C. Kaiser also presents this view in his book, *The Uses of the Old Testament in the New* (Chicago: Moody Bible Institute, 1986), p. 2.

9. Stendahl remarks concerning Mt. 5.31 that 'Matthew deviated both from the LXX and the MT to the extent of an allusion', although he includes it in quotations according to his definition that the sentence preceded by an introductory formula must be a quotation (*The School of St. Matthew*, p. 137).

10. Stendahl follows Swete by dealing with 'formula quotations' and conscious quotations without introductory formulas, 'judging from the context, or which agree verbatim with some passage in the O.T. in its Greek or Hebrew form'. He calls both 'strict quotations' (*The School of St. Matthew*, p. 46). Though investigating the OT quotation in Luke without defining the term 'quotation', T. Holtz betrays a similar position by dividing quotations into 'explicit quotations (Die selbständigen Zitate)' and 'quotations of variable origins (Zitate

In contrast, other scholars, recent ones in particular, define quotation strictly by saying that an alleged quotation must clearly point to a particular passage in the OT, with respect to both subject matter and vocabulary. Even the instances that contain the formulas introducing direct quotations, which scholars call 'formula quotation', can thereby be excluded. D. New, for example, excludes an instance in the Lukan infancy narrative which includes the introductory formula. According to him, πᾶν ἄρσεν διανοῖγον μήτραν ἅγιον τῷ κυρίῳ κληθήσεται in Lk. 2.23 cannot be a citation, although an introductory formula precedes the sentence (καθὼς γέγραπται ἐν νόμῳ κυρίου ὅτι).[11] New admits that the subject matter of Lk. 2.23 resembles that of Exod. 13.2 or 13.12 and that its wording is also similar to the two verses to some degree. However, the Lukan text does not correspond to either the LXX text or the Hebrew text of these two verses. A quotation, according to him, must be 'a passage which definitely corresponds closely to a particular OT passage and which is intended as a citation, whether or not there is an introductory formula' (*Old Testament Quotations*, p. 97). New defines quotation very strictly.

It may be true that the presence of an introductory formula itself cannot guarantee that the following phrase or sentence is a citation. For example, a possible introductory formula ἐρρέθη found in Mt. 5.31, 33 may not be an assurance of the author's intention to cite the OT. What follows the introductory formula in these instances cannot be found in the OT. Wilcox highlights another problem by pointing out that even in so-called 'formula quotations', references to OT books may be wrong. He cites, for instance, Jn 10.34 (ἀπεκρίθη αὐτοῖς [ὁ] Ἰησοῦς, Οὐκ ἔστιν γεγραμμένον ἐν τῷ νόμῳ ὑμῶν ὅτι Ἐγὼ εἶπα, Θεοί ἐστε;), where the quotation in fact is from a Psalm, not 'the Law'. In addition, even some of these explicit quotations do not always refer to a single passage in one OT book. For example, the quotation of Mk 1.2 (Καθὼς γέγραπται ἐν τῷ Ἡσαΐᾳ τῷ προφήτῃ, Ἰδοὺ ἀποστέλλω τὸν ἄγγελόν μου πρὸ προσώπου σου, ὃς κατασκευάσει τὴν ὁδόν σου) is attributed to Isaiah, though it is a composite quotation of both Isa. 40.3 and Mal. 3.1.[12] The quotation formula may be misleading.[13]

---

unterschiedlicher Herkunft)'. The second category clearly refers to 'allusions', but he includes them in quotations. For details, see his book, *Untersuchungen über die alttestamentlichen Zitate bei Lukas* (Berlin: Akademie, 1968), pp. 3–4.

11. D. New, *Old Testament Quotations in the Synoptic Gospels and the Two-Document Hypothesis* (Septuagint Cognate Studies, 37; Atlanta: Scholars Press, 1993), p. 90.

12. Despite these problems, Wilcox appears to regard only explicit quotations 'introduced by one of several more or less set formulae' as quotations, and others as allusion or reminiscence of the OT ('Text Form', p. 194).

13. Another possible example is found in some variants of Mt. 13.35, according to which the writer attributes the quotation to Isaiah, though the quoted text is from Ps. 78.2. For

While it is accepted that some of so called 'formula quotations' betray the problems suggested above, the presence of the introductory formulae must be seriously considered. For the use of the formula clearly indicates an author's intention to quote. Concerning New's explanation of Lk. 2.23, for example, the introductory formula καθὼς γέγραπται ἐν νόμῳ κυρίου ὅτι in this verse seems to mark what follows as an intended quotation. This formula is different from simple prefixing of the word ἐρρέθη. The formula includes the verb γράφω, a common one for introducing quotations,[14] and specifies the place where the following quotation appears by inserting ἐν νόμῳ κυρίου. Some quotations with the introductory formula may have been derived from the author's memory,[15] or the authors may have depended on different OT versions from ours.[16] Before excluding an example with an introductory formula, a scholar must examine it in order to trace a possible source and procedure for citation.[17]

How can 'quotation' then be delineated? Three criteria must be applied. First, all the phrases or sentences that are preceded by any kind of introductory formulae like καθὼς γέγραπται, (Ἠκούσατε ὅτι) ἐρρέθη (Mt. 5.21, 27, 31, 33, 38, 43), or (κατὰ τὸ) εἰρημένον ἐν τῷ νόμῳ (Lk. 2.24) can be counted as 'quotations'.[18] These formulas likely indicate the author's intention or opinion that what follows are quotations, at least from his own perspective. Second, the subject matter must correspond closely and discernibly to a couple of particular OT passages in order for a phrase or sentence to count as a quotation. Third, the wording must closely correspond to a couple of OT phrases or sentences. It is not necessary that phrases and sentences correspond only to one particular OT passage, as New insists. If the context and wording of two or three OT verses to which

---

details, see M.J.J. Menken, 'Isaiah and the "Hidden Things": the quotation from Psalm 78:2 in Matthew 13:15', in *The Use of Sacred Books in the Ancient World* (eds. L.V. Rutgers, P.W. van der Horst, H.W. Havelaar, and L. Teugels; Leuven: Peeters, 1998) pp. 61–77.

14. The use of the perfect tense of γράφω appears often in the NT to introduce a quotation: Mt. 4.4; 11.10; Mk 11.17; Acts 15.15; Rom. 1.17; 3.4; 10.15; 12.19; 1 Cor. 10.7; 1 Pet. 1.16 etc. In contrast, quotations in the Mishnah are always introduced by the verb of speaking. For details, see B. M. Metzger, 'The Formulas Introducing Quotations of Scripture in the NT and the Mishnah', *JBL*, 70 (1951), pp. 299–301.

15. Steyn admits that it is difficult to prove conclusively if formula quotations 'were quoted from some written source, or simply from memory.' He continues, however, that a careful examination will provide some indications (*Septuagint Quotations*, pp. 26–27).

16. For the discussion of the text form of the OT in the NT, see Wilcox, 'Text Form', p. 203.

17. It is possible that Luke thought he was quoting when he adopted the introductory formula. The possibility that Luke's concept of quotation differs from ours is high in the case of Lk. 2.23. We will deal with this verse later.

18. The majority of recent scholars, as noted above, tend to include only explicit quotations with introductory formulas in quotations. See above.

3. *A Close Examination of the Greek of the Infancy Narrative*   67

a NT passage refers are similar to each other, the NT sentence or phrase could be a citation that relies on two or three OT clauses.[19] Needless to say, an instance which sufficiently satisfies all three conditions can be considered a quotation. In addition, the combination of the second and third may indicate a quotation when the subject and wording strongly refer to a couple of OT phrases or sentences.[20] In contrast, examples with introductory formulas must not be eliminated from the category of quotation even if they do not have exact corresponding passages in the OT; only the example whose wording clearly deviates both from the LXX and the Hebrew OT text must be excluded from the category of quotations.[21]

With these criteria, the following study will examine possible quotations in the Lukan infancy narrative and decide whether they are quotations, or allusions or mere reminiscence.[22] In doing so, we will undertake the primary goal of this section, i.e., to determine whether quotations in the infancy story depend on the LXX or the Hebrew OT text. We will pay attention not only to the content of quotations but also to the manner of quotations like the introductory formula, if the quoted text is preceded by the formula; whether the manner of quotation stems from a source or from Luke's hand will also be examined.

---

   19. In his 'Isaiah in Luke', *Int*, 36 (1982), p. 151, J.A. Sanders, positing that the quotation in Lk. 4.18 pulls its wordings from both Isa. 58.6 and 61.11, attempts to explain this phenomenon by pointing out that to enlist wordings from two or more passages was not unusual in the first century. 'This was most often done by word tallying,' he continues on the same page, 'that is, each passage would have had in it one word at least that was the same.' Both Isa. 58.6 and 61.11, which Lk. 4.18 reflects, include the Greek word 'ἄφεσιν'. H. Ringgren, however, assumes in his 'Luke's Use of the Old Testament', *HTR*, 79 (1986), p. 229, that Luke quoted this verse from memory. The combined quotation is also found in other places like Acts 1.20 which obtains wordings from both Ps. 68 (69). 26 and Ps. 108 (109). 8 and Acts 3.22-23, where Deut. 18.15-20 and Lev. 23.29 are combined (cf. Steyn, *Septuagint Quotations*, p. 29). G.L. Archer and G.C. Chirichigno label them 'conflate quotations'. They remark that 'the NT authors found it useful to combine within one quotation sundry portions from Old Testament sources other than the principle passage that they were citing' (G.L. Archer and G.C. Chirichigno, *Old Testament Quotations in the New Testament* [Chicago: Moody, 1983], Introduction, p. xii).

   20. Rese emphasizes the importance of distinguishing between quotations introduced by the introductory formula and those without it (M. Rese, *Alttestamentliche Motive in der Christologie des Lukas* [Bonn: Rheinische Friedrich-Wilhelms-Universität, 1965], pp. 44–45).

   21. D.L. Bock presents a rather vague definition by saying that 'a passage will be treated as *a quotation*, either when it is introduced by a formula citation or is a substantial reproduction (more than a phrase) of a passage that by its function or precise form is clearly intended to be seen as a quotation' (D.L. Bock, *Proclamation from Prophecy and Pattern: Lukan Old Testament Christology* (JSNTSS 12; Sheffield: JSOT, 1987, p. 47).

   22. Stendahl points out that NA follows in most cases Westcott and Horton in identifying quotations (*The School of St. Matthew*, p. 45).

I. The Quotation in Lk. 2.23

Although most scholars agree that the sentence in Lk. 2.23, πᾶν ἄρσεν διανοῖγον μήτραν ἅγιον τῷ κυρίῳ κληθήσεται, is a quotation,[23] New argues that this clause has to be excluded from the category of quotations.[24] Attempting to determine the source of the possible quotation, the following study will try to respond to New's view.

2.22 Καὶ ὅτε ἐπλήσθησαν αἱ ἡμέραι τοῦ καθαρισμοῦ αὐτῶν κατὰ τὸν νόμον Μωϋσέως, ἀνήγαγον αὐτὸν εἰς Ἱεροσόλυμα παραστῆσαι τῷ κυρίῳ, 23 <u>καθὼς γέγραπται ἐν νόμῳ κυρίου ὅτι πᾶν ἄρσεν διανοῖγον μήτραν ἅγιον τῷ κυρίῳ κληθήσεται</u>,[25] 24 καὶ τοῦ δοῦναι θυσίαν κατὰ τὸ εἰρημένον ἐν τῷ νόμῳ κυρίου, ζεῦγος τρυγόνων ἢ δύο νοσσοὺς περιστερῶν.

22 And when the days of their purification had been fulfilled according to the Law of Moses, they brought him up to Jerusalem to present (him) to the Lord, 23 *as it has been written in the Law of the Lord that every (first-born) male opening the womb will be called holy to the Lord*, 24 and (they went up to Jerusalem) to offer a sacrifice according to what has been said in the Law of the Lord 'a pair of turtledoves or two young (ones) of pigeons'.

There is also a quotation in v. 24 and we shall treat this in the next section.

(A) *The Manner of Quotation*

As noted above, we need to examine the manner of quotation in order to decide whether the Lukan text stemmed from Luke's hand or from a source. The introductory formula and the conjunction ὅτι, which is followed by (in)direct discourse,[26] appear in this verse.[27]

---

23. C.K. Barrett notes that 'the OT, so often echoed (in the infancy narrative), is quoted, with citation formulas, only here (2:23, 24)' (C.K. Barrett, 'Luke/Acts' in *It is Written: Scripture Citing Scripture: Essays in Honour of Barnabas Lindars* [eds. D.A. Carson and H.G.M. Williamson; Cambridge: University Press, 1988], p. 235).We may enumerate scholars' names for this position: Hodges and Farstad, Westcott and Hort, Bock, Fitzmyer, Marshall, Brown, etc.

24. For New's argument, see above.

25. One may argue that the presence of the article in this infinitive construction and its absence in the first infinitive παραστῆσαι (v. 22) to express the same idea, i.e., 'purpose', indicate Luke's contribution, on the ground that the same phenomenon is found in the NT only in Luke: 1.76 and 77 where the article is absent in the former verse and it appears in the latter verse (BDR 400. 6). However, this example occurs only in the Benedictus of the infancy narrative and thus does not constitute a proof.

26. All the English translations interpret the quoted part as a direct statement, though the quoted part can be either a direct statement or an indirect statement. For details, see below.

27. The use of different formulas in Luke probably derived from Luke's hand as various formulas appear in Luke-Acts: the use of various expressions in general is Luke's stylistic

3. A Close Examination of the Greek of the Infancy Narrative 69

(1) *Introductory Formula*[28]

In Lk. 2.23, a ὅτι clause is introduced by a quotation formula: καθὼς γέγραπται ἐν νόμῳ κυρίου.[29]

(i) καθὼς γέγραπται (ἐν): *Is this non-Lukan?*

The introductory formula καθὼς γέγραπται occurs 22 times outside of Luke-Acts (Mt. 26.24; Mk 1.2; 9.13; 14.12; Rom. 1.17; 2.24; 3.4, 10; 4.17; 8.36; 9.13, 33; 10.15; 11.8, 26; 15.3, 9, 21; 1 Cor. 1.31; 2.9; 2 Cor. 8.15; 9.9); one of these instances contains also the prepositional phrase beginning with ἐν namely, Mark 1.2, where a direct quotation follows:

<u>Καθὼς γέγραπται ἐν</u> τῷ Ἠσαΐᾳ τῷ προφήτῃ, Ἰδοὺ ἀποστέλλω τὸν ἄγγελόν μου πρὸ προσώπου σου, ὃς κατασκευάσει τὴν ὁδόν σου.

While the Gospel of Luke itself offers no further example of the formula καθὼς γέγραπται, Acts contains two (7.42; 15.15), one of them (7.42) also followed by a prepositional phrase beginning with ἐν (καθὼς γέγραπται ἐν βίβλῳ τῶν προφητῶν) as in Luke 2.23. Although the formula καθὼς γέγραπται appears in these two verses, Luke usually uses only the verb γέγραπται (Lk. 4.4, 8, 10; 7.27; 19.46)[30] or the verb with ὡς instead of καθὼς (Lk. 3.4; Acts 13.33) or with οὕτως (Lk. 24.46). At any rate, the formula καθὼς γέγραπται itself does not belong to non-Lukanisms, since it occurs twice in Acts.

(ii) ἐν νόμῳ κυρίου: *Does this indicate Luke's hand?*

a. *Is the phrase* νόμος κυρίου *itself a non-Lukanism?*

The phrase νόμος κυρίου appears only in the infancy narrative in the whole NT, with the article in 2.24, 39 and without the article in 2.23.

---

habit. See G. Mussies, 'Remarks on Quotation Formulas in Gospels and Acts' in *The Use of Sacred Books in the Ancient World* (eds. L.V. Rutgers, P.W. van der Horst, H.W. Havelaar, and L. Teugels; Leuven: Peeters, 1998), p. 57. Nonetheless, a detailed study of the formula is meaningful because it constitutes one of considerations which play a role in deciding whether the manner of quotation indicates Luke's hand or that of others.

28. 'Much less systematic attention has been paid,' as Mussies points out, 'to the various formulas used by the NT writers to introduce or mark an OT quotation' ('Remarks on Quotation Formulas', p. 52).

29. Archer and Chirichigno classify this quotation as category 'Ba' which 'consists of those passages in which the LXX is somewhat closer to the MT than the NT. They comment that Luke does not follow the exact wording of the LXX in Exod. 13.12, but rather employs the basic sense in Lk. 2.23 (*Old Testament Quotations*, Introduction, p. xxv).

30. All instances that have only the verb γέγραπται appear in the common parts with Matthew, which always includes the verb, suggesting that this formula is probably not Luke's. However, the formula in Acts 23.5 (γέγραπται γὰρ ὅτι) proves that the formula belongs to Luke which means that he did not necessarily obtain it from a source.

Also important is that another phrase for the meaning 'the law,' i.e., (ὁ) νόμος Μωϋσέως, occurs four times in Luke-Acts outside of Luke's first two chapters (24.44; Acts 13.38; 15.5; 28.23; cf. Lk. 2.22 where the phrase appears), which is found only twice apart from Luke-Acts (Jn 7.23; Heb. 10.28).[31] The omission of the article with the noun νόμος in Lk. 2.23 is also non-Lukan.[32] The phrase νόμος κυρίου is thus a non-Lukanism.

b. *The use of the phrase* ἐν νόμῳ κυρίου *as indicating the source of the quotation*

Concerning the use of ἐν νόμῳ κυρίου after an introductory formula, it needs to be pointed out that this is the only place where Luke intends (or claims) to quote from 'the Law of the Lord.' Lk. 10.26 may be an exception where a quotation from Deuteronomy occurs in the following verse:

26 ὁ δὲ εἶπεν πρὸς αὐτόν, Ἐν τῷ νόμῳ τί γέγραπται; πῶς ἀναγινώσκεις;
26 He said to him, 'What is written *in the law*? What do you read there?'

27 ὁ δὲ ἀποκριθεὶς εἶπεν, Ἀγαπήσεις κύριον τὸν θεόν σου ἐξ ὅλης [τῆς] καρδίας σου καὶ ἐν ὅλῃ τῇ ψυχῇ σου καὶ ἐν ὅλῃ τῇ ἰσχύϊ σου καὶ ἐν ὅλῃ τῇ διανοίᾳ σου, καὶ τὸν πλησίον σου ὡς σεαυτόν;
27 He answered, 'You shall love the Lord your God with all your heart, and with all your soul, and with all your strength, and with all your mind; and your neighbour as yourself'. (NRSV)

However, only the phrase ἐν τῷ νόμῳ appears, thus without the modifying word κυρίου and the phrase is connected with the quoted text only indirectly.[33] Moreover, it seems that the phrase was derived from a common source of Matthew and Luke. The parallel verse in Mt. 22.35 reads:

---

31. See 1 Cor. 9.9 where ἐν γὰρ τῷ Μωϋσέως νόμῳ appears (cf. Mk 12.26 – ἐν τῇ βίβλῳ Μωϋσέως and Jude 9 – περὶ τοῦ Μωϋσέως σώματος). The way of expressing the construction in 1 Corinthians, (ὁ) Μωϋσέως νόμος instead of (ὁ) νόμος Μωϋσέως, which is usually used by classical authors, may indicate the Semitic origin of the phrase. However, the phrase clearly reflects the influence of the LXX where it occurs [1 Kgs 2.3; 1 *Esd.* 9.39; *Tob.* 7.13; Dan. (TH) 9.11 etc].
32. This feature will be treated in detail below.
33. In Lk. 10.27, no introductory formula appears; γέγραπται is used in v. 26 in a question: Ἐν τῷ νόμῳ τί γέγραπται; 'What has been written in the law?' In v.27 where the lawyer answered, the direct statement appears: ὁ δὲ ἀποκριθεὶς εἶπεν, Ἀγαπήσεις κύριον 'and he (the lawyer) answered and said, "Love the Lord...".' However, ὁ δὲ ἀποκριθεὶς εἶπεν is not an introductory formula and γέγραπται is indirectly connected with this direct statement.

3. A Close Examination of the Greek of the Infancy Narrative 71

35 καὶ ἐπηρώτησεν εἷς ἐξ αὐτῶν [νομικὸς] πειράζων αὐτόν,
and one of them, a lawyer, asked him a question to test him.

36 Διδάσκαλε, ποία ἐντολὴ μεγάλη *ἐν τῷ νόμῳ*;
'Teacher, which commandment *in the law* is the greatest?'

37 ὁ δὲ ἔφη αὐτῷ, Ἀγαπήσεις κύριον τὸν θεόν σου ἐν ὅλῃ τῇ καρδίᾳ σου καὶ ἐν ὅλῃ τῇ ψυχῇ σου καὶ ἐν ὅλῃ τῇ διανοίᾳ σου.[34]
He said to him, 'You shall love the Lord your God with all your heart, and with all your soul, and with all your mind.'

Furthermore, while Luke quotes from the Law (= the Pentateuch) elsewhere,[35] he never uses the phrase 'the Law of the Lord' to introduce such a quotation. Luke cites from the Pentateuch in the following verses with various introductory formulas:

Luke 4.4: Γέγραπται[36] ὅτι (γέγραπται in its parallel, Mt. 4.4): Deut. 8.3

4.8: Γέγραπται (γέγραπται γάρ in its parallel, Mt. 4.10): Deut. 6.13; 10.20

4.12: Εἴρηται (Πάλιν γέγραπται in its parallel, Mt. 4.7):[37] Deut. 6.16

10.27: Ἐν τῷ νόμῳ γέγραπται in v. 26:[38] Deut. 6.5; Jos. 22.5

18.20: τὰς ἐντολὰς οἶδας (the identical phrase is found in Mk 10.19): Exod. 20.12-16; Deut. 5.16-20

20.28: Μωϋσῆς ἔγραψεν ἡμῖν (the identical locution appears in Mk 12.19): Deut. 25.5[39]

---

34. In his 'The Biblical Quotations in Matthew', *HTR*, 36 (1943), p. 147, S.E. Johnson argues that the Lukan text depended on Q while Mt. conflated Mk and Q.

35. νόμος, as Metzger points out, sometimes refers to writings other than the Pentateuch outside of Luke-Acts, as in 1 Cor. 14.21, where νόμος stands for Isa. 28.11, and in Jn 10.34 where it points to Ps. 82.6 ('The Formulas', p. 302). See also Jn 15.25, which quotes Ps. 35.19. However, νόμος in Luke is always used to indicate the law of Moses, even when the phrase 'of Moses' does not appear with it (J. Reiling and J.L. Swellengrebel, *A Translator's Handbook on the Gospel of Luke* [Leiden: E.J. Brill, 1971], p. 125).

36. The capital letter indicates that the word is the first one in the direct statement.

37. The use of a saying verb in Lk. 4.12, different from the parallel in Mt. 4.7, is due to Luke's habit 'to vary his vocabulary and idiom wherever he can' (Mussies, 'Remarks on Quotation Formulas', p. 57).

38. This verse is different from the parallels in Mt. 22.36 and Mk 12.28 where the phrase ἐν τῷ νόμῳ γέγραπται does not appear.

39. All the instances in the Gospel appear to depend on Mark or a common source of Luke and Matthew.

Acts 3.21–22. 21 ... ὧν ἐλάλησεν ὁ θεὸς διὰ στόματος τῶν ἁγίων ἀπ'αἰῶνος αὐτοῦ προφητῶν. Μωϋσῆς μέν εἶπεν ὅτι: Deut. 18.15–20; Lev 23.29

3.25: λέγων πρὸς Ἀβραάμ: Gen. 22.18

7.3: καὶ εἶπεν πρὸς αὐτόν: Gen. 12.1

7.6: ἐλάλησεν δὲ οὕτως ὁ θεὸς ὅτι: Gen. 15.13

7.27: ὁ δὲ ἀδικῶν τὸν πλησίον ἀπώσατο αὐτὸν εἰπών: Exod. 2.14

7.31: ἐγένετο φωνὴ κυρίου: Exod. 3.6

7.33: εἶπεν δὲ αὐτῷ ὁ κύριος: Exod. 3.5, 7–10

7.35: Τοῦτον τὸν Μωϋσῆν, ὃν ἠρνήσαντο εἰπόντες: Exod. 2.14

7.37: οὗτός ἐστιν ὁ Μωϋσῆς ὁ εἴπας τοῖς υἱοίς Ἰσραήλ: Deut. 18.15

7.40: εἰπόντες τῷ Ἀαρών: Exod. 32.1, 23

23.5: γέγραπται γὰρ ὅτι: Exod. 22.27

As the above list shows, Luke-Acts does not attest an example for the use of the introductory phrase ἐν (τῷ) νόμῳ κυρίου to quote from the Torah. Luke indicates Μωϋσῆς as the origin of quotations from the Torah three times (Lk. 20.28; Acts 3.22;[40] 7.37) and ὁ κύριος once (Acts 7.33). ὁ θεός is also used as the subject of a saying verb in Acts 3.25; 7.3, 6. In contrast, Luke never even introduces a quotation with the phrase ἐν νόμῳ κυρίου nor with the locution ἐν (τῷ νόμῳ) Μωϋσῆς. The use of ἐν νόμῳ κυρίου to indicate the Torah as a quoted text is therefore a non-Lukanism.

(2) *The conjunction ὅτι[41] and the omission of indicators for direct discourse*

All instances of the verb γέγραπται with the preposition ἐν are followed by direct quotation, if the quoted text is a direct statement, without the conjunction ὅτι in Luke-Acts without exception (Lk. 3.4; Acts 1.20; 7.42;

---

40. In Acts 3.21, ὁ θεός appears without immediately quoting, but Μωϋσῆς is found in the following verse where the quotation starts. See above.

41. Winter argues that the conjunction here as well as in 1.25 is not recitative (that) but causal (because) on the basis of the Vulgate reading *quia* (P. Winter, 'Hoti "recitativum" in Lc 1, 25.61; 2, 23', *ZNW*, 46 [1955], pp. 261–63). While it is impossible to disprove his argument, most scholars and English versions interpret it as ὅτι recitativum introducing a direct quotation. See Holtz, *Untersuchungen*, p. 83 and Fitzmyer, *Luke I–IX*, p. 425. See also Brown, *The Birth of the Messiah*, p. 437.

13.33; 15.15).[42] By contrast, in Lk. 2.23 we find the conjunction. It is especially noteworthy that both examples in Acts 7.42 and 15.15, where the introductory formula καθὼς γέγραπται also appears, are followed by direct discourse without the conjunction ὅτι (as in Mk 1.2), while the instance in Lk. 2.23 involves it. The parallels of four verses illustrate the similarities and the differences between them.

| Καθὼς γέγραπται ἐν τῷ Ἠσαία τῷ προφήτῃ, ἰδοὺ ἀποστέλλω τὸν ἄγγελόν μου πρὸ προσώπου σου, ὃς κατασκευάσει τὴν ὁδόν σου (Mk 1.2) | καθὼς γέγραπται ἐν βίβλῳ τῶν προφητῶν, Μὴ σφάγια καὶ θυσίας προσηνέγκατέ μοι ἔτη τεσσεράκοντα ἐν τῇ ἐρήμῳ, οἶκος Ἰσραήλ; (Acts 7.42) | καὶ τούτῳ συμφωνοῦσιν οἱ λόγοι τῶν προφητῶν, καθὼς γέγραπται, 16 Μετὰ ταῦτα ἀναστρέψω καὶ ἀνοικοδομήσω τὴν σκηνὴν Δαυὶδ τὴν πεπτωκυῖαν καὶ τὰ κατεσκαμμένα αὐτῆς ἀνοικοδομήσω καὶ ἀνορθώσω αὐτήν (Acts 15.15–16) | καθὼς γέγραπται ἐν νόμῳ κυρίου ὅτι Πᾶν ἄρσεν διανοῖγον μήτραν ἅγιον τῷ κυρίῳ κληθήσεται (Lk. 2.23) |

First and second personal pronouns, μοι and σου, and first and second person verb forms in the first three passages are clear indicators of direct statement with the absence of the conjunction ὅτι. Most of these indicators are found in the quoted OT verses of the LXX and all of them reflect the Hebrew text except for μου in Mk 1.2; only the second σοῦ in Mk 1.2 and the first person verb form ἀνορθώσω in Acts 15.16 are not from the LXX. In contrast, Luke 2.23 leaves the following sentence ambiguous, either direct or indirect statement, by inserting the conjunction ὅτι, and more importantly by omitting some clear indicators of direct statement, which the two possible quoted verses in the LXX Exodus include:[43]

Exod. 13.2ff. ἁγίασόν μοι πᾶν πρωτότοκον πρωτογενὲς διανοῖγον πᾶσαν μήτραν ἐν τοῖς υἱοῖς Ἰσραὴλ ἀπὸ ἀνθρώπου ἕως κτήνους ἐμοί ἐστιν

---

42. γέγραπται occurs without the preposition and with the conjunction ὅτι in Luke-Acts: Lk. 4.4, 10 and Acts 23.5. A saying verb is used with the conjunction ὅτι in Acts 3.22 and 7.6. In all these instances, if the quoted verses include indicators of direct statement, they are always kept.

43. This does not confirm that the quotation in this verse is from these two verses, but simply suggests that they represent possible quoted texts. For more details, see below.

Exod. 13.12ff. καὶ ἀφελεῖς πᾶν διανοῖγον μήτραν τὰ ἀρσενικά τῷ κυρίῳ πᾶν διανοῖγον μήτραν ἐκ τῶν βουκολίων ἢ ἐν τοῖς κτήνεσίν σου ὅσα ἐὰν γένηταί σοι τὰ ἀρσενικά ἁγιάσεις τῷ κυρίῳ.[44]

The Lukan text in 2.23 avoids the first and second personal pronouns and the second person verb form in the above verses; they reflect the Hebrew text except for the σοι in Exod. 13.12. This kind of practice does not appear in Lk. 3.24 and Acts. The use of the conjunction and the omission of the direct discourse indicators thus point to non-Lukanisms.[45]

(3) *Does the introductory formula reflect Semitic syntax?*

Considering the above factors, Luke seems to have depended upon a Greek source for the introductory formula καθὼς γέγραπται ἐν νόμῳ κυρίου ὅτι in Lk. 2.23. The issue now centres on whether or not the formula is ultimately derived from a Semitic original.

(i)   The phrase 'ἐν νόμῳ κυρίου'

a.   *Is this a translation of a Semitic construction?*

This phrase demands attention, since the Semitic phrase בתורת־יהוה probably forced the translator to adopt the phrase.[46] The possibility of that translation, however, is not high when considered with the phrase ἐν τῷ νόμῳ κυρίου in the following verse. The phrase in v. 24 includes the article, while it is omitted in v. 23 for the same phrase.[47] Significant is that the same construction appears twice in one passage, once with the article (v. 24) and the other time without it (v. 23). This inconsistency makes it difficult to suppose that Luke or the composer translated a Hebrew original for the phrase ἐν τῷ νόμῳ κυρίου and ἐν νόμῳ κυρίου both of whose corresponding Hebrew

---

44. Some scholars, like Holtz and Bock, assume that Lev. 13.15b may have played a role in the composition of this quotation. This verse also includes the personal pronoun μοῦ. For their argument, see below.

45. It is true, as noted above, that 'Luke is an author who really loves to vary his vocabulary and idiom wherever he can' (Mussies, 'Remarks on Quotation Formulas', p. 57. See also his article, 'Variation in the Book of Acts', *Filologia Neotestamentaria* 4 [1991], pp. 165–82). The peculiarity of the introductory formula in 2.23, however, is too weighty to simply regard it as a variation of the Lukan style.

46. After pointing out that the Evangelists use always νόμος with the article except at Lk. 2.23, W. Gotbrod explains the absence of the article in this verse by stating that the combination of two words νόμος κυρίου may be influenced by Hebrew construction תורת־יהוה (*TDNT*, vol. 4, p. 1059). However, he adds in note 162 that the Greek locution is found with the article in Lk. 2.39.

47. Among commentators, only Brown observes the absence of the article in v. 23. He notices the difference between the noun νόμος without the article in v. 23 and with the article in vv. 22, 24, 27, 39. He denies, however, the possibility that a different hand intervenes here, since the difference is too trivial (*The Birth of the Messiah*, p. 437).

constructions lack the article. It is unlikely that Luke or the composer translated the same Semitic phrase בתורת־יהוה without the article in v. 23 and then with the article in the following verse v. 24, both of which are in one passage.

A possible refutation of this argument would be that Luke three times did exactly the same thing for the phrase ἄγγελος κυρίου (Lk. 1.11,13; 2.9,10; Acts 12.7, 8). In these verses, the noun ἄγγελος appears without the article in the first verses (Lk. 1.11; 2.9; Acts 12.7) and with the article in the second ones (Lk. 1.13; 2.10; Acts 12.8). It is possible to interpret that the first one is used indefinitely and the second one definitely:[48] 'an angel of the Lord' and 'the angel of the Lord' which refers to the first mentioned angel.[49] However, while the indefinite use of 'an angel' makes sense, the indefinite use of 'a law of the Lord' does not seem to be correct, because the Law of the Lord is definite. 'τὸν νόμον Μωϋσέως' in v. 22, which Luke probably inserted,[50] also makes it difficult to regard the Law of the Lord in v. 23 as being used indefinitely by Luke. If the Law of Moses is definite, the Law of the Lord is also definite. In 2.39, 'the Law of the Lord' is accompanied by the article again. It is also remarkable that Luke did not use the noun νόμος, which occurs nine times in Luke and seventeen times in Acts, without the article except at Acts 13.38 (νόμῳ Μωϋσέως), where Luke seems to have obtained it from his source,[51] and at 18.15 where the omission of the article for the previous two nouns seems to lead Luke to omit the article for the noun νόμος.[52] This is true also for Matthew and John[53] (the noun does not occur in Mark at all). It is also interesting to observe that in

---

48. See also Lk. 8.43, 44, where the same phenomenon appears for a different phrase: 43 καὶ γυνὴ οὖσα ἐν ῥύσει αἵματος ἀπὸ ἐτῶν δώδεκα ..., 44 ... παραχρῆμα ἔστη ἡ ῥύσις τοῦ αἵματος αὐτῆς. This may be from Mk 5.25.29, where a different noun is used in the second phrase: 25 καὶ γυνὴ οὖσα ἐν ῥύσει αἵματος δώδεκα ἔτη 29 καὶ εὐθὺς ἐξηράνθη ἡ πηγὴ τοῦ αἵματος αὐτῆς. Luke seems to have altered the noun πηγή to another one ῥύσις.

49. This usage of the noun 'angel' belongs to Septuagintalisms because it occurs in the LXX Judg. 6.11 and 12: in v. 11, the article is absent and in v. 12, the article appears for the noun 'angel' in the phrase ἄγγελος κυρίου.

50. This phrase is a Lukanism, as shown above.

51. γνωστὸν ἔστω with the dative in Acts 13.38 is, according to Wilcox, most probably from tradition. Luke seems to have depended on independent tradition (*The Semitisms in Acts*, pp. 90-91, 161). This consideration, along with the awkwardness of the omission of the article, makes it more probable that the phrase νόμῳ Μωϋσέως in Acts 13.38 may have derived from tradition.

52. Acts 18.15 εἰ δὲ ζητήματά ἐστιν περὶ λόγου καὶ ὀνομάτων καὶ νόμου τοῦ καθ᾽ ὑμᾶς.

53. Only one exception is found in Jn 19.7, where νόμος occurs twice: Ἡμεῖς νόμον ἔχομεν καὶ κατὰ τὸν νόμον ὀφείλει ἀποθανεῖν, ὅτι υἱὸν θεοῦ ἑαυτὸν ἐποίησεν. The noun, however, means 'a law' not 'the Torah'. Thus, the first one denotes 'a law' and the second one is used to define the first one: 'the law'.

Acts 21.20, 24, νόμος appears twice in one paragraph, and both nouns are accompanied by the article. The omission of the article in v. 23, thus, is different from Luke's style; this omission is 'a non-Lukanism'. These observations make more probable the thesis that Luke adopted the phrases 'Law of the Lord' in v. 23 and 'the Law of the Lord' in v. 24 from his source.[54] Then, was his source a translation from a Semitic original? The inconsistent usage of the article, as noted above, may make it less probable that the composer of Luke's source translated a Semitic source, though it is impossible to refute this possibility completely.

b. *The omission of the article in the LXX*
More important is that the LXX translators often omitted the article with the noun νόμος in the expression 'in the Law of the Lord' which indicates that its absence belongs to secondary Septuagintalisms.[55] In the Greek Old Testament, the phrase ἐν τῷ νόμῳ κυρίου itself occurs three times (2 Chron. 31.3; *1 Esd.* 1.31; Ps. 1.2), and the phrase ἐν νόμῳ κυρίου five times (2 Kgs 10.31; 1 Chron. 16.40; 2 Chron. 35.26; *Sir.* 46.14; Ps. 118.1).[56] There is no difference in meaning between these two phrases. The latter reflects Hebrew construction which does not have the article whereas the former may echo the way of the LXX by adopting the article. The composer of Luke's source probably imitated LXX style for the two phrases in v. 23 and v. 24, because both phrases, with and without the article, belong to Septuagintalisms. This explanation is at least logically more consistent than the translation theory because the latter does not provide a proper answer to the question of why the composer translated the same Hebrew locution once with the article and other time without the article in adjacent verses.[57]

---

54. The absence of the article in Lk. 2.23 bothered some copyists, who inserted it (D 1071). NA does not deal with these variations. See *The Gospel According to St. Luke* (The New Testament in Greek, III, Part One; ed. The American and British Committees of the International Greek New Testament Project; Oxford: Clarendon, 1984), p. 44.

55. It is possible for the author of the infancy story to have imitated the LXX for the phrase νόμος κυρίου without and with the article in v. 23 and v. 24 respectively as both appear in the LXX (with the article: Exod. 13.9; 1 Chron. 22.12; 2 Chron. 25.4, 31.3; *1 Esd.* 1.31; 8.7, 8, 9; 9.48; Ps. 1.2; Amos 2.4; Isa. 5.24; without the article: 2 Kgs 10.31; 1 Chron. 16.40; 2 Chron. 17.9, 34.14, 35.26; Neh. 9.3; Ps. 118.1; *Sir.* 46.14; Jer. 8.8).

56. In 2 Chron. 31.3 and 35.26, the prepositional phrase 'in the Law of the Lord' appears with the perfect participle form of γράφω. The article is absent in 2 Chron. 31.3, while it appears in 2 Chron. 35.26.

57. A possible suggestion would be that an unknown person translated the Semitic phrase once echoing the Hebrew syntax and then not reflecting it. Why did he do so? He probably

(ii) The whole formula καθὼς γέγραπται ἐν νόμῳ κυρίου

a. Is this from a Hebrew original?
This whole phrase may echo the Hebrew idiom in 2 Chron. 31.3; 35.26: ככתוב בתורת יהוה 'as (it is) written in the law of the Lord.'[58] The LXX translated the form into (εἰς τὰς ἑορτὰς) τὰς γεγραμμένας ἐν τῷ νόμῳ κυρίου '(for the festivals) that are written in the law of the Lord' in 2 Chron. 31.3, and ([ἦσαν] οἱ λόγοι Ἰωσια καὶ ἡ ἐλπὶς αὐτοῦ) γεγραμμένα ἐν νόμῳ κυρίου '(the acts of Josiah and his hope [are]) written in the law of the Lord' in 2 Chron. 35.26. However, the form in these two examples is not used to introduce quotations, but simply to indicate that the content of the verses is from the Law of the Lord. In addition, the literal translation echoing Hebrew syntax would be 'κατὰ τὸ γεγραμμένον ἐν νόμῳ κυρίου' (cf. Ezra 3.4; Neh. 8.15), since the verb form in Hebrew is a participle.[59]

b. Is the whole formula from the LXX?
As pointed out above, the phrase ἐν (τῷ) νόμῳ κυρίου is probably from the LXX. The question is whether Luke depended on the LXX to compose the formula καθὼς γέγραπται (ἐν). This formula appears in the LXX twice to introduce quotations in 2 Chron. 23.18 and 25.4 and twice to indicate allusions, in 2 Kgs 14.6 and Dan. (TH) 9.13. In two of these four instances, ἐν νόμῳ Μωυσῆ[60] is found (2 Chron. 23.18; 2 Kgs 14.6). However, the phrase in Lk. 2.23, ἐν νόμῳ κυρίου does not appear with the locution καθὼς γέγραπται (ἐν) in the LXX. In addition, the conjunction ὅτι does not follow the formula in these four instances, but only ὡς in 2 Chron. 25.4 and 2 Kgs 14.6.

The above observations indicate that the quotation formula as a whole neither originated from the LXX exactly or from the Hebrew OT, nor represents Luke's characteristic style. In other words, this formula is a non-Septuagintalism as well as a non-Lukanism, and a 'hard core non-Lukanism', which makes difficult Luke's direct composition in the imitation of the LXX and may indicate Luke's dependence on a Greek source. However, each of the phrases καθὼς

---

followed the LXX, where both locutions are used without distinction. Even in this case, he ultimately depended on the LXX. As noted in Chapter 2, the issue centres on which side – Semitic side or Greek side one lays the emphasis.

58. J. Nolland, *Luke 1–9:20* (WBC, 35A; Dallas: Word Books, 1989), pp. 117–18.

59. It is true that the Hebrew phrase ככתוב בתורה could be rendered with a finite verb as in Neh. 10.35–36: ὡς γέγραπται ἐν τῷ νόμῳ. The bottom line is, however, that the Greek sentence does not exactly reflect the Hebrew phrase.

60. A different declinable noun is used in these verses of the LXX; the genitive of 'Moses' is not Μωϋσέως as in Luke, but Μωυσῆ. In sixteen verses of the LXX, Μωϋσέως is also used (Judg. 1.6; 1 Kgs 2.3; *1 Esd.* 5.48; etc.).

γέγραπται and ἐν νόμῳ κυρίου probably originated from the LXX rather than the Hebrew OT.

In sum, the accumulated evidence in the manner of the quotation – the introductory formula and the conjunction ὅτι as well as the omission of the indicators for direct discourse in the quoted text – supports Luke's dependence on a Greek source for v. 23.[61] It is less probable that the source is translated from a Semitic source; it was more probably composed directly in Greek depending on the LXX for the phrase νόμῳ κυρίου.

Now, we turn to the content of the quotation to examine whether it depended on the LXX or the Hebrew OT. If the quotation is closer to the LXX, the dependence of the introductory formula on a source directly composed in Greek rather than a source translated from a Semitic original will be more probable along with the considerations mentioned above. For it is less probable that the composer of the source wrote the introductory formula in Hebrew, while depending on the LXX for the content of the quotation.

(B) *The Content of the Quotation*

(1) *The problem and proposals for a solution*

Some scholars count Lk. 2.23 a formal quotation of Exod. 13.2,[62] while others regard it as depending on Exod. 13.12.[63] This confusion arises from the wording of 2.23 not being identical to either Exod. 13.2 or 13.12:

---

61. Though it is hardly possible to completely refute the argument that Luke's source for the manner of the quotation had originated from a Semitic original, this solution represents a less probable one.

62. Böhl suggests Exod. 13.2 as well as Num. 18.15 as quoted texts (*Alttestamentlichen Citate*, p. 89). Bock, *Luke 1:1–9:50*, p. 237, suggests Reicke's explanation in *TDNT* as a base for his argument that Lk. 2.23 is from Exod. 13.2, though Reicke mentions also 13.12–15 (see *TDNT*, vol. 5, p. 84). Knox notes that 'the quotation is a free one from 13:2' (*The Interpreter's Bible*, p. 60). See also Fitzmyer, *Luke I–IX*, p. 426. G. Bratcher regards Exod. 13.2 as a quoted text in his book, *Old Testament Quotations in the New Testament* (London: United Bible Societies, 1961), p. 16.

63. See Swete's list in *An Introduction to the Old Testament in Greek*, p. 386. See also Johnson, *Luke*, p. 54. Nolland notes that 'the quotation is closest to Exod. 13:12', while adding 'ἅγιον – κληθήσεται "shall be called holy" paraphrases the consecration language of Exod. 13:2' whose wording echoes Lk. 1.35 (*Luke 1–9:20*, p. 118).

3. A Close Examination of the Greek of the Infancy Narrative 79

Πᾶν ἄρσεν
διανοῖγον
μήτραν (ἅγιον)
τῷ κυρίῳ κληθήσεταί
(Lk. 2.23)

(ἁγίασόν) μοι πᾶν
πρωτότοκον πρωτογενὲς
διανοῖγον πᾶσαν μήτραν
ἐν τοῖς υἱοῖς Ἰσραὴλ
ἀπὸ ἀνθρώπου ἕως
κτήνους ἐμοί ἐστιν
(Exod. 13.2)

καὶ ἀφελεῖς πᾶν διανοῖ-
γον μήτραν τὰ ἀρσενικὰ
τῷ κυρίῳ πᾶν διανοῖγον
μήτραν ἐκ τῶν
βουκολίων ἢ ἐν τοῖς
κτήνεσίν σου ὅσα ἐὰν
γένηταί σοι τὰ ἀρσενικά
(ἁγιάσεις) τῷ κυρίῳ
(Exod. 13.12)

The following differences between the Lukan text and the possible quoted texts may be noted:

a. πᾶν directly modifies ἄρσεν in Luke, while the pronoun modifies πρωτότοκον in Exod. 13.2 and διανοῖγον in 13.12;
b. the adjective ἅγιον appears with κληθήσεται in Luke, while the imperative ἁγίασον appears in Exod. 13.2 and the future indicative indicating command in Exod. 13.12a (ἀφελεῖς) and in 13.12b (ἁγιάσεις);
c. the Lukan text, as mentioned above, avoided certain indicators of direct discourse. It omitted μοι and ἐμοί in Exod. 13.2 and the second person verbs and personal pronouns, σου and σοι in Exod. 13.12.

These differences may argue against the theory that the Lukan text depended on the LXX, since it does not follow the wording of the LXX Exod. 13.2 or 13.12. In fact, Holtz interprets this citation as originating from Jewish tradition (*Untersuchungen*, pp. 82–3). Following Holtz when comparing with the Greek and Hebrew OT texts of these three verses, Bock insists that the Lukan text does not rely on the LXX as a whole, but on Semitic tradition which summarizes Exod. 13.2, 13.12a, and 13.15a.[64]

(2) *Another proposal*
The following elements make it probable to argue that the possible quoted text in Lk. 2.23 relied on LXX Exod. 13.2 or more probably Exod. 13.12:

a. the sentence in Lk. 2.23 is preceded by the introductory formula and its subject matter, if not the precise wording, is identical to Exod. 13.12, and shares the same topic: consecration of a firstborn male;
b. πᾶν is used as a modifying word in Lk. 2.23 and Exod. 13.12 of the LXX;

---

64. See Bock's *Proclamation from Prophecy and Pattern*, p. 83. He asserts in his recent commentary that 'the syntax of the Lukan citation is very different from that of the LXX', suggesting a 'non-Hellenistic origin' (*Luke 1.1–9.50*, p. 237).

c. all the vocabulary in Luke occurs in Exod. 13.12 of the LXX except for the verb κληθήσεται;[65]
d. a neuter participle (διανοῖγον) is used for a male in both verses;
e. in both Exodus and Luke, μήτραν is used for 'womb';
f. the phrase τῷ κυρίῳ and the word for 'male' appears in both verses: ἄρσεν in Luke and ἀρσενικά in Exodus. These two are not found in Exod. 13.2, but only in 13.12.

The last four elements require closer inspection.

(i) *The use of the passive indicative verb κληθήσεται with ἅγιον*
The last part of the sentence in Luke presents a problem: ἅγιον κληθήσεται. Different from the possible quoted text in Exod. 13.2 or 13.12, the passive form of the verb καλέω is used in Lk. 2.23. Nolland comments that this construction is a paraphrase of the purification language of Exod. 13.2 (*Luke 1–9:20*, p. 118). This explanation is possible, but the latter part of Exod. 13.12 may provide an answer, where the future indicative appears: ἁγιάσεις (τῷ κυρίῳ). Noteworthy is that the expression in Exod. 13.12, ἁγιάσεις τῷ κυρίῳ, is very close to the phrase ἅγιον τῷ κυρίῳ in Lk. 2.23. The composer may have intended to abridge the sentence in Exod. 13.12. The future indicative may have hinted at the use of the same root word as ἁγιάζω, but the adjective with a different verb echoing Lk. 1.35 (διὸ καὶ τὸ γεννώμενον ἅγιον κληθήσεται υἱὸς θεοῦ) emphasizes the holy character of the child.[66] As the result of the use of the passive verb, the accusative from the LXX, πᾶν διανοῖγον, becomes nominative in Luke, even though the forms are the same. Luke then has had to alter the voice of the verb from the active to the passive.[67] This process is probable, since the Lukan text does not follow the second part of Exod. 13.12, but abridges it.

(ii) *The participle διανοῖγον*
The word διανοίγω is mostly peculiar to Luke; it occurs six times in Luke-Acts (Lk. 24.31–32, 45; Acts 7.56, 16.14, 17.3), while only once does it appear outside of Luke-Acts in the NT (Mk 7.34). This verb occurs frequently in the LXX. More important is that the participle form διανοῖγον points to the influence of LXX Exod. 13.2

---

65. The first part of Lk. 2.23 is very close to that of Exod. 13.12. Compare the underlined part of the two verses.
66. Marshall notes that 'the phrase ἅγιον – κληθήσεται is repeated from 1:35' (*Luke*, p. 117).
67. In this process, either he employed a locution that occurs in Lk. 1.35, or quoted his LXX version which contains the verb καλέω.

3. *A Close Examination of the Greek of the Infancy Narrative* 81

or 13.12.⁶⁸ The corresponding Hebrew word contains the *masculine* פטר, while the LXX has the *neuter* in Exod. 13.2,12 (also in Exod. 13.13,15; 34.19; Num. 18.15; Ezek. 20.26 etc.). The participle is 'a hard core Septuagintalism'. Bock insists that although the phrase διανοῖγον μήτραν⁶⁹ appears to be influenced by the LXX, it may echo 'a technical idiom' as well (*Proclamation*, p. 83). He suggests the consistent occurrence of the phrase in the LXX as the basis of his argument. As even Bock admits, however, there are no 'Semitic or cultic Greek sources' to confirm his assumption. The phrase occurs only in the LXX as an idiomatic expression, but not in other Greek literature.⁷⁰ The use of the participle, therefore, indicates the influence of the LXX, most probably from possible quoted texts, either Exod. 13.2 or 13.12.

(iii)   *The word* μήτραν

μήτραν found in Lk. 2.23 is also found in Exod. 13.2 and 13.12 of the LXX. We must look closely at the word μήτρα because of its peculiarity. The noun means 'womb' in Lk. 2.23 and Exod. 13.2, 12. The common word for 'womb' in Luke-Acts is κοιλία which frequently appears also in the other NT books.⁷¹ While the noun κοιλία occurs four times outside of the narrative (Lk. 11.27, 23.29, Acts 3.2, 14.8), the noun μήτρα does not occur in Luke-Acts except in Lk. 2.23. The noun κοιλία is found five times also in the infancy narrative (1.15, 41-42, 44, 2.21). The noun μήτρα is thus 'a non-Lukanism' which calls into question Luke's translation;⁷² the noun is probably from a Greek source, i.e., the LXX of Exod. 13.2 or 12 in this case.

There remains, however, the possibility that Luke utilized the noun μήτρα since it could mean specifically the cervix of the orifice of

---

68. Holtz, *Untersuchungen*, p. 83, nt. 1.
69. For the discussion of the second word, see below.
70. Although it is not probable for Semitic intervention to happen in biblical Greek syntax, it is accepted that Semitic vocabulary influenced biblical Greek to the level of intervention. Even Porter, who denies the significant influence of Semitic languages on NT Greek, accepts a possible significant influence of Semitic languages on the NT in some vocabulary items (*Idioms of the Greek New Testament*, p. 13).
71. The noun κοιλία appears twelve times outside of Luke-Acts. In three verses, the noun means 'womb' (Mt. 19.12; Jn 3.4; Gal. 1.15) and 'stomach' in the rest of the verses (Mt. 12.40; 15.17; Mk 7.19; Jn 7.38; Rom. 16.18; 1 Cor. 6.13; Phil. 3.19; Rev. 10.9-10).
72. It is also less possible that other contemporary writers employed this noun while translating the Hebrew text; the noun μήτρα is further found only in Rom. 4.19b, which describes the story of Abraham and Sarah [Rom. 4.19b – καὶ τὴν νέκρωσιν τῆς μήτρας Σάρρας – 'and (he considered) the barrenness of Sarah's womb'].

the womb (Liddell and Scott, p. 1130): this may explain the reason why Luke, supposedly translating a Hebrew source, adopted this noun with the verb διανοίγω, just as the LXX translators did (Gen. 29.31; 30.22; Exod. 13.2,12,13,15; 34.19, etc.).

While it is possible that Luke did so, this pattern, i.e., the verb διανοίγω followed by the noun μήτρα as its object, appears frequently in the LXX.[73] More relevantly, the two possibly quoted verses, Exod. 13.2 and 13.12, use μήτρα for 'womb'.[74] The noun μήτρα thus belongs to 'non-Lukan Septuagintalisms' and the LXX presents the best explanation for the use of the noun μήτρα in Lk. 2.23.

The above considerations support the view that the author of the Lukan text adopted the word μήτρα, like διανοῖγον, ultimately from the LXX, either Exod. 13.2 or 13.12.[75]

(iv) *The phrase* τῷ κυρίῳ *and the use of the substantivized adjective* ἄρσεν[76]
The phrase τῷ κυρίῳ in Lk. 2.23 is found only in Exod. 13.12 and this clearly supports the dependence of the Lukan text on Exod. 13.12. The word meaning 'male' also occurs only in Exod. 13.12; but the substantivized adjective ἄρσεν poses another riddle which requires an explanation. While the neuter singular ἄρσεν is used in Luke, the neuter plural ἀρσενικά is found in Exodus. The possible corresponding Hebrew word in Exod. 13.12b, הזכרים, is a *masculine* and plural form which the LXX translated as τὰ ἀρσενικά, a *neuter* and plural form.

Concerning the use of ἄρσεν, Fitzmyer remarks that Luke, depending on the LXX of Exod. 13.2, added ἄρσεν, 'male' to make the meaning clear because Luke precisely grasped the topic of the verse, i.e., 'the consecration of the firstborn son'. His explanation

---

73. In the LXX, the term μήτρα is much more frequently used to denote 'womb' (35 times) than κοιλία, and always means 'womb', while κοιλία (107 times), which usually means something else, is also used to indicate 'womb' 7 times (Gen. 25.24; Ruth 1.11; *Tob.* 4.4; Job 31.15; *Wis.* 7.1; Hos. 12.4; Jer. 1.5). This is the case even in classical Greek where κοιλία means more frequently belly or intestines than womb (Liddell and Scott, pp. 966–67).

74. Also noteworthy is that μήτρα could have been used instead of κοιλία in the other Lukan verses. For the phrase ἐκ μήτρας ('from the womb' or 'from birth') instead of ἐκ κοιλίας in Lk. 1.15, Acts 3.2 and 14.8, see Ps. 21.11; *Sir.* 50.22 (cf. Job 3.16; Jer. 1.5; 20.18); for the phrase ἐν μήτρᾳ instead of ἐν τῇ κοιλίᾳ in Lk. 1.41,44 and 2.21, see *Sir.* 1.4; 49.7 and Jer. 20.17a. For the use of the word μήτρα instead of κοιλία itself to indicate 'womb' as in Lk. 11.27 and 23.29, see Gen. 49.25; Jer. 20.17b; Hos. 9.14, etc.

75. Other instances in Exodus and Numbers where μήτρα is used with the participle διανοῖγον to render the same Hebrew phrase פטר רחם are Exod. 34.19; Num. 3.12; 8.16; 18.15.

76. ἄρσην is prevalent in the NT and LXX, while the Attic Greek form ἄρρην occurs more frequently in the papyri (Liddell and Scott, p. 248).

3. *A Close Examination of the Greek of the Infancy Narrative* 83

that Luke relied on Exod. 13.2 seems inadequate. The alteration of the substantivized adjective ἀρσενικά in Exod. 13.12 to the substantivized adjective ἄρσεν provides a more probable solution. Exod. 13.2 does not, in contrast to Exod. 13.12, include the term τῷ κυρίῳ nor the term 'males', ἀρσενικά, while it contains the words μοι instead of τῷ κυρίῳ and πᾶσαν before μήτραν. In additon, πρωτότοκον πρωτογενές in Exod. 13.2, a seemingly redundant phrase for 'the firstborn', is lacking in Luke. It is more probable, therefore, that the Lukan text depended on Exod. 13.12 and thus the word ἄρσεν is from the alteration of the word ἀρσενικά in Exod. 13.12. The comparison of Lk. 2.23, Exod. 13.2 and 13.12 supports this assessment:

Exod. 13.12 καὶ ἀφελεῖς <u>πᾶν διανοῖγον μήτραν τὰ ἀρσενικά τῷ κυρίῳ</u> πᾶν διανοῖγον μήτραν ἐκ τῶν βουκολίων ἢ ἐν τοῖς κτήνεσίν σου ὅσα ἐάν γένηταί σοι τὰ ἀρσενικά ἁγιάσεις τῷ κυρίῳ

Lk. 2.23 <u>πᾶν ἄρσεν διανοῖγον μήτραν</u> ἅγιον τῷ κυρίῳ κληθήσεται

Exod. 13.2 ἁγίασόν <u>μοι πᾶν πρωτότοκον πρωτογενές διανοῖγον πᾶσαν μήτραν</u>

The disagreement of the number of the two words διανοῖγον (singular) and τὰ ἀρσενικά (plural) in Exod. 13.12, which reflects the Hebrew construction, may have bothered the composer of the Lukan text. He appears to assimilate the expression found in the LXX. In doing so, he changed the substantivized adjective τὰ ἀρσενικά in Exod. 13.12 to ἄρσεν, since the number of the adjective did not agree with the number of the participle διανοῖγον. This change explains why the composer altered τὰ ἀρσενικά to ἄρσεν, a correct word in the New Testament rather than inserting ἄρσεν, as Fitzmyer argues. It is also more probable that he changed only the number of the noun in the LXX from plural to singular rather than both the number and gender of the noun in the Hebrew OT. The change from ἀρσενικά to ἄρσεν instead of ἀρσενικόν is explained by the fact that the adjective ἀρσενικός in the LXX, where both words appear, is no longer used in the New Testament, where only the substantivized adjective ἄρσην appears (Mt. 19.4 = Mk 10.6 [quotation from Gen. 1.27 where ἄρσεν occurs]; Rom. 1.27; 1 Cor. 6.9; Gal. 3.28; 1 Tim. 1.10; Rev. 12.5, 13). It is remarkable that ἀρσενικά in Exod. 13.12 is neuter, while the corresponding Hebrew is masculine. With the masculine Hebrew noun of διανοῖγον, ἄρσεν could have been translated into a masculine if the Hebrew sentence in Exod. 13.12 had been more literally translated: πάντα ἄρσενα διανοίγοντα. Our argument makes it probable for the Lukan text to be based on the LXX rather than the Hebrew OT for the noun ἄρσεν.

(3) *Is Lk. 2.23 a summary of two or three verses?*

Some scholars have suggested that Luke (or his source) intended to summarize two or even three verses in Exodus: 13.2, 13.12, and 13.15.[77] It is accepted that the three verses are concerned with the same topic, i.e., the consecration of the first-born, and that some features like διανοῖον and μήτραν appear in all three verses. However, the Lukan text seems to have depended on and to have abridged Exod. 13.12 as shown above; the phrase τῷ κυρίῳ and the substantivized adjective for 'male' occur only in Exod. 13.12. The intention of the composer may have been to alter some awkward expressions in the LXX (πᾶν διανοῖγον μήτραν τὰ ἀρσενικά) and to emphasize the holiness of the child by omitting some irrelevant part (πᾶν διανοῖγον μήτραν ἐκ τῶν βουκολίων ἢ ἐν τοῖς κτήνεσίν σου ὅσα ἐὰν γένηταί σοι τὰ ἀρσενικά), and adding the verb καλέω.[78]

In conclusion, the way of quotation – a peculiar quotation formula and (in)direct discourse with the conjunction ὅτι – undermines the claim that Lk. 2.23 is Luke's direct composition, while features of content and wording – the neuter participle διανοῖγον and the noun μήτραν as well as ἄρσεν – support the conclusion that the quoted text in 2.23 was derived from the LXX rather than the Hebrew OT. The LXX text used is probably Exod. 13.12. Luke seems to have depended on his source, which included the introductory formula with the conjunction and relied on the LXX for the quoted text. The adoption of the conjunction ὅτι and a rather ambiguous (in)direct discourse may indicate that the composer of this sentence intended to abridge the sentence in the LXX Exod. 13.12.[79] The sentence in 2.23 πᾶν ἄρσεν διανοῖγον μήτραν ἅγιον τῷ κυρίῳ κληθήσεται, is counted, of course, as a quotation considering the following factors: 1) an introductory formula precedes it: καθὼς γέγραπται ἐν νόμῳ κυρίου; 2) it

---

77. Holtz, *Untersuchungen*, p. 83. Marshall and Bock follow Holtz. See Marshall, *Luke*, p. 117 and Bock, *Luke 1:1–9:50*, p. 237. Exod. 13.15 will be excluded from our discussion, since the basic wording is very different from Lk. 2.23: διὰ τοῦτο ἐγὼ θύω τῷ κυρίῳ πᾶν διανοῖγον μήτραν τὰ ἀρσενικά καὶ πᾶν πρωτότοκον τῶν υἱῶν μου λυτρώσομαι; 'Therefore I sacrifice to the Lord every male that first opens the womb, and every firstborn of my sons I will redeem.'

78. Some quotations in Acts show that the quoted text could be changed according to the author's intention. In Acts 13.34 (Δώσω ὑμῖν τὰ ὅσια Δαυὶδ τὰ πιστά), Luke changed and omitted some parts of the quoted text in Isa. 55.3 (διαθήσομαι ὑμῖν διαθήκην αἰώνιον τὰ ὅσια Δαυὶδ τὰ πιστά). For details, see Steyn, *Septuagint Quotations*, p. 178.

79. The following question may arise: Do the differences between the Lukan text and the LXX suggest that Luke depended on his memory? Having asked if the change of the verb in Jn 1.23 from ἑτοιμάσατε in Isa. 40.3, the quoted text, to εὐθύνατε happened 'because John quoted freely from memory,' M.J.J. Menken answers that 'it seems that such an explanation is only valid when no explanation can be found on the level of Johannine redaction' (M.J.J. Menken, *Old Testament Quotations in the Fourth Gospel: Studies in Textual Form* [Kampen: Kok Pharos, 1996]), p. 25. The same principle informs our study.

depends on one verse in Exod. 13.12, where the subject is the same as that in Luke and in which all the vocabulary in Luke is found except for the verb καλέω; 3) the differences can be explained as indicated above.

II. *The Quotation in Lk. 2.24*

22 Καὶ ὅτε ἐπλήσθησαν αἱ ἡμέραι τοῦ καθαρισμοῦ αὐτῶν κατὰ τὸν νόμον Μωϋσέως, ἀνήγαγον αὐτὸν εἰς Ἱεροσόλυμα παραστῆσαι τῷ κυρίῳ **23** καθὼς γέγραπται ἐν νόμῳ κυρίου ὅτι πᾶν ἄρσεν διανοῖγον μήτραν ἅγιον τῷ κυρίῳ κληθήσεται **24** <u>καὶ τοῦ δοῦναι θυσίαν κατὰ τὸ εἰρημένον ἐν τῷ νόμῳ κυρίου, ζεῦγος τρυγόνων ἢ δύο νοσσοὺς περιστερῶν</u>.

22 *And when the days of their purification had been fulfilled according to the Law of Moses, they brought him up to Jerusalem to present (him) to the Lord,* 23 *as it has been written in the law of the Lord that every (firstborn) male opening the womb will be called holy to the Lord,* 24 *and (they went up to Jerusalem) to offer a sacrifice according to what has been said in the Law of the Lord 'a pair of turtledoves or two young (ones) of pigeons'.*

(A) *The Manner of Quotation*

(1) *The introductory formula*

An introductory formula precedes the quoted phrase (ζεῦγος τρυγόνων ἢ δύο νοσσοὺς περιστερῶν): κατὰ τὸ εἰρημένον ἐν τῷ νόμῳ κυρίου.

(i) *The phrase* τὸ εἰρημένον

In Luke-Acts, this phrase occurs twice to introduce quotations in Acts 2.16 (τὸ εἰρημένον διὰ τοῦ προφήτου Ἰωήλ) and 13.40 (τὸ εἰρημένον ἐν τοῖς προφήταις), and once outside of Luke-Acts in Rom. 4.18 (κατὰ τὸ εἰρημένον). The two examples in Acts indicate that the use of τὸ εἰρημένον itself for quotation may not be a non-Lukanism as the use of καθὼς γέγραπται (ἐν) in the case of 2.23, though the presence of the preposition κατά possibly indicates its non-Lukan character.

(ii) *The prepositional phrase* ἐν τῷ νόμῳ κυρίου

However, ἐν τῷ νόμῳ κυρίου is 'a non-Lukanism' as shown in our discussion of 2.23.[80] It is less probable for Luke to either have composed the phrase or translated it from a Hebrew original.

(iii) *Is the introductory formula from the LXX?*

One may argue for Luke's imitation of the LXX for the phrase ἐν τῷ νόμῳ κυρίου because it appears in the LXX. It is accepted that the

---

80. For details, see above.

phrase itself may be included in hard core Septuagintalisms because the Hebrew text lacks the article of the LXX. However, the absence of the introductory formula (κατὰ τὸ εἰρημένον)[81] with the phrase ἐν τῷ νόμῳ κυρίου in the LXX makes it difficult to claim that the formula as a whole belongs to hard core Septuagintalisms. In sum, the introductory formula is a non-Septuagintalism and non-Lukanism which does not seem to derive from the translation of a Semitic original.[82] In other words, this belongs to 'hard core non-Lukanisms' and these support Luke's dependence on a written Greek source.

(2) *The quoted phrase:* ζεῦγος τρυγόνων ἢ δύο νοσσοὺς περιστερῶν

The seemingly quoted phrase ζεῦγος τρυγόνων ἢ δύο νοσσοὺς περιστερῶν betrays a peculiar character: while quotations always consist elsewhere of sentences in Luke-Acts, a phrase here follows the introductory formula. The use of a phrase for a quotation may thus point to a non-Lukanism. It may be true, however, that this element can be considered a non-Lukanism only after its confirmation as a quotation, since a phrase could form an allusion as in Lk. 20.37:

καὶ Μωϋσῆς ἐμήνυσεν ἐπὶ τῆς βάτου, ὡς λέγει κύριον τὸν θεὸν Ἀβραὰμ καὶ θεὸν Ἰσαὰκ καὶ θεὸν Ἰακώβ.[83]

In this instance, nevertheless, a verb form, the infinitive εἶναι is implied between κύριον and τὸν θεὸν. Thus, a phrase without any verb form, which is introduced by a quotation formula, does not appear in Luke-Acts. It is certain, therefore, that the use of the phrase instead of a full sentence for a quotation, if the phrase in Lk. 2.24 is a quotation, is 'a non-Lukanism', and that the use of the introductory formula for an allusion, even if the phrase forms only an allusion, is also non-Lukan. The phrase thus betrays a non-Lukan characteristic in any case.

---

81. Nolland points out that τὸ εἰρημένον is not Septuagintal because this phrase is not used for quotations in the LXX (*Luke 1–9:20*, p. 118). His statement is correct, but the LXX does not have the phrase because the MT does not have the corresponding phrase. In Gen. 45.21, κατὰ τὰ εἰρημένα ὑπὸ Φαραώ appears, but this is a paraphrase of a Hebrew construction: על־פי פרעה. This may indicate that the phrase κατὰ τὸ εἰρημένον itself is Septuagintalistic rather than Masoretic.

82. As pointed out above, the presence of the article in v. 23 and its absence in v. 24 for the same phrase 'the Law of the Lord' make it difficult to argue that the phrase is derived from a translation. For details, see the argument on v. 23.

83. The parallels in Mt. 22.32 and Mk 12.26 are quotations: Mt. 22.31b-32: οὐκ ἀνέγνωτε τὸ ῥηθὲν ὑμῖν ὑπὸ τοῦ θεοῦ λέγοντος, 32 Ἐγώ εἰμι ὁ θεὸς Ἀβραὰμ καὶ ὁ θεὸς Ἰσαὰκ καὶ ὁ θεὸς Ἰακώβ; Mk 12.26: ἐγείρονται οὐκ ἀνέγνωτε ἐν τῇ βίβλῳ Μωϋσέως ἐπὶ τοῦ βάτου πῶς εἶπεν αὐτῷ ὁ θεὸς λέγων, Ἐγὼ ὁ θεὸς Ἀβραὰμ καὶ [ὁ] θεὸς Ἰσαὰκ καὶ [ὁ] θεὸς Ἰακώβ. For more details, see Stendahl, *The School of St. Matthew*, pp. 71-72, and New, *Old Testament Quotations*, pp. 68-70.

3. A Close Examination of the Greek of the Infancy Narrative 87

In sum, the manner of quotation indicates that the use of the phrase ζεῦ γος τρυγόνων ἢ δύο νοσσοὺς περιστερῶν and the introductory formula are derived from Luke's source rather than from Luke's hand and that the source does not seem to be from a translation.

(B) *The Content of the Quotation*

(1) *Differences between the phrase in Lev. 12.8 of the LXX and that in Lk. 2.24*

The content of this verse seems to suggest a close connection to Lev. 12.8 which describes the purification of the mother after giving birth.[84] The offering originally includes a lamb as well as two turtledoves or young pigeons (Lev. 12.6), but the lamb can be exempted for the poor:

ἐὰν δὲ μὴ εὑρίσκῃ ἡ χεὶρ αὐτῆς τὸ ἱκανὸν εἰς ἀμνὸν καὶ λήμψεται δύο τρυγόνας ἢ δύο νεοσσοὺς περιστερῶν.
If her hand does not find enough for a lamb, then she shall take two turtledoves or two young (ones) of pigeons (Lev. 12.8).

However, the wording in Luke is not identical to that in Leviticus:

a. The Gospel contains a declinable noun ζεῦγος with the genitive τρυγόνων, resulting in the meaning 'a pair of turtle doves' (BAGD, p. 337), whereas Leviticus has an indeclinable noun δύο directly modifying the accusative τρυγόνας: 'two turtle doves';
b. another difference is related to a morphological variation on the noun νεοσσούς in Lev. 12.8 and νοσσούς in Luke.

(2) *Explanation of the differences*

(i) *The noun νεοσσούς in Lev. 12.8 and νοσσούς in Lk. 2.24*

The second difference is due to syncope, i.e., the loss of vowel before a vowel [BDF, p. 31.(3)]. Phrynichus, an Atticist of A.D. second century, labels νοσσός and cognate forms 'ἀδόκιμα' 'disreputable' (Liddell and Scott, p. 1169). The term occurs frequently in later Greek, but is not found at all in the LXX where syncope does not happen. In contrast, the NT contains three uses of the noun, including Lk. 2.24, and all are influenced by syncope (Lk. 13.14; Mt. 23.47). This tendency demonstrates that Luke could be expected to alter the noun in Leviticus, possibly because of the influence of the Greek of his time.

---

84. The expression 'the days of their purification' in Lk. 2.22 implies the purification motive for the following content.

(ii) ζεῦγος τρυγόνων *in Luke and* δύο τρυγόνας *in Leviticus*
The difference between ζεῦγος τρυγόνων and δύο τρυγόνας represents a more serious problem and thus requires explanation.

a. The Hebrew construction שתי תרים או־שני בני־יונה can be literally translated as 'δύο τρυγόνων ἢ δύο νοσσοὺς περιστερᾶς,' 'two of turtle doves or two young (ones) of a dove'.

b. The phrase 'two turtle doves or two young pigeons' occurs seven times in the LXX: Lev. 5.7, 11; 12.8; 14.22; 15.14, 29; Num. 6.10. All these instances, except Lev. 5.11, have the same Greek expression: δύο τρυγόνας ἢ δύο νοσσοὺς περιστερῶν. In contrast, Lev. 5.11 shows a different phrase for the first part: ζεῦγος τρυγόνων ἢ δύο νεοσσοὺς περιστερῶν; while Lev. 5.11 adopted ζεῦγος τρυγόνων 'a pair of turtle doves', all the other examples have δύο τρυγόνας 'two turtle doves'. But the underlying Hebrew construction is the same for these two Greek phrases.

Brown argues that this phrase in Lk. 2.24 derives from the LXX Lev. 12.8 (*The Birth of the Messiah*, p. 437).[85] It is true that Luke's context seems to correspond to Lev. 12.8.[86] Luke's wording, however, is exactly identical to that of Lev. 5.11: ζεῦγος τρυγόνων ἢ δύο νεοσσοὺς περιστερῶν apart from the spelling of νοσσός. Assuming that Luke tried to translate the Hebrew construction literally, some may argue that Luke translated Lev. 12.8 of the Hebrew text or depended on Semitic tradition, on the ground that the Hebrew construction of both verses in Leviticus is the same.[87]

c. As suggested above, however, the more probable literal translation would be δύο (τῶν) τρυγόνων ἢ δύο νοσσοὺς (τῆς) περιστερᾶς 'two of turtle doves or two young (ones) of a dove'. The Hebrew word for περιστερά is singular and its literal translation must be περιστερᾶς: 'of a dove'. Luke or the composer of his source did not have a reason to adopt ζεῦγος instead of δύο if he translated the Hebrew text, as the Hebrew word for both Greek words is the same: שתים. Why did he use ζεῦγος,[88] even though the Hebrew construction is the same for

---

85. Fitzmyer, *Luke I–IX*, p. 426, also notes that Luke picked up most of his wording from the LXX Lev. 12.8.
86. Marshall, *Luke*, p. 117, remarks that the content is close to Lev. 12.8, while the wording approximates to Lev. 5.11. He does not explain, however, why this phenomenon happens.
87. Bock, *Luke 1:1–9:50*, p. 237. Also Holtz, *Untersuchungen*, pp. 82–83.
88. Another instance for the word ζεῦγος appears only in Lk. 14.19 in the whole NT, where the noun can also mean simply 'two' (BAGD, p. 337).

3. *A Close Examination of the Greek of the Infancy Narrative* 89

δύο and ζεῦγος, if he translated the Hebrew text?⁸⁹ If he supposed that 'two' in the Hebrew text means 'pair', why did he not suppose the same for the next phrase שני בני-יונה, which he translated as δύο νεοσσοὺς περιστερῶν? It could have meant ζεῦγος τῶν νεοσσῶν τῶν περιστερῶν. A probable answer would be that he understood the first Hebrew word as indicating 'pair' and the second as 'two'. It is also possible that Luke or the composer had an LXX version, where ζεῦγος appeared in Lev. 12.8 instead of δύο. Another possibility is that he intended the meaning of Lev. 12.8, but borrowed the wording of Lev. 5.11 of the LXX.⁹⁰

(3) *The possibility that the phrase ζεῦγος τρυγόνων stemmed from solely Lev. 5.11 of the LXX*
However, the phrase ζεῦγος τρυγόνων may have been derived solely from the influence of Lev. 5.11 of the LXX, which deals with the sin offering:

ἐὰν δὲ μὴ εὑρίσκῃ αὐτοῦ ἡ ξεὶρ ζεῦγος τρυγόνων ἢ δύο νεοσσοὺς περιστερῶν.
But if her hand does not find a pair of turtledoves or two of the young of doves.

This possibility arises from the interpretation of the pronoun αὐτῶν in Lk. 2.22, which may indicate the sin offerings for Jesus' parents as well as for Jesus.⁹¹ The pronoun is problematic, since the meaning of the sentence would have been proper if the pronoun had been singular like αὐτοῦ or αὐτῆς, which refers to Jesus or Joseph and Mary respectively: 'the days of Jesus' (or Joseph's) purification' or 'the days of Mary's purification'. The context seems to point to the purification of women after giving birth. Some variants (76, the Complutensian Polyglot of 1514, some Italian manuscripts and Vulgate) thus use the singular αὐτῆς (or the Latin equivalent) instead of the plural in conformity with the purification law in Leviticus. Others (D, *pc.* lat sy sa) have αὐτοῦ (or the equivalent) which indicates Jesus or Joseph. The external evidence clearly stands against these two singular pronouns and supports the reading of αὐτῶν. The internal evidence also supports the plural pronoun, because it represents

---

89. Luke always employs δύο with the genitive plural in the rest of his Gospel and Acts except in Lk. 14.19; 7.18; 12.6; 19.29 (Cf. 24.13 where the phrase δύο ἐξ αὐτῶν appears); Acts 10.7; 19.22; 23.23. It is unlikely thus that Luke translated the Hebrew text.
90. Holtz, *Untersuchungen*, p. 83. He offers still another possibility, i.e., that Luke or his source did not follow the wording as it stands.
91. Sahlin claims that the supposed Hebrew text included a suffix pronoun: טהרה, 'τοῦ καθαρισμοῦ αὐτῆς' as in Lev. 12.4b, 6. Luke misunderstood this, according to him, as טהרה, 'τοῦ καθαρισμοῦ', as in Lev. 12.4a. Since this Greek expression was not satisfactory in polished Greek, he continues, Luke added the pronoun αὐτῶν. As a result, the Jewish meaning of the original text disappeared (*Der Messias*, p. 243). He does not suggest, however, why Luke had to add the pronoun αὐτῶν instead of αὐτῆς.

the most difficult reading. The original reading therefore is probably 'αὐτῶν'.

To whom, then, does this pronoun refer? Contextually, three alternatives are possible: Joseph and Mary, Jesus and Mary, or Jesus and Joseph. The context and background eliminate the last one because Mary should be included, given that she gave birth (Lk. 2.23) and needed to be purified according to Lev. 12.6–8. Historical background militates against the second interpretation which commentators since Origen have supposed to be correct.[92] Although both the mother and the baby were considered unclean in the Hellenistic world, that was not the case in the Palestinian world.[93] The first option is the most probable one when the grammar is considered. The main verb of the main clause in Lk. 2.22 indicates that the pronoun must point to Jesus' parents:

Καὶ ὅτε ἐπλήσθησαν αἱ ἡμέραι τοῦ καθαρισμοῦ αὐτῶν κατὰ τὸν νόμον Μωϋσέως, ἀνήγαγον αὐτὸν εἰς Ἱεροσόλυμα
When the days of *their* purification had been fulfilled according to Moses's law, *they* brought him up to Jerusalem.

The pronoun '*they*' clearly points to Joseph and Mary. It is most probable thus that the pronoun grammatically refers to 'Joseph and Mary'.

This interpretation allows for the possibility of the sacrifice in v. 24 as a sin offering for Mary and Joseph. What kind of sin, then, did Joseph commit? One possible explanation is that Joseph touched the blood of Mary as there was no midwife for Jesus' birth. Joseph must then be sanctified to present the child.[94] Another alternative is that both Joseph and Mary attended the sacrifice to purify their sins in general. In any case, Joseph is included as a participant in a sin offering. That may be why Luke or the composer adopted the phrase in Lev. 5.11, which is virtually identical to the phrase δύο τρυγόνας ἢ δύο νεοσσοὺς περιστερῶν as appears in Lev. 5.7, because he intended to describe a sin offering of uncleanness. Luke's wording may have originated from this passage, where ζεῦγος becomes a functional synonym for δύο.

(4) *Is this phrase a quotation?*

It is not easy to confirm that the sentence is a quotation. There are good reasons, however, to conclude that Luke intends a quotation. First, the introductory formula (κατὰ τὸ εἰρημένον ἐν τῷ νόμῳ κυρίου) signals Luke's intention to cite an OT passage (Lev. 12.8 or 5.11). The use of the verb

---

92. Fitzmyer, *Luke I–IX*, p. 424.
93. Marshall, *Luke*, p. 116. Fitzmyer also notes that the newborn child was not required to be purified (*Luke I–IX*, p. 424).
94. Bock, *Luke 1:1–9:50*, p. 236. According to the Mishnah, he notes, one who made contact with blood in the delivery had to give an 'offering of uncleanness'.

λέγω, here a perfect passive participle used as a noun, is not in itself proof that a quotation is to follow (see ἐρρέθη in Mt. 5.21, 27, etc.), but combined with the prepositional phrase ἐν τῷ νόμῳ κυρίου an intention to quote seems clear. Second, the context denotes the purification of a woman who has given birth corresponding, perhaps, to the content of Lev. 12.8. It may also refer to the purification of sins described in Lev. 5.11. Although the context of Lev. 12.8 is different from that of 5.11, both deal with sin offerings. The confusion in the Lukan text, if it existed, may have stemmed from these two verses. Luke or the composer probably relied on memory, while intending to quote Lev. 12.8. An even more probable answer is, however, that Luke or the composer intended to denote a sin offering because Joseph was included for that sacrifice. This indicates that Luke or the composer intended to quote Lev. 5.11. The adoption of ζεῦγος in Lk. 2.24 is explained by pointing to Lev. 5.7, dealing with sin offerings of 'two turtle doves and two young pigeons' and containing the same Hebrew phrase as that in 5.11, translated as δύο τρυγόνας. For the translator of the section of sin offerings in Leviticus, ζεῦγος is identical to δύο.[95] The Lukan text thus seems to have relied on the section Lev. 5.7–11 concerned with sin offerings. This interpretation provides a slight edge to the view that the phrase ζεῦγος τρυγόνων ἢ δύο νεοσσοὺς περιστερῶν is a 'quotation' with an introductory formula, referring to Lev. 5.11 of the LXX rather than to Lev. 12.8.[96]

[The Composition Procedure of Lk. 2.22-24]

Some scholars argue that apparent confusion about the purification of a mother who gives birth in Lk. 2.22-24 is derived from Luke's misunderstanding about Jewish customs or Jewish tradition.[97] However, the examination above has demonstrated that most of this section did not stem from Luke's hand but from the hand of others: a) the introductory formulas in v. 23 and 24 do not support the claim of Luke's direct composition; b) the manner of quotation, i.e., the use of the conjunction

---

95. Concerning the meaning of ζεῦγος, Reiling and Swellengrebel suggest that it means simply 'two' equivalent to δύο (*A Translator's Handbook on the Gospel of Luke*, p. 128). They seem to assume that the quotation is from Lev. 12.8. In contrast, BAGD, p. 337, suggest that ζεῦγος is from Lev. 5.11 and means 'pair'. However, ζεῦγος means 'a pair' in Leviticus (the two of a yoke) although it is a rendering of Hebrew 'two'.

96. Even in the case that Luke translated the Hebrew Text for this phrase, his adoption of two different Greek words for one and the same Hebrew word stemmed from Lev. 5.7–11 of the LXX.

97. R. Bultmann, *Die Geschichte der Synoptischen Tradition* (Göttingen: Vandenhoeck & Ruprecht, 1957; 9th edn, 1979), p. 326. Fitzmyer notes that 'Luke, not being a Palestine Jewish Christian, is not accurately informed about this custom of the purification of a woman after childbirth' (*Luke I–IX*, p. 424). See also Brown, who discusses this problem in detail (*The Birth of the Messiah*, pp. 447–50).

followed by a possible indirect discourse in v. 23 and the presence of mere phrase after the introductory formula in v. 24, indicates a non-Lukanism; c) as will be shown, the use of the verb πίμπλημι with time indicators in 2.22 is 'a non-Lukanism' as well as 'a non-Septuagintalism'.[98] If there is confusion about Jewish tradition, it mainly originated from Luke's source and not from his own hand, though it is impossible to rule out the possibility that Luke made his Greek source appear confused.[99] The seeming misunderstanding that results from Luke's sources may indicate non-Jewish tradition. The Hellenized form Ἱεροσόλυμα in 2.22 may also indicate a non-Jewish original.[100] This position refutes the argument that the Lukan source was embellished with Jewish tradition, which may ultimately support a Hebrew original theory for these verses. Luke depended on his source for most of these verses and the source does not rely on the Hebrew OT but the LXX for quotations.[101]

III. *The Quotation in Lk. 1.15*

ἔσται γὰρ μέγας ἐνώπιον [τοῦ] κυρίου, καὶ <u>οἶνον καὶ σίκερα οὐ μὴ πίῃ</u>, καὶ πνεύματος ἁγίου πλησθήσεται ἔτι ἐκ κοιλίας μητρὸς αὐτοῦ
for he will be great in the sight of the Lord and *he must never*[102] *drink wine and strong drink*; he will be filled with the Holy Spirit even from the womb of his mother.

---

98. For the argument on this last element, see the section 'Phraseology'.

99. If so, why did Luke do so? No clear answer can be given to this question. As a result, this possibility is less probable.

100. Ἱεροσόλυμα is used mostly by non-Jewish authors, while Ἱερουσαλήμ, a form close to Hebrew, is used by Jews. The former is sometimes used by Jews, but only for Greek readers (Marshall, *Luke*, p. 116). More important is that the latter appears in the following part (Lk. 2.25-45) five times without exception. This feature makes it less probable that Ἱεροσόλυμα is from Luke's hand, or the hand of a Jewish writer. However, it is still possible that Luke is the source of the noun Ἱεροσόλυμα, since it occurs twenty-five times in Acts, though it appears only four times in the Gospel of Luke.

101. Some possible Lukanisms in this paragraph may indicate Luke's participation: τὸν νόμον Μωϋσέως (see above) and ἀνάγω (3x in Luke; 17x in Acts; once in Matthew and in Mark respectively; once in the Pauline letters; once in Hebrews). As a result, it is probable that the confusion stemmed from Luke's hand. However, some inaccuracies did not stem from a confusion about the Jewish law, but from a different intention of the writer; he intended to describe the purification of Mary and Joseph.

102. Double negatives with the aorist subjunctive mean either emphatic denial or prohibition. A.T. Robertson believes that this construction in Lk. 1.15 has the implication of prohibition (A.T. Robertson, *A Grammar of the Greek NT in the Light of Historical Research* [Nashville: Broadman, 4th ed., 1934]), p. 933. Bock calls it 'emphatic command' (*Luke 1:1–9:50*, p. 85, nt. 43). In contrast, Turner interprets this construction as indicating emphatic denial in Lk. 1.15 (N. Turner, *A Grammar of NT Greek* (III, *Syntax*; Edinburgh: T. & T. Clark, 1963], p. 96). Most English versions translate the construction as indicating simple future negation. Only NRSV interprets the construction as denoting emphatic future

3. *A Close Examination of the Greek of the Infancy Narrative* 93

(A) *Is This a Quotation?*

It is recognized that an introductory formula does not precede the underlined clause, which includes a stereotyped expression in the OT (οἶνον καὶ σίκερα), and the subject matter does not fit any verse in the OT exactly.[103] Despite these elements, some scholars and Greek texts suggest that the clause in Lk. 1.15 is a quotation.

Westcott and Hort include the clause in their list of quotations, but their account needs not concern us given their tendency to count many allusions as quotations.[104] A more serious consideration is that NA[27] and UBS[4] regard it as a quotation and suggest Num. 6.3 and Lev. 10.9 as quoted texts by italicizing both the text and the references. Their treatment must be counted important because, different from Westcott and Hort, they make only this clause a quotation in the infancy story, apart from the sentence and phrase in 2.23 and 24. Archer and Chirichigno, following NA[26] and UBS[3],[105] also count the clause a quotation. They classify it as category A which renders 'quotations consist of reasonably or completely accurate renderings from Hebrew of the Masoraic text (MT) into the Greek of the Septuagint (LXX) and from there (apart from word order, which sometimes deviates slightly) into the New Testament passage in which the Old Testament is cited' (*Old Testament Quotations*, Introduction, p. xxv).[106] These factors make it imperative to critically scrutinize the clause to confirm or deny the decision of NA[27].

(B) *The Content of the possible Quotation*
(1) *The word* σίκερα

(i)   σίκερα *in the LXX*
    σίκερα is a Semitic loanword from Hebrew שכר and Aramaic שכרא,

---

prohibition. The above translation follows NRSV for the phrase 'must not'. The double negatives have the double implication: denial and prohibition. For the detailed discussion of double negatives with the subjunctive, see below.

103. Because of the absence of the formula, scholars suggest more than one verse as possible quoted texts (Num. 6.3; Lev. 10.4; Judg. 13.4, 7, 14). They also disagree on the subject matter: whether it refers to a Nazirite vow or to simple consecration before God. For detailed discussion, see below.

104. For their definition of quotations, see above.

105. NA[26] and UBS[3] have the same text as NA[27] and UBS[4], though they diverge in apparatus.

106. Considering that Archer and Chirichigno divide category A into three subcategories (A, A-, Ad), it is remarkable for Lk. 1.15 to be included in subcategory A. They add, of course, that the absence of the introductory formula indicates that the author did not intend to quote from the OT. This observation means that it could be also reminiscence or allusion. In other words, the phrase, according to Archer and Chirichigno, could belong to the category of accurate quotations or allusions. This points to the necessity to examine the phrase in order to decide whether it is a quotation or allusion.

ultimately traced to Akkadian *sikaru* (BAGD, p. 750).[107] It occurs only once in the present verse in the whole NT. It appears outside of the LXX neither in classical literature nor in Hellenistic literature except in Galenus's work where the noun is found once (Liddell and Scott, p. 1598). σίκερα does not even occur in extant papyri.[108] In contrast, the LXX translators used this term to transliterate the Hebrew word שכר fifteen times[109] (Lev. 10.9; Num. 6.3 [2x]; 28.7; Deut. 14.26; 29.5; Judg. [A][110] 13.4,7,14; Isa. 5.11, 22; 24.9; 28.7 [2x]; 29.9). The noun σίκερα appears with οἶνον in these verses and it is used in connection with a prohibition for consecration in five verses (Lev. 10.9; Num. 6.3; Judg. [A] 13.4,7,14). It is hard to decide whether the author of the Lukan infancy narrative adopted this word from the LXX while composing directly in Greek or translating Hebrew words into Greek. One thing is clear: even if he translated Hebrew into Greek, his source for this term is the LXX: since this word is not attested in classical literature and Hellenistic literature as well as in papyri, it is most likely that Luke adopted this word from the LXX.

Noteworthy is that σίκερα occurs once outside of the LXX in Galenus, a Hellenistic author, from the second century AD:

οὐκοῦν οὐδὲ τοῦ ψυχροῦ ὕδατος ἢ οἴνου ἢ ζύθου ἢ ἑτέρας σικέρας πόσις ἀβλαβής ἐστι.
Therefore drinking of cold water, wine, beer, or other alcoholic drink is never free from harm (19.693).[111]

It does not seem that Galenus adopted the noun from the LXX because he had no connection with Christianity.[112] σίκερα was probably used in non-Biblical Greek and the noun in Lk. 1.15 may have thus derived from non-Septuagint Greek. However, the noun σίκερα in Lk. 1.15 is most probably from the LXX; σίκερα is a *declinable feminine* noun in Galenus, while it

---

107. See also E. Klostermann, *Das Lukasevangelium*. Handbuch zum Neuen Testament 5 (Tübingen: Mohr, 1929; repr. 1975), p. 8.
108. This observation is resulted from the search of TLG.
109. The noun σίκερα occurs twice in non-canonical Judges of A text (13.4,7).
110. It is noteworthy that according to Swete the Evangelists depended on 'a recension of the LXX which came nearer to the text of cod. A than to that of our oldest uncial B' (*The Old Testament in Greek*, p. 395). Remarkably, Rahlf's LXX text places A text of Judges with B text together and A text is placed at the upper portion while B text at the lower portion. This study will take into account both A text and B text of Judges, if there is a difference between A and B text.
111. For the Greek text, see *Claudii Galeni Opera Omnia*, Tomus XIX (ed. C.G. Kühn; Hildesheim: Georg Olms, 1968).
112. For the date and brief information about Galenus, see M. Grant, *Greek and Latin Authors: 800 B.C.–A.D. 1000* (New York: The H.W. Wilson Company, 1980), pp. 171–74.

represents an *indeclinable neuter* noun in the LXX and *(in)declinable neuter* noun in Luke.[113] The Lukan text followed the LXX in using the (in)declinable *neuter* noun for the accusative form.[114] It is also noteworthy that the noun οἶνος occurs with σίκερα in Luke as in the LXX verses which deal with the prohibition for consecration. In other words, the noun is a Septuagintalism. This usage enhances the possibility that the Lukan text depended here on the LXX.[115]

(ii) μέθυσμα- *another translation of the Hebrew word* שכר *in the LXX*
The Hebrew word שכר was also translated as μέθυσμα eight times in the LXX and this noun always occurs with οἶνον[116] (Judg[B] 13.4,7,14; 1 Sam. 1.11,15; Hos. 4.11; Mic. 2.11; Jer. 13.13).[117] This usage may indicate that the Lukan text did not depend upon the LXX for the noun σίκερα, if it relied on one of these verses. The Lukan text, however, does not seem to depend on one of them. The last three examples can be excluded from consideration, because their context is totally different from Luke's. The first three instances in Judges need not detain us, since Codex Alexandrinus includes the

---

113. The gender of the noun σίκερα is neuter in the LXX because the neuter article is used for this noun in Isa. 5.11,22; 24.9 (BAGD 750). This means that the nominative is also σίκερα; in Greek, the nominative is the same as the accusative in neuter. BDF 58, remark that σίκερα represents an indeclinable word in the Greek OT. In most of the instances of the LXX, the accusative form is found (Lev. 10.9; Num. 28.7; Deut. 29.5; Judg. (A) 13.4,7,14; Isa. 5.11). The genitive form is used still in many instances (Num. 6.3; Isa. 5.22; 28.7; 29.9), while the dative occurs once in Deut. 14.26 and the nominative in Isa. 24.9. The indelinable form σίκερα is used in all these instances. The noun is an indeclinable neuter noun in the LXX. It is not easy to decide whether the noun is declinable or indeclinable in Luke, since only the accusative form occurs once in Lk. 1.15. The gender, however, is neuter in Luke. In contrast, the use in Galenus shows that the noun is a declinable feminine noun (for the use in Eusebius, see the next note).

114. Eusebius uses this noun once as a declinable noun; σίκερος is used as a genitive (BAGD, p. 750). The use of this form for the neuter genitive is a puzzle, since the neuter genitive should be most likely σικέρατος. Eusebius probably assumed that the gender of the noun is masculine and the nominative of the noun is σίκερ. Cf. Plummer who notes that Eusebius 'has gen. σίκερα and σικέρατος is also quoted; but σίκερα is usually undeclined' (*Luke*, p. 14).

115. Philo employs the noun σίκερα twice (*De ebrietate*, 127; 138), quoting from the LXX Lev. 10.9 where the noun οἶνος is also used: οἶνον καὶ σίκερα οὐ πίεσθε σὺ καὶ οἱ υἱοί σου μετὰ σου. The only difference between Philo's quotation and Lev. 10.9 is the use of the pronoun; while the genitive pronoun σου appears in Leviticus, the accusative pronoun σε in Philo.

116. The combination of these two words is not found in the pseudepigrapha at all. In contrast, οἶνον καὶ σίκερα occurs once in the pseudepigrapha in the *Testament of Ruben* 1.10 where abstinence is a token of repentance.

117. In Judg. (B) 13.14, the noun σίκερα appears with the noun μέθυσμα: οἶνον καὶ σίκερα μέθυσμα μὴ πιέτω.

noun σίκερα instead of μέθυσμα in these verses. This observation does not mean that these examples are excluded from possible quoted or alluded texts, but simply indicates that they can be excluded from our present consideration concerning the adoption of the noun μέθυσμα: even if the Lukan text relied on these three verses, it may have depended on the Alexandrian text, on which the Evangelists more probably depended.[118] The two uses in 1 Samuel require attention in two respects:

a. the context is similar to Luke: 1 Sam. 1.11–15 describes the future birth of Samuel, while Lk. 1.15 concerns the future birth of John;
b. both passages point to restrictions on the child's behaviour and upbringing, expressed by means of Greek locutions indicating future prohibition: οὐ μὴ πίῃ in Lk. 1.15 and οὐ πίεται in 1 Sam. 1.11. The noun οἶνον also appears in both verses:

Lk. 1.15: καὶ οἶνον καὶ σίκερα οὐ μὴ πίῃ
he shall (or must) never drink wine or strong wine.

1 Sam. 1.11: καὶ οἶνον καὶ μέθυσμα οὐ πίεται
he shall not drink wine or strong wine
[cf. 1 Sam. 1.15: οἶνον καὶ μέθυσμα οὐ πέπωκα]

These considerations indicate that the author perhaps relied on 1 Sam. 1.11. In this case, the difference between two verses – like the different terms μέθυσμα in 1 Samuel and σίκερα in Luke and different Greek locutions for future prohibition in the two verses[119] – may denote the possibility that the Lukan text did not follow the Greek OT but transliterated the Hebrew text of 1 Sam. 1.11. However, this speculation is doubtful. First, in 1 Sam. 1.11 the Hebrew OT differs from the Greek OT. The Hebrew text omits words corresponding to the Greek sentence καὶ οἶνον καὶ μέθυσμα οὐ πίεται, even though they may have been originally included. The absence of corresponding Hebrew words makes it difficult to confirm that the composer consulted the Hebrew OT for this phrase. Second, whereas the passage in 1 Samuel concerns a Nazirite vow, the passage in Luke does not. Luke's passage makes no mention of not cutting the child's hair and abstinence from defilement by a dead body.[120] The Lukan text does not seem to describe the birth of a Nazirite like Samuel or

---

118. For the relationship between A and B text of Judges, see above. The three verses in Judges will be treated below.
119. In A text, οὐ μὴ πιήτε appears. The construction for future prohibition will be treated below in detail.
120. Marshall, *Luke*, p. 57. See also Klostermann, *Das Lukasevangelium*, p. 9.

Samson.[121] The Lukan purpose was simply to point out John the Baptist's special task of preparing the way for Jesus; and he thus emphasizes John's purification. The Lukan text therefore does not appear to have exclusively depended on 1 Sam. 1.11 of either the LXX or the Hebrew OT.

(2) *The subjunctive with* οὐ μή

A more serious problem relates to the mood of the verb and the double negatives οὐ μή. All the examples from the LXX suggested above, which are related with future abstinence from 'wine and strong drink' for consecration, include future indicative with οὐ (Lev. 10.9; Num. 6.3; 1 Sam. 1.11), aorist imperative with μή (Judg. 13.14), or aorist subjunctive with μή (Judg. 13.4,7).[122] In contrast, the Lukan text uses the aorist subjunctive with οὐ μή.

(i) *Constructions for future emphatic prohibitions or denials in the NT*

In classical Greek, οὐ μή, with the future indicative and present or aorist subjunctive indicates emphatic future predictions[123] and prohibitions.[124] In the NT, οὐ μή occurs with the subjunctive more frequently and is much less emphatic than in classical Greek. In fact, οὐ μή, is used with the subjunctive in most cases (Mt. 18x; Mk 11x; Lk. 16x; Jn 16x; Acts 3x; Pauline letters 5x; non-Pauline letters 7x; Rev. 16x).[125] In contrast, examples of the future indicative are very rare: a certain example occurs only once in Mt. 16.22.[126] This

---

121. Plummer, however, asserts that John the Baptist was a Nazirite 'not only for a time, as was usual, but for all his life as Samson and Samuel.' 'This is not disapproved,' he continues, 'by the omission of the command not to cut his hair' (*Luke*, p. 14). See also Fitzmyer, *Luke I–IX*, p. 326 and Leaney, *Luke*, p. 41. However, other scholars are cautious to admit this argument. See Nolland who notes that John's abstinence 'expresses his consecration to God without necessarily implying a specific Nazirite vow' (*Luke 1–9.20*, p. 30). See also Brown, *The Birth of the Messiah*, p. 274 and Marshall and Klostermann noted above in nt. 1 20. Cf. Evans who is open to both possibilities (*Luke*, p. 149). See also Bock, *Luke 1.1–9.20*, p. 85. It is undeniable that the abstinence in Lk. 1.15 is not identical to that in the OT verses, which makes it difficult to confirm John's abstinence as a Nazirite vow.

122. In 1 Sam. 1.15, pluperfect indicative is used with οὐ to describe past deed.

123. Smyth, *Greek Grammar*, p. 2755.

124. For strong prohibitions, the aorist subjunctive is rarely used with the double negatives, while the future indicative is frequently used in classical Greek (Smyth, *Greek Grammar*, p. 2756).

125. Interestingly, the occurrence of the subjunctive with the double negatives is restricted mostly to quotations from the LXX, sayings of Jesus, or Revelation (Turner, *A Greek Grammar*, p. 96). See also BDF 356. There is a 'suspicion of "translation Greek"' in these parts (Moulton, *A Greek Grammar of New Testament Greek*. II, *Accidence and Word-Formation*, p. 23), but this construction belongs to normal Greek.

126. In some verses, 'the future forms are very similar to the aorist subjunctive and the text varies between the two' [BDF 365 (2)]. For example, such textual variations are found in Lk. 21.33. For details, see below nt. 129.

construction belongs to vulgar Koine as it appears in private documents in the Ptolemaic period [BDF 365 (2)].[127]

(ii) *Is this a non-Lukanism?*
How does Luke express emphatic future negation in Lk. 3–24 and Acts? The Gospel of Luke contains 16 examples of this idea outside of the infancy narrative (Lk. 6.37(2x); 8.17; 9.27; 10.19; 12.59; 13.35; 18.7,17; 21.18, 32-33; 22.16,18, 67, 68). Of 16, there is only one possible example of the future indicative in Lk. 21.33, which BDF [365 (1)] interpret as an attraction of the preceding verb παρελεύσονται:[128]

Lk. 21.33 ὁ οὐρανὸς καὶ ἡ γῆ παρελεύσονται, οἱ δὲ λόγοι μου <u>οὐ μὴ παρελεύσονται</u>.
Heaven and earth will pass away, but my words will never pass away.

The underlined part in Lk. 21.33, however, probably derives from Mk 13.31 where exactly the same expression appears according to NA[27].[129] In any case, the use of the future indicative with οὐ μή in Lk. 21.33 does not constitute proof that Luke uses the future indicative with οὐ μή for the future negation in the Gospel of Luke.

In all the rest of the instances of Luke, the aorist subjunctive appears; the use of the subjunctive with double negatives is possibly Lukan. The problem is, however, that most of them have parallels in Mark where this construction occurs. It is also true that in Acts, where three instances of the subjunctive appear (13.41; 28.26 [2x]),[130] all the three instances are from quotation of the OT.[131] Nevertheless, it is noteworthy that Luke inserted οὐ μή in two places whose parallels in Mark do not have it (Lk. 8.17 = Mk 4.22; Lk. 18.30 = Mk 10.30).[132] The use of double negatives thus, is

---

127. Future indicative, according to Turner, is not found in the Ptolemic papyri (*A Greek Grammar*, p. 96).
128. Many variants include the subjunctive (ACΘΨ*f*(1.13*m*)). NA[27] seems to have adopted the 'harder reading'.
129. BDF note that this use is perhaps merely 'a combination from the par(allels)' in Mt. 24.35 (οἱ δὲ λόγοι μου <u>οὐ μὴ παρέλθωσιν</u>) and Mk 13.31 (οἱ δὲ λόγοι μου <u>οὐ μὴ παρελεύσονται</u>). They do not suggest that the use of the future indicative with οὐ μή in Lk. 21.33 derives from Mk 13.31, since they do not follow the reading of NA[27] where the double negatives occur in Mk 13.31. They depend on the reading of other variants (B, D) which include only the negative οὐ with the future indicative (οἱ δὲ λόγοι μου <u>οὐ παρελεύσονται</u>).
130. Acts includes none of the indicative with the double negatives.
131. Concerning the double negatives οὐ μή, Jeremias argues that 'diese schwurartige Verneinung benutzt Lukas nur zurückhaltend.' He believes the double negatives stemmed from the tradition not from Luke's hand (*Die Sprache*, p. 36).
132. Luke omitted the double negatives in Lk. 21.6 whose parallel in Mk 13.2 includes two double negatives. The parallel in Mt. 24.2 has only one of the two double negatives in Mark.

probably Lukan. It is at least undeniable that Luke himself could use double negatives; this construction is not non-Lukan.

(iii) *The construction for emphatic future prohibition or denial in the LXX*
In classical Greek, the future indicative and the aorist subjunctive are used for future negation without any significant difference in frequency.[133] In contrast, οὐ μή with the subjunctive is usually used to express future negation with emphasis in the LXX; together with the imperative, the double negatives appear 559 times mostly with the subjunctive. The Hebrew original has the imperfect verb with the negative particle לא. This feature indicates that if literally translated from the Hebrew, οὐ μή could have been coupled with the future indicative (Jer. 37.14; 39.40; 40.8; 46.17; Isa. 7.12; 16.10 [2x]; 43.25; 65.22 [2x] etc.) or present indicative (Jer. 24.6; 49.10, etc.) as in some examples in the LXX, rather than with the aorist subjunctive.[134] The construction οὐ μή with the subjunctive is Septuagintalistic rather than Masoretic in the sense that it does not reflect the Hebrew construction and is frequently used in the LXX. If the composer of the double negative clause imitated LXX style, he most probably utilized the subjunctive as in Lk. 1.15.

In Lk. 1.15, the context requires a future negation with emphasis and Luke uses the aorist subjunctive with οὐ μή for that purpose in Luke-Acts. This observation indicates that Luke probably translated the Hebrew text according to his own style. Possible also is that a composer other than Luke may have adopted the subjunctive following current or LXX usage while translating the Hebrew OT as all the NT and the LXX authors mostly used the subjunctive. This possibility increases if the phrase is a quotation of the verses suggested above, whose Greek texts include the imperative with μή, the future indicative with οὐ, or the subjunctive with μή instead of the aorist subjunctive with οὐ μή as in Lk. 1.15. Thus, it is necessary to choose whether this phrase is quotation or allusion and upon which verses it depends.

This may indicate that the use of double negatives is not Lukan, but the above two instances lend support to the argument that it is Lukan. It is at least certain that one cannot assert that the use of double negatives is a non-Lukanism.

133. Smyth, *Greek Grammar*, p. 2755.

134. The use of the present indicative is not normal in Greek, though it possibly echoes the Hebrew imperfective. The future indicative, which could also reflect the Hebrew verb tense, is frequently used in non-Septuagintal Greek. The use of the present subjunctive with οὐ μή is also classical to express future negative prediction (Smyth, *Greek Grammar*, p. 2755).

(3) *Is this a quotation?*

Concerning the question of whether the phrase is a quotation or not, it is obvious that the phrase lacks an introductory formula. However, the wording is identical in some verses in which the subject matter seems to be the same as in Luke, suggesting that it may point to some OT verses. If so, which verse(s) does it refer to among those suggested? Nolland suggests Judg. 13.7 Alexandrian text (A) as being echoed in the phrase (*Luke 1–9.20*, p. 30):

ἰδοὺ σὺ ἐν γαστρὶ ἕξεις καὶ τέξῃ υἱὸν καὶ νῦν <u>μὴ πίῃς οἶνον καὶ σίκερα</u> καὶ μὴ φάγῃς πᾶσαν ἀκαθαρσίαν.
Behold, you shall conceive in your womb and bear a son and now *do not drink wine and strong drink* and do not eat anything unclean.

His decision depends upon the similarity of the wording between the phrase in Lk. 1.15 and that in Judg. 13.7(A); apart from the person of the verb, the only difference is the presence of οὐ in Lk. 1.15 which Judg. (A) 13.7 lacks. The subject matter, however, refutes his argument, because Judg. 13.7 is concerned with the abstinence of Samson's mother not Samson himself.

Fitzmyer interprets Judg. 13.4(A) as being quoted in Lk. 1.15, since both verses, in his view, deal with the topic related with a Nazirite:[135]

<u>μὴ πίῃς οἶνον καὶ σίκερα</u> καὶ μὴ φάγῃς πᾶν ἀκάθαρτον.
Do not drink wine and strong drink, and do not eat anything unclean.

The wording is identical to that of Judg. 13.7 (A). Similarly, O'Fearghail notes that Judg. 13.4 (A) and 13.14 (οἶνον καὶ σίκερα μὴ πιέτω – the abstinence of Samson's mother) have a closer linguistic agreement with Lk. 1.15 ('The Imitation of the Septuagint', p. 64). Their context, however, is different from Luke's. While Judg. 13.4 and 14 prohibit the mother from drinking wine now or at least from now on, Lk. 1.15 describes what the baby will not do in the future. If John's abstinence is not related to a Nazirite vow, it becomes unnecessary to suppose that the phrase in Luke refers to Judg. 13.4 or 14. 1 Sam. 1.11 describes the prohibition for the baby in the future, but as noted above, the wording is different from Luke. The subject matter of 1 Samuel is, in fact, also different from that of Luke.[136]

Archer and Chirichigno argue that the Lukan text quotes from Num. 6.3, which deals with a Nazirite vow. Though conceding that the wording of Num. 6.3 is different from that of Lk. 1.15, they assert that the sense is

---

135. Fitzmyer suggests that Num. 6.3 is also alluded to in Lk. 1.15 (*Luke I–IX*, pp. 325-26). For the discussion of the verse in Numbers, see below.
136. For details, see above.

3. *A Close Examination of the Greek of the Infancy Narrative* 101

the same. The phrase may derive from Num. 6.3, which concerns Nazirites, and possesses the same two words (οἴνου, σίκερα) and a Greek construction for the future prohibition:

ἀπὸ οἴνου καὶ σίκερα ἁγνισθήσεται ἀπὸ οἴνου καὶ ὄξος ἐξ οἴνου καὶ ὄξος ἐξ οἴνου καὶ ὄξος ἐκ σίκερα οὐ πίεται.
he shall separate himself from *wine and strong drink*; *he shall drink no* vinegar (made) from *wine* or vinegar (made) from *strong drink*.

As noted above, however, the Lukan text is not concerned about the Nazirite vow and the subject matter between Num. 6.3 and Lk. 1.15 could be different.

Similar is Lev. 10.9, where God announces the following prohibition for priests and their sons:[137]

οἶνον καὶ σίκερα οὐ πίεσθε σὺ καὶ οἱ υἱοί σου, ...
'*Drink no wine or strong drink*, neither you nor your sons ...' (NRSV)

It is possible that Luke just wanted to highlight the purification of John the Baptist as a son of a priest, but more likely simply to describe John's purification as pointing to his special task.

The above observations make it difficult to decide upon which verses the Lukan text depended. The author of the Lukan infancy narrative may not have depended on any single verse for the clause, but upon several: 1 Sam. 1.11; Lev. 10.9; Num. 6.3; Judg. (A) 13.4,7,14. In fact, to choose one may be a dubious undertaking. Comparison of the subject matter and wording of the sentence in Luke with those in the LXX would point the clause οἶνον καὶ σίκερα οὐ μὴ πίῃ in Lk. 1.5 toward an 'allusion' rather than a 'quotation'.

In summary, a) it is not preceded by an introductory formula; b) the clause does not refer to any one or two verses concerned with the same topic. All of them are different from each other in details, although they share one thing in common: they concern consecration before God. Although the LXX includes almost identical sentences in Judg. (A) 13.4, 14, the phrase οἶνον καὶ σίκερα is a stereotyped expression and the subjunctive mood represents a typical way of expressing future prohibition both in the LXX and in the NT. These considerations make it difficult to designate the sentence in Lk. 1.15 as a quotation.

---

137. 'Die Worte vom Verzicht auf Wein,' Bovon notes, 'stehen Lev 10,9 näher als Num 6,3, erinnern also eher an die Regel für Priester (und ihre Kinder!) zur Vorbereitung ihres Dienstes als an das Leben eines Nasiräers' (*Das Evangelium nach Lukas [1,1–9,50]*, p. 55).

(4) *Some possible explanations about the sentence in Lk. 1.15*

The Lukan clause was probably chosen to indicate simply the consecration of John without implying a Nazirite vow. The author does not intend to refer directly to one or two verses. In other words, he did not try to quote, but only allude to some verses suggested above (1 Sam. 1.11; Lev. 10.9; Num. 6.3; Judg. [A] 13.4,7,14). The author probably depended upon his memory of the LXX of these verses. It is fairly probable that he chose a more standard combination of two nouns in these verses, σίκερα and οἶνον, since this construction of the words occurs in five of the six verses, whereas οἶνον καὶ μέθυσμα appears only once according to text A (1 Sam. 1.11), or at best three times according to text B (Judg. 13.4,7). He may have employed the subjunctive mood in affinity with the LXX or current common usage. The author was not compelled to employ the exact wording of the verses alluded in Lk. 1.15 where the phrase σίκερα and οἶνον occurs, even if he relied on these verses, since their context is not identical to Luke's.

The composer here reveals his method of alluding to the OT. He depended on the LXX for word pair οἶνον καὶ σίκερα, but did not duplicate the exact wording of the LXX for the remaining of the sentence. He did not intend to quote, but merely to allude to some verses to highlight John's consecration. This is why the composer altered the second half of the sentence by employing the usual way to express future prohibition in the LXX. Otherwise, as a result of depending on his memory, he used the most frequent such phrase in the verses alluded to in Lk. 1.15, οἶνον καὶ σίκερα. Then he composed the second part by using the most frequent construction in the LXX for future prohibition. If Luke composed it, he adopted the most common expression in the LXX.

In sum, one cannot deny the possibility that Luke, or the composer of his source, translated Hebrew sources here. But in itself, this claim presumes too much. The dependence of the Lukan text on the LXX provides a more plausible explanation. The use of the (in)declinable neuter noun σίκερα, the word pair σίκερα and οἶνον, and the future prohibition with the subjunctive indicates that the composer was actively engaged in composition while relying on the LXX.

In conclusion, the author of the Lukan infancy narrative appears to be dependent on the LXX for quotations (and the allusion in 1.15).[138] The manner of quoting the OT in the infancy narrative indicates clearly that Luke depended on a Greek source for the quotations in vv. 2.22-24. That source itself seems to have used the LXX, not the Hebrew OT, for quotations from the OT. The composer of this source, writing in Greek,

---

138. The following statement does not include the consideration of the verse 1.15.

while adhering strictly to content, exercised freedom in altering the wording of LXX text where he thought it necessary.[139]

B. *Allusions*

It is difficult, as pointed out in the preceding section, to distinguish between quotations and allusions. However, allusions could simply refer to sentences and phrases which are reminiscent of the OT, and which cannot be counted as quotations according to our definition above.[140] The Lukan infancy story includes many such allusions, especially in the Magnificat and the Benedictus, which, though not including even one instance of quotation, are both full of reminiscence.[141] It is impossible and unnecessary to deal with all the allusions. This section will treat, therefore, only some relatively clear instances, most of which scholars have marshalled as evidence for the translation theory.[142]

I. *The Allusion in Lk. 1.17*

καὶ αὐτὸς προελεύσεται ἐνώπιον αὐτοῦ ἐν πνεύματι καὶ δυνάμει Ἠλίου, ἐπιστρέψαι καρδίας πατέρων ἐπὶ τέκνα καὶ ἀπειθεῖς ἐν φρονήσει δικαίων, ἑτοιμάσαι κυρίῳ λαὸν κατεσκευασμένον.

---

139. It seems a characteristic of Luke to alter the wording of the LXX when required by the context. As New points out, among the synoptic Evangelists, Luke most frequently corrects the others in the direction of the LXX. In contrast, 'Luke on his own apparently alters the LXX (*Old Testament Quotations*, p. 119).' This may imply that Luke composed the quoted text in Lk. 2.23-24. However, the quotations are not from Luke's hand, as the manner of quotations demonstrates (for details, see above). The composer other than Luke, thus, relied on the LXX for quotations in the infancy narrative.

140. Allusion is, S. Moyise argues, 'usually woven into the text rather than "quoted", and often rather less precise in terms of wording.' 'Naturally,' he continues, 'there is considerable debate as to how much verbal agreement is necessary to establish the presence of an allusion' (S. Moyise, 'Intertextuality and the Study of the Old Testament in the New Testament', in *The Old Testament in the New Testament: Essays in Honour of J.L. North* [ed. S. Moyise; JSNTSS, 189; Sheffield: Sheffield Academic Press, 2000], p. 18). He tries to define 'echo', which is different from allusion, as 'faint traces of texts that are probably quite unconscious but emerge from minds soaked in the scriptural heritage of Israel.' The distinction between allusion and echo presents another problem. For details, see his article, 'Intertextuality and the Study of the Old Testament', pp. 18–25.

141. Ringgren, 'Luke's Use of the Old Testament', p. 229.

142. Some other possible instances will be dealt with in the section 'Phraseology'.

and he himself will go before him in the spirit and power of Elijah, *to turn the hearts of fathers to (their) children* and the disobedient to the wisdom of the righteous, to make ready a people prepared for the Lord.

We shall first deal with the phrase ἐπιστρέψαι καρδίας πατέρων ἐπὶ τέκνα as a whole and then the construction ἐπιστρέψαι – ἐπί.

1. *Remarks on* ἐπιστρέψαι καρδίας πατέρων ἐπὶ τέκνα

(A) *The Problem*

(1) *To which verse does this sentence allude?*
This phrase seems to allude to the LXX Mal. 3.23 (the MT 4.6):

> v. 22 καὶ ἰδοὺ ἐγὼ ἀποστέλλω ὑμῖν Ἠλίαν τὸν Θεσβίτην πρὶν ἐλθεῖν ἡμέραν κυρίου τὴν μεγάλην καὶ ἐπιφανῆ 23 ὃς <u>ἀποκαταστήσει καρδίαν πατρὸς πρὸς υἱὸν</u> καὶ καρδίαν ἀνθρώπου πρὸς τὸν πλησίον...
>
> v. 22 and behold I myself will send you Elijah the Thesbite before the great and glorious day of the Lord comes 23 and *he will return (restore) the heart of the father to the son* and the heart of a man to the fellow man...

Malachi is concerned with the future role of Elijah and John the Baptist is cast in the role of Elijah in Luke. However, *Sir.* 48.10 also requires attention:

> ὁ καταγραφεὶς ἐν ἐλεγμοῖς εἰς καιροὺς κοπάσαι ὀργὴν πρὸ θυμοῦ <u>ἐπιστρέψαι</u>[143] <u>καρδίαν πατρὸς πρὸς υἱὸν</u> καὶ καταστῆσαι φυλὰς Ἰακωβ.
>
> (you) who it is written in refutation (ἐν ἐλεγμοῖς)[144] for the appointed times to calm the wrath of God before it breaks out in fury, *to turn the heart of the father to the son*, and to restore the tribes of Jacob. (RSV)

This verse refers to Elijah who is mentioned by name in *Sir.* 48.1,4:

a. its content is similar to Luke's verse as it describes what Elijah will do in the future;

---

143. The Greek infinitive ἐπιστρέψαι is corresponding to the Hifil infinitive להשיב in the Hebrew text. For the Hebrew text of Sirach, see P.C. Beentjes, *The Book of Ben Sira in Hebrew* (Leiden/New York/Koeln: E.J. Brill, 1997).

144. It is difficult to understand the meaning of this phrase. In some variants occurs ἕτοιμος, which means 'ready': 'who, it is written, are ready for...' For other readings, see *Septuaginta: Sapientia Iesu Filii Sirach* (ed. J. Ziegler Vetus Testamentum Graecum Auctoritate Societatis Litterarum Gottingsis Editum, vol. XII, 2; Göttingen: Vandenhoeck & Ruprecht, 1965), p. 351.

b. this verse contains the same verb as in Lk. 1.17: ἐπιστρέφω. The Lukan text therefore may allude to Sirach or Malachi, or perhaps to both.

(2) The core of the issue

In any case, the issue centres on the phrase καρδίας πατέρων ἐπὶ τέκνα '(the) hearts of fathers to (their) children' in Luke.

(i) In the Hebrew text of both Malachi and Sirach the Hebrew word for 'heart', לב, is singular and אבות for 'fathers' is plural, but the LXX translators altered the plural 'fathers' to the singular πατρός, 'father', while retaining the singular of the first noun καρδία: καρδίαν πατρός '(the) heart of (the) father'.

(ii) בנים 'sons' is plural, but the LXX presents the singular form υἱόν though the Lukan text uses the plural of a different noun τέκνον. This noun is preceded by the preposition ἐπί in Luke, different from the LXX where πρός appears. The Greek and Hebrew phrases need to be compared:

Greek phrases in Luke: καρδίας πατέρων '(the) hearts of fathers'
ἐπὶ τέκνα 'to (their) children'

Hebrew phrases in the OT: לב־אבות '(the) heart of fathers'
על־בנים 'to (their) sons (children)'

Greek phrase in the OT: καρδίαν πατρός '(the) heart of (the) father'
πρὸς υἱόν 'to (the) son'

In sum, the Lukan text, on the one hand, follows the MT in adopting the plural nouns 'fathers' (πατέρων) and 'children' (τέκνα) while deviating from it by using the plural 'hearts' (καρδίας) in place of the singular in Hebrew. The Lukan text, on the other hand, deviates from the LXX in three ways: three plural nouns (hearts, fathers, and children) for singular nouns; the use of the noun τέκνον instead of υἱός; preposition ἐπί for πρός.

(B) *Proposed Solutions*

(1) *Winter's view: the Lukan text depends on the Hebrew text of Malachi and Sirach*

The view accepted by the majority of the scholars is represented by Winter's argument that the two plurals in Luke, πατέρων and τέκνα, which echo the plurals in Hebrew, lend support to the hypothesis that the Lukan text depends on the Hebrew text of Malachi and Sirach rather than on the Greek text ('Some Observations on the Language', p. 114). The adoption of the plural καρδίας for the singular לב in Luke, according to him, indicates that the translator of Luke's Semitic source assimilated its number with the plural πατέρων, reflecting Hebrew plural אבות. In contrast, it is difficult to explain, he continues, why the Lukan text adopted these two plurals if it had relied on the LXX, either Malachi or Sirach, where singulars are used: καρδίαν πατρός. Fitzmyer, following Winter, assumes the plural 'fathers' and 'children' to reflect the influence of the MT rather than the LXX (*Luke I–IX*, p. 327).[145]

(2) *Turner's refutation*

Refuting Winter's argument that Luke's locution echoes the MT rather than the LXX, Turner points out that *Sirach* may reflect different text traditions, as it contains a common word and phrase for both Malachi and Luke: *Sirach* includes ἐπιστρέψαι found in Luke and πατρὸς πρὸς υἱόν in Malachi of the LXX ('The Relation of Luke I and II', p. 101). This phenomenon indicates, according to him, that Sirach's LXX developed in two different ways: Luke's LXX and our LXX. Luke's LXX, Turner continues, deviates from Sirach's by employing plurals and ἐπὶ τέκνα in Mal. 3.24, while our LXX deviates from *Sirach's* by changing the verb from ἐπιστρέψαι to ἀποκαταστήσει. He points out that the Lukan text deviates from the MT as well as the LXX because the Hebrew text has the singular for 'heart' for which the Lukan text has the plural. His refutation, however, is not effective because the plural noun for 'heart' in Luke could be explained as suggested by Winter, though it is still true that the Lukan text deviates from the Hebrew text in the use of the plural noun for 'heart'.

(C) *Another Proposal*

(1) καρδίαν πατρός '(a) heart of (a) father' in the LXX of Mal. 3.23

The LXX translated the Hebrew phrase לב־אבות 'heart of fathers' both in Mal. 3.23 and *Sir.* 48.10 as 'καρδίαν πατρός' '(a) heart of (a) father', making the number of the noun 'fathers' in Hebrew agree with that of the noun 'heart'. If the Hebrew לב־אבות is translated literally, it would be 'καρδίαν πατέρων', 'heart of fathers'. The Lukan phrase καρδίας πατέρων 'hearts of fathers' deviates both from the MT, as Turner points out, in altering the singular of καρδία to the plural and from the LXX in making both nouns plurals. It is noteworthy that the LXX translators do not always change the number of the modified noun καρδία, whose corresponding Hebrew noun is singular, to the plural to make it match

---

145. Recent scholars tend to accept this assessment as correct. Nolland argues for its dependence on the MT on the ground that the Lukan phrase deviates from the LXX in employing the plural (*Luke 1–9.20*, p. 31). Bock also declares in 1987 that this sentence in Luke's text reflects the MT because it has plurals for these two nouns (*Proclamation from Prophecy and Pattern*, p. 59, nt. 22). However, he adds without further explanation in 1994 that it is 'virtually a quotation of Mal. 3.24 LXX and *Sir.* 48.10' (*Luke 1.1–9.50*, p. 88).

3. A Close Examination of the Greek of the Infancy Narrative 107

the plural number of the modifying noun. They did so only occasionally (1 Kgs 8.47: ἐπιστρέψουσιν καρδίας αὐτῶν; 1 Sam. 6.6a τὰς καρδίας ὑμῶν; 10.26: καρδίας αὐτῶν; Ps. 32.15: τὰς καρδίας αὐτῶν, etc.), but they also kept the singular of this noun with the plural modifying noun or pronoun (1 Sam. 6.6b: τὴν καρδίαν αὐτῶν; *Jdt.* 8.27: τῆς καρδίας αὐτῶν; 13.19: καρδίας ἀνθρώπων; Ps. 9.38: τῆς καρδίας αὐτῶν [cf. *2 Macc.* 2.3: τῆς καρδίας αὐτῶν; *3 Macc.* 4.2: αὐτῶν τῆς καρδίας; both books were written directly in Greek]). The NT authors also ignore the apparent false concord of the number of the singular noun καρδία with the modifying plural noun: Mt. 15.8; Mk 3.5; 6.52; 7.6 (quotation from Isa. 29.13), 21; 8.17; Lk. 1.51, 66; 8.12 (parallels in Mt. 13.19 and Mk 4.15, but probably not from Mk or Mt.);[146] 9.47 (parallels in Mt. 18.2 and Mk 9.35, but not from Mk or Mt.);[147] 12.34 (in Mt. 6.21, singular pronoun and singular noun; from Matthew but different from each other);[148] 24.32, 38 (only in Luke); 2 Cor. 3.15; 6.11; Eph. 1.18; 4.18; 5.19; 6.5; Jas. 3.14; 1 Jn 3.19-20. Luke uses this seemingly false concord twice in the infancy narrative and five times in the remainder of the Gospel. Luke did not borrow this usage from Mark or the common source of Matthew and Luke. Rather, he may have taken it over from his peculiar source (cf. the instances in Lk. 24.32, 38), or he himself inserted the phrase as shown in Lk. 8.12, 9.47, and 12.34. With these considerations, it is certain that the apparent false concord was not problematic for Luke (nor for the other NT authors). This statement does not mean, of course, that the disagreement of the number is Lukan, since Luke also makes the number of the modifying noun agree with that of the modified seven times in the Gospel and nine times in Acts.[149] However, it becomes

---

146. Lk. 8.12 οἱ δὲ παρὰ τὴν ὁδόν εἰσιν οἱ ἀκούσαντες, εἶτα ἔρχεται ὁ διάβολος καὶ αἴρει τὸν λόγον ἀπὸ τῆς καρδίας αὐτῶν.

Mt. 13.19 παντὸς ἀκούοντος τὸν λόγον τῆς βασιλείας καὶ μὴ συνιέντος ἔρχεται ὁ πονηρὸς καὶ ἁρπάζει τὸ ἐσπαρμένον ἐν τῇ καρδίᾳ αὐτοῦ οὗτός ἐστιν ὁ παρὰ τὴν ὁδὸν σπαρείς.

Mk 4.15 οὗτοι δέ εἰσιν οἱ παρὰ τὴν ὁδόν· ὅπου σπείρεται ὁ λόγος, καὶ ὅταν ἀκούσωσιν, εὐθὺς ἔρχεται ὁ Σατανᾶς καὶ αἴρει τὸν λόγον τὸν ἐσπαρμένον εἰς αὐτούς.

The parallel in Mark has no expression for 'one's heart,' while the parallel in Matthew shows the agreement of the number between two nouns: τῇ καρδίᾳ αὐτοῦ.

147. Lk. 9.47 ὁ δὲ Ἰησοῦς εἰδὼς τὸν διαλογισμὸν τῆς καρδίας αὐτῶν, ἐπιλαβόμενος παιδίον ἔστησεν αὐτὸ παρ' ἑαυτῷ.

Mt. 18.2 καὶ προσκαλεσάμενος παιδίον ἔστησεν αὐτὸ ἐν μέσῳ αὐτῶν·

Mk 9.35 καὶ καθίσας ἐφώνησεν τοὺς δώδεκα καὶ λέγει αὐτοῖς, Εἴ τις θέλει πρῶτος εἶναι, ἔσται πάντων ἔσχατος καὶ πάντων διάκονος.

The parallels in Matthew and Mark do not include the phrase.

148. Lk. 12.34 ὅπου γάρ ἐστιν ὁ θησαυρὸς ὑμῶν, ἐκεῖ καὶ ἡ καρδία ὑμῶν ἔσται.

Mt. 6.21 ὅπου γάρ ἐστιν ὁ θησαυρὸς σοῦ ἐκεῖ ἔσται καὶ ἡ καρδία σου.

Interestingly, the singular noun θησαυρός is modified by the plural pronoun in Luke, while the singular pronoun modifies this singular noun in Mark.

149. It is interesting that Acts always makes the number of the modified noun καρδία agree with that of the modifying noun or pronoun without exception (nine times).

clear that Luke had no compelling reason to concord the number of the modified noun καρδία with the modifying noun if he had translated the Hebrew text. Then, he would have written (τὴν) καρδίαν πατέρων, i.e., '[the] heart of [the] fathers'. Luke as well as the other NT authors and the LXX translators did not have the dilemma Winter supposes in making the numbers of the nouns identical to each other. Therefore, it is unlikely that Luke depends on the MT for the phrase.

(2) *The absence of the article for the noun* καρδία

The absence of the article for the noun καρδία followed by modifying genitive noun is 'a non-Lukanism' as all the instances in Luke-Acts outside of the infancy narrative include the article without exception. This is also true for all the examples in the other NT books except for the quotations from the OT (1 Cor. 2.9; Heb. 8.10). This observation indicates that Luke, as well as the other NT authors, would have adopted the article if he had translated the Hebrew text or composed the phrase for himself. The omission of the article calls into question Luke's direct composition of the phrase in Lk. 1.17 and makes it less probable that Luke translated the Hebrew OT. The absence of the article for the noun καρδία at the same time belongs to secondary Septuagintalisms, reflecting Hebrew syntax. It is more probable that Luke depended on a Greek source for this construction or on the LXX.

One possible counter argument would be that Luke, translating the Hebrew text, omitted the article following Hebrew usage, while changing the singular to the plural for the noun 'heart'. Is it probable that Luke decided to reflect the absence of the article in the Hebrew OT, which makes the Greek expression awkward, while changing the number of a Hebrew noun, which is not at all awkward? Luke's direct dependence on the Hebrew text appears improbable. Another possible objection would be that an unknown person composed this phrase depending on the Hebrew OT. If someone translated the Hebrew text before Luke, he evidently did not share the view of the LXX and the NT authors that disagreement of the number in the phrase καρδίας πατέρων is tolerable. More importantly, his Greek is different from the Greek in the infancy narrative. Two different expressions in 1.51 (καρδίας αὐτῶν 'their heart') and 1.66 (ἐν τῇ καρδίᾳ αὐτῶν 'their heart') clearly indicate that the singular noun could be accompanied by a plural noun even without the article, as in 1.51. His Greek is different from that of the NT authors and of the composer of 1.51 and 1.66.

(3) *The plurals in Lk. 1.17*

If so, why did the Lukan text include the plurals for the phrase καρδίας πατέρων? The composer of the Lukan text altered καρδίαν πατρός in the LXX to καρδίας πατέρων probably because it was required by the context:

3. *A Close Examination of the Greek of the Infancy Narrative* 109

the nouns in the preceding verse and in the following lines are plurals. V. 16 contains two plurals, one in the phrase πολλοὺς (τῶν υἱῶν Ἰσραήλ) and the other in the phrase τὸν θεὸν αὐτῶν. The plural appears as 'children' τέκνα, 'the disobedient' ἀπειθεῖς and 'the righteous' δικαίων in the following line as well. All the nouns are plurals, and may justify Luke's alteration of the singular to the plural of the nouns in Sirach or Malachi of the LXX. It is accepted, of course, that the Greek plural τέκνα in v. 17, for which the LXX has the singular noun υἱός, might reflect the plural of the Hebrew noun and the Lukan text might depend on the Hebrew. However, it must be remembered that this is an allusion to the OT, not a quotation. The text of the OT could be changed according to the context more easily in allusions than in quotations. The change of the noun from υἱός in the LXX to τέκνον may indicate the Lukan intention to avoid a possible confusion over the presence of the former noun in v. 16:[150]

καὶ πολλοὺς τῶν υἱῶν Ἰσραὴλ ἐπιστρέψει ἐπὶ κύριον τὸν θεὸν αὐτῶν.
He will turn many of the sons of Israel to the Lord their God.

The context provides a plausible explanation for the change of the noun and its number.

Lk. 3.5 shows that Luke also altered the singular to the plural in line with the context even in a direct quotation. The Lukan verse reads as follows:

καὶ ἔσται τὰ σκολιὰ εἰς εὐθείαν καὶ αἱ τραχεῖαι εἰς ὁδοὺς λείας·
The crooked shall become straight and the rough roads smooth.

The Greek word αἱ τραχεῖαι is plural in Luke, whereas the corresponding verse Isa. 40.4 of the LXX includes the singular noun:

ἔσται πάντα τὰ σκολιὰ εἰς εὐθεῖαν καὶ ἡ τραχεῖα εἰς πεδία.
all the crooked shall be straight and the rough place plains.

The plural noun in Luke might reflect the plural of the Hebrew text. However, other factors make improbable dependence of the Lukan text on the Hebrew OT for the quotation in Lk. 3.5.[151] Luke changed ἡ τραχεῖα in Isa. 40.4 into αἱ τραχεῖαι to make it conform to the use of the plural forms of τὰ σκολιά and ὁδοὺς λείας. The Lukan text 'is too close to the LXX', as New concludes, 'in everything but the omission of πάντα and his own

---

150. Marshall, *Luke*, p. 59.
151. New raises the following question arguing for Luke's dependence on the LXX: if Luke had changed his LXX text in accordance with the Hebrew text, 'why does Luke not make other changes as well? For example, why did he not make the change many late minuscules made, ταπεινωθήσεται to ταπεινωθήσονται?' For more details, see his book, *Old Testament Quotations*, pp. 43–47.

stylistic change to αἱ τραχεῖαι to have used any other source' (*Old Testament Quotations*, p. 45).

Another example is found in Acts 3.22:

Μωϋσῆς μὲν εἶπεν ὅτι Προφήτην ὑμῖν ἀναστήσει κύριος ὁ θεὸς ὑμῶν ἐκ τῶν ἀδελφῶν ὑμῶν ὡς ἐμέ αὐτοῦ ἀκούσεσθε κατὰ πάντα ὅσα ἄν λαλήσῃ πρὸς ὑμᾶς.
Moses said, 'The Lord *your* God will raise up for *you* from *your* own people a prophet like me. You must listen to whatever he tells you'. (NRSV)

Deut. 18.15, the quoted text, reads:

προφήτην ἐκ τῶν ἀδελφῶν σου ὡς ἐμέ ἀναστήσει σοι κύριος ὁ θεὸς σου αὐτοῦ ἀκούσεσθε.
The LORD your God will raise up for you a prophet like me from among your own people; you shall heed such a prophet. (NRSV)

Three second person singular pronouns in Deut. 18.15 are replaced by three second person plural pronouns in Acts 3.22. The context explains why the author changed the pronouns. The speaker, Peter, addresses the crowd (3.12 – πρὸς τὸν λαόν) using the second person plural: "Ἄνδρες Ἰσραηλῖται, τί θαυμάζετε...'.[152] This feature forces the author to alter the singular pronouns to the plural.[153]

Deut. 18.15 is quoted again in Acts 7.37:

οὗτός ἐστιν ὁ Μωϋσῆς ὁ εἴπας τοῖς υἱοῖς' σραήλ (Προφήτην ὑμῖν ἀναστήσει ὁ θεὸς ἐκ τῶν ἀδελφῶν ὑμῶν ὡς ἐμέ.
This is the Moses who said to the Israelites, 'God (without 'your', which Deut. 18.15 includes) will raise up a prophet for you from your own people as he raised me up.'

The context in this verse also requires the plural for two pronouns. These examples illustrate that Luke changes the number of nouns or pronouns even in direct quotation.

(4) *Summary*

(i) It is unlikely that Luke translated the Hebrew text for the phrase καρδίας πατέρων ἐπὶ τέκνα or composed it for himself, since the singular noun καρδία with the plural modifying noun is evidently

---

152. In Deuteronomy, the speaker, Moses, addresses the Israelite people, but he uses the second singular pronouns in most cases. Luke appears to tend to change the number of nouns or pronouns in accordance with the context.

153. For more details, see Steyn, *Septuagint Quotations*, pp. 143–46. Enumerating all the second person plurals in 3.13-26, Steyn concludes that 'seen from this contextual viewpoint, the three changes in vv. 22-23 are compatible with the hearers, or subjects, who are addressed' (p. 146).

Lukan. He even inserts this construction in the sections where the parallels in Mark or Matthew do not include it. If he had translated the Hebrew text, he could have kept the singular noun καρδία.

(ii) The absence of the article of the noun καρδία makes it less probable for Luke to have relied on the Hebrew OT because Luke always uses the article with the noun καρδία.

(iii) The argument for Luke's dependence on the Hebrew OT rather than on the LXX lacks consistency. Its advocates claim that the Lukan text relied on the Hebrew text considering the plural nouns πατέρων and τέκνα; the plural καρδίας was adjusted to the plural πατέρων. It is certain that Luke had no compelling reason to avoid the expression καρδίαν πατέρων, which stemmed from a literal translation of the Hebrew.

(iv) The claim that an unknown person translated the Hebrew text before Luke is untenable as explained above. His Greek is different from other NT authors and even the author of the infancy narrative. These considerations make it probable that the Lukan text in 1.17 depends on either a Greek source or the LXX which includes the plural for all three nouns. Otherwise, Luke (or the composer) may have changed the number of all three singular nouns in the LXX without consulting the Hebrew OT. Luke usually changes the number of nouns or pronouns, if the context requires. The plural nouns and pronouns in vv. 16-17 seem to force Luke to alter the singular to the plural. The theory of the Lukan text's dependence on the LXX shows consistency in the contention that the author, without consulting the Hebrew OT, changed the numbers of three nouns from singular in the LXX to plural in accordance with the context. In contrast, if the Lukan text depended on the Hebrew OT, it is difficult to explain the plural noun for 'hearts'. The view of Luke's dependence on the LXX is at least more logically consistent than the theory of Luke's dependence on the Hebrew OT.[154]

2. *Remark on the construction* ἐπιστρέψαι – ἐπί

One more question needs to be answered: why did the Lukan text employ the preposition ἐπί instead of πρός which appears both in Malachi and *Sirach* of the LXX? The simple answer is that Luke altered the latter to the

---

154. Marshall recognizes that it is difficult to argue for Luke's independent translation of the MT or his dependence on the Greek text of *Sirach*. Luke's freedom in dealing with the OT, he concludes, makes it difficult to decide between two options, though he believes the first option is more probable given that other parts of the story support Luke's dependence on a non-LXX text (*Luke*, p. 59).

former since he preferred ἐπί when using the verb ἐπιστρέψαι. This construction is 'a hard core Lukanism', for it occurs elsewhere only in Acts in the whole of the NT (Acts 9.35; 11.21; 14.15; 15.19; 26.20). However, it is hardly possible to decide whether it echoes Hebrew syntax or not. Accordingly, it may support either Luke's translation theory or Luke's direct composition theory. In contrast, Luke apparently did not rely on a written source for this phrase. The examples in Acts demonstrate Luke's preponderant use of ἐπί with the verb. It is true that in two instances Luke uses the preposition πρός with this verb (Lk. 17.4; Acts 9.40), but in these cases the verb is not used to mean 'convert' or 'turn' in a metaphorical sense. In these two verses, it denotes a turning of the body. Given the five instances in Acts, Luke's use of the phrase ἐπιστρέψαι ἐπί is certainly habitual which may indicate Luke's possible intervention to change the preposition πρός in the LXX to ἐπί.

In conclusion, the argument that the plural nouns καρδίας, πατέρων, and τέκνα indicate the Lukan text's dependence on the Hebrew OT rather than the LXX is not convincing. The absence of the article and the use of the singular for 'heart', the context and the plural nouns in vv. 16-17 make it less probable for Luke or a composer[155] to have relied on the Hebrew OT than most scholars assume, though they do not clearly support dependence of the Lukan text on the LXX. At least, it is certain that the plural nouns in Luke do not support the dependence of the Lukan text on the Hebrew OT over the LXX.

II. *The Allusion in Lk. 1.37*

ὅτι οὐκ ἀδυνατήσει[156] παρὰ τοῦ θεοῦ πᾶν ῥῆμα.
because no word (or thing) from God will be impossible.[157]

(A) *The Problem*

(1) *Possible Semitisms*
The sentence in Lk. 1.37 betrays several possible Semitisms:[158]

---

155. As argued just above, the change of number of nouns and the use of the preposition ἐπί with the verb ἐπιστρέφω may indicate Luke's intervention in this verse.
156. The future tense of this verb is unusual because the context refers to the past act of making Elizabeth pregnant. Porter interprets this future as timeless future, which describes here God's timeless character, indicating 'nothing can be expected to be impossible for God' (*Verbal Aspect*, pp. 421–22). However, the future may be used to point to Mary's future pregnancy. See K. Stock, 'Die Berufung Marias (Lk. 1.26–38)', *Bib*, 61(1980), pp. 484–85.
157. This rather ambiguous translation is adopted here in order to show that the Greek text itself could be translated in various ways. For the various translations, see below.
158. Sahlin claims that the sentence is 'stark hebraisierend', alluding to Gen. 18.14 and Jer. 32.17, but he does not present details for his argument (*Der Messias*, p. 139). Winter

3. *A Close Examination of the Greek of the Infancy Narrative* 113

a. the reversed negative pattern of the sentence, i.e., the negative connected to the verb reflecting Hebrew לא – כל: οὐ – πᾶς;[159]
b. the use of ῥῆμα 'word', reflecting the Hebrew דבר 'word, thing'; and
c. παρὰ τοῦ θεοῦ as reflecting the Hebrew phrase מעם האלהים.

Allusions to two possible texts have been proposed: Gen. 18.14; Jer. 32.17 of the Hebrew text. The Greek phrase παρὰ τοῦ θεοῦ is not in accord with a possible allusion to the LXX, Gen. 18.14: μὴ ἀδυνατεῖ παρὰ τῷ θεῷ ῥῆμα; the preposition is followed by the dative in Gen. 18.14, but the genitive follows the preposition in Luke.

(2) *To which verse does the Lukan text allude?*

It may not be necessary to decide to which verse the Lukan text exactly alludes. Nolland, however, attempts to prove the Lukan text's dependence on Jer. 32.17 of the Hebrew text (39.17 in the LXX, where the translation completely deviates from the MT: οὐ μὴ ἀποκρυβῇ ἀπὸ σοῦ οὐθέν 'nothing will never be hidden from you [God])', rather than on Gen. 18.14 on the ground that the word order and syntax of Jer. 32.17 of the MT perfectly reflect those of Lk. 1.37 (*Luke 1–9.20*, p. 56). It must be accepted that the MT text in Jer. 32.17 (לא־יפלא ממך כל־דבר), 'nothing is impossible for you') discloses similarities with Lk. 1.37:

a. the sentence in Jeremiah is indicative as in Luke, while the sentence in Genesis is a question;
b. the position of the negative and the pronoun πᾶν in Luke exactly echo those in Jeremiah: לא – כל.

However, the Lukan context is totally different from that of Jeremiah. Nolland thus concedes that the usage in Jeremiah and Luke may be proverbial, but he still assumes the proverb to have been not in Greek but in Hebrew. A residual memory, he continues, may refer to the experience of Abraham, but the language derives from Jeremiah of the Hebrew OT as the proverb represents a fixed idea at the NT times. 'In any case,' he concludes, 'the language is Semitic, non-Septuagintal, and

---

argues in detail for the affinity of the Lukan text to the MT rather than the LXX. The following first and third suggestions are from Winter. See his article, 'Some Observations on the Language', pp. 115–16. Brown also insists that the sentence includes several Semitisms, suggesting the first and second elements (*The Birth of the Messiah*, p. 292). See also Bock who follows Brown (*Luke 1.1–9.50*, p. 126).

159. The expression οὐ πᾶς is classical Greek [BDF 302.2], where the negative is connected with πᾶς. In contrast, the negative connected with the verb in the locution οὐ – πᾶς reflects Hebrew syntax לא – כל. It is remarkable that this construction does not appear often in non-Biblical literature [BDF 302.1].

non-Lukan.'[160] Bock agrees with Nolland, arguing that 'Jer. 32:17 is close in force to the genitive expression (with here παρά).' He infers: 'so the genitive may reflect a Semitic original behind Luke and suggest that he is not responsible for the material in the section' (*Luke 1.1–9.50*, p. 126, nt. 49).

(B) *Solution*

(1) *Does the Lukan text allude to Jer. 32.17 of the Hebrew OT?*

Concerning the second problem, i.e., whether the Lukan text alludes to Jer. 32.17 of the Hebrew text or not, the Greek sentence in Luke reveals differences from the Hebrew text in Jer. 32.17:

a. the sentence in Jeremiah lacks the noun 'God' in Luke;
b. the subject matter is different, since Jeremiah ch. 32 does not deal with a miraculous pregnancy as Luke does;
c. the use of the verb ἀδυνατήσει for Hebrew פלא is not compelling, as ἀσθενήσει or ἀνενέργητον ἔσται could be used.[161]

In contrast, the Lukan text shares many common elements with Gen. 18.14 in the LXX: μὴ ἀδυνατεῖ παρὰ τῷ θεῷ ῥῆμα; 'Shall anything be impossible with God?':[162]

a. the subject matter of both is closely connected: the miraculous pregnancy of (old) women, Sarah in Genesis and Elizabeth or Mary in Luke;
b. both sentences begin with the negative, although μή is used in Genesis to indicate a question that anticipates a negative answer, and Luke adopted the normal οὐ for the indicative sentence;
c. the verb ἀδυνατέω is utilized in both verses and this verb is connected with a negative particle in both cases: οὐκ ἀδυνατήσει in Luke and μὴ ἀδυνάτει in Genesis;
d. both verses include the preposition παρά[163] and the noun ῥῆμα;
e. the basic word order is identical:

---

160. In contrast to Nolland, Jeremias believes the sentence in Lk. 1.37 has been redacted by Luke. For more details, see his book *Die Sprache*, p. 54.

161. F. Field, *Notes on the Translation of the New Testament* (Cambridge: University Press, 1899; repr. Hendrickson, 1994), p. 47. The verb ἀσθενέω means 'be weak', 'powerless', or 'be void of power', and the adjective ἀνενέργητον 'inactive' or 'inefficacious' (Liddell and Scott, pp. 256, 132).

162. Sanders comments on this verse that the wording of Lk. 1.37 duplicates those spoken by the heavenly visitors in Gen. 18.14 of the LXX ('Isaiah in Luke', p. 149).

163. Field suggests that ὑπερ τὸν θεόν must replace παρὰ τῷ θεῷ for the context of Gen. 18.14: 'is anything wonderful (hard) beyond God?' (*Notes on the Translation*, p. 46). He also observes on the same page that Aquila translated the preposition as 'ἀπό'.

οὐκ ἀδυνατήσει παρὰ τοῦ θεοῦ πᾶν ῥῆμα (Lk. 1.37)

μὴ ἀδυνατεῖ παρὰ τῷ θεῷ ῥῆμα (Gen. 18.14).

Most important is that even if the sentence, as Nolland contends, was a proverb, no fixed maxim existed, as other verses in the OT offer different expressions for the same thought: Job 10.13 (LXX); 42.2; Jer. 32.27; Zech. 8.6 [cf. Mt. 19.16 (parallel in Mk 10.27 and Lk. 18.27)]. This situation indicates that an author could choose an expression of various locutions in accordance with his context. Although the thought, then, is common in the OT, the wording here is based on Gen. 18.14, whose context is identical to Luke's.[164] Therefore, Nolland's argument that the Lukan text alludes to Jer. 32.17 in the Hebrew OT and its language is non-Septuagintal is not convincing,[165] though the problem of possible Semitisms in Gen. 18.14 of the LXX and Lk. 1.37 has yet to be resolved.

(2) *Explanations concerning first two points of the first problem*
The first two points of the first problem can be resolved without difficulty.

(i) *The use of the noun* ῥῆμα
The second point of the first problem, i.e., the use of the noun ῥῆμα with the double connotation of the Hebrew דבר, i.e., 'word' and 'deed or thing' stems from a confusion between Hebraisms and Septuagintalisms. It disappears if the use of the noun reflects LXX usage. This view supports the influence of the LXX more than that of the Hebrew OT, as Fitzmyer suggests that ῥῆμα delivers the meaning of the LXX, 'word, matter, thing' (*Luke*, p. 352).

(ii) *The reversed negative construction*
With respect to the first point, i.e., the reversed negative pattern, the LXX also displays the pattern in Ps. 142.2:

οὐ δικαιωθήσεται ἐνώπιόν σου πᾶς ζῶν (לא־יצדק לפניך כל־חי).
'no one living is righteous before you.'

---

164. F. Danker considers the phrase as a paraphrase of Gen. 18.14 (F. Danker, *Jesus and the New Age: A Commentary on St. Luke's Gospel* [Philadelphia: Fortress, 1988], p. 40). Marshall also argues for the dependence of the Lukan text on Gen. 18.14 (*Luke*, p. 72). Field claims that the Lukan text is 'undoubtedly a reminiscence of (if we may not say, a quotation from) Gen. xviii. 14' (*Notes on the Translation*, p. 46). Jeremias notes that the sentence in Lk. 1.37 is a free citation of Gen. 18.14 of the LXX (*Die Sprache*, p. 54). See also Wilcox, *The Semitisms of Acts*, p. 72, nt. 12.

165. Nolland appears to recognize that the Lukan text in 1.37 is closer to Gen. 18.14 of the LXX than that of the MT. He suggests Jer. 32.17 as an alluded text, because he argues for the dependence of the infancy narrative on Semitic sources.

This reversed negation, rare in non-biblical literature (BDR 303), occurs also in Pss. 9.3 and 17.27, and thus it belongs to secondary Septuagintalisms. Moreover, this pattern does not echo Gen. 18.14 of the Hebrew text. The Hebrew text has only the interrogative particle with the nifal verb: היפלא. The negative pattern echoes the LXX rather than the Hebrew OT of Gen. 18.14. Even if the reversed negative reflects the Hebrew OT of Jer. 32.17, it must be added that οὐ – πᾶς, as Winter points out, is frequent in the NT and a secondary Septuagintalism as shown above ('Some Observations on the Language', p. 115).[166] It is true that Gen. 18.14 of the Hebrew text and of the LXX does not have any corresponding word for πᾶς in Luke, though Jer. 32.17 of the Hebrew text has it. However, Luke typically adds πᾶς to strengthen the meaning, as Jeremias notes (*Die Sprache*, p. 54). Thus, Luke probably inserted the pronoun to the sentence in the LXX Gen. 18.14 in line with his own personal style (see Lk. 6.10; 6.17; 8.52; 9.1; 18.22; 21.29 in which Luke inserts πᾶς, which Mark does not include).

(3) *Proposal for the last problem*

The last speculation must be given serious consideration. Winter postulates that παρά with the genitive reflects the Hebrew construction מעם האלהים. Luke's verse with the phrase παρὰ τοῦ θεοῦ means, he claims, that 'Nothing [that comes] *from God* (= that has been caused by God) shall be impossible.' On the contrary, the LXX reads 'Not impossible is *to God* a thing' (or 'A word by God is not void') ('Some Observations on the Language', p. 116). The LXX, according to him, clearly differs from Luke. He continues to argue that the Hebrew version of Gen. 18.14 is to be translated as, 'Is anything [coming] *from God* wondrous?' Three sentences suggested by Winter need to be compared:

> Lk. 1.37: 'Nothing [that comes] *from God* (= that has been caused by God) shall be impossible.'

> The MT of Gen. 18.14: 'Is anything [coming] *from God* wondrous?'

> The LXX of Gen. 18.14: 'Not impossible is *to God* a thing' (or 'A word by God is not void')

Winter concludes that Luke's sentence is closer to the MT than the LXX.[167]

After pointing out the similarity between the Lukan text and the Septuagintal text, Turner refutes Winter's claim mainly by showing that the verb in the Hebrew text of Gen. 18.14 could mean 'to be too difficult

---

166. Mk 13.20, parallel in Mt. 24.22; Acts 10.14; Rom. 3.20; 1 Cor. 1.29; Rev. 21.27. etc.
167. This may indicate either Luke's dependence upon Hebrew originals or upon a non-LXX source. See Marshall, *Luke*, p. 72.

3. *A Close Examination of the Greek of the Infancy Narrative* 117

for' as in Deut. 10.11 and Jer. 32.17, 27 ('The Relation of Luke I and II', p. 102). The Hebrew verb, he continues, does not necessarily illuminate the meaning of the Lukan verb more than does the Greek verb of Gen. 18.14. The LXX translation conveys the correct meaning of the Hebrew verb, i.e., 'nothing is too difficult for God'. As a result, Turner concludes, the argument that the Lukan text is closer to the MT than the LXX is unconvincing, as both texts have the same meaning.

Turner's argument can be complemented:

(i) *Various translations*
   With the dative the preposition παρά denotes 'beside, by, or with'. παρά with the dative in variations of Lk. 1.37 and in Gen. 18.14 is almost equivalent to the dative alone (BAGD, p. 610). With the genitive it indicates 'from'. The various translations are worth noting:

   since nothing is impossible for God (Fitzmyer)[168]

   because nothing said by God can be impossible[169] (Brown)

   for with God nothing shall be impossible (KJV)

   for nothing will be impossible with God (NASB, NRSV)

   for nothing is impossible with God (NIV)

All the interpretations translate the prepositional phrase as 'with or for God', even though it must mean 'from God' in Greek. According to BAGD (p. 609), the preposition with the genitive denotes 'the one who originates or directs'. Various translations seem to rest on two elements: a) the preposition with the dative has the same meaning as with the genitive, or Greek variants containing the phrase παρὰ τῷ θεῷ, which may mean 'with God', are reliable;[170] and b) their decision as to the meaning of ῥῆμα results in that translation. All of them understand the noun as 'thing', and not 'word'.[171] It is intriguing to observe that the Old American Standard

---

168. Fitzmyer provides a literal translation as follows: 'for not impossible will be word (or thing) with God' (*Luke I–IX*, p. 352).
169. Brown uses the noun 'thing' to indicate the double connotation of the Hebrew word. He also suggests a literal translation: 'because not impossible will be every word [ῥῆμα] with God' (*The Birth of the Messiah*, p. 292).
170. Field follows the reading of the majority text 'παρὰ τῷ θεῷ' (*Notes on the Translation*, p. 46).
171. They seem to suppose that the sentence 'word from God is not impossible' does not seem to make good sense.

Version translated the phrase as 'from God': 'For no word from God shall be void of power.' This translation results from the interpretation of the noun as 'word'.

(ii) *Is the preposition followed by the genitive or dative?*

a. In order to resolve the problem of the preposition, a decision regarding the prepositional phrase must be made. Some variants read παρὰ τῷ θεῷ instead of παρὰ τοῦ θεοῦ. External evidence gives slightly more credence to the latter, although it is not decisive. ℵ$_2$ A C Θ ψ *f*(1)13 33 support the reading παρὰ τῷ θεῷ, while ℵ B D L W Ξ 565 *pc* read παρὰ τοῦ θεοῦ. Because proto-Alexandrian ℵ B and Western D lend support, the genitive is a better-attested reading than the dative. Internal evidence also indicates a preference of the former over the latter. The expression, παρὰ τοῦ θεοῦ, may have bothered copyists, since in Koine Greek παρά with the genitive τοῦ θεοῦ meant 'from God', while copyists assumed the context requires 'with or for God'. They probably supposed that the meaning of the Lukan text had been distorted by the preposition, or that the preposition should have been accompanied by the dative as in the LXX Gen. 18.14. If the principle *lectio difficilior* and the *canon of harmonization* are applied, the reading παρὰ τοῦ θεοῦ is preferable. Copyists had no reason to change παρὰ τῷ θεῷ to παρὰ τοῦ θεοῦ. If the original text of παρὰ τοῦ θεοῦ is retained, the phrase should denote 'from God'.

b. Some scholars argue that the preposition conveys the same meaning both with the genitive and with the dative.[172] However, if Luke had intended the meaning of the LXX Gen. 18.14, he should have kept the reading in the LXX: παρὰ τῷ θεῷ. A possible solution would be that the Hebrew text of Gen. 18.14 forced Luke to employ the genitive since the Hebrew text is closer to the meaning of the Lukan text than the LXX.

This suggestion, however, is not convincing, as Turner points out.[173] Moreover, the meaning in this case must be 'from God' not 'with God'. It is unlikely that the Lukan text was intended to deliver the same meaning as the LXX Gen. 18.14 with the genitive, which is

---

172. Marshall, refuting the argument by Tasker that the preposition should mean 'from God' with the genitive, claims that the preposition could mean 'for' with the genitive (*Luke*, p. 72). His argument is not convincing. He depends on the possibility that the meaning of the preposition can be flexible enough to mean 'for', but does not offer any example or reference. See also Bock, *Luke 1.1–9.50*, p. 131.

173. For details, see above.

different from the LXX and more importantly from classical and Hellenistic Greek, where the genitive occurs only rarely in place of the dative, if it does, and even in this case, the meaning is not 'with' but 'by' or 'near' (Liddell and Scott, p. 1302). These considerations make it less probable that the Lukan text was intended to mean 'nothing is impossible with God' with the genitive.[174]

(iii) *The meaning of the noun ῥῆμα in Lk. 1.37*
It is necessary to decide the meaning of the noun ῥῆμα to find an answer to the question of why the Lukan text includes the genitive instead of the dative. The noun occasionally means 'thing' in the infancy narrative (1.65; 2.15, 19, 51), but this use is balanced by cases where the noun means 'word' (1.38; 2.17, 29, 50). Noteworthy is that the noun is clarified when it appears twice in one passage and each use denotes a different meaning: περὶ τοῦ ῥήματος τοῦ λαληθέντος 'the word [message] which has been told' (2.17) and τὰ ῥήματα ταῦτα 'these things' (2.19).[175] 2.50 and 51 also display the same discrepancy: τὸ ῥῆμα ὃ ἐλάλησεν, 'the word which he said' (v. 50); πάντα τὰ ῥήματα, 'all these things' (v. 51). Turning to 1.37, ῥῆμα appears in the same passage in v. 38 and the noun ῥῆμα lacks any modifying word in these two examples. Thus, both nouns probably convey the same meaning

---

174. In Luke-Acts, the preposition παρά followed by the genitive always means 'from': Lk. 8.49; Acts 2.33; 3.2; 7.16; 9.14; 10.22; 17.9; 20.24; 26.10; 28.22. In contrast, it always means 'with or for' with the dative: Lk. 18.27; 19.7; Acts 9.43; 10.6.

175. Brown suggests that the word ῥῆμα in v. 17 and v. 19 as well as v. 15 delivers the double connotation of Hebrew דבר: 'word, deed' (*The Birth of the Messiah*, p. 405). While his argument is acceptable, it is more probable that the Greek word in v. 17 renders 'word' than 'deed':

ἰδόντες δὲ ἐγνώρισαν περὶ τοῦ ῥήματος τοῦ λαληθέντος αὐτοῖς περὶ τοῦ παιδίου τούτου. 'Then, having seen (it), they made known about the saying [word, message] which was told them concerning this baby.'

It is true that the Greek word in v. 19 could convey the double connotation of the Hebrew word. However, in this case, the word must be translated as 'event, or thing' rather than 'word'.

Concerning the word ῥῆμα in 2.50, Brown concedes that it means 'word'. He continues, however, that 'and yet to translate it thus would disguise from the reader the connection with previous uses.' 'Moreover,' he adds, 'the parents' lack of comprehension centres not only on the words of Jesus' question but on the whole course of action that leads to it' (Brown, p. 477). Here again, whereas it is impossible to completely refute his argument, a more probable meaning of the word here is 'word' than 'deed':

καὶ αὐτοὶ οὐ συνῆκαν τὸ ῥῆμα ὃ ἐλάλησεν αὐτοῖς, 'but they themselves did not understand the word which he told them.'

v. 50 deals with parents' lack of comprehension concerning Jesus' saying in v. 49, though the word in v. 51 could mean 'event' or 'word'. In this case, as shown above, the translation must be 'event', which includes Jesus' saying.

and the noun certainly means 'word' in v. 38. This observation adds credence to the interpretation that the author intended to render the same meaning of 'word' for both nouns. It is accepted, of course, that the word ῥῆμα could deliver the double connotation of Hebrew in v. 37. However, the word must be translated 'word' rather than 'event' as in 2.17 and 2.50. While the latter focuses on the aspect of 'deed, or matter', the former on the aspect of 'the message, or what is spoken'. The whole sentence may be reconstructed as follows: 'because no word from God will be impossible (disabled/ made void/ disempowered/ emptied of its power).' This rendition is strengthened by the noun ῥῆμα in the following verse (v. 38). It seems that the two sentences form a pair:

v. 37 because no *word from God* will be impossible (disabled/ made void/ disempowered/ emptied of its power).

v. 38 may it be done to me according to *your word* (ῥῆμα).

(4) *The composition procedure*

How did this sentence evolve, then? With Gen. 18.14 of the LXX in front of him or in his mind, Luke adapted the Greek OT because the context requires modification. First, the interrogative needed to be changed to the indicative. The verb tense then required the future to express Mary's future pregnancy. Luke wanted to have the sentence mean 'no word from God will be impossible' leading him to alter παρὰ τῷ θεῷ in Gen. 18.14 of the LXX to παρὰ τοῦ θεοῦ to indicate 'from God'.[176] He may have intended 'word' here by ῥῆμα, since the angel announced both John's (1.13) and Jesus' birth. It is also noteworthy that Acts 10.22 shows the phrase ῥήματα παρὰ σοῦ to mean 'words from you'.

In conclusion, it is not easy to determine whether the Lukan text in 1.37 relied on the LXX or the Hebrew OT, because the verse alludes to, but does not quote, the OT. However, the similarity between the Lukan text and Gen. 18.14 of the LXX shows the dependence of the Lukan text on the LXX. Differences exist, but as an allusion and not as a quotation, they cannot detract from the probable dependence of the verse upon Gen. 18.14 of the LXX.

---

176. The latter construction occurs 29 times in the LXX, while the former only three times.

III. The Allusion in Lk. 1.31

καὶ ἰδοὺ συλλήμψῃ ἐν γαστρὶ καὶ τέξῃ υἱὸν καὶ καλέσεις τὸ ὄνομα αὐτοῦ Ἰησοῦν.

and behold, you will conceive in (your) womb and bear a son, and you will call his name Jesus.

It is assumed by scholars that Lk. 1.31 alludes to Isa. 7.14 or Gen. 16.11.[177] Whether the Lukan text depends on the Hebrew OT or the LXX of these verses has been discussed by many scholars.[178]

(A) *The Problem*

(1) *Is the whole sentence in Lk. 1.31 an allusion or a quotation?*

In order to clarify the problem, we need to compare Lk. 1.31 with Gen. 16.11 and Isa. 7.14, the two texts frequently proposed by scholars as the source of Luke's language:

Lk. 1.31 καὶ <u>ἰδοὺ συλλήμψῃ ἐν γαστρὶ</u> καὶ <u>τέξῃ υἱὸν καὶ καλέσεις τὸ ὄνομα αὐτοῦ</u> Ἰησοῦν.

Gen. 16.11 <u>ἰδοὺ</u> σὺ <u>ἐν γαστρὶ</u> ἔχεις καὶ <u>τέξῃ υἱὸν καὶ καλέσεις τὸ ὄνομα αὐτοῦ</u> Ἰσμαὴλ ὅτι ἐπήκουσεν κύριος τῇ ταπεινώσει σου.

Isa. 7.14 <u>ἰδοὺ</u> ἡ παρθένος <u>ἐν γαστρὶ</u> ἕξει καὶ τέξεται <u>υἱὸν καὶ καλέσεις τὸ ὄνομα αὐτοῦ</u> Ἐμμανουηλ.

The words and phrases which are common to all three verses have been underlined to ease comparison.[179] Both verses in Gen. 16.11 and Isa. 7.14 use the verb ἔχω with the prepositional phrase ἐν γαστρί instead of the verb συλλαμβάνω in Luke. Despite the difference in the use of the verb, however, the following points support the view that the sentence in Luke is an allusion to these verses in Genesis and Isaiah:

---

177. Scholars are divided mainly into two groups; some argue for this Lukan verse's dependence on Genesis while others argue for its dependence on Isaiah. For their arguments, see below.

178. For their opinions, see below.

179. To the verses in Gen. 16.11 and Isa. 7.14, the margin of NA[27] adds Judg. 13.3 (of A Text, ἐν γαστρὶ ἕξεις καὶ τέξῃ υἱόν) as a possible alluded verse. Judg. 13.5, 7 (A) also contain the same locution: (ἰδοὺ σὺ) ἐν γαστρὶ ἕξεις καὶ τέξῃ υἱόν (in B, the tense of the first verb is the present). While these verses in Judges are possibly alluded to in Luke, the absence of the last part (καὶ καλέσεις τὸ ὄνομα αὐτοῦ + name) makes it less probable to assume the Lukan verse alludes to them. Our following discussion thus will exclude these verses from consideration.

a. All three verses are concerned with the conception, birth and naming of a baby;
b. apart from the question of which one is closer to the Lukan text, it is striking that the content of the second part of three sentences in Luke, Genesis, and Isaiah is identical to each other:

and someone ('you' in Gen. 16.11 and Lk. 1.31; 'she' in Isa. 7.14;) will bear a son and call his name 'Jesus' (Luke), 'Ishmael' (Genesis), or 'Immanuel' (Isaiah). [in the LXX: καὶ τέξῃ (τέξεται in Isaiah) υἱὸν καὶ καλέσεις τὸ ὄνομα αὐτοῦ[180] + name; in the Hebrew text: וקראת שמו בן (וילדת) in Isaiah) וילדת].

There are also ἰδού and ἐν γαστρί in the first part of these sentences. These considerations make it highly probable that the whole sentence in Lk. 1.31 is an allusion to the LXX Isa. 7.14 or Gen. 16.11.[181] In fact, we have to ask whether Luke's text is really a quotation, given the arguments with respect to the LXX of both Isa. 7.14 and Gen. 16.11.

However, the use of a different verb συλλαμβάνω in Luke makes it difficult for the sentence to be a quotation based on the LXX verses. More importantly, the use of the verb makes it doubtful whether Luke depended on the LXX of Isa. 7.14 or Gen. 16.11.

(2) *The phrase* συλλήμψῃ ἐν γαστρί

It has been shown above that the phrase συλλήμψῃ ἐν γαστρί in Luke differs from the locution in the possible alluded verses as well as in other verses of the LXX. This observation may cast doubt on the claim that the whole sentence alludes to some Greek OT verses like Gen. 16.11 or Isa. 7.14. Regardless of which verse the Lukan text relies on, the issue centres on the phrase συλλήμψῃ ἐν γαστρί because the phrase is peculiar: the LXX and Luke as well as other NT authors use different constructions.

---

180. The use of the article for the noun ὄνομα followed by the modifying genitive seems inevitable. However, the article is omitted in Lk. 1.63 ('Ιωάννης ἐστὶν ὄνομα αὐτοῦ) and Acts 16.18 (ἐν ὀνόματι Ἰησοῦ χριστοῦ). This may indicate that the article in the phrase τὸ ὄνομα αὐτοῦ could have been omitted, if the phrase had been translated from a Hebrew original which must have lacked the article.

181. Most commentaries regard this verse as an allusion, some even as a quotation. E.E. Ellis notes in his commentary *The Gospel of Luke* (Grand Rapids: Eerdmans, n.e., 1981), p. 73 that 'the verse is virtually a quotation of Isa. 7.14 with "Immanuel" changed to Jesus.' W.L. Liefield also comments that 'the wording is virtually identical to the "virgin" passage in Isa. 7.14 (LXX) and to the assurance the angel of the Lord gave the fugitive Hagar (Gen. 16.11, LXX).' 'The word "virgin" is not, however,' he continues, 'mentioned in the allusion to Isaiah, though Mary's question (v. 34) shows she was a virgin, a fact that Luke has mentioned in v. 27' (W.L. Liefield *Matthew, Mark, and Luke*. The Expositor's Bible Commentary, vol. 8 [Grand Rapids, Zondervan, 1985], p. 831). Nolland and Bock deny that Lk. 1.31 alludes to Isa. 7.14 and interpret Lk. 1.31 as alluding to Gen. 16.11. For more details, see below.

3. *A Close Examination of the Greek of the Infancy Narrative* 123

(i) *The use of the construction outside of Luke-Acts*
The whole phrase does not appear in the NT outside of Luke's writings. The verb συλλαμβάνω, however, occurs five times: Mt. 26.55; Mk 14.48; Jn 18.12; Phil. 4.3; Jas 1.15. In all the examples, the verb does not convey the meaning 'conceive' but 'seize or arrest'. There is an apparent exception in Jas 1.15:

εἶτα ἡ ἐπιθυμία συλλαβοῦσα τίκτει ἁμαρτίαν, ἡ δὲ ἁμαρτία ἀποτελεσθεῖσα ἀποκύει θάνατον.
'then, when that desire has conceived, it gives birth to sin, and that sin, when it is fully grown, gives birth to death.'[182]

The verb here is not used literally, however, but figuratively. In addition, the verb is not used with the prepositional phrase ἐν γαστρί or ἐν τῇ κοιλίᾳ.[183]

(ii) *The use in Luke-Acts*
In Luke-Acts, there are eleven examples of the verb (seven in Luke of which four occur in the infancy story and four in Acts). Remarkably, only the four instances in the infancy narrative are used to mean 'conceive' (without the prepositional phrase in 1.24, 36; with ἐν γαστρί in 1.31; with ἐν τῇ κοιλίᾳ 2.21). In the rest of the Gospel and Acts, it means 'arrest'. The use of the verb itself to denote 'conceive' is therefore a possible non-Lukanism which casts doubt on Luke's direct composition or translation on the one hand or supports the possibility that the ultimate Lukan source depended on a Semitic original on the other hand.

(iii) *The phrase in the LXX*
A more serious problem emerges with the recognition that the LXX, even in the possible alluded to verses, uses different locutions for the meaning 'conceive'. It is true that the verb συλλαμβάνω, although it denotes 'take, or arrest' in the rest of the Greek OT, means 'conceive' in Genesis and Song of Solomon. However, the verb is always used alone, i.e., without the prepositional phrase ἐν γαστρί (Gen. 4.1, 17,

---

182. Interestingly, 22 words appear only in James and Luke-Acts among the whole of the NT books. In addition, 38 words in James occur only in Luke-Acts, but not in Matthew and Mark. It seems that there is a connection between Luke and James. For more detailed statistics and argument, see J. B. Adamson, *James: The Man and his Message* (Grand Rapids: Eerdmans, 1988), pp. 173–94. He does not list the verb συλλαμβάνω as a peculiar vocabulary that appears only in Luke and James. He seems to take into account only the occurrence of words. The verb, as mentioned in the text, occurs four times outside of James and Luke-Acts.
183. The latter is another possible phrase for the meaning 'in the womb' as in Lk. 1.41, 44; 2.21.

25; 16.4; 19.36; 21.2; 25.21; 29.32-35; 30.5, 7, 10, 12, 17, 19, 23; 38.3-4; Song of Solomon 3.4; 8.2). ἐν γαστρί is used to indicate 'conceive' with verbs like λαμβάνω (Gen. 25.21; 38.18; Exod. 2.2, 22; Num. 11.12; 2 Sam. 11.5; 4 Kgs 4.17; 1 Chron. 7.23; Job 15.35; Isa. 8.3, 26.18; *Tob.* 15.35) or ἔχω (Gen. 16.4–5,11; 38.24-25; Job 21.10; 2 Sam. 8.12; 4 Kgs 15.16; 13.3,5,7; Judg. 13.5,7; Exod 21.22; Hos. 14.1; Amos 1.3, 13; Isa. 7.14, 40.11). Noteworthy is that in the possible alluded to verses like Gen. 16.11, Isa. 7.14, or even Judg. 13.3 the prepositional phrase ἐν γαστρί is used, but the phrase is not accompanied by the verb συλλαμβάνω. Thus, the construction συλλαμβάνω ἐν γαστρί is a non-Septuagintalism. One may thus ask: Is the phrase συλλαμβάνω ἐν γαστρί influenced by the LXX or not in any sense?

(B) *Proposed Solutions*

Emphasizing that the phrase συλλήμψη ἐν γαστρί is not found in the whole LXX as well as in the verses to which Luke alluded, many scholars have interpreted it as indicating a Semitic or Palestinian origin.[184] In contrast, those who deny that theory have kept silent about it or do not provide a sufficient answer.

(1) *The theory that Lk. 1.31 is dependent on the Hebrew OT or a Semitic original*

(i) Concentrating on the prepositional phrase ἐν γαστρί, Laurentin gives a detailed argument for this view (*Luk I–II*, pp. 68–70, 72). The construction συλλαμβάνω ἐν γαστρί, according to him, presents an abnormal addition to the verb συλλαμβάνω especially in view of the locutions in 1.24 (συνέλαβεν Ἐλισάβετ ἡ γυνὴ αὐτοῦ) and 1.36 (συνείληφεν υἱόν) where the verb συλλαμβάνω appears without the

---

184. Mary's response to angel's annunciation in v. 34 is a puzzle: 'How can this be, since I do not know a man?' According to v. 27, Mary was engaged to Joseph, a descendent of David and the angel predicts Mary's future conception and birth of a baby. Some scholars try to solve this problem by assuming that the future verb συλλήμψη in v. 31 is a mistranslation of a Semitic source. The verb, according to them, is a participle in the Semitic original. The translator misunderstood Hebrew and translated the participle as indicating future time, though it in fact refers to the present. While this interpretation is not impossible, the text needs to be interpreted as it stands. Although the alleged translator might have misunderstood Hebrew, it would be less probable for him to have failed to recognize the awkwardness of the meaning of the translated Greek sentence. For details, see J.G. Machen, *The Virgin Birth of Christ* (New York: Harper & Brothers, 1930), pp. 145–46. See also Brown, *The Birth of the Messiah*, p. 289, who notes that 'Luke's future verb cannot be explained away as a misunderstanding of a putative Semitic original, for the verbs in 1.35 are also future.'

3. A Close Examination of the Greek of the Infancy Narrative 125

prepositional phrase. He concludes that this Greek phrase echoes a Hebrew original: בקרבך. He supposes that a Hebrew construction forced the composer to adopt the Greek locution in 1.31 while the constructions in 1.24 and 1.36 were composed by him. Laurentin tries to explain the locution in 2.21 (πρὸ τοῦ συλλημφθῆναι αὐτὸν ἐν τῇ κοιλίᾳ) by assuming that Luke took over a redundant expression from 1.31 while changing γαστήρ to κοιλία, since κοιλία was 'a more formal, elegant and Greek expression, and habitual to Luke' (*Luk I–II*, p. 70).[185]

(ii) Bock argues for a possible Semitic and Palestinian tradition on the grounds that the Lukan text includes συλλαμβάνω, a verb different from the alluded to verses of the LXX: Gen. 16.11 and Isa. 7.14. The phrase συλλαμβάνω ἐν γαστρί points to a non-Septuagintal tradition and thus probably to a Semitic origin in his view (*Proclamation from Prophecy and Pattern*, p. 296, nt. 36).[186] His argument convinces to the extent that the LXX contains no example for the verb συλλαμβάνω with the prepositional construction. After attempting to refute the view that the Lukan text depends verbally on the LXX of Isa. 7.14, he claims it to be probable that the phrase συλλαμβάνω ἐν γαστρί reflects the influence of the Hebrew text of Isa. 7.14. Bock bases this argument on the fact that the LXX translators frequently adopted the verb συλλαμβάνω to translate the Hebrew adjective הרה, which appears also in the Hebrew OT of Isa. 7.14 and Gen. 16.14 (*Proclamation*, p. 62). In other words, the Greek word in Luke must be a translation of the Hebrew adjective.

(iii) Refreshing the Semitic original theory with a cautious attitude, Nolland cites Audet's argument that the phrase συλλαμβάνω ἐν γαστρί occurs in the works of Hippocrates three times[187] and represents a normal construction. He emphasizes, however, that this locution is a non-Septuagintalism. Nolland interprets Gen. 16.11, where 'the trio of conception, birth, and naming' appears, as similar to Lk. 1.31, since in both verses these three motives take place in an 'angel message'. Rejecting the view that Lk. 1.31 reflects Isa. 7.14, he argues that the wording of Lk. 1.31 is closest to that of Gen. 16.11 of the

---

185. 'L'expression plus formelle, plus élégante en grec, et chez lui habituelle' (*Luk I–II*, p. 70). For more information about the use of these two nouns, see below. Plummer argues for Luke's redaction or composition of 2.21 (*Luke*, p. 61). Sahlin, who claims that Luke translated a Hebrew source for the infancy narrative, suggests that 2.21 was written in Greek by Luke, not derived from Luke's Hebrew source (*Der Messias*, pp. 241–42). In contrast, Gaechter claims a Hebrew original for this verse. See Laurentin, *Luk I–II*, p. 70, nt. 3.

186. See also his commentary, *Luke 1:1–9:50*, p. 111.

187. This will be treated below in detail.

MT. In 1.26-38, he concludes, Luke relied on a written source most probably translated from a Hebrew original, though his substantial intervention makes this argument less conclusive (*Luke 1–9.20*, p. 43).[188] According to Nolland, then, the Lukan text in 1.31 depended on Gen. 16.11 of the MT.

(2) *The theory that Lk. 1.31 is dependent on the LXX*

(i) According to Marshall, the original reading of Isa. 7.14 was ἐν γαστρὶ λήμψεται. Text variation appears in this verse: while MS A contains ἕξει, BLC exhibits λήμψεται, which Marshall accepts. Both verbs are commonly used in the LXX. Marshall seems to assume that Luke could easily add the prefix συν to the future form of the verb in the LXX. He interprets Luke's locution as a conflation of the phrase ἐν γαστρὶ λήμψεται and 'the more usual LXX usage of συλλαμβάνω absolutely' (*Luke*, p. 66). In other words, Luke depended on Isa. 7.14 of the LXX but he changed the verb λαμβάνω to the compound verb συλλαμβάνω which is more commonly used for the meaning 'conceive' in the LXX.[189]

(ii) Pointing to the fact that the Hebrew adjective הרה was translated with both present and future tenses in the LXX, Fitzmyer argues that the future tense in Luke reflects the Septuagintal usage. While the Hebrew text includes only an adjective in all the possible alluded verses, the LXX has examples where it is translated with the future verb as in Isa. 7.14 or Judg. 13.3, 5[190] (*Luke I–IX*, pp. 346–47). H. Schürmann also notes that Lk. 1.31 depends on Isa. 7.14 of the LXX, since a Hebrew phrase הנך הרה corresponding to ἰδοὺ συλλήμψῃ does not necessarily indicate the near future. Thus, Luke's dependence on the Hebrew text is dubious.[191]

---

188. Nolland does not clearly suggest the Hebrew original theory in his comment on the section 1.26-38, but only mentions the possibility of a written source. Dealing with the source problem at the beginning of the section for 1.4–2.52, however, he notes that 'special attention has been directed to the source question in 1.5-25 and 1.26-38 and in these texts at least a strong case can be made for extended Hebrew documentary sources' (*Luke 1–9.20*, p. 22).
189. The verb συλλαμβάνω (22x) occurs in the LXX more frequently than the other two verbs, λαμβάνω (12x) and ἔχω (19x) for the meaning 'conceive'.
190. Text A includes this phrase while text B omits it in Judg. 13.3. In Judg. 13.5, text B has the present tense while text A includes the future tense for the verb.
191. H. Schürmann, *Das Lukasevangelium: Kommentar zu Kap. 1:1–9:50* (Herders Theologischer Kommentar Zum Neuen Testament, Freiburg/Basel/Wien: Herder, 1969), p. 46.

3. A Close Examination of the Greek of the Infancy Narrative

(C) *Evaluation of the Suggested Solutions*

(1) *Does the prepositional phrase appear in classical Greek?*

The view that the prepositional phrase represents an abnormal addition (Laurentin) has been discarded as it can be shown that the phrase συλλαμβάνω ἐν γαστρί itself is acceptable Greek. It occurs three times in Hippocrates:

Ὁκόσαι παρὰ φύσιν παχεῖαι ἐοῦσαι μὴ συλλαβάνουσιν ἐν γαστρί, ταύτῃσι τὸ ἐπίπλοον τὸ στόμα τῶν ὑστερέων ἀποπιέζει
when unnaturally fat women cannot conceive in womb, it is because the fat presses the mouth of the womb. (Aphorisms 5.46.2)[192]

γίνεται δὲ καὶ τοῦτο αἴτιον τοῦ μὴ συλλαμβάνειν ἐν γαστρί.
and even this is responsible for not conceiving in (one's) womb. (The Diseases of Women, III. 213.027)[193]

γυναῖκα θεραπεῦσαι, ὥστε ξυλλαβεῖν ἐν γαστρί.
to pay a woman's attention, so that she may conceive in her womb.[194]
(The Diseases of Women, I. 075.007)

Hence, it seems that there is no need to posit Semitic Vorlage.

(2) *Non-Septuagintal aspect of the phrase* συλλαμβάνω ἐν γαστρί

Scholars like Bock and Nolland emphasize the non-Septuagintal aspect of the phrase συλλαμβάνω ἐν γαστρί. While it is admitted that the use of the verb is non-Septuagintal, it needs to be examined whether the whole phrase reflects the Hebrew text or not. The mere absence of this construction in the LXX does not necessarily indicate the Lukan text's dependence on the Hebrew text. Positive evidence is required to prove a possible influence of a Hebrew construction which corresponds to the Greek of Luke.

(3) *The Lukan text's dependence on the LXX*

Concerning the theory of the Lukan text's dependence on the LXX, its advocates (Marshall, Fitzmyer, and Schürmann) tend to overlook the difference between the phrase in Luke and that in the LXX. Though Marshall tries to explain the difference, his explanation is insufficient. He

---

192. For the text of Aphorisms, see *Hippocrates*, vol. IV in The Loeb Classical Library. Concerning the meaning of ἐπίπλοον, it notes that the word 'means literally the fold of the peritoneum' (p. 171).
193. For the text of this and the last instance, see *Concordantia in Corpus Hippocraticum*, Tome V (eds. Gilles Maloney and Winnie Frohn; Hildesheim/Zürich/New York: Olms-Weidmann, 1986), pp. 4109–10. This concordance provides the sentence in which a word appears.
194. For details, see below.

needs to explain why Luke, if he consulted the LXX, employed συλλαμβάνω with the prepositional phrase, whereas it is always used without the prepositional phrase in the LXX.[195] Whereas it is accepted that the verb συλλαμβάνω (22x), as Marshall insists, occurs more frequently than the verb λαμβάνω (12x) in the LXX, the reason why Luke decided to change the verb must be clarified. With respect to the tense of the verb (Fitzmyer and Schürmann), the context probably provides a reason to adopt the future.

(D) *Another Proposal*

As for the whole phrase, most scholars do not pay attention to the fact that it is a possible non-Lukanism which may indicate the dependence of the Lukan text on a Greek source. That source could well be the LXX as the argument below will suggest.

(1) *The possibility of Luke's direct translation or composition: Is the phrase* συλλαμβάνω ἐν γαστρί *a non-Lukanism?*

Luke's use of the prepositional phrase ἐν γαστρί with the verb συλλαμβάνω may be classical as the construction συλλαμβάνω ἐν γαστρί occurs three times in Hippocrates. Thus, if Luke did use a Semitic source, or the Hebrew OT, he used a classical expression to translate the Hebrew phrase תהרי בקרבך or הרה.

(i)   *The verb* συλλαμβάνω

The verb συλλαμβάνω probably belongs to Lukanisms, since other verbs are not used to convey the meaning 'conceive' in the rest of Luke's corpus. It is true that the Gospel includes one example in 21.23 where one verb ἔχω occurs with the prepositional phrase ἐν γαστρί for this meaning. This verse, however, has parallels in Mk 13.17 and Mt. 24.19. Luke appears to have relied on his source, Mark or Matthew, for the verb ἔχω in this verse.[196] The only difference between the Gospel of Luke and the other two Gospels is found in the absence/presence of the conjunction δέ.[197] Thus, apart from this one verse, Luke did not use another verb for the meaning

---

195. G.M. Soares Prabhu notes that the verb συλλαμβάνω is Septuagintal, different from ἔχω, which is, in his view, more New Testament style than Septuagintal in the sense that ἔχω, found in the LXX less frequently than συλλαμβάνω, is the verb for the meaning 'conceive' in the New Testament outside of the Lukan infancy narrative (G.M. Soares Prabhu, *The Formula Quotations in the Infancy Narrative of Matthew* [Rome: Biblical Institute Press, 1976], p. 245).

196. Of course, this may not be the case; Luke could be the source for Mark and Matthew. At any rate, it is still possible that Luke depended on Mark or Matthew.

197. Lk. 21.23 οὐαὶ ταῖς ἐν γαστρὶ ἐχούσαις καὶ ταῖς θηλαζούσαις ἐν ἐκείναις ταῖς ἡμέραις:
Mk 13.17 οὐαὶ δὲ ταῖς ἐν γαστρὶ ἐχούσαις καὶ ταῖς θηλαζούσαις ἐν ἐκείναις ταῖς ἡμέραις.
Mt. 24.19 οὐαὶ δὲ ταῖς ἐν γαστρὶ ἐχούσαις καὶ ταῖς θηλαζούσαις ἐν ἐκείναις ταῖς ἡμέραις.

'conceive' outside of the infancy narrative. This makes it unclear whether the verb συλλαμβάνω in the Lukan infancy narrative is non-Lukan or Lukan. Lukan vocabulary for 'conceive' could well be συλλαμβάνω, but this cannot be proven. The verb itself, therefore, does not refute the possibility that Luke himself translated or composed the phrase.[198]

(ii) *The phrase* συλλαμβάνω ἐν γαστρί

The juxtaposition of the verb with the prepositional phrase ἐν γαστρί, however, is probably a non-Lukanism. Luke does not use γαστήρ but κοιλία for the meaning 'womb'. The noun γαστήρ occurs only once apart from in the present verse in the whole of Luke-Acts, in Lk. 21.23, where the prepositional phrase is accompanied by the verb ἔχω. But this verse has parallels in Mark and Matthew as explained above. Luke probably took over the phrase ἐν γαστρί with the verb ἔχω from Mark or Matthew. As a result, Luke himself did not use the noun γαστήρ for 'womb'. In contrast, the Greek noun κοιλία is frequently used for the same meaning in Luke-Acts (Lk. 1.15, 41-42, 44, 2.21; 11.27; 23.29;[199] Acts 3.2; 14.8). κοιλία appears twelve times in the rest of the NT apart from Luke-Acts (Mt. 12.40; 15.17; 19.12; Mk 7.19; Jn 3.4; 7.38; Rom. 16.18; 1 Cor. 6.13; Gal. 1.15; Phil. 3.19; Rev. 10.9-10). Of these twelve examples, the noun means 'womb' only in three instances (Mt. 19.12; Jn 3.4; Gal. 1.15). It denotes 'belly or stomach' in the other places. By contrast, it always denotes 'womb' in Luke-Acts. Luke, different from other NT authors, uses κοιλία only with the meaning 'womb'. These observations suggest that the noun γαστήρ is a non-Lukanism.[200]

A possible counter argument would be that Luke probably used the dative noun γαστρί with the preposition ἐν to denote 'in the womb' as the other NT authors did, but he employed the other noun κοιλία for all other

---

Luke inserted the sentence ἔσται γὰρ ἀνάγκη μεγάλη ἐπὶ τῆς γῆς καὶ ὀργὴ τῷ λαῷ τούτῳ in the last part, but the following verses in Mark and Matthew have a different content from Luke. Thus, only the first part of the Lukan text needs to be compared.

198. Plummer regards the verb συλλαμβάνω as a word peculiar to Luke on the grounds that the verb for the meaning 'conceive' occurs only in the Lukan infancy narrative in the NT (*Luke*, p. 19). He does not consider the possibility that Luke depended on the source for the verb in the story.

199. The last two examples do not have parallels in Mark or Matthew.

200. In classical Greek, ἐκ γαστρός, not ἐκ κοιλίας is used to denote 'from the womb, or from infancy' (Liddell and Scott, p. 339). In the LXX, ἐκ κοιλίας is used more frequently than ἐκ γαστρός. The former occurs fifteen times: with the genitive μητρός to indicate 'from the mother's womb' six times (Judg. 16.17 (A); Job 1.21, 38.8; Ps. 21.11; 70.6; Isa. 49.1) and without it three times (Job 10.18; Isa. 46.3; 48.8). The latter appears only eight times and three times with μητρός (Ps. 138.13; Job 31.18; *Sir.* 40.1).

instances. Other authors did not use ἐν (τῇ) κοιλίᾳ but ἐν γαστρί for that meaning: γαστήρ appears seven times in the NT apart from two instances in Luke (Mt. 1.18, 23; 24.19; Mk 13.17; 1 Thess 5.3; Tit. 1.12; Rev. 12.2), and all of them except for the instance in Titus are used idiomatically with the preposition ἐν to mean 'in the womb'.[201] Luke did not utilize ἐν κοιλίᾳ outside of the infancy narrative, while keeping ἐν γαστρί in Lk. 21.23, taking it over from Mk 21.23. Luke probably decided to keep the prepositional phrase in Lk. 21.23 because that was also his locution to express 'in the womb'. However, the phrase in Lk. 21.23, as pointed out above, appears to be from a source used by Luke (Mark, Matthew, or the common source for Matthew and Luke). The Lukan vocabulary for 'womb' is exclusively κοιλία outside of the infancy narrative. More importantly, ἐν τῇ κοιλίᾳ for the meaning 'in the womb' occurs three times in the Lukan infancy narrative itself (1.41, 44; 2.21). Especially in 2.21 (πρὸ τοῦ συλλημφθῆναι αὐτὸν ἐν τῇ κοιλίᾳ), this prepositional phrase, i.e., ἐν τῇ κοιλίᾳ, is used with the verb συλλαμβάνω. Luke appears to have utilized here the phrase ἐν τῇ κοιλίᾳ with the verb συλλαμβάνω, an awkward combination in Greek,[202] simply because his word for 'womb' was κοιλία. With these considerations, it is difficult to accept the claim that the Lukan expression for 'in the womb' was 'ἐν γαστρί'. It is clear at least that Luke himself is probably not the source of the phrase ἐν γαστρί. It follows that he has not translated a Semitic source (if there was one) himself.

(2) The source of the phrase

It has become clear that Luke himself was probably not the source of the phrase. This would mean that Luke depended on a Greek source for the phrase. What kind of source did Luke hold before himself, then? The composer of the source used by Luke may have translated the Hebrew text of Isa. 7.14 or Gen. 16.11. It is also probable that the Lukan text relied on the Greek OT of one of these two verses for the phrase. In this case, the following question must be answered: why is the verb συλλαμβάνω used instead of ἔχω?

(i)   *Translation of the Hebrew OT?*

It must be pointed out that the Hebrew Text does not have a corresponding construction for the prepositional phrase ἐν γαστρί in Gen. 16.11 and Isa. 7.14 as well as in other verses.[203] Scholars who argue for the translation theory tend to overlook this aspect, while emphasizing the use of a non-Septuagintal verb in Lk. 1.31. It is clear

---

201. In Tit. 1.12, the plural noun is used for the meaning 'glutton'.

202. The verb συλλαμβάνω is nowhere else in a Greek source accompanied by the prepositional phrase ἐν τῇ κοιλίᾳ.

203. In the LXX, ἐν γαστρί is used with two verbs – ἔχω and λαμβάνω – to denote 'conceive' 30 times. In these 30 instances, the Hebrew text includes only the adjective הרה (13x) or the verb ה-ר-ה

3. *A Close Examination of the Greek of the Infancy Narrative* 131

that the addition of the prepositional phrase indicates the influence of the LXX rather than the Hebrew OT.

(ii) *A different LXX?*
Luke's LXX may have employed the verb συλλαμβάνω with the prepositional phrase. While this possibility cannot be completely excluded, the use of the verb ἔχω in Mt. 1.23 (Ἰδοὺ ἡ παρθένος ἐν γαστρὶ ἕξει καὶ τέξεται υἱόν), a quotation of Isa. 7.14, makes it clear that Matthew's LXX of Isa. 7.14 has the verb ἔχω. It is also noteworthy that no variation of the LXX shows the verb συλλαμβάνω with the prepositional phrase in the examples which include ἔχω or λαμβάνω with ἐν γαστρί.[204] These considerations make it less probable that Luke's LXX contained the construction συλλαμβάνω ἐν γαστρί.

(iii) *Did Luke change the verb in the LXX?*
The following points seem to make it less probable for Luke to have altered the verb ἔχω in the LXX to συλλαμβάνω: (a) Luke, who never used the noun γαστήρ for the meaning 'womb' except in Lk. 21.23, adopted it in Lk. 1.31 from the LXX, if he depended on the LXX, though his word for 'womb' is κοιλία which appears five times even in the story. If he did not change γαστήρ into κοιλία, we must ask why he would change the verb into συλλαμβάνω. (b) More important, as shown above, is that Luke did not change the verb ἔχω in 21.23 where he appears to have relied on Mark or Matthew. Thus, it seems less probable that Luke altered ἔχω τὸ συλλαμβάνω while depending on the LXX for the adoption of the prepositional phrase ἐν γαστρί.

Nevertheless, it is possible for Luke, consulting the LXX, to have changed the verb. Possible quoted verses, Gen. 16.11 and Isa. 7.14, contain the construction ἔχω + ἐν γαστρί. As explained above, the prepositional phrase ἐν γαστρί is a non-Lukanism which indicates Luke's dependence on a Greek source. Interestingly, two possible alluded verses of the LXX include the prepositional phrase ἐν γαστρί which does not appear in the Hebrew text of Gen. 16.11 or Isa. 7.14. This may imply that Luke's Greek source was the LXX.[205]

(12x) or יהם (only once in Gen. 30.41) without exception (in four instances, there is no corresponding Hebrew word: Exod. 2.22; Job 21.10; Amos 1.3; Isa. 40.11). In contrast, if the LXX uses ἔχω or λαμβάνω, it is always accompanied with the prepositional phrase ἐν γαστρί.

204. The Sistine version of the LXX (1587) contains συνέλαβεν ἐν γαστρί in Gen. 25.21 in which all the other variations include ἔλαβεν ἐν γαστρί. It seems that the variation was influenced by Lk. 1.31. See Laurentin, *Luk I–II*, p. 68, nt. 4.

205. As Schürmann and Fitzmyer insist, the future tense of the verb συλλαμβάνω may indicate the influence of the LXX of Isa. 7.14, though it could not be a strong argument. See the section 'Evaluation of the Suggested Solutions'.

(iv) *Why did Luke alter the verb ἔχω to συλλαμβάνω?*
In order to demonstrate that the whole phrase συλλήμψῃ ἐν γαστρί has been derived from the LXX of Gen. 16.11 or Isa. 7.4, the question of why Luke changed the verb ἔχω in these verses to the verb συλλαμβάνω needs to be answered. If Luke or the composer had translated the Hebrew text of the OT, he could have used only the verb συλλαμβάνω as in 1.24. Three alternatives emerge: 1) Luke probably altered the verb ἔχω in the LXX to συλλαμβάνω since the latter was the verb for the meaning 'conceive' in his sources for the infancy narrative (1.24, 36; 2.21); 2) he did so since the verb was his own vocabulary for 'conceive'; 3) the composer of the source used by Luke changed ἔχω to συλλαμβάνω because the latter was the correct word for the meaning 'conceive' to him. The second alternative represents the least probable given that Luke did not change the verb ἔχω in Lk. 21.23. Without special reason, Luke would have kept ἔχω. It seems that the third alternative is most probable. However, it is also probable for Luke, consulting the LXX, to have been influenced by his source. The repeated occurrence of the verb συλλαμβάνω in his Greek source before and after 1.31 (1.24, 36), may have caused Luke to change the verb in the LXX.[206]

In conclusion, if the Lukan text in 1.31 relied on the OT, the Bible was more probably the LXX than the Hebrew text as the Hebrew text, in contrast to the LXX, has no prepositional phrase. The verb συλλαμβάνω was adopted since it was the verb for the meaning 'conceive' in the infancy narrative.

Finally, the author of the Lukan infancy narrative appears to have relied on the LXX for allusions. The instances which scholars believe support the translation theory indicate in reality that they derived from the LXX rather than the Hebrew OT. A partial investigation seems to support the dependence of allusions in the infancy narrative on the Hebrew OT, but the examination from the whole perspective lends support to the dependence of the allusions on the LXX.

C. *Phraseology*

The preceding section has dealt with quotations and allusions, a study which is important in examining whether the Lukan infancy story is a translation of Semitic sources or a direct composition dependent on the

---

206. If Luke depended on the LXX versions which include λήμψεται in Isa. 7.14, he could change the verb more easily by adding the prefix συν to it.

3. *A Close Examination of the Greek of the Infancy Narrative* 133

LXX.[207] Now this section will treat phrases and expressions which some scholars have suggested indicate an underlying Semitic source. The study of such phrases and expressions therefore also constitutes an important part of our investigation. It is true, of course, that one can hardly separate the search for phraseology from that for allusions. For allusions usually echo phrases and expressions of the OT and most of the locutions which shall receive attention in this section of the investigation also reflect OT expressions. However, a clear difference may be recognized between these two categories; while expressions in allusions stem from one or two, or at most several fixed OT verses, those for the study of phraseology do not stem from fixed OT verses. As a result, the search for allusions focuses on comparing expressions in the infancy story with those in some specific OT verses, whereas the study of phraseology focuses on scrutinizing such locutions by looking at their usage in the OT in general. This consideration justifies dealing with phraseology separately from allusion.

There is a consensus among scholars that the infancy narrative includes expressions (words and phrases) which indicate the influence of a Semitic language, i.e., Hebrew.[208] There are two main explanations for this influence. The first is that the Lukan infancy narrative is the translation of a Semitic original;[209] in this case, the influence of Hebrew on Luke's Greek would be direct.[210] The second explanation is that such constructions only

207. As noted in the section 'Quotations', if the Lukan infancy narrative depends on the LXX for quotations and allusions, it is less possible for the writer to have translated a Semitic source.
208. Some scholars like Zimmerman argue for an Aramaic original. However, most scholars, especially recent scholars claim that the Semitisms in the infancy narrative are not Aramaisms but Hebraisms [for details, see Chapter 1, B]. Thus, this study will mention only Hebrew without including Aramaic when Semitic languages need to be mentioned.
209. The Semitic source theory presupposes that there was a pre-Lukan Semitic source and that it was translated either by Luke himself or by an unknown person before him.
210. For the detailed argument, see Sahlin's *Der Messias und das Gottesvolk*, p. 70, where he declares that 'die Phraseologie ist idiomatisch hebräisch'. 'Dies erklärt sich leichter,' he continues, 'durch die Annahme, *Proto*-Lukas habe den Satz idiomatisch hebräisch abgefasst, als etwa dadurch, dass *Lukas* den LXX – Stil imitiert hätte – und an dieser Stelle gleichwohl dem hebräischen Grundtext näher als der LXX gekommen sei.' Nolland also provides many locutions which he believes support the existence of a Semitic original in his commentary *Luke 1–9:20*, pp. 13–135. Laurentin and Winter must also be added to this list. Concerning Winter's contribution to the search for original sources, Nolland claims that Winter's argument for a Hebrew original remains 'essentially unanswered' (*Luke 1–9.20*, p. 22). Winter discusses the following constructions: προβεβηκότες ἐν ταῖς ἡμέραις in 1.7; καρδίας πατέρων ἐπὶ τέκνα in 1.17; παρὰ τοῦ θεοῦ in 1.37 Ἐποίησεν κράτος ἐν βραχίονι αὐτοῦ in 1.51; ἀγραυλοῦντες in 2.8; πλῆθος στρατιᾶς οὐρανίου in 2.13. He also deals with the use of the noun κύριος and the parallelism of the Hebrew original in 1.13. For his argument, see his article 'Some Observations on the Language in the Birth and Infancy Stories of the Third Gospel', *NTS*, 1 (1954–55), pp. 111–21. The examples in 1.17 and 1.37 have been discussed in the preceding section 'Quotations and Allusions'. Some of the remaining instances will be treated below.

point to the influence of the LXX, which means that the influence of Hebrew on Luke's Greek is indirect, mediated by the LXX.[211] The first explanation involves the use of a Semitic original, while the second an imitation of the Greek of the LXX. It is not necessary here to reiterate general arguments by the proponents of the Semitic original theory on the one side and by the advocates of the LXX imitation theory on the other.[212] As pointed out in Chapter 2.1.B, 'The definition of Semitisms and Septuagintalisms', the emphasis has to be laid not on the side of the Semitic language (Hebrew) but on the side of Greek in explaining this phenomenon. That is, the starting point of the investigation into phrases and expressions has to be the Greek, not the supposed Hebrew underlying it. This requires that we define Semitisms precisely, as we have above, and that we distinguish between a Semitism and a Septuagintalism. According to our definition, all the constructions that are found in the LXX, even if only in a few places, are to be counted as 'Septuagintalisms' rather than as 'Semitisms'. That means in investigating phraseology we have to determine first whether a phrase is a Septuagintalism before we can conclude that it is a Semitism. If it is the former, it is not the latter by our definition.

While the debate on Septuagintal expressions is rather simple, a more complicated argument arises concerning so-called 'non-Septuagintal expressions', expressions which do not exactly follow LXX style but come close.[213] The proponents of the translation theory tend to interpret such expressions as refuting the imitation theory and supporting the translation theory. They assume that if a Greek locution does not exactly follow LXX style and seems to echo Hebrew style, the locution is a translation of the Hebrew text.[214] The possibility that the writer composed the construction directly in Greek must be considered first, however. Here its possible occurrence in other Greek literature has to be investigated. One needs also to consider whether the locution reflects a Semitic construction in an absolute sense. Otherwise, one could count some seemingly non-Septuagintal but good Greek locutions as

---

211. From Dalman, Harnack, and Moulton to Turner early this century, Fitzmyer, Brown, and many others more recently.

212. See section B of Chapter 1, 'A Survey of Scholarly Views on the Greek of the Lukan Infancy Narrative'.

213. In order to resolve this problem, some scholars like O'Fearghail introduce the concept 'the Septuagintal-type expressions', which are similar to the LXX locutions but not exactly identical to them. We prefer to call them 'non-Septuagintal expressions' unless it is explained that they reflect expressions in the LXX. For details, see section B of Chapter 1, 'A Survey of Scholarly Views on the Greek of the Lukan Infancy Narrative'.

214. One of the main arguments of the translation theory is that if a Greek locution, being a non-Septuagintalism, represents a natural translation from the Hebrew original, it is a translation. The emphasis is thereby placed on the Semitic language.

3. A Close Examination of the Greek of the Infancy Narrative 135

Semitisms.[215] It is also necessary to examine whether seemingly non-Septuagintal constructions are variations of Septuagintal expressions. Here again, seemingly non-Septuagintal expressions which have been used to support the translation theory may actually belong to normal Greek usage to the extent that they are attested in classical and Hellenistic Greek and their deviation from the LXX is thus explained.[216] Possible composition procedures for such constructions will be suggested below in order to show how they were composed directly in Greek. In order to clarify the procedure as much as possible, this study will investigate whether those expressions are Lukan or non-Lukan. Non-Lukanisms[217] most probably do not stem directly from Luke's hand and indicate Luke's dependence on Greek sources.[218]

It is impossible and unnecessary to deal with all the constructions which scholars have suggested as indicating the influence of a Hebrew original. It will suffice to treat some important examples.[219]

I. *Constructions in Lk. 1.5*

Lk. 1.5 Ἐγένετο ἐν ταῖς ἡμέραις Ἡρῴδου βασιλέως τῆς Ἰουδαίας ἱερεύς τις ὀνόματι Ζαχαρίας ἐξ ἐφημερίας Ἀβιά,[220] καὶ γυνὴ αὐτῷ ἐκ τῶν θυγατέρων Ἀαρὼν καὶ τὸ ὄνομα αὐτῆς Ἐλισάβετ.

In the days of Herod the king of Judah, there was a certain priest named Zechariah, of the division of Abia, and his wife (was) of the daughters of Aaron and her name was Elizabeth.

---

215. For some phrases, the translation theory assumes that the author of the infancy narrative translated Hebrew constructions with more idiomatic Greek locutions than LXX Greek locutions. For examples, see below.

216. With regard to the term 'imitation', it has to be pointed out that the imitation theory does not mean that the writer imitates the LXX style for every word and every sentence. In this sense, the imitation theory must be understood as the 'pastiche' theory. See Chapter 1.B.

217. For the definition of non-Lukanisms, see Chapter 2.B.

218. It is possible to assume that Luke, not following his own style, perhaps imitated LXX style for non-Lukan locutions. This may be the case only when it is not clear if some expressions belong to Lukanisms. In most cases, however, this is less probable except for the examples where Luke directly depended on the LXX as in the case of quotations and allusions.

219. 'Important examples' are those phrases which some scholars believe can only be explained as translations from a Hebrew source. Also included are examples which have been treated by other scholars, but insufficiently and ineffectively.

220. Jeremias regards the construction of the so-called anarthrous genitive, like ἐξ ἐφημερίας Ἀβιά, as reflecting the LXX. In other words, such construction stemmed from the LXX. He affirms that 'wir es nicht mit alltäglicher Sprache, sondern mit einer biblizistischen Konstruktion zu tun haben' (*Die Sprache*, p. 20).

136   *The Original Language of the Lukan Infancy Narrative*

We will focus our attention on the following:

1. Ἐγένετο ἐν ταῖς ἡμέραις Ἡρῴδου βασιλέως τῆς Ἰουδαίας ἱερεύς τις
2. (ἱερεύς τις) ὀνόματι Ζαχαρίας
3. καὶ τὸ ὄνομα αὐτῆς Ἐλισάβετ

1. *Remarks on* Ἐγένετο ἐν ταῖς ἡμέραις Ἡρῴδου βασιλέως τῆς Ἰουδαίας ἱερεύς[221]

(A) *The Problem and Suggestions*

The issue revolves around how the verb ἐγένετο is to be translated, and whether or not it is a Semitism or a Septuagintalism. There are two possible translations:

a. 'It happened (that) in the days of Herod the king of Judea, (there was) a certain priest …' In this translation, ἐγένετο is an impersonal expression: the verb (ἦν) is assumed or must be supplied between Ἰουδαίας and ἱερεύς.
b. 'There was a certain priest in the days of Herod the king of Judea ….' In this case, ἐγένετο is the main verb (= was) and ἱερεύς is the subject.

Scholars agree that the phrase ἐγένετο ἐν ταῖς ἡμέραις Ἡρῴδου βασιλέως τῆς Ἰουδαίας (ἱερεύς τις) betrays Semitic features. However, they disagree in explaining the reason why these features occur. Some scholars suggest that they betray the direct influence of the Hebrew OT on Luke's Greek. Others argue that the phrase ἐγένετο ἐν ταῖς ἡμέραις Ἡρῴδου βασιλέως τῆς Ἰουδαίας is reminiscent of the style of the LXX. The debate centres on the verb ἐγένετο and the following phrase ἐν ταῖς ἡμέραις + anarthrous modifying genitives.

(1) *Views that argue for direct Semitic influence*

(i) Plummer contends that ἐγένετο, alongside ἐν ταῖς ἡμέραις, is Hebraistic (*Luke*, p. 7). He notes that it is not necessary to suppose the imperfect form of εἰμί (ἦν) or another verb to be implied so that the sentence may mean 'it happened that there was–'. The verb, according to him, simply means 'there was'.
(ii) Brown regards the phrase ἐν ταῖς ἡμέραις Ἡρῴδου βασιλέως τῆς Ἰουδαίας as 'a semitized Greek expression'[222] except for the article

---

221. Evans notes that the expression ἐν ταῖς ἡμέραις Ἡρῴδου βασιλέως τῆς Ἰουδαίας is non-Lukan, since Luke usually suggests a specific year as in Lk. 2.1-3 and 3.1-2. In contrast, Fitzmyer remarks that 'the vague dating used here is probably derived by Luke from a characteristic OT expression; see *Tob.* 1.16; *Jdt.* 1.1; cf. 2 Chron. 14.1' (*Luke I–IX*, p. 322). The vague dating seems to stem from the LXX.

222. He does not explicitly state that the expression is derived from a Semitic original. He also does not mention that it occurs in the LXX. In contrast, he frequently notes concerning

3. *A Close Examination of the Greek of the Infancy Narrative*   137

before βασιλέως[223] and Ἰουδαίας (*The Birth of the Messiah*, p. 257),[224] though he does not take the aorist verb ἐγένετο into account.[225]

(iii) Following Brown, Nolland comments that all the elements in the phrase including ἐγένετο are Semitisms (*Luke 1–9.20*, p. 25). While recognizing the possible influence of the LXX,[226] Nolland still emphasizes the Semitic aspect of the phrase by saying that 'only Luke's definite article before Ἰουδαίας "Judah" is not Semitic.'[227] He assumes that an imperfect form of the verb εἰμι is implied, in contrast to Plummer, and he translates the sentence as follows: 'it happened that in the days of Herod, king of Judea, there was a certain priest ...' Interpreting ἐγένετο as 'it happened (that)', which he thinks may render Hebrew יהי, he includes it in the category of Semitisms.

(2) *Views that consider the LXX as the source of the constructions*

(i) Marshall notes that 'Luke's style changes abruptly from that of the preface to one strongly reminiscent of the LXX' and suggests Judg. 13.2 of the LXX as having a similar form to the whole of this verse (*Luke*, p. 51). Translating ἐγένετο as 'there was', he suggests that the verb is used for the same meaning in Lk. 4.36 and Jn 1.6.

(ii) Concerning the opening phrase ἐν ταῖς ἡμέραις Ἡρῴδου βασιλέως τῆς Ἰουδαίας, O'Fearghail claims that Luke consulted Jeremiah, Amos and others of the LXX for it ('The Imitation of the Septuagint', p. 61). Bock also remarks that the phrase is reminiscent of LXX style and ethos (*Luke 1.1–9.20*, p. 75).

---

other expressions that they are good LXX Greek or that they appear in the LXX. For his position toward Semitisms in the Lukan infancy narrative, see Chapter 1.2.B, 'The Imitation Theory'.

223. Brown accepts the text supported by ACD have Θ, where the noun 'king' is preceded by the article.

224. The article before Ἰουδαίας, according to Brown, represents 'a classical touch'. While his statement is possibly true, it needs to be pointed out that all the examples in the NT include the article before the noun. Moreover, a better explanation could be found by attributing it to the influence of the LXX where the noun is always accompanied by the article as well.

225. He seems to accept the translation 'there was' for this verb, which probably causes him to exclude the verb from the category of Semitisms. His position is accurate, if this is the case. For a detailed discussion on the use of the verb, see below.

226. He points to the LXX of Jer. 1. 2-3 to indicate the possible influence of the OT in setting the background of Luke in the period of the kings of Judah.

227. The text of NA[27] is accepted by Nolland. See above nt. 223 and 224.

(B) Evaluation of the Suggestions

(1) ἐν ταῖς ἡμέραις *and the omission of the article*

According to our definition, any phrase that appears in the LXX must be included in the category of Septuagintalisms. The phrase ἐν ταῖς ἡμέραις and the omission of the article in the phrase Ἡρῴδου βασιλέως are well attested in the LXX. Jeremiah and Amos have the same expression:

Jer. 1.3: καὶ ἐγένετο ἐν ταῖς ἡμέραις Ἰωακίμ υἱοῦ Ἰωσία βασιλέως Ἰούδα;[228]

Amos 1.1: ἐν ἡμέραις Ὀζίου βασιλέως Ἰούδα καὶ ἐν ἡμέραις Ἱεροβοαμ τοῦ Ἰωας βασιλέως Ἰσραήλ.

As a result, these features are to be classified as Septuagintalisms.[229]

(2) *The use of the verb*

Concerning Nolland's suggestion that ἐγένετο means 'it happened (that)', it is possible that the imperfect verb ἦν is implied somewhere in the sentence, most probably between Ἰουδαίας and ἱερεύς. This insertion, however, is not necessary because the sentence makes a good sense without ἦν, if ἐγένετο is interpreted as indicating 'there was'. In addition, the omission of the imperfect verb ἦν in this construction, i.e., 'ἐγένετο δὲ or καὶ ἐγένετο', is not attested in the NT[230] nor in the LXX where the Greek conjunction reflects the Hebrew original.[231] Moreover, in all the examples of the NT as well as the LXX, the conjunction καί or δέ is used before and after ἐγένετο for this construction, even in the very first verse of a book

---

228. The apparent similarity of the verb usage in Jer. 1.3 to that in Lk. 1.5 is denied by the fact that the meaning of the verb is different in each verse. While the verb means '(a word) came or happened' in Jeremiah, it denotes 'there lived (somebody)' in Luke. In addition, Jer. 1.3 is not the first sentence of a story and thus includes the conjunction before the verb. For the precise meaning of the verb in Lk. 1.5, see below.

229. The presence of the article in ἐν ταῖς ἡμέραις does not reflect the corresponding Hebrew phrase which does not involve the article. This probably is from Luke's hand, as he always uses the article except for two examples in the infancy narrative (1.25; 2.36), while other Evangelists omit it twice (Mt. 2.1; 1 Pet. 3.20).

230. Outside of Luke-Acts, there are only nine examples of this construction in the whole NT: Mt. 7.28; 9.10; 11.1; 13.53; 19.1; 26.1; Mk 1.9; 2.23; 4.4. In all the examples in Matthew, the same expression appears except in 9.10: καὶ ἐγένετο ὅτε ἐτέλεσεν ὁ Ἰησοῦς.

231. Fitzmyer suggests that εἰμί needs to be supplied in Lk. 9.29 (*Luke I-IX*, p. 119). However, ἐγένετο means 'became' here (see Marshall, *Luke*, p. 383, and Nolland, *Luke 9.21–18.34*, p. 498). Another possible example is found in Lk. 5.12 where καὶ ἰδού appears: Καὶ ἐγένετο ἐν τῷ εἶναι αὐτὸν ἐν μιᾷ τῶν πόλεων καὶ ἰδοὺ ἀνὴρ πλήρης λέπρας. In this case, however, the verb must be supplied because a καὶ ἰδού clause is connected with καὶ ἐγένετο. In addition, καὶ ἰδού is used with the sense 'there is' in Luke-Acts: Lk. 7.37; 11.31; 13.11; 19.2; 23.50; Acts 8.27 (Fitzmyer, *Luke I-IX*, p. 574). See Judg. 19.1, where εἰμί appears with the conjunction: καὶ ἐγένετο ἐν ταῖς ἡμέραις ἐκείναις καὶ οὐκ ἦν βασιλεὺς ἐν Ἰσραήλ.

3. A Close Examination of the Greek of the Infancy Narrative 139

(Judg. 1.1; Josh. 1.1; 2 Sam. 1.1).²³² The aorist verb ἐγένετο, thus, has to be interpreted as indicating 'there was or appeared' rather than 'it happened (that)'. Most importantly, even if the construction means 'it happened (that)', it belongs to 'hard core Septuagintalisms'.²³³

Plummer's assertion that ἐγένετο, even though it means 'there was', is Hebraistic is not sufficiently supported. He does not elucidate the reason why the verb must be Hebraistic if it does not mean 'it happened' but 'there was'.²³⁴

In sum, the use of the verb needs to be closely examined in order to decide whether it indicates the direct influence of the Hebrew language.

(C) *A detailed Suggestion with respect to the Construction,* γίνομαι *with the personal Subject*

(1) *Does this verb usage appear in non-Biblical Greek?*

γίνομαι primarily means 'come into being', 'come to be', 'happen', or 'originate' (Liddell and Scott, p. 349; BAGD, p. 158). It means in Lk. 1.5 'appear', 'exist', 'there is', or 'there lives' with the nominative which is the subject (BAGD, p. 160). This usage of the verb γίνομαι with the personal subject to indicate 'there appears (somebody)', 'there lives (somebody)', or 'there is (somebody)' does not appear in classical Greek. A classical author would employ the verb εἰμί.²³⁵ Does this verb usage appear in non-Biblical Hellenistic Greek? With regard to the aorist verb ἐγένετο in Lk. 1.5, Bovon, following Lagrange,²³⁶ notes that ἐγένετο is not used with the personal subject in Greek.²³⁷ A search of the TLG database brought no example of this construction, i.e., the aorist verb ἐγένετο with the personal subject, to light in non-Biblical Greek literature. However, other forms of the verb γίνομαι appear with the personal subject in Hellenistic Greek. This usage is attested in Hellenistic authors like Diodorus Siculus (3.52.4: γέγονε μὲν οὖν

---

232. In Luke-Acts, the construction is usually used at the beginning of a story. See Lk. 1.59; 2.1,15; 5.1,12,17; 7.11; 8.1, 22; 9.18, 28, 37, 51; 11.1,14, 27; 14.1; 17.11; 18.35; 19.29; 20.1; Acts 5.7; 9.19.

233. The Hebrew construction includes the conjunction before the finite verb while the LXX omits it occasionally. For details, see the next section.

234. For its use in Hellenistic Greek, see below. Cf. Brown's position above in nt. 225.

235. The verb γίνομαι is used to denote 'be' in classical literature, but it is accompanied by the genitive or dative noun or prepositional phrase, not by the nominative noun (Liddell and Scott, pp. 349–50).

236. M.-J. Lagrange, *Évangile selon Saint Luk* (Paris: Gabalda, 2nd edn 1927), p. 8. He notes that 'ἐγένετο avec une personne n'existe probablement pas en grec où l'on dirait ἦν.'

237. 'ἐγένετο mit persönlichen Subjekt ist niet griechisch' (*Das Evangelium nach Lukas [Lk 1,1–9,50]*, p. 52).

πλείω γένη γυναικῶν: there have been a number of races of women),[238] according to BAGD (p. 160).[239] Josephus also uses the verb γίνομαι with the same meaning in *Ant.* 18.63, where Josephus makes use of the historical present in place of the aorist ἐγένετο:

γίνεται δὲ κατὰ τοῦτον τὸν χρόνους Ἰησοῦς σοφὸς ἀνήρ[240]
and around this time there appears (appeared) Jesus a wise man.

The personal subject, Ἰησοῦς, is utilized here and the historical present is used to describe more vividly what happened in the past. This construction occurs also in the NT: Mk 1.4; Jn 1.6; 1 Jn 2.18; 2 Pet. 2.1; Rev. 16.18 (BAGD, p. 160). The verb usage, thus, belongs to Hellenistic Greek. Luke himself might have used the verb to denote 'there is' or 'there appears', as do other Hellenistic authors. Nevertheless, we need to examine if this usage is Lukan in order to confirm this possibility.

(2) *Is the verb usage Lukan?*

The present and aorist forms of the verb γίνομαι appear in Luke-Acts, but the question is whether their meaning is identical to that in Lk. 1.5 and whether another verb is used in Lk. 3–24 and Acts for the meaning of the verb in Lk. 1.5, 'there is', 'there live', or 'there exists'.

(i) *The use of the present form* γίνομαι

The present form of the verb γίνομαι, mainly in non-indicative moods, occurs in Luke-Acts, but the meaning is always 'become' except in Lk. 15.10:

οὕτως, λέγω ὑμῖν, γίνεται χαρὰ ἐνώπιον τῶν ἀγγέλων τοῦ θεοῦ ἐπὶ ἑνὶ ἁμαρτωλῷ μετανοοῦντι.

In this way, I tell you, there is joy [joy occurs] in the presence of the angels of God in the case of one sinner who repents.

The precise meaning of the verb, however, is 'occur or happen' (BAGD, p. 159) and the subject is not a person.[241] The usage of the verb in this verse, therefore, is different from that in Lk. 1.5.

---

238. BAGD shows only the core part of the sentence and its translation: γέγονε γένη γυναικῶν, 'there have been nations of women'. Of course, the basic idea of the original text is well demonstrated in this sentence.

239. In *Appianus. Maced.* 18.3, according to BAGD, the verb means 'exist': τὸ χρυσίον τὸ γιγνόμενον, 'the gold that was at hand'. In the context, however, the verb could mean 'come': 'the gold that was coming (into him)'.

240. In this context, he emphasizes the appearance of Jesus from the historical horizon. Josephus employs the verb εἰμί to mean 'there is' in other places.

241. 'γίνομαι something ἐπί someone' is an idiomatic expression which means 'something happens in the case of or to a person' (BAGD, p. 159).

3. *A Close Examination of the Greek of the Infancy Narrative* 141

The aorist form ἐγένετο

The aorist verb ἐγένετο occurs in 202 places in the whole NT, of which Luke-Acts includes 122 examples. Such a high number partly derives from the overuse of the construction (καὶ) ἐγένετο (δέ), which is found 58 times in Luke-Acts.[242] Even after these 58 examples in Luke-Acts are excluded, however, its frequency is still high in Luke's corpus compared to the rest of the NT: it takes place 64 times in Luke-Acts and 80 times in the whole of the remaining NT.

Of 64 instances, Luke-Acts includes some examples which seem to support the use of the aorist verb ἐγένετο to denote 'there was' or 'there appeared':

Lk. 4.36: καὶ ἐγένετο θάμβος ἐπὶ πάντας
and amazement was on all of them,[243] (and amazement happened to all of them)

Acts 8.8: ἐγένετο δὲ πολλὴ χαρὰ ἐν τῇ πόλει ἐκείνῃ
and there was a great joy in that city (and a great joy occurred in that city).

Acts 16.26: ἄφνω δὲ σεισμὸς ἐγένετο μέγας.
'and suddenly there was a great earthquake' (and suddenly a great earthquake happened).

The precise meaning of the aorist verb ἐγένετο in the above examples, however, is not 'there was', but 'happened', or 'occurred', as the bracketed translations suggest. The verb emphasizes the happening of something rather than its existence as in Lk. 1.5. Moreover, the subject is not a person but a thing in these examples. It is clear that Luke does not utilize the aorist verb ἐγένετο except for Lk. 1.5 to indicate 'there was somebody (or something)' or 'somebody (or something) existed' in his Gospel and Acts.

The use of the verb εἰμί

Further, Luke employs a form of the verb εἰμί (usually the imperfect ἦν) in order to express 'there is (was)' or 'there lives (lived)' in his Gospel:[244]

---

242. This construction is followed by 1) infinitive (Luke 5x, Acts 17x); 2) finite verb (Luke 22x); 3) καί + finite verb (Luke 12x; Acts 2x). The statistics are based on Fitzmyer. See Moulton, who suggests that the number of the construction is 55. The difference between Fitzmyer and Moulton happens because Moulton does not include one example in Luke (9.28) and two examples in Acts (5.7; 9.19) for category 3). For details, see Moulton, *A Grammar of New Testament Greek*, vol. I; *Prolegomena*, p. 16.

243. Marshall suggests that Lk. 4.36 is an example where the verb means 'there is' (*Luke*, p. 51). For the precise meaning of the verb in Lk. 4.36, see the translation in brackets. Marshall also points to John 1.6 which will be dealt with later.

244. All the first four examples in Luke have parallels in Mark and the verb is always placed before the subject in both Gospels. The position of the verb probably indicates the

4.33 – καὶ ἐν τῇ συναγωγῇ ἦν ἄνθρωπος[245]

6.6 – καὶ ἦν ἄνθρωπος ἐκεῖ[246]

8.32 – Ἦν δὲ ἐκεῖ ἀγέλη χοίρων[247]

9.27 – εἰσίν τινες τῶν αὐτοῦ ἑστηκότων[248]

16.1 – <u>Ἄνθρωπός τις ἦν</u> πλούσιος

16.19 – <u>Ἄνθρωπος δέ τις ἦν</u> πλούσιος

16.20 – <u>πτωχὸς δέ τις ἦν ὀνόματι</u> Λάζαρος ὃς ἐβέβλητο[249]

18.2 – <u>Κριτής τις ἦν</u> ἔν τινι πόλει

18.3 – χήρα δὲ ἦν ἐν τῇ πόλει ἐκείνῃ

18.29 – οὐδείς ἐστιν ὃς ἀφῆκεν οἰκίαν

Underlined instances in the listed verses call for our attention,[250] as they display similar expressions to Lk. 1.5: noun + indefinite pronoun τις + ἦν with the meaning 'there was (lived) a certain man (or disciple, widow …)'.[251] In Lk. 16.20, the dative noun ὀνόματι appears as in Lk. 1.5.[252] Only in 8.32, does the imperfect verb[253] mean 'there was (is) something'.[254] In all

---

influence of Hebrew in which the verb frequently occurs before both the subject and object. However, this does not necessarily point to the direct Semitic influence as the LXX also includes examples for this word order (for similar examples to this word order with the imperfect verb ἦν see Exod. 2.1 and *2 Macc.* 4.13). For a detailed discussion on the word order in the NT, see N. Turner, *A Grammar of New Testament Greek*, vol. IV; *Style* (Edinburgh: T. & T. Clark, 1976), pp. 17–19.

245. The parallel in Mk 1.23 contains the same verb form ἦν.
246. The parallel in Mk 3.1 shows the same verb form ἦν.
247. The parallels in Mk 5.11 and Mt. 8.30 include ἦν.
248. The parallels in Mk 9.1 and Mt. 16.28 contain εἰσίν.
249. Variations A P W Θ include the verb εἰμί between τις and ὀνόματι and the relative pronoun ὅς between Λάζαρος and ἐβέβλητο, while P_{75} ℵ B D L Ψ do not contain the verb and the pronoun.
250. See also underlined instances in Acts below.
251. This word order, i.e., noun + τις + ἦν appears in the LXX (*Wis.* 7.16) and without the pronoun τις in Job 1.1.
252. This construction occurs also in Acts 9.10, 36; 16.1. For the detailed study on the noun ὀνόματι, see below.
253. Only in 9.27, 18.29, the verb tense is present.
254. This usage probably derived from Mark, Matthew, or the common source for Matthew and Luke.

the rest of the instances, it denotes 'there was somebody'. In 16.1, 16.19,[255] and 18.2,3, ἦν is used at the beginning of parables to indicate 'there lived, or there was'. The infancy narrative also includes examples for 'there is' in 1.61 (Οὐδείς ἐστιν ἐκ τῆς συγγενείας σου), and 'there was (lived)' in 2.25 (Καὶ ἰδοὺ ἄνθρωπος ἦν ἐν Ἰερουσαλήμ) and 2.36 (Καὶ ἦν Ἄννα προφῆτις).

Because the first four instances, i.e., 4.33, 6.6, 8.32, 9.27, have parallels in Mark and/or Matthew, they do not necessarily represent Lukan style. Although the remaining six examples do not have parallels in Mark or Matthew, this does not necessarily mean that the expressions in these examples present Lukan style, since they probably reflect the Greek style of the source peculiar to Luke. However, these six examples may be interpreted as reflecting the style of Luke, if we find some examples in the book of Acts, especially in the second part of the book, i.e., chs 16–28.

In Acts, the imperfect form of the verb εἰμί is used to indicate 'there was somebody':

4.34 – οὐδὲ γὰρ ἐνδεής τις ἦν ἐν αὐτοῖς·

9.10 – Ἦν δέ τις μαθητὴς ἐν Δαμασκῷ ὀνόματι Ἀνανίας

9.36 – Ἐν Ἰόππῃ δέ τις ἦν μαθήτρια ὀνόματι Ταβιθά

13.1 – Ἦσαν δὲ ἐν Ἀντιοχείᾳ κατὰ τὴν οὖσαν ἐκκλησίαν προφῆται καὶ διδάσκαλοι

16.1 – καὶ ἰδοὺ μαθητής τις ἦν ἐκεῖ ὀνόματι Τιμόθεος

19.14 – ἦσαν δέ τινος Σκευᾶ Ἰουδαίου ἀρχιερέως ἑπτὰ υἱοί

In 9.10, 9.36, and 16.1, as in some instances of the Gospel of Luke (16.1,19; 18.2-3), the imperfect form of the verb εἰμί is used at the beginning of the story to introduce a main character: 'there was (or lived) somebody'. Interestingly, Luke utilizes the imperfect verb of εἰμί in the second part of Acts: 16.1; 19.14. The use of the verb, therefore, is certainly Lukan. If Luke had translated a Semitic source in Lk. 1.5, he would probably have employed the imperfect of the verb εἰμί to indicate the meaning 'there was a person' as he did in the rest of the infancy narrative and of the Gospel and Acts.

(3) *Is ἐγένετο in Lk. 1.5 still from Luke's hand?*

In spite of the above consideration, it is still possible to ascribe ἐγένετο in Lk. 1.5 to Luke. He probably used the aorist verb ἐγένετο in order to depict the appearance of Zechariah to the front of the history at the very first part

---

255. In some variations, the conjunction δέ is omitted.

of a book, beginning a narrative.[256] The Gospel of John employs ἐγένετο to express 'there appeared, there was' in 1.6. Jn 1.6 seems to contain the same verb usage as Lk. 1.5:

ἐγένετο ἄνθρωπος ἀπεσταλμένος παρὰ θεοῦ.
there appeared (or came, or was) a man sent from God.

Remarkably, John also does not use the verb γίνομαι but εἰμί in the rest of his Gospel without exception when he intends to indicate 'there is somebody': 3.1; 4.46; 5.5; 12.1.[257] However, there is a clear reason why the verb γίνομαι is adopted in Jn 1.6. The verb is used to introduce John the Baptist as a person who is contrasted with Jesus. In 1.1–5, the author of the Gospel of John utilizes the verb εἰμί for Jesus to emphasize the comparison between Jesus and John: while John the Baptist 'appeared', Jesus had existed.[258]

Mk 1.4 also seems to start with the verb ἐγένετο:

ἐγένετο[259] Ἰωάννης [ὁ] βαπτίζων ἐν τῇ ἐρήμῳ καὶ κηρύσσων[260] βάπτισμα μετανοίας εἰς ἄφεσιν ἁμαρτιῶν.

John the Baptist appeared in the desert and proclaimed a baptism of repentance for the forgiveness of sins.

---

256. As pointed out in Chapter 2 (The Definition of Lukanisms and non-Lukanisms), a possibly non-Lukan expresssion has to be excluded from non-Lukanisms, if it is proven that the expression originates from Luke's intentional change.

257. In 5.1, the verb is used to indicate 'there is something'.

258. Carson, *John*, p. 114. See also L. Morris, who notes that 'while in this verse (v. 5) there is no particular emphasis on the act of creation (we may well accept the translation 'came'), yet the use of this word must be held to point a contrast between Jesus and John' (L. Morris, *The Gospel according to John*, NICNT [Grand Rapids: Eerdmans, 1995], p. 79). Cf. Brown, who remarks that the verb 'is not the ἦν, "was", used of the word in vvs. 1-2, but the ἐγένετο used of creation in vvs. 3-4. John the Baptist is a creature.' (R. Brown, *The Gospel According to John I–XII* (The Anchor Bible; Garden City: Doubleday & Company, 1966, p. 8).

259. R. A. Guelich notes that 'ἐγένετο stands as the main verb in a Semitic construction' (R. A. Guelich, *Mark 1–8:26* [WBC, 34a; Dallas: Word Books, 1989], p. 16). His comment appears unclear. Pointing out that the verb is not connected with the participle, he translates it as 'appeared'. Then, what is the Semitic construction? Does it render the periphrastic participial construction? If not, what is Semitic? He seems inconsistent in explaining the construction. Without explanation, H. Anderson also remarks that the verb itself is a Semitism (Hugh Anderson, *The Gospel of Mark* [New Century Bible Commentary; Grand Rapids: Eerdmans, 1981], p. 69). These comments indicate the widespread unclarity and imprecision about Semitisms.

260. The presence of the article with βαπτίζων seems awkward with the conjunction before the participle κηρύσσων. The normal construction is to be formed by omitting the article or the conjunction. In fact, some variations omit the article while others the conjunction. However, this alternation is not necessary because such construction is attested in Herodotus VIII. 72: οὗτοι μὲν ἦσαν οἱ βοηθήσαντες καὶ ὑπερρωδέοντες [τῇ Ἑλλάδι κινδυνευούσῃ]. For details, see M. Reiser, *Syntax und Stil des Markusevangeliums im Licht der Hellenistischen Volksliteratur* (Tübingen: Mohr, 1983), p. 135.

3. A Close Examination of the Greek of the Infancy Narrative 145

The verb indicates the appearance of John the Baptist as the fulfilment of the prophecy in Isa. 40.3, which is quoted in Mk 1.2b-3. In Jn 1.6 and Mk 1.4, the use of the verb γίνομαι is appropriate in their contexts. It clearly emphasizes John's appearance.

Compared with the usage in Mark and John, the Lukan context does not provide a clear reason for the use of the aorist verb ἐγένετο. The usage in John and Mark[261] probably differs from that in Lk. 1.5 where the aorist verb simply means 'there was or lived'. Thus the use of the aorist verb ἐγένετο in Lk. 1.5 is 'a non-Lukanism', though it is possible for Luke to have used ἐγένετο to emphasize the appearance of Zechariah to the historical horizon at the first part of a book, beginning to tell a narrative, as John and Mark did.[262]

(4) *A Septuagintalism?*

Hebrew narratives typically start with the expression 'there was a person' as in 1 Sam. 1.1 ('there was a certain man of—'איש אחד מן־הרמתים ויהי) and Job 1.1 ('there was a man in—'איש היה בארץ־עוץ).[263] The Greek texts of both verses do not utilize the aorist form of γίνομαι but the imperfect of εἰμί – ἄνθρωπος ἦν in 1 Samuel and ἄνθρωπός τις ἦν in Job 1.1. This observation seems to make it difficult to accept the claim that Luke depended on the LXX for the aorist verb ἐγένετο in Lk. 1.5.

However, the use of the aorist verb ἐγένετο to indicate 'there was or appeared (a person)' occurs three times in the LXX at the start of a narrative: Judg. 13.2 (A);[264] 17.1; 19.1.[265] All these verses include the same phrase καὶ ἐγένετο ἀνήρ.[266] As 1 Sam. 1.1 and Job 1.1 demonstrate, the use

---

261. See also the use of the verb in Josephus *Ant* 18.23, where the verb clearly means 'there appears'. For the text and the translation, see above.

262. Lk. 1.5 is undoubtedly the virtual start of the story of the Gospel after the introductory statement in 1.1–4.

263. This is pointed out by Barnabas Lindars, *The Gospel of John* (London: Marshall, Morgan and Scott, 1972), p. 88.

264. The setting of Lk. 1.5-7 is similar to Judg. 13.2-3; both concern the sterility of someone's wife (both Lk. 1.7 and Judg. 13.2 include the noun στεῖρα); an angel appears in both passages (Lk. 1.13 and Judg. 13.3. Cf. Judg. 13.6). It is also noteworthy that Judg. 13.3 is alluded to in Lk. 1.31 and the non-Lukan verb τίκτω in Lk. 1.31 occurs in Judg. 13.3 and 13.2. The verb appears only in the infancy narrative throughout the whole of Luke's Gospel and Acts (for the statistics, see below). These factors make it probable that the Lukan text is dependant on the LXX of Judg. 13.2-3. Concerning the problem of the text variation, Luke depended on 'A' text, as pointed out in the preceding section, for his quotation and allusion. See the sections 'Quotations' and 'Allusions'.

265. Many books in the Greek OT start with καὶ ἐγένετο: Jos. 1.1; Judg. 1.1; 2 Sam. 1.1; *1 Macc.* 1.1; Mic. 1.1; Jon. 1.1; Ezek. 1.1. etc. Needless to say, numerous narratives also begin with the same locution: Gen. 6.1; 22.1; Num. 7.1, etc. However, the expression καὶ ἐγένετο is followed by the finite verb to mean 'and it happened that—'.

266. The Greek text reflects the Hebrew text: ויהי איש אחד.

of the verb γίνομαι in these verses is not obligatory; the translator could have used ἦν here. Perhaps, the translator adopted ἐγένετο to give an implicit nuance of the appearance of somebody as in the Lukan context. ἐγένετο is certainly a Septuagintalism as much as ἦν is.

Two points have become manifest: (1) the verb usage is clearly Septuagintal; (2) the use of ἐγένετο probably does not reflect Luke's own style ('a non-Lukanism'). Luke appears to have depended on the Greek of the LXX for this verb or on a Greek source which was dependent on the LXX. In any case, it is 'a Septuagintalism'.

(D) *The Absence of the Conjunction* καί *or* δέ

The absence of the conjunction has not drawn much attention among scholars. If the writer has translated a Semitic source, however, he could have used the conjunction καί or δέ after ἐγένετο, reflecting the Hebrew construction, ויהי. The absence of the conjunction is probably to be explained as an intentional omission. This observation requires further scrutiny.

(1) *The Hebrew construction* ויהי

In the Hebrew Bible, if the verb יהי[267] appears as the first word at the start of a narrative which tells about what happened in the past, it must be accompanied by the conjunction ו:[268] Gen. 6.1; 2 Sam. 7.1; 13.1; 1 Kgs 21.1; 2 Chron. 20.1; Ezra 1.1; Jon. 1.1; Ruth 1.1; Est. 1.1; Neh. 1.1b.[269] If the writer of Lk. 1.5 has translated a Semitic source, he could have used a corresponding Greek conjunction, καί or δέ, as in the LXX Gen. 6.1; 2 Sam. 7.1, etc.

In sum, the absence of the conjunction in Lk. 1.5 does not reflect the common Hebrew construction.[270]

---

267. If the imperfect has the shortened form, the Waw Consecutive is accompanied by this form. Thus, יהי, a shortened imperfect form of יהיה, appears with the conjunction ו to constitute ויהי. See J. Weingreen, *A Practical Grammar for Classical Hebrew* (Oxford: Clarendon, 2nd edn, 1972), pp. 92, 114.

268. This is the case even at the start of a clause. In the case that a clause is not concerned about what happened in the past, יהי can appear at the beginning of a clause without the conjunction. This useful information is given and confirmed by Prof. T. Muraoka of the Near Eastern Studies Department at Leiden University.

269. Dr. Booij of the Semitic Language Department at Vrije University provided this list for me.

270. In Deut. 1.1, the Hebrew text does not include the conjunction:
אלה הדברים אשר דבר משה; οὗτοι οἱ λόγοι οὓς ἐλάλησεν Μωϋσῆς

However, Deut. 1.1 does not lend support to the argument that the Hebrew OT can begin a book without the conjunction. First, the sentence in Deuteronomy does not have a verb at the

3. *A Close Examination of the Greek of the Infancy Narrative* 147

(2) *The LXX rendering of* ויהי *in 1 Sam. 1.1*

The LXX omits the conjunction in 1 Sam. 1.1, even though the Hebrew text has it:

ἄνθρωπος ἦν ἐξ Ἀρμαθαιμ Σιφα ἐξ ὄρους Ἐφραιμ—. ויהי איש אחד מן־הרמתים

The above observation illustrates that the LXX may omit the conjunction as in 1 Sam. 1.1 in the very first verse of a book which is the start of the narrative part of the book as Lk. 1.5.[271] The translator of 1 Sam. 1.1, however, does not place the verb as the first word, but a noun. This makes it difficult to posit that the omission of the conjunction in 1 Sam. 1.1 is identical to that in Lk. 1.5.

Nonetheless, the following conclusion is certain: the absence of the conjunction makes the Semitic original theory less probable, while the LXX of 1 Sam 1.1 shows that the first story of a book could start without the conjunction.[272]

(3) *Contemporary Greek parallels*

ἐγένετο appears in Jn 1.6 without a conjunction to introduce a person (John the Baptist).[273] However, the absence of the conjunction in Jn 1.6 is probably due to John's style because asyndeton is 'an important element in Johannine Greek'.[274] John omits the conjunction in many places where it normally would be expected, even in the beginning of a paragraph (1.9, 29,

---

first place, though the 'be' verb is implied. The narrative of Deuteronomy begins in 1.3 after an introductory statement in 1.1-2:,

ויהי בארבעים שנה; καὶ ἐγενήθη ἐν τῷ τεσσαρακοστῷ ἔτει

In this verse, the Hebrew 'be' verb appears with the conjunction.

271. The instance in Job 1.1 (see also Mal. 1.1 and cf. Gen. 25.19b) suggests that a noun can be the first word of the first sentence in the Hebrew text:

איש היה בארץ־עוץ; ἄνθρωπός τις ἦν ἐν χώρᾳ τῇ Αυσίτιδι.

One may argue that the alleged Semitic original in Lk. 1.5 contained the noun like ἱερεύς before the verb היה and did not have the conjunction, as in Job 1.1. However, this proposal presupposes too much. It is difficult to explain why a translator – if he existed – would have placed a noun like ἱερεύς in the middle of the sentence, if his alleged Semitic source had had it at the first place [see the underlined examples of Luke-Acts in C]. He should have translated it like "Ἱερεύς τις ἦν ….' The alleged Hebrew source, if it existed, should have contained the conjunction with the verb, ויהי, and he would have translated it as 'καὶ ἐγένετο'.

A possible resolution would be that the translator attempted to avoid the confusion between the verb ἐγένετο and the Septuagintalistic 'καὶ ἐγένετο'. If that was the case, however, he could have used a common verb form 'ἦν' instead of καὶ ἐγένετο.

272. Some variations add καί or δέ in Lk. 1.5: the Armenian version and the Ethiopian version for καί and Old Latin version, Coptic version, and Georgian version for δέ.

273. Jn 1.6 is the virtual start of the narrative in the Gospel of John as Lk. 1.5 is in the Gospel of Luke.

274. Turner, *A Grammar of New Testament Greek*, vol. IV, p. 70.

35, 43; 2.11; 3.31, etc.). This tendency does not exist in Luke at all.[275] Even though the evidence in Jn 1.6 seems to show, therefore, that the conjunction could be omitted at the start of a narrative to introduce persons, this does not explain the absence of the conjunction for the aorist verb ἐγένετο in Lk. 1.5.

In Mk 1.4, we find another example where ἐγένετο occurs without the conjunction. The absence of the conjunction, however, is appropriate here, since v.4 is preceded by a subordinate clause:[276] (v.2) 'As it has been written in the prophet Isaiah ..., (v.4) John the Baptist appeared in the desert ....'[277] Here again, the absence of the conjunction is not the same as in Lk. 1.5.[278]

(4) *Luke's Contribution?*

The absence of the conjunction is probably Luke's responsibility. The conjunction is also absent at the beginning of parable narratives in 15.11; 16.1[279] and 18.2, etc. The problem lies in the fact, however, that those verses occur at the beginning of direct discourse. While the conjunction in the beginning of direct discourse is usually absent in Luke, it appears always in the case of narrative in Luke.[280] Thus, it is less likely that the omission of the conjunction is a Lukan stylistic feature; it is probably 'a non-Lukanism'.

---

275. For details, see below.

276. The punctuation of Mk 1.1-4 has generated discussion among scholars. Some scholars regard the first verse as an independent sentence, while others consider it as connected with the following verse. The advocates of the former interpret vv. 2-3 as a subordinate clause and v. 4 as a main clause: 'The beginning of ... (v 1). As it is written ... (vv. 2-3), John the Baptist appeared ... (v. 4)'. The second view assumes that a new sentence begins in v. 4: 'The beginning of ... (v. 1), as it is written ... (vv. 2-3). John the Baptist appeared ... (v. 4)'. The vast majority of commentators follow NA[27] which supports the first view. However, some scholars still believe that the first verse can be considered as connected with the following verses. For more details, see J.K. Elliott, 'καθώς and ὥσπερ in the New Testament', *Filologia Neotestamentaria* 7 (1991), pp. 55–58 and Guelich, *Mark 1–8.26*, p. 6.

277. As Guelich notes, '"appeared" (ἐγένετο) in conjunction with 1.1-3 connotes the "happening" of what had been promised and sets the Baptizer's appearance within redemptive history as an event that comes to pass' (*Mark 1–8.26*, p. 18).

278. Even if Mk 1.4 starts the narrative independently, this probably stems from the style of Mark. Asyndeton occurs more frequently in Mark than in Matthew or Luke. According to V. Taylor, there are 25 cases where both Luke and Matthew have parallels to Mark concerning the asyndeton and 'Luke retains the asyndeton twice and Matthew never' (V. Taylor, *The Gospel According to St. Mark: the Greek text with Introduction, notes, and indexes* [London: Macmillan, 1952], p. 49).

279. See also 16.19, where some variations omit the conjunction δέ.

280. Luke utilizes a conjunction not only at the beginning of a narrative but also at the start of a paragraph without exception. The asyndeton appears only twice in Luke, one in the sayings (12.20), one in the middle of a narrative (8.3).

In summary, 1) the verb usage certainly belongs to Septuagintalisms; 2) the verb is probably non-Lukan, though it is possible that Luke, following the LXX [or John and Mark], used the verb to signify the appearance of Zechariah, just as the translator of Judges did in Judg. 13.2, 17.1 and 19.1 and John and Mark did in Jn 1.6 and Mk 1.4; 3) the absence of the conjunction is certainly non-Hebraistic and probably non-Lukan. The absence of the conjunction is possibly a Septuagintal characteristic in the sense that the LXX can omit it at the beginning of a narrative, as in 1 Sam. 1.1.[281] However, the evidence is not strong enough to assert that the Lukan text follows LXX style. It is at least certain, at any rate, that the verb usage belongs to Septuagintalisms as well as to Hellenistic Greek, while the absence of the conjunction does not lend support to the translation theory, because the supposed Hebrew construction would have the conjunction.

2. *Remarks on* ἱερεύς τις[282] ὀνόματι Ζαχαρίας *and* καὶ τὸ ὄνομα αὐτῆς Ἐλισάβετ[283]

1) ὀνόματι Ζαχαρίας *'with respect to name, Zechariah'*

(A) *The Problem*

The dative ὀνόματι is used as the 'dative of respect' to mean 'with respect to name, or by name' (BDR 197.2). It appears between 27 and 30 times in

---

281. If Luke or the composer of the pre-Lukan Greek source translated a Hebrew original, he did not use the conjunction intentionally. This denotes that he was a deliberate editor. Is it possible, then, for this deliberate editor to keep the preposition ἐν in the construction προβαίνω ἐν ταῖς ἡμέραις in 1.7, 18; 2.36, which is never attested in Greek? This is not probable. For the detailed argument on the construction προβαίνω ἐν ταῖς ἡμέραις, see below.

282. The adjective τις also occurs frequently in Luke-Acts while it is rarely found in the other New Testament books: 102 times in Luke-Acts and only 18 times in the rest of the New Testament. The order of the words ἱερεύς τις, Nolland argues, is non-Septuagintal. Nolland goes one step further by saying that the use of τις after the noun belongs to Lukanisms and non-Septuagintal Semitisms (*Luke 1–9.20*, pp. 25–26). In contrast to Nolland, Brown asserts that the phrase ἱερεύς τις is a 'good LXX Greek' expression (*The Birth of the Messiah*, p. 258). Brown's judgement is correct, because the usage appears at least three times in the LXX: Job 1.1 – ἄνθρωπός τις ἦν; *2 Mac.* 4.13 – ην δ'ο οὕτως ἀκμή τις Ἑλληνισμοῦ; *Bel* 1.2 – ἄνθρωπός τις ἦν ἱερεύς ᾧ ὄνομα Δανιηλ. These examples nullify Nolland's argument that the use of τις after the noun is a non-Septuagintal Semitism.

283. In this verse, Elizabeth is also called 'γυνὴ ἐκ τῶν θυγατέρων Ἀαρών' of v. 5, 'from the female descendants of Aaron'. Nolland believes that the use of the noun θυγάτηρ is Semitic (*Luke 1–9.20*, p. 26). The noun is used to refer to the descendant rather than the direct daughter. In the NT, υἱός is used to indicate not direct offspring, but descendant: Lk. 1.16; 19.9; Acts 5.21; 7.23, 37; 9.15; 10.36; Rom. 9.27; 2 Cor. 3.7, 13; Heb. 7.5; 11.22 (BAGD, p. 833). In contrast, θυγάτηρ is rarely used to refer to the female descendant. This usage, however, appears twice in Luke (1.5; 13.16) and three times in the LXX (Gen. 24.3; 2 Chron. 2.13; *4 Macc.* 15.28). As a result, it is a Lukan Septuagintalism.

Luke-Acts,²⁸⁴ and only twice in the rest of the NT. These statistics seem to indicate that it is Lukan. In fact, scholars agree that the use of the dative ὀνόματι as a 'dative of respect' is Lukan. In contrast, as the following arguments will show, they betray differences concerning the question whether the usage is Septuagintal.

1. Following Machen's assertion that the dative ὀνόματι does not appear in the Septuagint,²⁸⁵ Nolland notes that the dative ὀνόματι is Lukan and non-Septuagintal (*Luke 1–9.20*, pp. 25–26). Luke, according to him, depends on a Hebrew original for v. 5a where ושמו 'and his name' occurs, but he obscures the Hebrew construction in v. 5a by using ὀνόματι 'to avoid a repetition of the καὶ τὸ ὄνομα αὐτῆς' in v. 5b.

2. Concerning the dative noun ὀνόματι, Brown simply points to the fact that it occurs more than twenty-five times in Luke-Acts (*The Birth of the Messiah*, p. 258). Marshall insists that the use of the dative ὀνόματι before the name is Lukan²⁸⁶ but he does not investigate whether it belongs to non-Septuagintalisms (*Luke*, p. 52). He seems to assume that ὀνόματι does not indicate direct Semitic influence; he thus does not examine whether or not it is Septuagintal.

(B) *Solution*

(1) *General survey*

Several other locutions could have been used instead of ὀνόματι Ζαχαρίας for '(and) his name was Zechariah':

---

284. Brown suggests that there are over 25 examples for this usage in Luke-Acts (*The Birth of the Messiah*, p. 258). Nolland quotes Brown's statistics without examining them. In contrast, BDR note that the dative appears six times in Luke and 21 times in Acts respectively (128.3). There may be as many as 30 instances when textual variations are taken into account. For the list of the verses and the difference of variations, see below, nt. 292.

285. G. Machen, 'The Origin of the First Two Chapters of Luke', *PTR*, 10 (1912), p. 213. He notes that 'there is perhaps not a single case of ὀνόματι where the text is perfectly certain'.

286. With regard to the Greek word ὀνόματι, BDF cite M. Johannessohn by saying that 'the NT has a predilection for placing ὀνόματι first' before somebody's name (197). The following observation does not nullify this statement, but complements it. While all the examples in the Gospel of Luke justify the assessment of BDF with regard to the position of the word ὀνόματι, some examples in Acts do not. The number of the instances in which ὀνόματι is placed after a person's name reaches six in Acts. This word order, according to J. Heimerdinger, is intentionally chosen (J. Heimerdinger, 'Word order in Koine Greek: Using a Text-Critical Approach to Study Word Order Patterns in the Greek Text of Acts', *Filologia*, 9[1996], p. 153). The name is placed before ὀνόματι when 'the name of the person in question is necessary information, provided by the speaker for the purpose of identification'. 'Most of the other occurences of the formula with ὀνόματι,' she continues, 'introduce a participant with the indefinite τίς, or with an indefinite anarthrous noun (e.g. a servant [Acts] 12.13; a centurion 27.1).'

3. *A Close Examination of the Greek of the Infancy Narrative* 151

a. (καὶ) τὸ ὄνομα αὐτοῦ Ζαχαρίας (see 1.5b);[287]
b. ᾧ ὄνομα Ζαχαρίας (compare with the locution in 1.26, 27a; 2.25; 8.41;[288] 24.13; Acts 13.6);
c. ὀνόματι καλουμένος Ζαχαρίας (see 10.39; 19.2);
d. καλουμένος Ζαχαρίας (compare this with the expression in Lk. 6.15; 19.29; 21.37; 22.3; 23.33; Acts 1.23; 15.22, 37; 27.8,16);
e. λεγόμενος Ζαχαρίας[289] as in Lk. 22.1,47; Acts 3.2.[290]

In classical literature, the second construction b) (dative pronoun + ὄνομα in the nominative + name of a person) is usually used. In the LXX, the first construction a) that reflects a Hebrew original appears and the second b) occurs most frequently (Gen. 16.1; Exod. 3.13; 15.3, etc) as in classical Greek.

(2) *A confirmation of the judgement that it is Lukan*
The dative falls into the category of 'the dative of respect' which 'takes the place, in Hellenistic Greek, of the classical accusative'.[291] Luke's two books involve seven and 22 instances respectively [Lk. 1.5; 5.27; 10.38; 16.20; 19.2; 23.50; 24.18; Acts 5.1, 34; 8.9; 9.10-12, 33, 36; 10.1: 11.28; 12.13; 16.1,14; 17.34; 18.2, 7, 24; 19.24; 20.9; 21.10; 27.1; 28.7].[292] Remarkably, two instances in Lk. 10.38 (γυνὴ δέ τις ὀνόματι Μάρθα) and 16.20 (πτωχὸς δέ τις ὀνόματι Λάζαρος) exhibit exactly the same construction,

---

287. Matthew includes four instances for the construction τὸ ὄνομα + genitive: 1.21, 23, 25; 6.9. However, the construction is always accompanied by the verb καλέω.
288. Lk. 8.41 (καὶ ἰδοὺ ἦλθεν ἀνὴρ ᾧ ὄνομα Ἰάϊρος) has a parallel in Mk 5.22 (καὶ ἔρχεται εἷς τῶν ἀρχισυναγώγων, ὀνόματι Ἰάϊρος). Interestingly, Luke's favourite expression, i.e., the dative of respect, is found in Mark while Luke uses his second favourite locution.
289. Matthew usually uses the participial form of the verb λέγω for this usage: 1.16; 4.18; 9.9; 10.2; 26.14; 27.16-17, 22, 33 (a,b); 26.3.
290. In Mk 14.32, we find the following construction: (εἰς χωρίον) οὗ τὸ ὄνομα Γεθσημανί. The parallel in Mt. 26.36 has a different locution: (εἰς χωρίον) λεγόμενον Γεθσημανί. Matthew does not use the construction τὸ ὄνομα with the genitive pronoun, but the participle of λέγω. The Lukan parallel in 22.39 omits the name, probably because the Aramaic name was meaningless for Luke's readers (Marshall, *Luke*, p. 830). At any rate, no example is found for the construction τὸ ὄνομα + genitive pronoun + name in Luke except in Lk. 1.5. For details, see below.
291. Zerwick, *Biblical Greek*, pp. 52–53.
292. The passages listed follow NA[27]. Jeremias, *Die Sprache*, p. 15, notes that the dative of respect appears seven times in Luke and 21 times in Acts respectively, without listing verses. In contrast, A. George remarks that the construction appears eight times in Luke and 22 times in Acts without suggesting verses (A. George 'Jean-Baptiste et Jesus en Lc 1–2', in *Mélanges Bibliques*, FS B. Rigaux [eds. A. Descamps and R.P. André de Halleux; Gembloux: Duculot, 1970], p. 166). According to NA[27], George's count concerning Acts is correct while Jeremias' count is correct concerning the Gospel. The text variation in Lk. 24.18 seems to produce the difference between Jeremias and George with regard to the Gospel. The difference concerning Acts is probably due to the text variation in 18.7 or 19.24. It seems that Jeremias depends on

i.e., noun + τις + ὀνόματι, as the one in Lk. 1.5. By comparison, the dative of respect appears only twice in the whole NT outside of Luke and Acts. Mt. 27.32; Mk 5.22. These statistics confirm that the use of the dative noun ὀνόματι in Lk. 1.5 as 'a dative of respect' is mostly peculiar to Luke.

(3) A translation?

The possibility of translation is dubious given that the dative noun ὀνόματι does not reflect a Hebrew construction. In the Hebrew OT, the corresponding construction is as follows: the noun שם followed by the possessive pronoun, e.g, שמה or שמו. They can be literally translated into Greek as ὄνομα αὐτῆς or ὄνομα αὐτοῦ, as the LXX translators in fact did in some places.[293] Such considerations make it unlikely that the Greek construction is a translation of a Hebrew original.[294]

(4) Is this construction attested in non-Biblical Greek?

Some examples of the dative 'ὀνόματι' used as the dative of respect occur in Greek literature outside of the Greek Bible. Two examples are found in Xenophon:

> καὶ πόλις αὐτόθι ᾠκεῖτο μεγάλη καὶ εὐδαίμων θάψακος ὀνόματι[295]
> and a city, by name Thabsakos, was being inhabited on the spot greatly and blessedly [*Anabasis* I.iv.11 (v. 4)].

> ἐστρατήγει δὲ αὐτῶν Σάμιος ὀνόματι Ἱππεύς.
> and Samios, by name Ippes, became their general [*Historia Graecae* I, vi, p. 29].

D in 18.7 or A in 19.24. Interestingly, Brown remarks that the construction occurs over 25 times and Nolland quotes this statistics (*Luke 1–9.20*, p. 26). This statement, though not incorrect, is imprecise, since it takes place 29 times in Luke-Acts.

293. For the passages, see below.

294. The exponents of the translation theory could argue that Luke used a free translation in v. 5a to avoid the repetition of the construction in v. 5b: τὸ ὄνομα αὐτῆς Ἐλισάβετ. See Nolland, *Luke 1–9.20*, p. 26, who follows Machen. While everything can be explained in this way, this argument is not probable, or at least less probable than the alternative. It is possible that Luke employed the dative because of the adjective τις. He always uses the dative ὀνόματι after the adjective τις without exception [Lk. 10.38; 16.20; Acts 5.1, 34; 8.9; 9.10, 33; 16.14; 18.2, 7, 24; 19.24; 20.9; 21.10]. Further, the dative ὀνόματι occurs only here in the whole Lukan infancy narrative. It would thus be more reasonable to suppose that Luke composed v. 5 rather than that he or somebody else made a translation from Hebrew. For more argument, see below.

295. There are text variations. While Cpr and D include ὄνομα, FMBC contains ὀνόματι. According to Liddell and Scott, p. 1232, the nominative ὄνομα was also used absolutely in prose to mean 'by name'. This usage is found in Xenophon: διὰ μέσον δὲ ῥεῖ τούτων ποταμὸς Κάρσος ὄνομα; 'and a river, Karsos by name, flows between these' [*Anabasis*, I.iv.4]. This usage appears also in *Anabasis*, I.v.10 and *Historia Greacae*, I.iv.2. For the references, see F.W. Sturz, *Lexicon Xenophonteum* (Hildesheim: Georg Olms, 1964).

Plutarch also used this construction:

ἐπεὶ δὲ Λούσιος ὁ ἀδελφιδοῦς, αὐτοῦ τὸ δεύτερον ὑπατεύοντες, ἐβιάζετο τῶν ἐν ὥρᾳ στρατευομένων τινὰ ὀνόματι Τρεβώνον, ὁ δὲ ἀπέκτεινεν αὐτόν.
When he was in the second consulship, Lusius, his nephew, was attempting to attack one of the soldiers in the army at that time, by name Trebonius, but he killed Lusius [*Moralia*, III. 202.B].[296]

One more example is found in Diodorus Siculus:

μιγεῖσα δὲ τῷ Ἡρακλεῖ ἐγένησεν υἱὸν ὀνόματι Γαλάτην.
and having sexual intercourse, she bore to Heracles a son, by name Galates [5.24.3].[297]

Demosthenes, a classical author, adopted a similar expression 'τις ὀνόματι ἀδελφός'.

The dative ὀνόματι as a dative of respect also appears in Josephus, BJ 6.186.1 (νεανίας, ὀνόματι Λογγος).[298] He also utilized the construction identical to that in Lk. 1.5 in BJ 4.37.1:

ἑκατοντάρχης δέ τις Γάλλος ὀνόματι

and in AJ 11. 145.2:

Ἀχόνιός τις ὀνόματι πρῶτος τῶν Ἱεροσσολυμιτῶν.

The only difference between the example in BJ 4.37.1 and that in Luke's verse is the position of the last two words.[299]

The use of the dative ὀνόματι is also attested in the other sources. *Acta Joannis*, the first-century document, also includes this construction: Ἰωάννης τις ὀνόματι (work #3.2). *Acta Pauli*, from the second century,

---

296. This reference is from Daniel Wyttenbach's *Lexicon Plutarcheum* (Hildesheim: Georg Olms Verlagsbuchhandlung, 1962).
297. Also in 16.41.1; 18.40.2. This text is found in *Diodorus Siculus* (ed. J. Iain McDougall; Hildesheim/Zürich/New York: Georg Olms, 1983).
298. Josephus usually uses the nominative ὄνομα. BJ. 2.118: ἀνὴρ Γαλιλαῖος, Ἰούδας ὄνομα. See also 1.432; 2.481; 2.585; 4.155. See also BJ. 6.201: γυνή τις... Μαρία τοὔνομα.
299. Some may argue that the use of this construction in Josephus supports the translation theory on the ground that Josephus translated his work 'Jewish War' from Aramaic to Greek. This argument ignores some important points: 1) Josephus composed his other works directly in Greek; 2) it is generally accepted that his professional Greek helper corrected his composition or translation (See Mussies, 'Greek in Palestine and the Diaspora', p. 1041, where he notes that 'Josephus ... wrote first in Aramaic or Hebrew, probably while still in Palestine. He translated his 'War' into Greek at Rome and had the result revised by professional correctors'.) It is likely, therefore, that the corrector altered awkward Greek phrases except for inevitable ones. The present construction was not abnormal in the eyes of the Greek professional corrector.

also contains three examples: τις ἀνὴρ ὀνόματι Ὀνησιφορος *(work # 4, 2.1)*, συριάρχης τις Ἀλεξανδρος ὀνόματι *(work # 4, 26.3)*, τις βασίλισσα πλουσία ὀνόματι Τρύφαινα *(work # 4, 27.6)*. Also in Publius Aelius Phlegon *(work # 2b, 257, F. 36.356)*: Φιλωτὶς γάρ τις ὀνόματι παρθενός. This evidence indicates that the expression was widespread among the Hellenistic writers.

The above examples support the view that the use of ὀνόματι as 'a dative of respect' is well attested in non-Biblical Greek.[300]

(5) *A non-Septuagintalism?*

In the whole of the Septuagint, the dative of the noun ὄνομα occurs 191 times, and most of them are accompanied by the preposition ἐν. There are, however, many instances with the article to indicate 'indirect object' (1 Kgs 8.33, 35), 'dative of purpose' (2 Sam. 7.13; 1 Kgs 3.2; 5.17; 5.19; 8.17-18, etc.) or 'dative of means' (Lev. 19.12; Deut. 6.13; 10.21; 18.7, etc.). Only four instances occur without both the preposition and the article. One example is found in Prov. 27.16:

> βορέας σκληρὸς ἄνεμος ὀνόματι δὲ ἐπιδέξιος καλεῖται.
> The north wind is sharp, but it is called by name 'propitious'.

Interestingly, the corresponding Hebrew text discloses a different construction:

> צפניה צפן־רוח ושמן ימינו יקרא:
> to restrain her is to restrain the wind or to grasp oil in the right hand.

The meaning of the words in the LXX, ὀνόματι δὲ ἐπιδέξιος καλεῖται, has no counterpart in the Hebrew text. It is supposed that the translator did a free translation or had a Hebrew text different from the present Hebrew OT. At any rate, the LXX of Prov. 27.16 includes ὀνόματι which is used as 'the dative of respect'.

Sirach has one instance in 37.1:

> πᾶςφίλος ἐρεῖ ἐφιλίατα κἀγω, ἀλλ' ἔστινφίλος ὀνόματι μόνονφίλος
> Every friend will say, 'I also was a friend (of yours)' but a friend is a friend in name only.

Though the usage here is not exactly identical to Lk. 1.5 as only a common noun 'friend' appears, the dative represents 'dative of respect'. This verse is found in the Hebrew text:[301]

---

300. The locution also appears in papyri. However, most of those instances are excluded because of their unclear date. The geographical distribution includes Macedonia and Italy. For Macedonia, see SEG. 27. 292–93 and for Italy, see West. IG 14.237. There is one example from the second century, A.D. 167 [Pfam Tebt. 37]. All the references are based on TLG.

301. The text depends on Beentjes, *The Book of Ben Sira in Hebrew*.

3. A Close Examination of the Greek of the Infancy Narrative 155

כל אוהב אומר אהבתי אך יש אהב שם אהב
Every friend says that "I am your friend", but there is a friend (who is) a friend only in name.

The Hebrew word שם corresponds to the Greek word ὀνόματι. The use of the dative ὀνόματι in this verse at least belongs to secondary Septuagintalisms.

Examples closer to that in Lk. 1.5 are found in *4 Maccabees* which was composed directly in Greek and in Tobit whose original language is ambiguous:[302]

4 Macc. 5.4 πολλῶν δὲ συναρπασθέντων εἷς πρῶτος ἐκ τῆς ἀγέλης ὀνόματι Ἐλεάζαρος;
And when many were captured, there was a prominent (figure) in the herd by name Eleazar (NRSV).

Tob. 6.11 καὶ ἔστιν αὐτῷ θυγάτηρ μονογενὴς ὀνόματι Σάρρα.
and there is for him an only daughter to him, by name Sarah.

These four examples indicate that the dative ὀνόματι without the article and preposition used as 'a dative of respect', is attested in LXX Greek.

(6) From Luke's hand?

The construction 'ὀνόματι + name' does not necessarily stem from Luke's hand, though that is probable,[303] since it occurs twice in the other Gospels (Mt. 27.32 and Mk 5.22). However, the construction 'noun + adjectival τις[304] + ὀνόματι + name' is uniquely Lukan in the New Testament and in the whole Greek Bible. This construction appears only in

---

302. D.C. Simpson notes that the original language of *Tobit* possibly is Aramaic, but this is uncertain as he accepts. See his article, 'The Book of Tobit', in *The Apocrypha and Pseudepigrapha of the Old Testament in English* (ed. R.H. Charles; repr. 1963 Oxford: Clarendon, 1913), pp. 174–75. However, C. Moor notes that 'with the discovery of one Hebrew and four Aramaic copies of Tobit in Cave 4 at Qumran, the century-long debate as to whether Tobit was originally composed in Greek or a Semitic language has now been settled in favour of the latter' (C. Moor, *The Anchor Bible Commentary*, vol. 6 [ed. D.N. Freedman; New York: Doubleday, 1992], pp. 590–91).

303. The construction 'ὀνόματι + name' is a hard core Lukanism which very probably came from Luke's hand.

304. Classical authors use the pronoun τις after the noun. I found some examples in Thucydides. 3.36.4. καὶ τῇ ὑστεραίᾳ μετάνοια τις εὐθὺς ἦν αὐτοῖς; 'And the following day a regret immediately was to them'. 4.39.2. καὶ ἦν σῖτός τις ἐν τῇ νήσῳ; 'and there was a certain grain in the island.' 7.42.2. στρατεύματι τῶν Ἀθηναίων ὡς ἐκ κακῶν ῥώμη τις ἐνεγένετο; 'To a soldier of Athenians, a certain power sprang up as from evils'. 7.49.4. ἀτιλέγοντος δὲ τοῦ Νικίου ὄκνος τις καὶ Μέλλησις ἐνεγένετο; 'But when Nikos spoke in opposition, a certain hesitation and delay sprang up'. For references, this study depends on the book, *Thucydides: Concordantia Thucydidea* by Carlos Schrader (Hildesheim; Zürich; New York: Olms-Weidmann, 1998).

Luke-Acts, and thus it is 'a hard core Lukanism': the same or almost same locution occurs twice in the remainder of the Gospel:

10.38 – γυνὴ δέ τις ὀνόματι Μάρθα

16.20 – πτωχὸς δέ τις ὀνόματι Λάζαρος

It is very frequently found in Acts:

5.1 – Ἀνὴρ δέ τις Ἀνανίας ὀνόματι

5.34 – τις ἐν τῷ συνεδρίῳ Φαρισαῖος ὀνόματι Γαμαλιήλ

8.9 – Ἀνὴρ δέ τις ὀνόματι Σίμων

9.10 – Ἦν δέ τις μαθητὴς ἐν Δαμασκῷ ὀνόματι Ἀνανίας

9.33 – ἄνθρωπόν τινα ὀνόματι Αἰνέαν

9.36 – τις ἦν μαθήτρια ὀνόματι Ταβιθά

10.1 – Ἀνὴρ δέ τις ἐν Καισαρείᾳ ὀνόματι Κορνήλιος

16.1 – μαθητής τις ἦν ἐκεῖ ὀνόματι Τιμόθεος

16.14 – τις γυνὴ ὀνόματι Λυδία

18.2 – τινα Ἰουδαῖον ὀνόματι Ἀκύλαν

18.7 – τινὸς ὀνόματι Τιτίου Ἰούστου

18.24 – Ἰουδαῖος δέ τις Ἀπολλῶς ὀνόματι

19.24 – Δημήτριος γάρ τις ὀνόματι

20.9 – τις νεανίας ὀνόματι Εὔτυχος

21.10 – τις ἀπὸ τῆς Ἰουδαίας προφήτης ὀνόματι Ἄγαβος.[305]

Even in the second part of Acts (chs 16–28), which Luke probably himself composed without depending on other sources, it occurs eight times. These considerations, along with the fact that the use of the dative does not

---

305. In some places, only the dative ὀνόματι appears without τις: Lk. 5.27; 19.2; 23.50; 24.8; Acts 9.11-12; 11.28; 12.13; 17.34; 27.1; 28.7.

reflect a Hebrew construction, indicate that Luke himself is the source of the construction.

In conclusion, it has been demonstrated that Nolland's argument that the use of the dative ὀνόματι in Lk. 1.5 is non-Septuagintal is incorrect. This construction is 'a hard core Septuagintalism' since it has no Hebrew counterpart. Further, in Lk. 1.5, the construction with ὀνόματι is certainly 'a hard core Lukanism' as we have shown above. It does not seem probable that Luke relied upon a Semitic source for the phrase ἱερεύς τις ὀνόματι Ζαχαρίας.[306]

2) καὶ τὸ ὄνομα αὐτῆς Ἐλισάβετ:[307] *'and her name (was) Elizabeth'*

This sentence has the construction καὶ τὸ ὄνομα + genitive + (ἐστιν) + name. Similar expressions to this construction appear in 1.27b (καὶ τὸ ὄνομα τῆς παρθένου Μαριάμ) and 1.63 (Ἰωάννης ἐστὶ [τὸ] ὄνομα αὐτοῦ).[308]

(A) *The Problem and Suggestions*

1. About a century ago, V.H. Stanton suggested that the construction καὶ τὸ ὄνομα αὐτῆς Ἐλισάβετ in Lk. 5b is a non-Lukan expression. This causes him to deny Luke's direct composition of the infancy narrative.[309]

2. Recently, Brown has also noted that this expression is non-Lukan, but he stresses that it appears in the LXX of Gen. 17.5, 15 (*The Birth of the Messiah*, p. 258).[310]

---

306. It is impossible to completely rule out the possibility that Luke translated the Semitic source adopting his favourite expression, 'noun + adjectival τις + ὀνόματι + name'. However, this represents the least likely possibility.

307. In Lk. 1.13, 31, we find the construction καλέσεις τὸ ὄνομα αὐτοῦ Ἰωάννην (Ἰησοῦν) [also in Mt. 1.21]. A form of the verb καλέω is accompanied by ὄνομα followed by the genitive pronoun in in Mt. 1.23, 25). This construction is called a Semitism by Brown (*The Birth of the Messiah*, p. 130). It occurs frequently in the LXX.

308. There are textual variations. ℵ A B₂ C D W Θ Ψ $f_{1,13}$ 33 include the article before the noun ὄνομα, while P4 B* L C 565. 579. 700. l2211 *pc*; Or omit the article. The external evidence does not support either of the two readings. The internal evidence, however, supports the omission of the article; Luke usually uses the article before this noun when the genitive modifies it (1.5b, 13, 27, 31, 49, 59; 2.21; 6.22; 9.48, etc.). NA²⁷ omits the article seemingly due to the internal evidence.

309. V.H. Stanton, *The Gospel as Historical Documents: Part II, The Synoptic Gospels* (Cambridge: University Press, 1909), p. 294.

310. Brown notes that this construction 'is unusual for Luke, being found only in the parallel annunciation of Jesus' birth', namely, in Lk. 1.27. Brown fails to mention that this construction occurs again in 1.63 (cf. 1.49).

3. Concentrating on the phrase καὶ τὸ ὄνομα + genitive noun itself without considering the implied verb ἐστιν, Nolland also emphasizes that it is non-Lukan (*Luke 1–9.20*, p. 26). He recognizes that this phrase occurs in the LXX, quoting the results of George's research that it occurs some eighteen times there.[311] Nonetheless, he still tries to emphasize the possibility that Luke does not follow the LXX exactly. He points to the Hebrew construction ושמו, 'and his name' in 1 Sam. 1.1. The LXX translator rendered it not as καὶ ὄνομα αὐτοῦ but as καὶ ὄνομα αὐτῷ; the LXX of 1 Sam. 1.1 does not adopt the genitive pronoun as in Luke 1.5b but the dative pronoun.[312]

(B) *Lack of Clarity*

Before we continue our investigation, we need to clarify some points. First, Brown's claim that Gen. 17.5, 15 of the LXX includes the same construction as the one found in Lk. 1.5b is imprecise. The two instances in Genesis do not have the conjunction καί but ἀλλά. In a strict sense, the construction καὶ τὸ ὄνομα αὐτῆς + (ἐστι) + name in Lk. 1.5b is not found in Gen. 17.5, 15, but only the locution τὸ ὄνομα αὐτῆς + (ἐστι) + name is.

Second, another source of the lack of clarity is that some scholars take only the phrase καὶ τὸ ὄνομα αὐτῆς itself into account (George and Nolland). It is true that this phrase is important for the investigation of the whole construction καὶ τὸ ὄνομα αὐτῆς + (ἐστι) + name, but a more important question is whether the phrase (καὶ) τὸ ὄνομα αὐτῆς is the subject. These matters need to be clarified first before we can decide whether this construction is Septuagintal or not.

(C) *Solution*

(1) *A confirmation that this is non-Lukan*

Luke usually expresses the meaning '(and) one's name (was or is) something' by using the Greek construction in 1.5a: ὀνόματι + name.[313] The phrase καὶ τὸ ὄνομα + the genitive (pro)noun + (ἐστι) name does not appear in Luke-Acts outside of the infancy narrative. In fact, this construction is

---

311. George remarks that the locution καὶ τὸ ὄνομα (αὐτῆς) in 1.5, 27 'est une formule des Septante' ('Le parallèle entre Jean-Baptiste et Jésus en Lc 1–2', p. 166).

312. Nolland argues unsuccessfully, as we have seen previously, that the noun ὀνόματι in v. 5a is non-Septuagintal, even though he believes that the construction τὸ ὄνομα + genitive pronoun in v. 5b is Septuagintal. He probably supposes that if both expressions are from the LXX, his argument for Semitic sources in this section will be weakened.

313. The conjunction καί is, in fact, implied in this construction. For example, the sentence in 5a, Ἐγένετο ἐν ταῖς ἡμέραις Ἡρῴδου βασιλέως τῆς Ἰουδαίας ἱερεύς τις ὀνόματι Ζαχαρίας virtually means 'there lived a certain priest... (and) his name was Zechariah'.

3. A Close Examination of the Greek of the Infancy Narrative 159

found only in the Lukan infancy narrative in the NT[314] except Mk 14.32 (Καὶ ἔρχονται εἰς χωρίον οὗ τὸ ὄνομα Γεθσημανῆ).[315] This observation indicates that the phrase is a non-Lukanism; Luke seems to have depended on a source. Now, the question is, what kind of source did he use?

(2) *Did this come from the imitation of the LXX?*

The construction καὶ τὸ ὄνομα + the genitive noun or pronoun, according to George, occurs some 18 times in the LXX. In fact, there are 31 instances of the phrase[316] [Gen. 48.16; Exod. 1.15; 6.3; 18.4; Lev. 24.11; Num. 17.18; 26.30, 59; Judg. 1.10; 13.6; 1 Kgs 10.1; 14.21; 2 Chron. 3.17; *Tob.* 5.12(S); Ps. 24.14; 79.19; 114.4; 115.4; *Wis.* 2.4; *Sir.* 37.26; 39.9; 44.14; 46.12; Zech. 14.9; Mal. 1.14; Isa. 66.22; Jer. 11.19; 14.9; Ezek. 20.39; 39.7; 48.35]. The context in most of these instances is different from that in Lk. 1.5; the construction is not used to constitute 'and one's name is (or was) X'. However, the phrase used for 'and one's name is X' appears in some verses: Exod. 1.15; 18.4; Lev. 24.11; Num. 26.30; 26.59; 1 Kgs 14.21; 2 Chron. 3.17; *Tob.* 5.12; Zech. 14.9; Ezek. 48.35 (10x).

In addition, the expression (without the conjunction) τὸ ὄνομα + the genitive pronoun + (ἐστι) + name appears in the LXX [Gen. 17.5,15; 32.27-28; 35.10; Num. 25.14; Judg. 1.11, 23; Dan. 4.5,16; 1 Sam. 8.2; 1 Kgs 11.26; 12.24; 14.31; 15.2, 10; 16.28; 18.31;[317] 2 Kgs 8.26; 12.1; 14.2; (cf.15.2; 18.2); 1 Chron. 2.29; 4.3; 7.15; 9.35 (cf. 8.29); 2 Chron. 12.13; 27.1; 36.2, 5] (27x).

In the LXX, the construction καὶ τὸ ὄνομα + the genitive noun (+ ἐστι) + name for the meaning 'and one's name is X' and the construction τὸ ὄνομα + the genitive pronoun (+ ἐστι) + name are normal expressions, which reflect Hebrew constructions.

In brief, the construction καὶ τὸ ὄνομα + the genitive noun (or pronoun) (+ ἐστι) + name in Lk. 1.5b is a secondary Septuagintalism.

---

314. It is remarkable that even Revelation, in which many scholars discern numerous Semitisms, does not include examples of the construction. The author of Revelation uses the very common construction ὄνομα + dative + name in 6.8; 9.11, which, as we pointed out, most frequently occurs in classical and Septuagint Greek.

315. Jeremias remarks that 'καὶ τὸ ὄνομα αὐτῆς ... mit fehlender Kopula im NT nur 2 mal, beide Belege in der lukanischen Kindheitsgeschichte: 1, 5.27b'. He does not take Mk 14.32 into account.

316. This construction appears twice in non-canonical Judges (1.11; 13.6).

317. This verse has the same construction as Lk. 1.69 (Ἰωάννης ἐστὶν ὄνομα αὐτοῦ): Ἰσραηλ ἔσται τὸ ὄνομά σου.

II. πλῆθος στρατιᾶς οὐρανίου 'a Multitude of the Heavenly Army' in Lk. 2.13

Lk. 2.13 καὶ ἐξαίφνης ἐγένετο σὺν τῷ ἀγγέλῳ πλῆθος στρατιᾶς οὐρανίου αἰνούντων[318] τὸν θεὸν καὶ λεγόντων,
and suddenly, there appeared with the angel a multitude of the heavenly army, (of those) praising God and saying,

(A) *The Problem and Suggestions*

The heart of the problem lies in the fact that the locution στρατιὰ οὐράνιος in Lk. 2.13 is different from the expression in the LXX where the construction, arthrous noun ἡ στρατιά + arthrous genitive noun τοῦ οὐρανοῦ, occurs in nine places (1 Kgs 22.19; 2 Chron. 33.3, 5; Jer. 7.18; 8.2; 19.13; Hos. 13.4; Zeph. 1.5; *2 Esd.* 19.6).[319] This difference leads some scholars to argue that the locution in Lk. 2.13 was not derived from the imitation of the LXX but from the translation of the Hebrew locution צבא השמים in the Hebrew OT even though the second noun of the Hebrew expression is definite.

(1) *The Hebrew original theory*

Winter argues that the Greek locution στρατιὰ οὐρανίου in Luke is 'certainly a suitable rendering for the Hebrew construction צבא השמים' ('Some Observations on the Language', p. 118).[320] In contrast, the LXX, he continues, uses the arthrous noun οὐρανοῦ instead of the anarthrous adjective οὐράνιος: ἡ στρατιὰ τοῦ οὐρανοῦ. Because the composer of the Lukan infancy narrative,[321] Winter avers, relied on the Hebrew OT for this

---

318. The plural participle αἰνούντων grammatically modifies the singular noun πλῆθος (Fitzmyer and Marshall) or στρατιᾶς (Brown). This is *constructio ad sensum* which 'was very widespread in Greek from early times and is found in the NT as in the papyri' (BDF 134). It is really harsh, according to BDF, that a plural circumstantial participle is joined to a singular noun. However, this usage is Lukan, since two of the three examples in the NT, apart from Lk. 2.13, for the same construction appear in Acts (5.16; 21.36) [BDR 134.b]. For details, see below.
319. Scholars omit some of these nine instances. Fitzmyer omits four instances (Jer. 7.18; 8.2; Zeph. 1.5; *2 Esd.* 19.6), while Marshall omits two instances (Jer. 7.18; Hos. 13.4). Marshall appears to omit these two instances since the Hebrew locution צבא השמים, which occurs in all the other instances, does not occur in their Hebrew texts. Nolland also omits some instances (Jer. 7.18; 8.2; Zeph. 1.5; *2 Esd.* 19.6). For Winter's list, which also omits some instances, see below.
320. Nolland also notes that 'στρατιᾶς οὐρανίου, "heavenly host," reflects צבא השמים.' He points out that the LXX does not use the genitive adjective οὐρανίου but the genitive noun οὐρανοῦ (*Luke 1–9.20*, p. 108).
321. Winter does not postulate that Luke translated the Hebrew original. He simply asserts that the original source of the Lukan infancy narrative was in Hebrew.

construction without consulting the LXX, he used στρατιὰ οὐρανίου, a different Greek locution from that in the LXX. The anarthrous adjective οὐράνιος in Lk. 2.13 instead of τοῦ οὐρανοῦ of the LXX, according to Winter, reflects the influence of the Hebrew text rather than that of the LXX. If the author had imitated LXX style, Winter continues, he should have employed the expression in the LXX, where the noun οὐρανοῦ appears with the article without exception – ἡ στρατιὰ τοῦ οὐρανοῦ (1 Kgs 22.19; 2 Chron. 33.3, 5; Jer. 8.2; 19.13; Zeph. 1.5). 'If, as alleged, the writer of the Lukan Infancy Narrative', he argues, 'intentionally imitated the biblicisms of the Septuagint in his supposed desire of writing "in Biblical style", one might ask: why was not his effort of imitating carried out consistently?' ('Some Observations on the Language', pp. 117–18). Winter concludes that the author of the Lukan infancy story did not imitate LXX style, but translated a Hebrew original, צבא השמים, for the expression in Lk. 2.13, στρατιᾶς οὐρανίου.

(2) *The view which interprets the phrase as a variation of the LXX expression*
Recognizing that the phrase in Lk. 2.13, πλῆθος στρατιᾶς οὐρανίου, is an unusual locution compared with the locution in the LXX, Marshall suggests that πλῆθος στρατιᾶς τοῦ οὐρανοῦ is the usual expression according to LXX style. Without elucidating why and how the construction in Lk. 2.13 was composed, he notes that Luke probably adapted here the usual locution of the LXX (*Luke*, p. 111). In the same way, Fitzmyer considers the phrase in Lk. 2.13 στρατιὰ οὐρανίου, 'the heavenly host' simply a variation of the LXX expression ἡ στρατιὰ τοῦ οὐρανοῦ 'the host of heaven' (*Luke I–IX*, p. 410).

(B) *Evaluation of the Suggested Solutions*

(1) *The view of the LXX influence*
The locution in Lk. 2.13, as Marshall and Fitzmyer assume, could be a simple variation which resulted from the adaptation of an LXX locution. However, a proper explanation for the alteration of the arthrous noun in the LXX, τοῦ οὐρανοῦ, to the anarthrous adjective in Lk. 2.13, οὐρανίου, must be given.

(2) *The translation theory*
Concerning Winter's view, it is accepted that the Hebrew construction צבא השמים could underlie the Greek expression στρατιᾶς οὐρανίου in Lk. 2.13, even though the locution in Luke deviates from LXX style. Winter's argument, however, that the Greek locution in Luke stemmed from the translation of a Hebrew original is not convincing. He has to provide positive evidence to show that a Semitic original underlies the expression in Lk. 2.13. This expression could represent a good Greek locution which was

composed by Luke himself. In addition, the second noun of the Hebrew locution is definite. Therefore, his view needs to be closely re-examined.

(C) *Re-examination*

(1) *A non-Lukan Expression?*
Following Gersdorf, Machen regards the construction στρατιὰ οὐρανίου in Lk. 2.13 as a Lukanism ('The Origin', p. 243).[322] However, Luke does not seem to have followed his own style for this expression. If Luke had composed it, he could have employed the expression τῆς στρατιᾶς τοῦ οὐρανοῦ as in Acts 7.42a (τῇ στρατιᾷ τοῦ οὐρανοῦ), or 'τῆς οὐρανίου στρατιᾶς' following the expression in Acts 26.19 (τῇ οὐρανίῳ ὀπτασίᾳ). The locution in Acts 7.42a is exactly the same as the one in the LXX: arthrous noun στρατιά + arthrous modifying genitive noun οὐρανοῦ. In Acts 26.19, the adjective οὐράνιος is used as in Lk. 2.13, but it is placed between the article and the noun ὀπτασίᾳ; in contrast, the adjective οὐράνιος appears after the noun στρατιά in Lk. 2.13. These factors may demonstrate that the locution in Lk. 2.13, στρατιᾶς οὐρανίου, is non-Lukan and that it is less probable that Luke himself was the source of this phrase.

However, the case is not decisive. In Acts 7.42a, Luke probably looked up the LXX, attempting to allude to Jer. 7.18, 8.2, or 19.13;[323] before he directly quoted the LXX of Amos 5.25-27 in Acts 7.42b-43, he probably consulted with the LXX of Jer. 7.18, 8.2, or 19.13 in Acts 7.42a.[324] Concerning the expression τῇ οὐρανίῳ ὀπτασίᾳ in Acts 26.19, Luke's use of the adjective οὐρανίου indicates that the adjective belongs to Luke's

---

322. Nolland also suggests the possibility that the adjective οὐρανίου is Lukan, though he argues that it is non-Septuagintal. His suggestion is based on its occurrence in Acts 26.19 (*Luke 1–9.20*, p. 108). See also Jeremias, *Die Sprache*, p. 83, who argues that πλῆθος is a Lukanism and that a Greek locution for the meaning 'der himmlischen Heerschar' appears only in Luke-Acts in the NT (Acts 7.42a). The expression in Lk. 2.13, he continues, is different from that in Acts 7.42 but the locution in Lk. 2.13 came from the LXX; he admits that Luke does not exactly follow the expression in the LXX, but he interprets this as indicating that Luke adapted the LXX expression in Lk. 2.13 as in Lk. 1.13. For details, see *Die Sprache*, pp. 33–34.

323. Wilcox notes that Acts 7.42 alludes to Jer. 8.2 or 7.18 (*The Semitisms of Acts*, p. 103). Marshall suggests that 2 Chron. 33.3 and Jer. 8.2 were alluded to in Acts 7.42; 2 Chron. 33.3 also includes the phrase ἡ στρατιὰ τοῦ οὐρανοῦ (H. Marshall, *The Acts of the Apostles: An Introduction and Commentary* [Tyn NTCs; Grand Rapids: Eerdmans, 1980], p. 144). This study follows NA[27] which suggests three verses in Jeremiah as alluded to in Acts 7.42a.

324. Winter notes that Luke consulted the LXX in Acts 7.42a before he directly quoted the OT in the following verses, vv. 42b-43 ('Some Observations', p. 118. nt. 1). In contrast, the writer of the Lukan infancy narrative, according to him, did not consult the LXX for the phrase in Lk. 2.13.

vocabulary because this verse is Luke's direct composition.[325] Moreover, the word order in Acts 26.19, the article + adjective + noun, could change to the word order noun + adjective in Lk. 2.13.[326] Thus, it is hardly possible to confirm that the locution as a whole is non-Lukan.[327]

(2) *Translation?*

The Semitic original theory for the expression in Lk. 2.13, πλῆθος στρατιᾶς οὐρανίου, appears at first glance to be convincing. The following factors, however, mitigate against this suggestion.

First, scholars tend to concentrate on the expression in the LXX and argue that the usual expression should be 'τῆς στρατιᾶς τοῦ οὐρανοῦ';[328] they assume that the noun οὐρανοῦ must appear with the article after τῆς στρατιᾶς, although the anarthrous adjective οὐρανίου after στρατιᾶς in Lk. 2.13 represents a normal Greek expression.[329]

Secondly, the anarthrous adjective οὐρανίου in Lk. 2.13 does not reflect the Hebrew construction which consists of the noun and the article: השמים. The Hebrew phrase could be translated as 'τοῦ οὐρανοῦ' as in the LXX or literally 'τῶν οὐρανῶν'. Strikingly, the adjective οὐρανίου in Lk. 2.13 does not have the article, even though the Hebrew construction includes the article for the noun שמים. If a translator had translated a Semitic source, he would have not avoided the expression τοῦ οὐρανοῦ or τῶν οὐρανῶν, as in 2 Esd. 19.6.[330] These considerations call into question the argument that the Greek construction reflects the Hebrew construction.[331]

In brief, the phrase in Lk. 2.13 must not be considered a translation from a Semitic source. There may be another explanation, direct composition in Greek or dependence on the LXX.

---

325. Apart from the examples in Lk. 2.13 and Acts 26.19, the adjective οὐράνιος appears seven times elsewhere in the NT books always in Matthew. In Matthew, the adjective is always used in a stereotyped expression 'ὁ πατὴρ ὑμῶν (or μου) ὁ οὐράνιος' (Mt. 5.48; 6.14, 26, 32; 15.13; 18.35; 23.9). Hagner interprets this unique way of 'referring to God as ὁ πατὴρ ὑμῶν (or μου) ὁ οὐράνιος' as reflecting Matthew's Jewish milieu (*Matthew 1–13*, p. 135).

326. For the word order, see below.

327. Though postulating that the Greek locution in Lk. 2.13 echoes the Hebrew construction and differs from the LXX expression, Nolland admits that the adjective itself is probably Lukan, as it occurs in Acts 26.19 (*Luke 1–9.20*, p. 108).

328. As pointed out above, Marshall omits the article for the genitive noun στρατιᾶς due to the anarthrous noun πλῆθος. The problem concerning the article in this construction will be dealt with.

329. For a detailed argument on the phrase στρατιᾶς οὐρανίου, see below.

330. No Hebrew or Aramaic version of *2 Esdras* remains, but most scholars agree that this book was originally written in a Semitic language. For details, see J.M. Myers, *I and II Esdras* (The Anchor Bible; New York: Doubleday, 1985), pp. 115–19.

331. The advocates of the translation theory may argue that the translator omitted the article intentionally. However, there is no clear reason of why he did so.

(D) *A possible Explanation of the Reason why the Lukan Expression deviates from the LXX Phrase*

As we have seen, two differences between the expression in the LXX and that in Lk. 2.13 are clearly suggested: 1) while the noun οὐρανοῦ is used in the LXX, the adjective οὐρανίου appears in Lk. 2.13; 2) the locution in the LXX includes the article both for the first and the second noun: ἡ στρατιὰ τοῦ οὐρανοῦ. In comparison, the expression in Luke has the article neither for the noun nor for the adjective: στρατιᾶς οὐρανίου. Now we will deal with these differences.

(1) *The absence of the article for the noun στρατιά in the expression πλῆθος στρατιᾶς*

It seems that the noun στρατιά has the article in the LXX partly because the article of the second noun οὐρανοῦ reflects the Hebrew construction of the OT.[332] The article for the noun στρατιά occurs also partly because the prenominal adjective πᾶς was included in all the instances of the LXX except Zeph. 1.5:[333] πᾶσα ἡ στρατιὰ τοῦ οὐρανοῦ, 'all the heavenly host'. The article could be omitted after the pronoun πᾶς, but the pronoun does not mean 'all or whole' but 'every' in this case (BDF 275).

In contrast to the locution in the LXX, the phrase στρατιᾶς οὐρανίου in Lk. 2.13 is preceded by the anarthrous noun πλῆθος instead of πᾶς.[334] This anarthrous noun may provide an explanation to the question of why the article is omitted for the noun στρατιά; the anarthrous noun πλῆθος requires an anarthrous genitive noun in Luke-Acts. The noun πλῆθος occurs in 32 places in the NT and 25 examples of it are found in Luke-Acts.[335] Of these 25, nine examples do not have the article for the noun πλῆθος (Lk. 2.13; 5.6; 6.17; 23.27; Acts 5.14; 14.1; 17.4; 21.22;[336] 28.3) and the article is omitted with the following noun, except in Lk. 6.17 and 23.27. In these two

---

332. οὐρανοῦ will be treated in detail below.
333. The prenominal adjective πᾶς does not appear in this verse, but only the phrase τῇ στρατιᾷ τοῦ οὐρανοῦ, which corresponds to the Hebrew text.
334. Most scholars overlook the question of why Luke did not use the article for the genitive noun στρατιᾶς. Marshall, for example, suggests 'πλῆθος στρατιᾶς τοῦ οὐρανίου' as the usual expression (*Luke*, p. 111). He omits the article for the noun στρατιά without any explanation.
335. Luke's preponderance of this word is evident. This will be dealt with below.
336. There appear textual variations in this verse and NA[27] adopts the variations which omit the sentence δεῖ συνελθεῖν πλῆθος and the particle γάρ [B C*vid 36. 453. 614. 1175. 1505. 1739* *pc* sy(p) co]: πάντως ἀκούσονται ὅτι ἐλήλυθας. NA[27] seems to follow the shorter reading. The external evidence, however, supports the insertion of them [P[74] ℵ (*) A (C2) D E Ψ 33. 1739 v. 1 latt]: πάντως δεῖ πλῆθος συνελθεῖν, ἀκούσονται γὰρ ὅτι ἐλήλυθας. Bruce notes that the longer reading is probable and attractive (*The Acts of the Apostles*, p. 446).

instances, the phrase πλῆθος πολὺ τοῦ λαοῦ appears. The article before the noun λαός in these verses can be easily explained by pointing to the fact that the singular noun λαός almost always occurs with the article in Luke-Acts. The singular noun λαός appears 63 times in Luke-Acts, and only in four cases is the article omitted (Lk. 1.17; 2.32; Acts 5.37; 15.14). The first two examples appear in the infancy story, and these examples are excluded from our consideration because they may have been derived from Lukan sources.[337] The use of the anarthrous noun λαός in the other two examples, Acts 5.37 and 15.14, is appropriate in their context,[338] since the noun means 'a crowd' and 'a people'[339] respectively. In brief, the article is maintained for the noun λαός in Luke-Acts unless the context requires otherwise. It is thus certain that the article with the noun λαός in Lk. 6.17 and 23.27 appears because of the peculiarity of the noun λαός. Aside from Lk. 6.17 and 23.27, therefore, the anarthrous πλῆθος is always followed by an anarthrous noun in Luke-Acts.[340] Thus, the absence of the article for the noun στρατιᾶς in Lk. 2.13 is explained by the absence of the article for the noun πλῆθος.

In the LXX, πλῆθος occurs frequently with the article and an arthrous noun always follows anarthrous πλῆθος in this case. However, whenever πλῆθος appears without the article, the accompanying noun usually does not have the article either (Gen. 17.4; 27.28; 48.19; 1 Kgs 1.16; Ps. 32.16; 36.11; 63.2; 71.7; 76.17; *Jdt.* 1.16; 2.5; Eccl. 1.18; Job 33.19; *Wis* 6.24;

---

337. The first one is in Gabriel's message of the annunciation of Jesus' birth (1.17) and the other in Simeon's song of praise (2.32). [In Simeon's song, according to BDF 259 (3), Semitic colouring is strong.]

338. The instance in Acts 5.37 (καὶ ἀπέστησε λαὸν ὀπίσω αὐτοῦ; 'and he incited a crowd to revolt after him') is the direct statement of Gamaliel and Acts 15.14 (Συμεὼν ἐξηγήσατο καθὼς πρῶτον ὁ θεὸς ἐπεσκέψατο λαβεῖν ἐξ ἐθνῶν λαὸν τῷ ὀνόματι αὐτοῦ. 'Simeon has related how God first looked favourably on the Gentiles, to take from among them a people for his name' [NRSV]) records James' speech at the Jerusalem Council. In both cases, they probably spoke in Hebrew or Aramaic.

339. Bruce notes that λαός is regularly used for the Jewish people in Acts as in the NT and the LXX (*Acts*, p. 133). However, this noun, according to him, 'comprises believing Gentiles' in Acts 15.14 (*Acts*, p. 339).

340. Seven instances for the noun πλῆθος appear outside of Luke-Acts, and they also support this conclusion. Of these seven instances, the noun is followed by a genitive noun in four of them (Jn 5.3; 21.6; Jas 5.20; 1 Pet. 4.8). In Jn 21.6, the noun πλῆθος has the article and the arthrous noun follows it (τοῦ πλήθους τῶν ἰχθύων). In Jas 5.20 (πλῆθος ἁμαρτιῶν) and 1 Pet. 4.8 (πλῆθος ἁμαρτιῶν), the anarthrous πλῆθος is followed by an anarthrous noun. Jn 5.3 is the only apparent exception. In this case, an arthrous participle follows an anarthrous πλῆθος (πλῆθος τῶν ἀσθενούντων). The article here seems to be employed to clearly indicate that the participle is used as a substantive. Most instances in the NT use the article for the substantivized participle [BDF 264 (6)]. More importantly, the Gospel of John has no instance where the article is omitted for the substantivized participle (BDR 413.2).

11.17; 18.15, etc.).³⁴¹ Thus, the construction of the phrase πλῆθος στρατιᾶς, that is, anarthrous πλῆθος + anarthrous genitive noun, was usual; it is also found in the LXX.

Why then did the writer not use the article for the noun πλῆθος? According to Plummer, he intended to denote '*a multitude* of the throng of the heavenly host' (*Luke*, p. 57).³⁴² He may thus have employed πλῆθος without the article to indicate 'a multitude', which fits for the context, and the absence of the article for πλῆθος caused him then to choose an anarthrous genitive noun στρατιᾶς. This being the case, the issue of Luke's deviation from the LXX, thus, centres on the latter part of the phrase, the anarthrous adjective οὐρανίου.

(2) *The use of the adjective* οὐρανίου *instead of the noun* οὐρανοῦ *and the absence of the article for the adjective*

(i)   *the position of the adjective* οὐράνιος

As mentioned above, the adjective οὐράνιος is placed between the article and a noun in Acts 26.19 (τῇ οὐρανίῳ ὀπτασίᾳ).³⁴³ Is the word order of στρατιᾶς οὐρανίου in Lk. 1.5 non-Greek? According to BDF, 'an anarthrous adjectival attribute usually follows its substantive' [BDF 474(1)].³⁴⁴ This rule also applies to the adjective οὐράνιος in classical Greek:³⁴⁵ θεὸν οὐράνιον (*Appianum*. C2. 146.607); καὶ Διὸς οὐρανίου (Herodotus 6.056.01); ἄστρων οὐρανίων [Hippocrates,

---

341. The word order varies in the LXX. In *Sir*. 16.1, for example, the word order is a noun + πλῆθος + adjective modifying the noun without article: τέκνων πλῆθος ἀχρήστων. In *Isa*. 17.12, the word order is πλῆθος + noun + adjective: πλῆθος ἐθνῶν πολλῶν. In *Wis*. 11.15, πλῆθος is followed by the adjective + noun: πλῆθος ἀλόγων ζῴων.

342. It is noteworthy that Herodotus made use of πλῆθος with the noun στρατός, στρατοῦ πλῆθος, to mean 'a multitude of the army', a paraphrase of στρατὸς πολύς (Liddell and Scott, p. 1417). Herodotus did not add the article for πλῆθος, neither for στρατός.

343. 'Hebrew favored the postposition of the adjective' (BDF 474.1).

344. This word order is well attested in Luke-Acts; it is sufficient to show some examples in Acts (2.2; 2.5b; 5.12; 8.1; 13.32, 48; 18.14; 22.3a). It is also found outside of Acts: Mt. 25.46 (ζωὴν αἰώνιον 'eternal life') [αἰώνιος tends to be placed after the modified word, especially in John: Jn 3.15–16; 4.4, etc. Another representative example is πνεύματος ἁγίου which appears many times in the NT: Mt. 1.18; 3.11; Mk 1.8; Lk. 1.15; Jn 1.30; Acts 1.2, etc.]; 2 Thess. 2.16 (παράκλησιν αἰωνίαν 'eternal comfort'); 1 Tim. 6.9 (ἐπιθυμίας πολλὰς ἀνοήτους καὶ βλαβεράς; 'many foolish and harmful lusts'). The word order anarthrous noun + anarthrous adjective is as normal for the NT authors as for classical.

345. Concerning the use of the adjective οὐρανίου in Lk. 2.13, Jeremias notes that Luke Graecizes the expression in the LXX by altering the phrase τοῦ οὐρανοῦ to an adjective οὐρανίου without the article (*Die Sprache*, p. 34). This implies that the phrase in Luke, στρατιᾶς οὐρανίου, belongs to normal Greek usage.

3. *A Close Examination of the Greek of the Infancy Narrative*

EdmHi 1 (Lette de Democe a Hippocrate)].³⁴⁶ It is true that the reversed word order οὐράνιος + noun also occurs in classical Greek. However, the word order, noun + οὐράνιος, is more frequently used.³⁴⁷ In sum, the word order of the phrase στρατιᾶς οὐρανίου is normal in Greek.³⁴⁸

(ii) *Why is the adjective* οὐρανίου *used in Lk. 2.13 instead of the noun* οὐρανοῦ *in the LXX?*

In the LXX, the expression ἡ στρατιὰ τοῦ οὐρανοῦ refers to sun, moon, or stars in all the instances except in 1 Kgs 22.19.³⁴⁹ Interestingly, Luke uses this LXX phrase in Acts 7.42a to refer to sun, moon, and stars.³⁵⁰ In contrast, the phrase in Lk. 2.13, στρατιὰ οὐρανίου, is employed to refer to the heavenly army. If Luke composed the construction στρατιὰ οὐρανίου in Lk. 2.13, he probably intended to avoid a confusion between this construction and the LXX phrase ἡ στρατιὰ τοῦ οὐρανοῦ; Luke probably utilized the adjective οὐρανίου with the noun στρατιά in Lk. 2.13 on purpose in order to render 'heavenly spirits'.³⁵¹ Otherwise, Luke probably altered the arthrous noun τοῦ οὐρανοῦ in the LXX to the anarthrous adjective οὐρανίου in Lk. 2.13 in order for the phrase στρατιά οὐρανίου to mean clearly 'heavenly army', not 'heavenly bodies'. This interpretation is strengthened by the observation that Luke never used the genitive τοῦ οὐρανοῦ for metaphorical meaning; Luke used the genitive noun οὐρανοῦ only for the literal meaning 'of sky' or 'of air', not for the metaphorical meaning 'of heaven' (Lk. 8.5; 9.58; 10.21; 12.56; 13.19;³⁵² Acts 10.12; 11.6; 17.26).³⁵³ These elements may have led Luke to change the noun οὐρανοῦ in the LXX to the adjective in Lk. 2.13.

---

346. A similar expression is found in Hippocrates, Vic 4 [Le regime. Livre IV] 00. 089. 130: Διὶ οὐρανίου where the genitive adjective is used as a substantive: 'to Zeus of heaven'.

347. For a detailed list, see Traub, *TDNT*, vol. 5, p. 536.

348. In the LXX, the adjective occurs eight times, but there is no example for the word order, anarthrous noun + anarthrous adjective οὐράνιος. It seems that the word order in the expression of Lk. 2.13 may have occurred under the influence of the LXX expression ἡ στρατιὰ τοῦ οὐρανοῦ.

349. In *2 Esd.* 19.6, αἱ στρατίαι τῶν οὐρανῶν means the heavenly host(s), but this example is excluded from our consideration because the nouns are plurals.

350. See Bruce, *The Acts of the Apostles*, p. 203 and Marshall, *The Acts*, p. 144.

351. For more details, see below.

352. The genitive noun in this verse is included in the quotation of Ps. 103.12.

353. In Lk. 21.26, the plural noun seems to be used to refer to spiritual beings: αἱ γὰρ δυνάμεις τῶν οὐρανῶν σαλευθήσονται 'for the powers of the heavens will be shaken'. The expression, αἱ γὰρ δυνάμεις τῶν οὐρανῶν, however, probably refers to the objects of the sky rather than to spiritual beings. This interpretation is strengthened by the reference to sun, moon, and stars in v. 25. For the interpretation of the phrase, see Marshall who notes that the

(iii) *The omission of the article before the adjective* οὐρανίου
Needless to say, the adjective οὐρανίου modifies the noun στρατιᾶς in Lk. 2.13. The gender, number, and case of the adjective is identical to those of the modified noun στρατιᾶς: female, singular, genitive.[354] If the adjective used in post-position modifies the anarthrous noun, the modifying adjective normally does not include an article. It is true, as BDF remark, that 'it is also possible for an attributive adjective used in postposition with an anarthrous substantive to take the article' (BDF 270.3).[355] However, there is no instance in Luke-Acts for the use of the arthrous adjective used in the post-position to modify the anarthrous noun.[356] This probably provides an explanation to the question of why the locution in Lk. 2.13, if Luke composed it, does not have the article for the adjective οὐρανίου. Remarkably, οὐρανίος does not include the article in the construction, noun + οὐρανίου, in most instances of classical authors.

(E) *Other Evidence which supports Luke's Direct Composition*

This construction thus is probably from Luke's hand. Apart from the adjective οὐρανίου, there are many Lukan words and usage in Lk. 2.13:

1. The verb αἰνέω occurs six times in Luke-Acts (Lk. 2.13, 20; 19.37; Acts 2.47; 3.8-9)[357] while it is found only twice in the rest of the NT, in Rom. 15.11 where it occurs in a quotation of Ps. 117.1 of the LXX (MT 116.1), and in Rev. 19.5 which is a possible allusion to the LXX Ps. 21.24 (MT 22.24).

   The plural circumstantial participle αἰνούντων modifies the singular noun στρατιά in Lk. 2.13.[358] This harsh construction

---

noun δύναμις means 'a heavenly body' (*Luke*, p. 775). Cf. Hagner, who argues that αἱ γὰρ δυνάμεις τῶν οὐρανῶν does not refer to spiritual beings but to the objects of the sky in Mt. 24.29, the parallel verse of Lk. 21.26 (*Matthew 14–28*, p. 713).

354. In classical Greek, the feminine genitive is οὐρανίας. Luke uses the masculine form of this adjective with the feminine noun again in Acts 26.19 (οὐρανίῳ). This change occurs already in the LXX [Dan. (Th) 4.26; *3 Macc.* 6.18; *4 Macc.* 9.15; 11.3].

355. BDR add that Mayer sees the literary manner of Hellenistic age in this construction (270.3).

356. In Luke-Acts, there are some examples in which the arthrous participle in post-position modifies the anarthrous noun: Lk. 23.49; Acts 7.35; 9.22. While there are textual variations which support the presence of the article for the noun in Lk. 23.49 and Acts 9.22, there is no textual variation in Acts 7.35. In Jn 14.27, the arthrous adjective used in post-position modifies the anarthrous noun.

357. In variations of Lk. 24.53, this verb appears.

358. Marshall (*Luke*, p. 111) and Fitzmyer (*Luke I–IX*, p. 410) note that the plural participle is joined with the noun στρατιά in Lk. 2.13 (also Bock and Greijdanus). In contrast,

3. A Close Examination of the Greek of the Infancy Narrative 169

appears only three times in the NT apart from Lk. 2.13 (BDR 134.b);[359]

Mt. 15.31: ὥστε τὸν ὄχλον θαυμάσαι βλέποντας κωφοὺς λαλοῦντας
'so that the crowd was amazed when they saw the mute speaking'

Acts 5.16: συνήρχετο δὲ καὶ τὸ πλῆθος τῶν πέριξ πόλεων Ἰερουσαλὴμ φέροντες ἀσθενεῖς.
'And even the people of the cities around Jerusalem was gathering bringing the sick'.

Acts 21.36: ἠκολούθει γὰρ τὸ πλῆθος τοῦ λαοῦ κράζοντες Αἶρε αὐτόν.
'For the multitude of the people was following, crying out "away with him".'
Two of the three instances occur in Acts.

2. πλῆθος occurs 25 times in Luke-Acts, only seven times in the rest of the NT.

3. In the whole NT, ἐξαίφνης occurs in five verses, of which four are in Luke's writings (Mk 13.36; Lk. 2.13; 9.39; Acts 9.3; 22.6). It is also noteworthy that the tendency to add the adverb 'suddenly' exists only in Luke. Luke appears to have inserted ἐξαίφνης in Lk. 9.38-39, while the parallels in Mk 9.18 and Mt. 17.15 do not have it:

Lk. 9.38-39: καὶ ἰδοὺ ἀνὴρ ἀπὸ τοῦ ὄχλου ἐβόησεν λέγων, Διδάσκαλέ δέομαί σου ἐπιβλέψαι ἐπὶ τὸν υἱόν μου, ὅτι μονογενής μοί ἐστιν, καὶ ἰδοὺ πνεῦμα λαμβάνει αὐτὸν καὶ ἐξαίφνης κράζει,

Mk 9.17-18: καὶ ἀπεκρίθη αὐτῷ εἷς ἐκ τοῦ ὄχλου, Διδάσκαλε, ἤνεγκα τὸν υἱόν μου πρὸς σέ, ἔχοντα πνεῦμα ἄλαλον· καὶ ὅπου ἐὰν αὐτὸν καταλάβῃ ῥήσσει αὐτόν,

Mt. 17.15: καὶ λέγων, Κύριε, ἐλέησόν μου τὸν υἱόν, ὅτι σεληνιάζεται καὶ κακῶς πάσχει·
Although ὅπου ἐὰν in Mark could produce a sense of the meaning of the adverb,[360] Luke added the adverb to denote 'suddenly'. This tendency appears only in Luke.

Brown regards πλῆθος as the modified noun. While the meaning is the same in both cases, it appears that Marshall and Fitzmyer's explanations are more precise than Brown's; the case of the participle is identical to the noun στρατιά (genitive).
359. BDF suggest only one example in Acts 21.36 (134.1b).
360. Marshall, *Luke*, p. 91.

4. Concerning the preposition σύν, Plummer notes that 'Luke greatly prefers σύν to μετά or καί (*Luke*, p. 34). Luke-Acts includes 72 instances of the preposition σύν (Lk. 23; Acts 49), while it occurs only 13 times in Matthew, Mark, and John and 37 times in the whole Pauline corpus. Two more instances are found in James and 2 Peter. More importantly, Luke uses σύν, according to Plummer, in some verses whose parallels in Matthew and Mark include μετά or καί: 8.38, 51; 10.1; 22.14, 56.[361]

Lk. 2.13, καὶ ἐξαίφνης ἐγένετο σὺν τῷ ἀγγέλῳ πλῆθος στρατιᾶς οὐρανίου αἰνούντων τὸν θεὸν καὶ λεγόντων, includes ten words, excluding conjunctions and articles. Of these ten, five are particularly Lukan and two grammatical elements are also Lukan, while there is no non-Lukanism and no construction that reflects a Hebrew construction.[362] With all these considerations, we may conclude that Luke himself composed the sentence in 2.13, including the phrase πλῆθος στρατιᾶς οὐρανίου.

In summary, the Greek locution στρατιᾶς οὐρανίου[363] does not reflect the Hebrew construction and is not awkward at all.[364] In addition, the composition procedure can be well explained, and Lukan style is patent in Lk. 2.13, as we have shown above. Therefore, the expression needs to be regarded as Luke's direct composition.

III. *The Usage of the Passive Form of the Verb* πίμπλημι *with* ἡμέρα *or* χρόνος

The passive form of the verb πίμπλημι is used with ἡμέρα or χρόνος to indicate the fulfilment of a certain period of time five times in the Lukan infancy narrative: 1.23, 57; 2.6, 21, 22.

---

361. Plummer concludes that 'it is not likely that an interpolator would have caught all these minute details in Luke's style' (*Luke*, p. 34).

362. Brown notes that 'there may be a Semitic influence on the word order (BDF 472.1d)' (*The Birth of the Messiah*, p. 403). His remark, however, appears groundless.

363. In the word order, anarthrous noun + anarthrous adjective, the adjective does not convey an important meaning while in the construction adjective + noun, the adjective is underlined (Heimerdinger, p. 157). If this is the case, the author of the infancy narrative used στρατιᾶς οὐρανίου without emphasizing the adjective 'heavenly'. The phrase 'with the angel' which occurs just before the phrase πλῆθος στρατιᾶς οὐρανίου may have made it useless to emphasize the adjective 'heavenly'.

364. It is impossible here again to completely refute the argument that Luke translated his Semitic source considering the elements explained above. We may conclude, however, that it is unnecessary to assume that Luke translated this phrase from a Semitic original simply because an expression deviates from LXX style.

3. A Close Examination of the Greek of the Infancy Narrative 171

1.23 – καὶ ἐγένετο ὡς ἐπλήσθησαν αἱ ἡμέραι τῆς λειτουργίας αὐτοῦ
and it happened (that) when the days of his service were fulfilled.

1.57 – Τῇ δὲ Ἐλισάβετ ἐπλήσθη ὁ χρόνος τοῦ τεκεῖν αὐτήν[365]
And for Elizabeth the time (for her) to give birth was fulfilled.

2.6 – ἐγένετο δὲ ἐν τῷ εἶναι αὐτοὺς ἐκεῖ ἐπλήσθησαν αἱ ἡμέραι τοῦ τεκεῖν αὐτήν
and it happened (that) when they were there, the days for her to give birth were fulfilled.

2.21 – Καὶ ὅτε ἐπλήσθησαν ἡμέραι ὀκτὼ τοῦ περιτεμεῖν αὐτόν
'And when eight days were fulfilled for circumcising him.'

2.22 – Καὶ ὅτε ἐπλήσθησαν αἱ ἡμέραι τοῦ καθαρισμοῦ αὐτῶν κατὰ τὸν νόμον Μωϋσέως
And when the days of their purification were fulfilled according to the law of Moses.

(A) *The Problem and Proposals for a Solution*

The verb πίμπλημι occurs eight times in the Lukan infancy narrative, five times in the above verses for the completion of a period of time and three times for a filling with the Holy Spirit (1.15, 41, 67). In Lk. 3–24 and Acts, there are fourteen further instances of this verb (it thus appears twenty-two times in total in Luke-Acts). There are only two instances in the rest of the NT. These statistics indicate that the verb is characteristically Lukan. The passive form of the verb πίμπλημι, however, is never used of the completion of a time period outside of the infancy narrative, though it is utilized for different meanings.[366] Further, no instance of this usage is found in the LXX. For the fulfilment of a time period, another verb, πληρόω, is used in Lk 3–24 and Acts (5x)[367] as well as in the LXX (14x).[368] The use of the verb πίμπλημι for the fulfilment of a time period, therefore, deviates from both Lukan and LXX style.[369]

---

365. With respect to the phrase ἐπλήσθη ὁ χρόνος τοῦ τεκεῖν αὐτήν, P. Benoit remarks that it 'représente une grécisation Lukanienne de l'hébraïsme-septuagintisme normal αἱ ἡμέραι (Gen. 25.24)' ['L'enfance de Jean-Baptiste selon Luc I,' *NTS*, 3 (1956–57), p. 175]. This article is republished in his book, *Exégèse et Théologie, III* (Paris: Les Éditions de Cerf, 1968), pp. 165–96].

366. For other usages, see below.

367. This construction occurs only in Mk 1.15 in the NT, apart from the verses in Luke-Acts. This indicates that the use of the verb πληρόω for the completion of a time period is almost exclusively Lukan. For details, see below.

368. Detailed information about the use of the verb πληρόω will be given below.

369. The verb πίμπλημι is not utilized for this concept even by classical authors who employ the verb πληρόω for it.

(1) *A non-Lukanism*

There is no dissenting voice against the view that this usage of the verb is non-Lukan. In connection with the fulfilment of a time period, the verb πίμπλημι appears in the NT only in the infancy narrative whereas the verb πληρόω is used with this meaning outside of the Lukan infancy story.[370]

(i) Most scholars assume that this usage of the verb did not stem from Luke's hand but from his source. Jeremias argues that this construction originates from the tradition used by Luke (*Der Sprache*, p. 45). Depending on Jeremias's observation, Nolland claims that this non-Lukan usage points to a Semitic pre-Lukan source (*Luke 1–9.20*, p. 78).

(ii) In contrast, Benoit regards this verb as possibly coming from Luke's hand. Listing some non-Lukanisms, including the use of πίμπλημι for the fulfilment of a time period, he asks, 'do such a few <non-Lukanisms> suffice to require someone's hand other than Luke's?'[371] His answer is 'absolutely not'. Emphasizing that the verb πίμπλημι is Luke's peculiar word, he suggests that 'the peculiarity of chs 1–2 is only in its more frequent occurrence [8 of 22 instances in Luke-Acts] and in its application to the time.'[372]

(2) *The non-Septuagintal character of the usage*[373]

It is indisputable that the usage of the verb πίμπλημι in the five verses of the Lukan infancy narrative is different from LXX style; this is a non-Septuagintalism.[374] However, O'Feargail tries to show that this construction comes from the influence of the LXX. Though recognizing that the verb usage differs from that in the LXX, he posits that the phrase ὡς

---

370. Benoit is the first scholar who recognized the peculiarity of the verb usage. 'πίμπλησθαι dit du temps qui s'accomplit,' he notes, 'employé cinq fois dans les deux chapitres de l'évangile de l'Enfance.' 'Mais jamais ailleurs dans l'Évangile,' he continues, 'ni dans les Actes, où Luk use normalement de πληροῦσθαι.' ('L'enfance de Jean-Baptiste selon Luc I,' p. 175).

371. 'Ces quelques <non-Lukanismes> suffisent-ils pour requérir une main autre que celle de Luc?' (*Exégèse et Théologie III*, p. 173).

372. 'la particularité des ch. 1–2 est seulement dans sa plus grande fréquence (8 cas sur 22 de Luk-Actes) et dans son application au temps' (*Exégèse et Théologie III*, p. 173).

373. This usage of the verb πίμπλημι is also different from classical Greek. See Benoit's article, 'L'enfance de Jean-Baptiste selon Luc I,' p. 175. Liddell and Scott, p. 1420, list some examples for the use of the active form of the verb πληρόω with the time indicator. The passive form of this verb, however, does not appear in classical Greek though the use of the active form probably paved the way to the use of the passive verb in Luke.

374. Interestingly, many scholars do not recognize the non-Septuagintal character of this verb usage. See Brown, Fitzmyer, Bock, Jeremias, and Nolland. Only Benoit and O'Fearghail acknowledge that the verb usage is non-Septuagintal.

3. A Close Examination of the Greek of the Infancy Narrative 173

ἐπλήσθησαν αἱ ἡμέραι in 1.23 is 'a septuagintal-type phrase' which means 'a septuagintal expression which is cast in the mould of a septuagintal expression but which does not have an exact parallel there, or represents an inaccurate or unsuccessful attempt at reproducing a septuagintal expression.'[375] Luke, according to this description, unsuccessfully attempted to imitate LXX style. Emphasizing that the verb itself represents a typical Lukan word, he labels it 'a Lukan created septuagintal-type phrase' ('The Imitation,' p. 62).

(B) *Evaluation of the Suggested Proposals*

(1) *Did the non-Lukan verb usage stem from a Semitic source or Luke's hand?*

It is conceded that the usage of the verb πίμπλημι deviates both from Lukan and LXX style, which does seem to indicate the influence of a pre-Lukan source. This does not necessarily imply, however, that the source was Semitic. One needs to try to find another possible explanation for the origin of the verb usage before concluding that it is derived from a Semitic source.

Benoit's argument that the verb probably stemmed from Luke's hand requires more evidence: he does not show why Luke used the verb πίμπλημι for the complement of a time period only in the infancy narrative, while using another verb (πληρόω) in Luke (21.24) and Acts (7.23; 7.30; 9.23; 24.27).

(2) *Is this Septuagintal-type expression created by Luke?*

Concerning O'Fearghail's view, it is admitted that the verb itself is typically Lukan; it may thus be from Luke's hand. However, the verb used of the completion of a time period is not a Septuagintal-type phrase, but a non-Septuagintal expression. The usage of the verb πίμπλημι does not reflect the style of the LXX where πληρόω is used of the fulfilment of a time period without exception.[376] The discrepancy between its usage in the LXX and that in Luke 1–2 is too weighty to be solved by simply identifying it as an unsuccessful Septuagintalism. More importantly, Luke uses the verb πληρόω in the rest of his writings, following LXX style; Luke has no discernible reason to unsuccessfully imitate LXX style for this construction in the infancy narrative. The theory that the Lukan phrase is 'a Lukan created Septuagintal-type phrase' thus does not provide a convincing solution. In order to argue that the expression is a Septuagintal-type

---

375. 'The Imitation of the Septuagint in Luke's Infancy Narrative', p. 52. For his argument on the imitation theory, see Chapter 1.B.

376. For detailed statistics, see below.

expression, a more adequate explanation is required. This issue therefore requires an approach different from O'Fearghail's.

(C) *A Detailed Study*

Before suggesting a probable solution, we need to scrutinize the use of the verb πίμπλημι in Luke-Acts in detail. Along with the verb πίμπλημι, the verb πληρόω, which is used of the fulfilment of a period of time in Lk. 3–24 and Acts, also requires close examination. In order to confirm that the usage is non-Septuagintal, the LXX verses, where the verb πληρόω appears with time indicators, will be listed. On the basis of these detailed statistics, we will make some observations and then proceed to make a proposal.[377]

(1) *Confirmation that the verb itself is Lukan vocabulary*

πίμπλημι occurs 16 times in the NT outside of the Lukan infancy narrative. Of these 16 instances, 14 are found in Luke-Acts. The frequency indicates that the verb itself stemmed most probably from Luke's hand.[378]

(2) *The use of the verb πίμπλημι and πληρόω in Luke-Acts*[379]

(i) the use of πίμπλημι in Luke-Acts

The verb πίμπλημι used to indicate the fulfilment of a certain period of time is found only in the infancy narrative; it is never used in this way in Lk. 3–24 and Acts (14x). This verb appears also in connection with the Holy Spirit in the infancy narrative (Lk. 1.15, 41, 67), which is well attested also in Acts (Acts 2.4; 4.8, 31; 9.17; 13.9). Outside of the infancy narrative, it also occurs in connection with feelings like

---

377. In order to look at the statistics at a glance, some explanations, which were already given above, will be repeated.

378. The two instances of the verb πίμπλημι both occur in the Gospel of Matthew and the verb does not indicate the completion of a certain time period there: 22.10 (ἐπλήσθη ὁ γάμος ἀνακειμένων: 'and the wedding hall was filled with the guests'); 27.48 (λαβὼν σπόγγον πλήσας τε ὄξους: 'having taken a sponge and filled it with sour wine'). Mt. 22.10 and 27.48 have parallels in Lk. 14.23 and Mk. 15.36 respectively. In the verses of Mark and Luke, the verb γεμίζω is used. Matthew seems to have intended to avoid the use of the verb γεμίζω, since that was not his vocabulary; this verb does not appear in Matthew. (In Jn 19.29, a parallel of Mt. 27.48, some variations inserted, 'οἱ δὲ πλήσαντες ὄξους') In the Gospel of Matthew, πληρόω is used only in the connection with a fulfilled promise without exception. Matthew thus avoids using πληρόω in 22.10 and 27.48, utilizing πίμπλημι instead.

379. B.J. Koet points out that πληρόω, πίμπλημι as well as τελειόω were used distinctively: 'a) to indicate the end of a certain period; b) to describe the realization of certain prophecies or obligations from the Scripture or on the basis of the Scriptures; c) to clarify a certain state of mind, especially the fullness of the Spirit' (B.J. Koet, *Five Studies on Interpretation of Scripture in Luke-Acts* [Studiorum Novi Testamenti Auxilia, XIV; Leuven: University Press, 1989], p. 36). This classification is not accurate as the following study shows.

anger, jealousy, or fear (Lk. 4.28; 5.26; 6.11; Acts 3.10; 5.17; 13.45; 19.29). In the active form of the verb, this means 'fill' in Lk. 5.7. Luke makes use of this verb even for the fulfilment of the OT in Lk. 21.22,[380] which deviates from his own style.[381]

(ii) *the use of* πληρόω *in Luke-Acts*
In the infancy narrative, the verb πληρόω appears twice in 1.20; 2.40: in Lk. 1.20, the verb conveys the connotation of fulfilment (οἵτινες πληρωθήσονται εἰς τὸν καιρὸν αὐτῶν), and in 2.40, 'wisdom' is the object (πληρούμενον σοφίᾳ), which consists with the usage in Acts 2.28; 13.52. The verb πληρόω occurs five times for the completion of a period of time in Lk. 3–24 and Acts: Lk. 21.24; Acts 7.23; 7.30; 9.23; 24.27. The compound verb συμπληρόω occurs in Lk. 9.51 and Acts 2.1 with the time indicator ἡμέρα.[382] The majority of the examples are connected with the concept 'fulfilment of the (promised) word or thing' as in Lk. 1.20; Lk. 4.21; 7.1; 9.31; 22.16; 24.44; Acts 1.16; 3.18; 19.21.

(3) *A non-Septuagintal construction*
In the LXX, the passive form of the verb πληρόω occurs frequently with αἱ ἡμέραι or ἔτη as the subject (Gen. 25.24, 29.21; Lev. 8.33; 12.4; Num. 6.5, 13; 1 Kgs 18.16; 2 Kgs 7.12; 1 Chron. 17.11; *Tob.* 8.20; 10.1; Jer. 32.34; 41.14; Lam. 4.18).[383] No example of the verb πίμπλημι appears with time indicators in the LXX.

From the above observations, the following points have become clear: i) the verb πίμπλημι itself is vocabulary mostly peculiar to Luke; ii) the usage of the verb πίμπλημι with time indicators in the infancy story deviates from Lukan and Septuagintal style;[384] iii) the use of the verb πληρόω with time indicators is almost exclusively Lukan as it appears only in Luke-Acts in the NT except in Mk 1.5; iv) for the concept 'fulfilment of the promise', Luke uses the verb πληρόω and the only exception is found in Lk. 21.22

---

380. In some textual variants of Lk. 1.20, where the concept of the fulfilment of the promise appears, this verb, πίμπλημι, is used instead of the verb πληρόω. Some copyists seem to have assumed that only the verb πίμπλημι is used in the infancy narrative. The verb πληρόω occurs only once more in the infancy narrative apart from Lk. 1.20 (2.40).
381. The use of the verb πίμπλημι in Lk. 21.22 will be examined below to show that Luke possibly used a seemingly wrong verb intentionally.
382. As noted above, this construction is found also in Mk 1.15, where καιρός is the subject (Πεπλήρωται ὁ καιρός).
383. The noun ἔτη is the subject in Jer. 41.14 and the active form of the verb is used in Gen. 50.3 and *1 Macc.* 3.50. All the others had αἱ ἡμέραι as the subject.
384. This usage is probably different from the style of Mark in which the verb πληρόω is used for it in Mk 1.5.

where the verb πίμπλημι appears for this concept. The last point seems to provide a hint concerning our investigation and we will return to this observation below.

(D) *A probable Proposal*

The following question arises: why did Luke who uses the verb πληρόω (and its compound) outside of the infancy story for the fulfilment of a certain period with ἡμέρα or ἔτη as the subject employ the verb πίμπλημι in the first two chapters of the Gospel in connection with the completion of a time period?

(1) *Luke's intentional adoption of the verb πίμπλημι*[385]
Luke probably intended to avoid a possible confusion which could have come from the use of the same verb for two different meanings in a pericope; after adopting πληρόω to express fulfilment of what has been said in 1.20, Luke used a different verb, πίμπλημι, in v. 23 in order to avoid using one verb for two different meanings.[386] Afterwards, Luke decided to keep this usage in the infancy narrative.

(2) *The instance which supports this interpretation*
This kind of practice is found in Lk. 21.22-24 where both the verb πληρόω and the verb πίμπλημι occur:

22 ὅτι ἡμέραι ἐκδικήσεως αὗταί εἰσιν τοῦ <u>πλησθῆναι πάντα τὰ γεγραμμένα</u>.
'for these are days of vengeance *for all that is written to be fulfilled.*'

---

385. The attitude of early Church Fathers demonstrates that the use of the verb πίμπλημι with time indicators in the Lukan infancy narrative bothered them. Their attitudes are mixed: some follow Luke's way, whereas others alter the verb into 'πληρόω'. The Church Fathers of the first three centuries absolutely prefer πίμπλημι to πληρόω, when these verbs appear with time indicators. For example, Origen utilizes the latter with time indicators only once (work# 017, 56.3) while utilizing the former many times. This tendency changes in A.D. 4–6; the verb πληρόω is then dominant. The Church Fathers of this period alter the former to the latter, even when they quote or allude to the verses in the Lukan infancy story. See Joannes Chrysostomus, work# 137, 50.809.1 which quoted Lk. 2.22. The same verse is quoted in 137, 50. 809. 6 and 442, 58. 29. Work# 304, 61.738. 45 clearly refers to Lk. 2.6 and it alters the verb to πληρόω. For the case of non-quotations or allusions, see Palladius #001, 70.3.8, and Theodoretus #026, 81.637.89 and #026, 81.804.10. Their attitude indicates that the verb usage bothered them (Source: TLG).
Some copyists also try to alter the verb πίμπλημι to πληρόω (Θ 33 *pc* in 2.21) or the verb τελέω and its compound verb (D in 2.6 and 2.21). Interestingly, D alters the verb πληρόω to πίμπλημι in 1.20.

386. Fitzmyer suggests that the verb πίμπλημι was taken to convey the idea that there is no connotation of fulfilment (*Luke I–IX*, p. 329).

23 οὐαὶ ταῖς ἐν γαστρὶ ἐχούσαις καὶ ταῖς θηλαζούσαις ἐν ἐκείναις ταῖς ἡμέραις· ἔσται γὰρ ἀνάγκη μεγάλη ἐπὶ τῆς γῆς καὶ ὀργὴ τῷ λαῷ τούτῳ,
'Woe to those who are pregnant and to those who are nursing infants in those days! For there will be great distress on the earth and wrath against this people;'

24 καὶ πεσοῦνται στόματι μαχαίρης καὶ αἰχμαλωτισθήσονται εἰς τὰ ἔθνη πάντα, καὶ Ἰερουσαλὴμ ἔσται πατουμένη ὑπὸ ἐθνῶν, ἄχρι οὗ <u>πληρωθῶσιν καιροὶ ἐθνῶν</u>.
'they will fall by the edge of the sword and be taken away as captives among all nations; and Jerusalem will be trampled on by the Gentiles, until *the times of the Gentiles are fulfilled*.' (NRSV)

The usage of the verb πίμπλημι in v. 22 is different from that in Luke-Acts and the other NT books as well as in the LXX; for the connotation of the fulfilment of the prophecy and promise, the verb πληρόω or τελέω is always used in Biblical Greek.[387] Moreover, πάντα τὰ γεγραμμένα, exclusively a Lukan expression, occurs four times in Luke-Acts apart from Lk. 21.22 and the verb πληρόω (Lk. 24.44) and τελέω (Lk. 18.31; Acts 13.29) are utilized with this phrase.[388] Why is then seemingly an inappropriate verb, i.e., πίμπλημι, used in Lk. 21.22?

The use of the verb πληρόω in v. 24 probably suggests an answer; Luke might have intended to avoid using the same verb, πληρόω, for two different meanings in v. 22 and v. 24. It appears for Luke to have depended on his peculiar source for v. 24 while composing the sentence in v. 22.[389] In other words, Luke used the verb πίμπλημι in v. 22 because of the use of the verb πληρόω in v. 24 which was in his source.[390]

This instance demonstrates that Luke probably made use of the verb πίμπλημι or πληρόω, whose usage is different from his own style in order to

---

387. For detailed statistics of the verb πληρόω, see above. The verb τελέω appears for the connotation of fulfilment in Lk. 2.39, 18.31, 22.37, and in Acts 13.29.

388. The instance in Acts 24.14, where this phrase appears, is not connected with the fulfilment of things that are written. In Lk. 22.37, τοῦτο τὸ γεγραμμένον occurs with the verb τελέω.

389. Marshall notes concerning Lk. 21.22 that 'the language suggests Lukan formulation' though 'there may be a traditional basis in the first part of the verse' (*Luke*, p. 773). The phrase πάντα τὰ γεγραμμένα in this verse appears only in Luke-Acts (Lk. 18.31; 24.44; Acts 13.29; 24.14). The rhetorical use of πάντα is also Lukan (Fitzmyer, *Luke X–XIV*, p. 1345).

390. Lk. 21.20-24 has a parallel in Mk 13.14-20, but there are many differences between them. Some scholars argue that Luke rewrote Mark (Creed, Danker, etc.), while others claim that the Lukan text is independent of Mark (Dodd, Manson, etc.). It does not seem that Luke was solely dependent on Mark. For detailed argument, see Marshall, *Luke*, pp. 770–71. He concludes that 'Luke has made use of traditional material in rewriting this paragraph from Mk' (*Luke*, p. 771).

avoid using one of the two verbs for two different meanings in a pericope.[391]

(3) *The use of the verbs in Lk. 1.20 and 23*

The usage in Lk. 21.22 and 24 may explain the usage of the same two verbs, i.e., πίμπλημι and πληρόω, in Lk. 1.20 and 23. The verb πληρόω is used in v. 20 for the connotation of fulfilment: οἵτινες πληρωθήσονται εἰς τὸν καιρὸν αὐτῶν. This verb in v. 20 may have originated from a Lukan source or Luke may have employed the verb πληρόω in v. 20 for the fulfilment of what have been said after using πίμπλημι for the Holy Spirit in v. 15. This usage might have led Luke to use a different verb, πίμπλημι, in v. 23 to indicate the completion of a time period; he intended to avoid using the same verb for a different concept.[392] And then Luke retained this usage in the infancy narrative.[393]

(4) *A last question: Is this from a translation?*

It is true that the non-Lukan and non-Septuagintal character of this expression seems to support the theory that the phrase stemmed from the translation of a Semitic source.[394] While it is possible that an unknown person translated a source for the usage of the verb πίμπλημι in the Lukan infancy narrative, we can hardly suggest a proper explanation about why this usage, which is not attested in any Greek literature, was adopted by him.

Another possible answer is that Luke, while translating a source, did the same thing as the above composition procedure suggests: while translating a source, he employed the verb πίμπλημι, which itself is typical of Luke, in v. 23 after utilizing the verb πληρόω in v. 20 in order to avoid using the same verb for two different meanings. Whereas this explanation is possible,

---

391. Otherwise, he depended on his peculiar source for the use of both verbs in v. 22 and v. 24. In this case, Luke did not change the verb usage, but adopted it from his source. This explanation, however, cannot be proven correct.

392. In Lk. 1.23, there is a Lukan phrase: καὶ ἐγένετο ὡς. This construction appears once outside of the Lukan infancy narrative in Lk. 19.29 whose parallels in Mt. 21.1 and Mk 11.1 include a different construction καὶ ὅτε. In addition, there is no non-Lukan expression in Lk. 1.23. Luke might have composed this verse.

393. Otherwise, Luke adopted πίμπλημι in v. 23 which was in his source. Even in this case, there is no strong reason to believe somebody else translated a Hebrew original. He probably did the same thing as Luke did in Lk. 21.22 and 24.

394. One may defend the translation theory with the peculiarity of the usage of πίμπλημι in the infancy narrative. Indeed, Bock, commenting on the use of the verb συλλαμβάνω in Lk. 1.31 argues that 'Luke's use of the term συλλαμβάνω (in Lk. 1.31) points to a possible Semitic and Palestine origin behind this part of the tradition, since the LXX verb ἔχω is not used' (*Luke 1.1–9.50*, p. 111). According to this logic, the adoption of the verb πίμπλημι with time indicators could indicate a possible Semitic original.

it presumes too much. Most importantly, the use of the verb πίπλημι does not indicate a Semitic original; it only signifies that its usage differs from that in all the other Greek authors.[395]

In conclusion, Luke intentionally employed the passive form of the verb πίμπλημι to indicate the fulfilment of a certain time period in the infancy narrative. This usage is a non-Lukanism in the sense that it deviates from the usage in Lk. chs 3–24 and Acts. The probable explanation for this deviation is given when one supposes that Luke himself employed the verb πίμπλημι, which itself is typical of Luke, in v. 23 because of the verb πληρόω in v. 20. The verb πληρόω in v. 20 was probably from Luke's Greek source. Otherwise, Luke simply utilized the verb πληρόω here in accordance with his style, after employing another verb πίμπλημι in 1.15. Then, Luke used the verb πίμπλημι for the completion of a time period in other verses of the infancy narrative.[396]

IV. *The Construction* προβαίνω + ἐν (ταῖς) ἡμέραις (εἰμι)

The phrase προβαίνω + ἐν (ταῖς) ἡμέραις appears three times in the NT. All three instances are found in the Lukan infancy narrative: 1.7,18; 2.36.

1.7 – καὶ οὐκ ἦν αὐτοῖς τέκνον, καθότι ἦν ἡ Ἐλισάβετ στεῖρα, καὶ ἀμφότεροι <u>προβεβηκότες ἐν ταῖς ἡμέραις αὐτῶν ἦσαν</u>.
'But they had no child, because Elizabeth was barren, and both *were advanced in their days*.'

1.18 – Καὶ εἶπεν Ζαχαρίας πρὸς τὸν ἄγγελον, κατὰ τί γνώσομαι τοῦτο; ἐγὼ γάρ εἰμι πρεσβύτης καὶ ἡ γυνή μου <u>προβεβηκυῖα ἐν ταῖς ἡμέραις αὐτῆς</u>.
'And Zechariah said to the angel, "How will I know this thing? For I myself am an old man, and my wife *is advanced in her days*".'

2.36 – Καὶ ἦν Ἅννα προφῆτις, θυγάτηρ Φανουήλ, ἐκ φυλῆς Ἀσήρ· αὕτη <u>προβεβηκυῖα ἐν ἡμέραις πολλαῖς</u>, ζήσασα μετὰ ἀνδρὸς ἔτη ἑπτὰ ἀπὸ τῆς παρθενίας αὐτῆς
'And there was Anna, a prophetess, the daughter of Phanuel, of the tribe of Asher. She *was advanced in many days*, having lived with her husband seven years from her virginity.'

---

395. We cannot completely rule out the possibility that somebody translated a source. However, there is no clear reason to believe so and more importantly, the composition procedure is well explained as we do above. In this case, the emphasis has to be laid on the direct composition.

396. The verb πίμπλημι in other verses possibly derived from Luke's sources. In this case, however, no proper explanation is to be suggested.

(A) *The Problem and Proposals for a Solution*

The presence of the preposition ἐν with the noun ἡμέρα after the verb προβαίνω in the above instances has generated much discussion. The preposition is never used in the construction, προβαίνω + time indicators, by other Greek writers. In classical Greek, the verb προβαίνω occurs with time indicators other than ἡμέρα without the preposition ἐν. The use of the noun ἡμέρα as a time indicator is found seven times in the LXX, four times with a genitive plural (Gen. 18.11; 24.1; Josh. 13.1[2x]) and three times with a dative plural (Josh. 23.1; 23.2; 1 Kgs 1.1). The instances in the LXX do not involve the preposition ἐν.[397] In contrast, the corresponding Hebrew phrase in the OT includes the preposition ב with ימים in all seven instances. Here are two examples cited, one with the genitive, the other with the dative in the LXX translation:

Gen. 24.1a LXX καὶ Αβρααμ ἦν πρεσβύτερος <u>προβεβηκὼς ἡμερῶν</u>

MT ואברהם זקן <u>בא בימים</u>

Jos. 23.1c LXX καὶ Ἰησοῦς πρεσβύτερος <u>προβεβηκὼς ταῖς ἡμέραις</u>

MT ויהושע זקן <u>בא בימים</u>

Scholars give two main explanations for the expression προβαίνω + ἐν (ταῖς) ἡμέραις in Luke. Some scholars regard it as reflecting a Hebrew original while others interpret it as a variation of the LXX locution ultimately derived from Luke's own hand.

(1) *The view that the Greek preposition ultimately reflects the Hebrew preposition* ב

(i) The attempt to interpret the construction as reflecting a Hebrew original began in the beginning of the last century when Plummer called it 'Hebraistic' (*Luke*, p. 10). He notes that classical authors use τῇ ἡλικίᾳ instead of ἐν ταῖς ἡμέραις. Plummer's remark is ambiguous, however. It is not clear whether 'Hebraistic' points to the Hebrew OT text or the LXX.

(ii) Sahlin claims that the prepositional phrase is not Septuagintal because the Hebrew construction בא בימים was translated as προβεβηκὼς ἡμερῶν or προβεβηκὼς (ταῖς) ἡμέραις in the LXX, thus without using the preposition ἐν. The expression in Lk. 1.7 is a free revision of the expression which was in the proto-Lukan source.[398] The proto-Lukan

---

397. Needless to say, the genitive cannot be accompanied by the preposition ἐν.
398. Sahlin notes that the expression is 'eher eine etwas freie Wiedergabe des protolukanischen Ausdrucks' (*Der Messias*, p. 72).

source of the Lukan infancy narrative, according to Sahlin, was written in Hebrew.³⁹⁹ Sahlin recognizes that the modifying adjective πολλαῖς in 2.36 seems to make the translation theory less probable. However, he still believes that even the expression in 2.36 as well as those in 1.7 and 1.18 is from a Semitic original.⁴⁰⁰

(iii) Though Lagrange admits that ἐν might be added as in *2 Macc.* 8.8,⁴⁰¹ he nevertheless argues for the Semitic original of this phrase, because the use of 'days' (ἡμέραις) instead of 'years' or 'ages' indicates Semitic influence (*Saint Luc*, p. 11).

(iv) After a detailed study on this Greek construction, Winter postulates that it is 'more Hebraistic than the Septuagint'.⁴⁰² The Greek preposition in Luke, according to him, echoes the Hebrew preposition 'b' in the construction of the MT, בא בימים, which the LXX translators did not include in their translation.⁴⁰³ The presence of the preposition in Luke, in his view, supports the argument that the Lukan expression is dependent on the MT rather than the LXX.⁴⁰⁴

(v) Noting that the construction, προβαίνω + ἐν (ταῖς) ἡμέραις, is attested neither in the LXX nor in Josephus nor in extra-Biblical Greek,

---

399. Sahlin believes Lk. 3.1-7a is also a translation from the Hebrew original (*Der Messias*, p. 9). For his argument on the original language of Luke-Acts, see Chapter 1.

400. Though recognizing that 'man hat das πολλαῖς als unsemitisch betrachten wollen,' Sahlin argues that 'jedoch scheint mir dieses Skepsis gegenüber πολλαῖς übertrieben' (*Der Messias*, p. 283). 'Offenbar bezeichnet προβεβηκυῖα ἐν ἡμέραις πολλαῖς,' he concludes, 'ein höheres Alter als einfach προβεβηκυῖα ἐν ταῖς ἡμέραις (vgl. Lk. 1.7 und 18), und warum hätte dieser höhere Grad auf hebräisch nicht durch רבים ausgedrückt werden können?'

401. The meaning of the preposition ἐν in *2 Macc.* 8.8 is different from that in Lk. 1.7, 18, or 2.36: ἐν ταῖς εὐημερίαις προβαίνοντα; 'going ahead in happiness (or success)'. The dative in *2 Macc.* is used as 'the dative of means', while the dative in the Lukan phrase indicates either 'dative of respect' or 'dative of time'. Lagrange seems to understand the noun εὐημερίαις as related to ἡμέραις.

402. 'Some Observations on the Language in the Birth and Infancy Stories of the Third Gospel', *NTS*, 1 (1954-55), p. 114.

403. Winter adds that ἐν ἡλικίᾳ would be a better Greek locution than ἐν ἡμέραις, since the noun ἡλικία is used by classical authors, though they employ this noun without the preposition. He omits one example in the LXX: Josh. 23.2.

404. It is interesting to observe that Nolland, a strong advocate for the translation theory of the Lukan infancy narrative, considers the possibility that Luke inserted the preposition before ταῖς ἡμέραις. He also notes, of course, that 'Luke's insertion of ἐν (contrast LXX) probably reflects the ב of a Hebrew source' (*Luke 1–9.20*, p. 27). His attitude is balanced, but he suggests no further explanation.

Jeremias concludes that this expression should be regarded as a Hebraism (*Die Sprache*, p. 25).[405]

(2) *The view which denies the Semitic original theory*

(i) Without any proper explanation, some scholars either assume that the expression is Septuagintal or deny the dependence of the Lukan phrase on the Hebrew text. Fitzmyer notes in brief that the expression occurs frequently in the Septuagint (*Luke I–IX*, p. 323).[406] Though acknowledging that the construction does not appear in the LXX, Bovon rejects the view that the Lukan phrase depends on a Hebrew original.[407]

(ii) Conceding that Luke inserted the preposition ἐν against the LXX, Turner still attempts to refute the translation theory. He lists some factors that may support the influence of the LXX;[408] he points to non-inevitable adoption of προβαίνω for the Hebrew word בוא and ἡμέραι for ימים. Luke's LXX, he adds, was different from ours and his version included the preposition.[409]

(iii) Considering Turner's response to Winter's argument pertinent, Benoit suggests another possible solution by regarding the locution as resulting from Luke's fondness for the prepositional phrase ἐν ταῖς ἡμέραις: Luke always uses the dative plural (ταῖς) ἡμέραις with the preposition ἐν except in 1.75 of the Benedictus which Luke did not directly compose.[410]

---

405. Brown also explicitly labels this locution as 'a Hebrew expression' (*The Birth of the Messiah*, p. 259). Bock, who ambiguously observes that the expression in 1.7 is 'stylistically' ... like some OT phrases, e.g., 'advanced in days' (*Luke 1.1–9.50*, p. 78), also clearly calls the expression in 2.26 a Hebraism (*Luke 1.1–9.50* p. 251).

406. See also Evans, *Saint Luke*, p. 146, where he describes the locution as 'a LXX expression'.

407. 'Das ἐν (Lk. 1.7), das in der Septuaginta fehlt,' Bovon notes, 'bedeutet nicht, daß Lukas sich auf einen hebräischen Text stützt' (*Das Evangelium nach Lukas: Lk. 1.1–9.50*, p. 52, nt. 38).

408. 'The relation of Luke I and II to Hebraic Sources and to the Rest of Luke-Acts,' p. 101.

409. For details, see Chapter 1. 2.B.

410. 'La présence ici de ἐν,' Benoit concludes, 'pourrait bien n'être due qu'à sa manière d'écrire et ne rejoindre que matériellement la tournure de l'hébreu' (*Exégèse et Théologie*, III, p. 170). His explanation is accepted by recent commentaries. See Marshall, *Luke*, p. 53 and Nolland, *Luke 1–9.20*, p. 27.

(B) *Evaluation of the suggested Proposals*

(1) *The argument for a Hebrew original*

Scholars who argue for a Hebrew original understand the heart of the problem concerning the phrase προβαίνω + ἐν (ταῖς ἡμέραις): the presence of the preposition in this phrase may reflect the Hebrew preposition ב in the corresponding Hebrew construction of the OT, while the preposition is absent in the LXX. Nevertheless, their argument overlooks some important features of the OT texts. First, the Hebrew text in the OT includes זקן which the LXX translators render as 'πρεσβύτερος' (see the two examples, Gen. 24.1a and Josh. 23.1c, quoted above). Second, the Hebrew OT passages have no counterpart to the modifying pronoun in Lk. 1.7,18 (αὐτῶν and αὐτῆς) and adjective in Lk. 2.36 (πολλαῖς). Their argument thus is not as convincing as it may at first appear.

(2) *The argument for dependence on the LXX*

The views which argue for the dependence on the LXX instead of translation from a Hebrew source seem plausible; for instance, the use of the plural dative noun ἡμέραις with the verb προβαίνω is Septuagintal. However, they fail to provide a sufficient and close examination of the phrase. Fitzmyer's opinion overlooks the peculiarity of the phrase, i.e., the presence of the preposition which does not appear in the LXX. Bovon does not explain why the presence of the preposition does not indicate that Luke used a Hebrew source. Benoit's solution is attractive, but it does not offer a sufficient explanation. Although his explanation may be better than Fitzmyer's and Bovon's, a more detailed study is required to resolve the problem of the preposition. Turner's approach is probably more realistic than the others', but the phrase itself, apart from the problem of the transmission of the LXX, needs to be closely examined from a different point of view.[411]

(3) *Is the construction προβαίνω + ἐν (ταῖς) ἡμέραις non-Lukan?*

As noted above, this construction appears only in the Lukan infancy story (1.7, 1.18; 2.36). In all three examples, the verb προβαίνω is followed by the preposition ἐν and the time indicator ἡμέρα.[412] This observation seems to indicate that the expression is a non-Lukanism. However, Luke does not use any other Greek locution for 'be old, or advanced in age' in

---

411. For the evaluation of Turner's argument, see Chapter 1. 2.

412. BDF interpret the use of the preposition as connected with 'the dative of respect' (BDF 197). The dative alone indicates 'dative of respect' without the preposition ἐν in classical and Septuagint Greek, but the preposition is added in the infancy narrative. There is no change in meaning due to the preposition and the phrase is translated as 'advanced in age (with respect to age)'. For details, see below.

Lk. 3–24 and Acts. Thus, it is impossible to determine whether or not the phrase in the Lukan infancy narrative is non-Lukan.[413]

(4) *A close examination of the examples in the LXX and the Hebrew OT*

(i)   *The usage in the LXX*

In the LXX, the verb προβαίνω appears with time indicators ἡμέρα, ἡλικία, or χρόνος.[414] The preposition ἐν, however, is not used with these time indicators. The LXX translates the Hebrew prepositional phrase in the construction בא + בימים into two ways as we noted above. (a) with the genitive plural of the noun ἡμέρα (Gen. 18.11; 24.1; Jos. 13.1[2x]),[415] and (b) with the dative plural of the noun ἡμέρα (Josh. 23.1, 23.2 and 1 Kgs 1.1). No instance in the LXX includes the preposition ἐν as in Luke. This indicates that the phrase προβαίνω + ἐν (ταῖς) ἡμέραις is a non-Septuagintalism.

In (b), the dative is used as 'the dative of respect' (BDF 197). In contrast, the usage of the genitive in (a) is really enigmatic; there is no 'genitive of respect' in Greek. The best interpretation is to understand the genitive as a 'genitive of time', and in this case, the meaning of the phrase is 'advanced within (or in) days'.[416] In fact, 'the dative and genitive of time are sometimes employed with only a slight difference' in classical Greek.[417] More important is the fact that the use of the verb προβαίνω with the plural dative noun ἡμέραις is Septuagintal.

---

413. For 'be old,' NT authors use the word πρεσβύτης in Lk. 1.18a ('I am an old man') and Phlm. 1.9. See also Heb. 11.11 where παρὰ καιρὸν ἡλικίας appears for the meaning 'past the normal age'.

414. The accusative singular of ἡλικία is used in *2 Maccabees*, which was composed directly in Greek (*2 Macc.* 4.40; 6.18). The accusative is 'the accusative of respect'. The noun ἡλικία reflects the usage of non-biblical Greek in which προβαίνω is accompanied by this noun without the preposition (Lysias 24.16; Diodor 12.18; 13.89, etc. See Liddell and Scott, p. 1470). Χρόνος appears only in Job 2.9 where it is used as a subject in the genitive absolute construction: χρόνου δὲ πολλοῦ προβεβηκότος 'after much time passed'. This construction is classical (Liddell and Scott, p. 1470).

415. In Judg. 19.11, ἡμέρα is the subject which reflects the Hebrew text והיום רד מאד: ἡ ἡμέρα προβεβήκει σφόδρα 'The day had far advanced'.

416. Another possibility is 'the genitive of quality' which is related also to 'the dative of measure'. The 'be' verb, however, is usually used for this usage. See Smyth, *Greek Grammar*, pp. 1320–21, 1325–27. No biblical Greek grammar suggests how the genitive is used in this phrase.

417. Smyth, *Greek Grammar*, p. 1543.

3. *A Close Examination of the Greek of the Infancy Narrative* 185

(ii) *The Hebrew corresponding locution. Is the phrase in Luke from the Hebrew OT?*
Since all the examples in the Hebrew OT include the preposition ב whereas the preposition is omitted in all the examples of the Greek OT, the view that the preposition reflects the Hebrew OT text rather than the LXX seems convincing. Nevertheless, the following elements make it difficult to assert that the Lukan phrase depended on the Hebrew OT text.

a. If the Lukan text had been a translation of the Hebrew construction found in the Hebrew OT, it should have included the Greek word πρεσβύτερος, used by the LXX translators to render the Hebrew word זקן:[418]

Gen. 18.11   LXX   'Αβρααμ δὲ καὶ Σαρρα <u>πρεσβύτεροι</u> προβεβηκότες ἡμερῶν
             MT   ואברהם ושרה <u>זקנים</u> באים בימים

b. This Hebrew noun occurs in all the examples except Jos. 23.2 and there is no reason to believe that the Lukan text relied exclusively on Josh. 23.2. It appears, in fact, that Lk. 1.7 and 1.18 allude to Gen. 18.11, not to Jos. 23.2.

c. As noted above, the presence of the modifying genitive pronouns in 1.7 (αὐτῶν) and 1.18 (αὐτῆς) and of the adjective in 2.36 (πολλαῖς) makes the view that the Lukan text depended on the Hebrew text of the OT less probable. The pronoun or adjective never occurs in the construction προβαίνω + a form of ἡμέρα in the LXX, nor does the Hebrew OT contain counterparts to these words. The expression in 2.36 is also more problematic than those in 1.7 and 1.18; in the two instances of Chapter 1, the phrase makes good sense (with respect to their or her days [age]), but the meaning of the phrase in 2.36 seems slightly awkward. 'with respect to many days (age)'.[419]

---

418. This word is the comparative of πρέσβυς 'old man'. The comparative primarily means 'the older one', and thus can mean 'elder' (Liddell and Scott, p. 1462). This form completely loses the comparative meaning in Josephus and can thus mean simply 'old man' (BAGD, p. 699). The word means 'elder' in most of the instances of the LXX.
419. Marshall notes that 'πολλαῖς is redundant, perhaps to give a contrast with 1.7, 18' (*Luke*, p. 125). Brown remarks that 'this is a more emphatic form of the expression used to describe Zechariah and Elizabeth in 1.7' (*The Birth of the Messiah*, p. 442). Bock suggests that the literal translation of the phrase in 2.36 is 'she was very old in her many days (*Luke 1.1–9.50*, p. 251)'. This translation, however, is not exactly a literal translation; there are no Greek words corresponding to 'very old' and 'her'.

d. Scholars who argue for the translation theory do not clarify why Luke, the final editor, decided to keep the preposition in this case, although this locution is not attested in any other Greek literature.[420] In addition, if the supposed translator consciously omitted the word זקן in the Hebrew OT, he could also easily have omitted the preposition.

These considerations point to the peculiarity of the phrase in the Lukan infancy narrative; this peculiarity makes it difficult to argue that the Lukan phrase depended on the MT rather than the LXX. If a proper explanation about the composition of the phrase is to be given, therefore, the argument for the dependence of the Lukan phrase on the Hebrew text has to be surrendered. We shall investigate the possibility that the Lukan expression derived from the influence of Hellenistic Greek or LXX Greek.

(C) *Another Explanation*[421]

The preposition ἐν in 1.7, 18 and 2.36 is awkward in two ways.

a. if the dative is used as 'the dative of respect' (BDR 197),[422] the use of the preposition for this usage is unusual in Greek;[423]

b. the verb προβαίνω is not followed by the prepositional phrase ἐν + time indicating dative noun in classical and Septuagint Greek; the dative noun appears unaccompanied.

(i) *The possibility that the phrase is influenced by Hellenistic Greek*
Are these seemingly awkward features from the influence of Hellenistic Greek? The following phenomena are observed in Hellenistic Greek.

a. The preposition ἐν could be added to the dative noun even when the dative is used as 'the dative of respect'.[424]

---

420. While Luke was not competent in Hebrew, his Greek was superior to that of the average Hellenistic writers. For details, see Chapter 1 'Introduction'.

421. One way to tackle this problem is to research the use of the verb in Hellenistic Greek. The result, however, is disappointing because to my knowledge Hellenistic Greek literature provides no instance for the construction προβαίνω ἐν + time indicating nouns. Even papyri do not include it. For the research of Greek constructions in Hellenistic Greek and papyri, this study uses TLG.

422. See also Turner, *A Greek Grammar*, vol. III, p. 220. The dative is probably not a 'dative of respect', but a 'dative of time'. For details, see below.

423. In Job 15.10 and 32.4, the dative plural ἡμέραις is used as 'the dative of respect' ('in age') without the preposition ἐν, but the verb προβαίνω does not appear.

424. The dative in the expression προβαίνω ἐν ταῖς ἡμέραις, according to BDR, is 'the dative of respect', 'advanced in (with respect to) age'. Is the preposition ἐν used for this usage? In classical

b. The prepositional phrase, κατά or εἰς followed by the accusative of nouns indicating time, could be a substitute for dative nouns indicating time after the verb προβαίνω.[425]

On the basis of the above observations, one may suggest some possible solutions concerning the use of the preposition in the Lukan phrase.

a. Luke probably made use of the preposition ἐν for the usage of 'the dative of respect', following Hellenistic authors. The 'dative of respect', however, does not occur with the preposition ἐν in Lk. 3–24 and Acts nor in the rest of the NT.[426] A more convincing explanation, therefore, has to be suggested.
b. Prepositions like κατά or εἰς occur with the verb προβαίνω in Hellenistic Greek, which is not found in classical Greek. The use of these prepositions may have led Luke to use the preposition ἐν. There is no instance, however, for the use of the preposition ἐν with time indicating nouns after the verb προβαίνω and prepositions κατά or εἰς are not used with the noun ἡμέρα in Hellenistic Greek. A more

---

Greek, the preposition ἐν is not used for the dative of respect. In the NT, it is found only in the expression προβαίνω ἐν ταῖς ἡμέραις. It appears once in 2 Cor. 7.11, but only in some textual variants. ἐν παντὶ συνεστήσατε ἑαυτοὺς ἁγνοὺς εἶναι (ἐν) τῷ πράγματι. 'At every point you have proved yourselves guiltless in (with respect to) the matter' (NRSV). D Ψ m d sy include the preposition before τῷ πράγματι (BDR. 197.5).

Hellenistic authors utilize the preposition ἐν for 'the dative of respect'. An interesting example occurs in Diognes Laertius, a third century writer, who uses the verb προβαίνω with the preposition ἐν for the dative of respect, although the meaning of the verb is not related to age.

καὶ τοὺς προβεβηκότας δὲ ἱκανῶς ἐν τῇ τῶν ὅλων ἐπιβλέψει 'and those who advanced sufficiently in (with respect to) the inquiry of all (things or persons)' (Vit. 10.35.7).

A similar expression is found in *2 Macc.* 8.8, but the preposition is not used there for 'the dative of respect', but 'the dative of means'. [For the date of Hellenistic Greek authors, this study depends on M. Grant, *Greek and Latin Authors. 800 B.C.–A.D. 1000* (New York: The H.W. Wilson Company, 1980)].

425. The second-century Hellenistic author Galenus uses the perfect form of the verb προβαίνω several times. One example appears with the dative ταῖς ἡλικίαις. Two instances contain the preposition κατά: κατὰ τὴν ἡλικίαν (#001, 3.641). Josephus also employs the same preposition in Vit. 266.4. καλεύω τοὺς καθ' ἡλικίας προβεβηκότας. Alexander of Aphrodisias, a second-century author, also includes the use of the preposition κατά three times (#013, 141.20; #013, 142.7; #013, 142.16). Another second-century author Dionius Casius uses the preposition εἰς in 68.4. προβαίνω εἰς πεντήκοντα ἔτη 'advanced to fifty years'.

426. In some verses of Acts, this usage occurs without the preposition ἐν: 4.36; 7.51; 14.8; 16.5; 18.5, 25. Turner notes that the preposition ἐν is frequently used for 'the dative of respect', suggesting only the three instances in the infancy narrative (*A Grammar of New Testament Greek*, vol. III, p. 220). The problem is, however, that no instance is found except these three in the NT. His statement is thus imprecise.

probable and detailed influence thus needs to be traced with regard to the preposition ἐν.

(ii) *Did the preposition occur because the phrase* ἐν ταῖς ἡμέραις *(+ modifying word) is Lukan?*
The preposition is probably used, as Benoit suggested, due to the noun ἡμέραις; for this plural dative noun, Luke always employs the preposition ἐν except in 1.75 (πάσαις ταῖς ἡμέραις ἡμῶν).[427]

a. ἐν ταῖς ἡμέραις + *modifying word: a phrase typical of Luke*
The phrase ἐν ταῖς ἡμέραις is a Lukanism. Luke utilizes the phrase ἐν ταῖς ἡμέραις in Lk. 3–24 and Acts much more frequently than the other NT authors. 28 times in Luke (18x) and Acts (10x), 16 times in the rest of the NT (Matthew 5x; Mark 4x; the remainder 7x).[428] Luke adds it even when he seems to have depended on the Gospel of Mark or the common source with Matthew as his source.[429] The presence of the article before ἡμέραις in Lk. 1.7, 18 is also Lukan, which does not reflect the Hebrew OT.[430] The modifying adjective

---

427. Jeremias interprets the omission of the preposition in 1.75 as originating from the tradition. However, the use of the dative for the concept of 'the extent of time' is Lukan (cf. Lk. 20.9 and 21.37 where the accusative is used as the 'accusative of the extent of time'). For details, see below.

428. The phrase ἐν τρισὶν ἡμέραις appears four times in the NT (Mt. 27.40; Mk 15.29; Jn 2.19; 2.20), but the noun ἡμέρα indicates the literal meaning 'day' not 'time' as in the phrase ἐν (ταῖς) ἡμέραις: 'in three days'.

429. See Lk. 6.12 whose parallels in Matthew and Mark do not have the expression ἐν ταῖς ἡμέραις ταύταις; in both parallels, the whole phrase 'in these days' is omitted. Luke also employs this phrase in 17.26 (καὶ καθὼς ἐγένετο ἐν ταῖς ἡμέραις Νῶε), while the parallel verse in Mt. 24.37 contains the nominative of ἡμέρα: ὥσπερ γὰρ αἱ ἡμέραι τοῦ Νῶε.

430. The use of the article in Luke-Acts is different from some instances in the other NT books. The article always occurs in the phrase ἐν ταῖς ἡμέραις followed by the demonstrative pronoun in the NT. However, the phrase ἐν (ταῖς) ἡμέραις appears without the article when it is modified by the genitive noun outside of Luke-Acts. Mt. 2.1 (Τοῦ δὲ Ἰησοῦ γεννηθέντος ἐν Βηθλέεμ τῆς Ἰουδαίας ἐν ἡμέραις Ἡρῴδου τοῦ βασιλέως. See also 11.22, 24 and 12.36 where the singular noun of ἡμέρα occurs with the genitive noun without the preposition); 1 Pet. 3.20 (ἀπειθήσασίν ποτε ὅτε ἀπεξεδέχετο ἡ τοῦ θεοῦ μακροθυμία ἐν ἡμέραις Νῶε κατασκευαζομένης κιβωτοῦ εἰς ἣν ὀλίγοι). Both examples do not include the article (cf. Jeremiah, *Die Sprache*, p. 17). On the contrary, the article appears for the noun ἡμέραις followed by the genitive noun in all the examples of Luke-Acts, which indicates the effect of the LXX: Lk. 1.75; 4.25; 17.26; 17.28; Acts 5.37; 12.41. It is also intriguing that the phrase 'in the last days', which appears only three times in the NT, includes the article in Acts 2.17 (ἐν ταῖς ἐσχάταις ἡμέραις), while the article is absent in the remaining two examples. 2 Tim. 3.1 and Jas 5.3 (ἐν ἐσχάταις ἡμέραις). In Acts 2.17, Peter speaks to people quoting Joel 2.28ff. In the LXX of Joel 2.28, ἐν ταῖς ἐσχάταις ἡμέραις does not occur but μετὰ ταῦτα is used. 'Peter regards', Marshall notes, 'Joel's prophecy as applying to the last days' (*Acts*, p. 73). The insertion of the article may point to Luke's hand. All these observations indicate that Luke prefers to add the article compared with the other NT authors.

(Lk. 2.36) and genitive pronoun (1.7,18) after the prepositional phrase also indicate Luke's style; this prepositional phrase appears always with the modifying adjective, demonstrative pronoun or genitive noun in Luke-Acts.[431] This is probably why Luke, deviating from LXX as well as Hebrew OT locution for 'advanced in age',[432] inserted the modifying genitive noun for this locution 'advanced in age', (προβαίνω + (ἐν) ταῖς ἡμέραις) in 1.7 and 1.18 and the adjective in 2.36.[433] If Luke, following his own style and deviating from LXX style, inserted the modifying word for this construction, he could also add the preposition to the phrase in accordance with his peculiar phrase, i.e., ἐν ταῖς ἡμέραις.

b. *The meaning of the preposition ἐν: Does its meaning make the above suggestion less probable?*

Though the solution suggested above seems probable, there remains a problem. The phrase ἐν ταῖς ἡμέραις means 'within (or in) the days (of)' in all the examples in Lk. 3–24 and Acts. This is the case also in the LXX;[434] there is no instance which does not include the preposition for the plural dative noun ἡμέραις when it means 'in the days (of)' (about 220x). As a result, it is possible to argue that the preposition in 1.17–18 and 2.36 appears due to Luke's fondness of the phrase ἐν ταῖς ἡμέραις or the influence of the LXX. The problem is, however, that the prepositional phrase after the verb προβαίνω in 1.17-18 and 2.36, according to BDF (p. 197), does not indicate 'within the days', but 'with respect to days'. If the dative is 'the dative of respect', therefore, the consistent use of the preposition ἐν with ἡμέραις in Luke-Acts does not support the argument that the preposition in the construction προβαίνω + ἐν ταῖς ἡμέραις occurs because the phrase ἐν ταῖς ἡμέραις is Lukan. In addition, the dative plural ταῖς ἡμέραις appears without the preposition ἐν in 1.75; the omission of the preposition in this verse also requires an explanation.

---

431. Even in the LXX, ἐν ταῖς ἡμέραις is used with modifying genitive pronouns without exception (e.g., 1 Kgs 11.12; 16.34; 20.29; 2 Kgs 8.20; 15.19; 20.19; 23.29; 24.1; 1 Chron. 22.9; 2 Chron. 36.5; *Sir.* 44.7; [48.12; 48.18 without article]; 49.12; 50.1,3, 23.24; Ps. 17.32, 37; Hab. 1.5; Isa. 39.8; Jer. 16.9; 23.6; *Bar.* 4.20; Ezek. 12.25; 28.15).

432. The phrase ταῖς ἡμέραις, when it is used with the verb προβαίνω, is not followed by any modifying pronoun either in the Hebrew OT or in the LXX.

433. The genitive of names is used to modify the phrase in Luke as well as in the LXX as pointed out above. Lk. 1.5; 4.25; 17.26, 28. The genitive pronoun is found in Acts 13.14; ἐκείναις in Lk. 2.1; 4.2; Acts 2.18; 7.14; 9.37; ταύταις in Lk. 6.12; 24.18; Acts 1.15; simple noun in Lk. 17.26; Acts 5.37.

434. Even in classical Greek, the preposition ἐν could be used with the noun ἡμέρα, indicating 'in' or 'during' (Smyth, *Greek Grammar*, p. 1542).

(iii) *Answers to the final questions*
Two questions raised above need to be answered: the omission of the preposition in Lk. 1.75 and the usage of the dative in the phrase in 1.7, 18 and 2.36.

a. *The omission of the preposition in Lk. 1.75*
In 1.75, if the dative is the correct reading,[435] Luke omits the preposition ἐν in accordance with his style: the dative in this verse is used as 'the dative of extent of time' and Luke always employs the dative alone for this usage. Noteworthy is that this usage appears in the NT only in Luke-Acts: Lk 8.27, 29 and Acts 13.20 (Acts 28.12 of B).[436] While this dative implies 'for', the preposition ἐν with ἡμέραις indicates 'within', or 'during'. In the LXX, there are two instances in which the preposition is omitted before ἡμέραις and the dative indicates 'for' in these instances (2 Chron. 7.8;[437] 3 *Macc.* 6.38) as in Lk. 1.75.[438] In sum, the preposition is omitted in 1.75 because the absence of the preposition to indicate 'for' is 'Lukan and Septuagintal'.[439]

b. *Is the dative in the Lukan phrase used as 'the dative of respect'?*
The issue now centres on whether or not Luke had a reason to omit the preposition ἐν in Lk. 1.7,18 and 2.36 as in 1.75. This question is related with the question of the usage of the dative in those verses. In order to answer this question, we need to re-examine phrases for the meaning 'advanced in age' in the LXX. In the LXX, the genitive noun ἡμερῶν occurs with the verb προβαίνω in four out of seven instances[440] and the use of the genitive, as noted above, is enigmatic:

---

435. Many textual variants support the accusative instead of the dative. In case of the accusative, the absence of the preposition is normal.

436. This usage of the dative appears in Jn 14.9 (Τοσούτῳ χρόνῳ μεθ' ὑμῶν εἰμι – I am with you for such a long time) where the external evidence supports another reading, τοσοῦτον χρόνον. *P*66.75 ℵ1 AB Θ Ψ f1.13 33 *m* support this reading. It seems that the internal evidence is interpreted as supporting the dative (harder reading); the dative of time is never used in the Gospel of John whereas the accusative of time is used in Jn 2.12 (how long) and 4.52 (when) [BDR 161].

437. In 2 Chron. 7.8, the Hebrew text includes the preposition ב.

438. All the instances in the LXX include the preposition ἐν for the use of the dative of time 'within, or in', which reflects the Hebrew preposition. Ps. 89.4; 114.2; *Sir* 23.15; 48.12 (cf. *2 Macc.* 5.14; Jdt. 8.15).

439. This observation makes less probable Benoit's argument that the phrase in 1.75 is not from Luke's hand. Now it is clear that Luke omitted the preposition in 1.75 according to his style as well as LXX style.

440. Two instances in *2 Macc.* are excluded from our consideration since they are not from translation.

3. *A Close Examination of the Greek of the Infancy Narrative* 191

there is no 'genitive of respect' in Greek. Noteworthy is that the verb προβαίνω is not accompanied by the genitive noun indicating time in other Greek literature (Liddell and Scott, p. 1470; BAGD, p. 702). Possibly the genitive is a 'genitive of quality', but this case is not strong as the 'be' verb is used for this usage.[441] The genitive is to be interpreted as 'the genitive of time'.[442] Luke was probably well acquainted with the expressions in the LXX: the use of the verb προβαίνω and the dative plural noun ἡμέραις is Septuagintal. The usage of the dative in the Lukan construction προβαίνω ἐν (ταῖς) ἡμέραις is ambiguous, namely either 'dative of respect' ('with respect to one's or many age') or 'dative of time' ('in one's or many days') and this ambiguity probably stemmed from the use of the genitive noun in the LXX. If Luke consulted the LXX where either the genitive or the dative is used for the expression 'advanced in age', he may have interpreted the dative as indicating 'dative of time'. This interpretation becomes more probable with the consideration of the phrase in Lk. 2.36 where the use of the dative cannot be 'the dative of respect'; 'advanced in many days'. The dative in Lk. 2.36 indicates 'time' ('advanced within [to] many days') rather than 'respect' ('advanced with respect to many days'). The use of the dative in Luke, therefore, is at least ambiguous. If this is the case, Luke had no reason to omit the preposition for the expression ἐν ταῖς ἡμέραις in Lk. 1.7, 18 and 2.36.[443] Rather, he must have included the preposition ἐν.[444]

In sum, Luke always uses the preposition ἐν with ταῖς ἡμέραις to indicate 'within'. He omits the preposition in 1.75 where the dative is used as 'the dative of the extent of time', and this is Lukan and Septuagintal. In contrast, there is no clear reason for Luke to omit the preposition in the locution in 1.7,18 and 2.36 as the use of the dative is ambiguous, which probably reflects the indirect influence of the LXX.

In conclusion, the view that the Lukan expression originated from the translation of the Hebrew locution in the OT is not convincing given that

---

441. For the genitive of quality, see Smyth, *Greek Grammar*, pp. 1320–21 and 1325–27.
442. The genitive noun probably appears due to the preposition πρό in the compound verb προβαίνω (Smyth, *Greek Grammar*, p. 1384). Even in this case, the usage of the genitive is a riddle.
443. The use of the preposition with the verb προβαίνω is non-Septuagintal, but it is hardly possible to decide whether the phrase is Lukan or not.
444. Luke could have employed either the genitive ἡμερῶν or the dative ἡμέραις, as both are used in the LXX; he appears to have used his favorite phrase (ταῖς) ἡμέραις with the preposition in accordance with his style.

the Lukan locution does not exactly echo the Hebrew text. The prepositional phrase itself is certainly Lukan: the phrase probably stemmed from Luke's fondness for it and the modifying words derived from Luke's style. The use of the article also indicates Luke's hand. In fact, there is no evidence that proves that the whole expression in Luke is a non-Lukanism. The use of the genitive plural noun ἡμερῶν in the LXX with the verb προβαίνω might have influenced the interpretation of the dative plural noun ἡμέραις with the same verb in the LXX and Luke; the ambiguous use of the dative might have led Luke to keep the preposition. The phrase in Lk. 2.36 supports this interpretation. With these considerations, we may conclude that the phrase ἐν (ταῖς) ἡμέραις after the verb προβαίνω occurred ultimately due to Luke's style and the influence of the LXX.[445] This conclusion is supported by the attitude of the Church Fathers[446] and

---

445. The bottom line is that even if the dative is used as 'the dative of respect', the preposition could be employed for 'the dative of respect' in Luke as in some Hellenistic authors.
446. The Church Fathers utilize the Lukan locution, quoting or alluding to Lukan verses.
a) Gregorius Nyssenus (fourth century) has one quotation of Lk. 2.36 where he inserts the article ἡ before the noun 'prophetess', which the Lukan text lacks: ἡ προφῆτις. On the contrary, he keeps the preposition ἐν for the phrase ἐν ἡμέραις πολλαῖς. He also alludes to Lk. 2.36 and adopts the Lukan expression: ὡς δὴ προβεβηκυῖα ἐν ἡμέραις πολλαῖς. b) Epiphanius utilizes the locution in *Anc.* 80.2.3 where he abridges the story about the parents of John the Baptist in Lk. 1.6–7 (ὅτι ἦσαν ἅγιοι δίκαιοι προβεβηκότες ἐν ταῖς ἡμέραις ἄμεμπτοι). Intriguingly, Epiphanius keeps the preposition in an arbitrary allusion, though he makes the sentence more usual by omitting the pronoun αὐτῶν. His writings also include one quotation of Lk. 1.18 where he employs the construction in Luke. c) Quoting the LXX of Gen. 17.19, Origen (third century) follows its wording which does not include the preposition ἐν (#48, 12.116.27). He adopts the exact wording in alluding to Lk. 1.18 (#005, 6.17.97.3). The instance in # 078, 17.316.34n which quotes Lk. 1.7 draws our attention, where he alters the word order of ἦν ἡ Ἐλισάβετ in Lk. 1.7 to ἡ Ἐλισάβετ ἦν; in contrast, he does not omit the preposition ἐν. Although Origen could correct the locution προβεβηκότες ἐν ταῖς ἡμέραις by deleting the preposition, as he changes the word order of ἦν ἡ Ἐλισάβετ, he keeps it. It seems that the usage of the preposition appears correct to Origen. d) One instance in Joannes Chrysostomus (fourth century) calls attention (#112. 53.383.34). He seems to quote the story of Abraham in Gen. 18.1 at a glance:
Ἀβρααμ δὲ καὶ Σαρρα προβεβηκότες ἦσαν ἐν ταῖς ἡμέραις αὐτῶν.
However, Gen. 18.11 is different from this sentence:
Ἀβρααμ δὲ καὶ Σαρρα πρεσβύτεροι προβεβηκότες ἡμερῶν (ἐξέλιπεν δὲ Σαρρα γίνεσθαι τὰ γυναικεῖα).
Chrysostomus intends to allude to Gen. 18.11 here and he adopted Luke's way to express 'advanced in age': προβεβηκότες ἦσαν ἐν ταῖς ἡμέραις αὐτῶν instead of πρεσβύτεροι προβεβηκότες ἡμερῶν in the LXX. This may imply the following things: i) Chrysostomus held before him a LXX text different from ours, but identical to Luke's, where the preposition occurs with the verb προβαίνω; ii) Chrysostomus imitated the style of Luke as Epiphanius did. Another instance is also concerned with Abraham's story (#072, 51.233.16) and he employed the LXX locution this time (προβεβηκὼς ἡμερῶν). His writings include seven more instances for the allusion and quotation which include the expression. Two of them require a close look: #131, 50.788.18 and #132, 50.790.8. The first one, the quotation of Lk. 1.18 changes μοῦ in Luke to μοι: καὶ ἡ γυνή μοι προβεβηκυῖα ἐν ταῖς ἡμέραις αὐτῆς. The second one, a quotation of Lk. 1.7, altered the word order

copyists⁴⁴⁷ toward this expression; none of them tried to delete the preposition at all. All these considerations indicate that the expression may be the Lukan variation of the LXX rather than the result of the translation of the Hebrew phrase in the OT.

V. *Words and Phrases in Lk. 1.13b*

διότι εἰσηκούσθη ἡ δέησίς σου, καὶ ἡ γυνή σου Ἐλισάβετ γεννήσει υἱόν σοι καὶ καλέσεις τὸ ὄνομα αὐτοῦ Ἰωάννην.⁴⁴⁸

'because your prayer has been heard, and your wife Elizabeth will bear a son to you and you will call his name John.'

(A) *The Problem and Proposals*

Some elements of this verse are interpreted as supporting the Hebrew original theory or at least as militating against the theory of the dependence of the Lukan text on the LXX.

(1) *Hebrew etymological parallelism*⁴⁴⁹

(i)   Winter posits that this verse provides a conclusive proof for the argument that the Lukan infancy story 'was not originally conceived in Greek' ('Some Observations', p. 120). There is a clear connection, according to him, between the Hebrew name 'John', יוחנן, which means 'Yahweh is gracious', and the sentence 'your prayer has been heard'. He postulates that 'there is a parallelism of the thought:

---

as Origen did: ἡ Ἐλισάβετ ἦν instead of ἦν ἡ Ἐλισάβετ. However, Chrysostomus kept the preposition ἐν for the phrase προβεβηκυῖα ἐν ταῖς ἡμέραις.

The above investigation has demonstrated that this locution was not strange to the Church Fathers. Although they altered words or word order or inserted the article in some cases, they kept the locution, προβαίνω ἐν (ταῖς ἡμέραις). In addition, alluding to Luke and the LXX, Epiphanius and Chrysostomus employ the preposition ἐν.

447. It is also striking that no copyist has ever tried to eliminate the preposition ἐν in all three instances. This may indicate that the usage of the preposition did not seem to be wrong even to the copyists.

448. The second part, καὶ ἡ γυνή σου Ἐλισάβετ γεννήσει υἱόν σοι καὶ καλέσεις τὸ ὄνομα αὐτοῦ Ἰωάννην, alludes to Gen. 17.19 (so in the margin of NA²⁷), and thus could be treated in the section 'Allusions'. However, we have decided to treat this material here for reasons to be discussed below.

449. Not all the scholars who argue for etymological allusions claim that these allusions support the existence of a Hebrew original. For example, F.C. Burkitt, who assumes the existence of etymological allusions in the Lukan infancy narrative, believes the narrative derived from Luke's hand. See F.C. Burkitt, 'Who Spoke the Magnificat?', *JTS*, 7 (1906), pp. 220–27.

"God has granted to thee fulfilment of thy prayer," and, *propter ea*, "the name of thy child shall be John (= Yahweh is gracious)".' Because this parallelism makes sense only in Hebrew, he concludes, this verse must have been originally written in Hebrew.

(ii) Following Laurentin,[450] Farris examines instances for etymological allusions. Having rejected other instances by Laurentin, Farris suggests that an etymological allusion possibly exists between the root of the Hebrew word for John, i.e., חנן, and the sentence 'your prayer has been answered' (*The Hymns of Luke's Infancy Narratives*, pp. 42–45). The angel announces, he argues, that Zechariah's prayer has been answered, though the narrative has not previously described Zechariah's prayer at all. 'The word "prayer", δέησις,' he argues, 'corresponds most frequently in the LXX to one of two words derived from חנן.' 'The answer to Zechariah's prayer,' he continues, 'is the gift of a son, John.' In this way, there could be an etymological allusion between the Hebrew name of John and the sentence 'your prayer has been answered'.[451]

The argument for a possible Hebrew etymological connection in Lk. 1.13b may gain strength from the following elements, which may in turn lend support to the Hebrew original theory.

(2) *The expression '(and) you will call one's name X'*

The expression (καὶ) καλέσεις τὸ ὄνομα αὐτοῦ + name, which does not occur in the rest of the Gospel and Acts, echoes a Hebrew construction, name + וקראת את־שמו (BDF 157.2).[452]

(3) *The use of a different verb from Gen. 17.19*

The latter part of Lk. 1.13b apparently alludes to Gen. 17.19 but there are some differences between the LXX text and the Lukan text:

---

450. Laurentin, 'Traces d'allusions etymologiques en Luc I–II,' *Biblica*, 37 (1956), pp. 435–56; 'Traces d'allusions etymologique en Luc I–II,' *Biblica*, 38 (1957), pp. 1–23.
451. Farris admits, however, that the prayer is mentioned 'due to the influence of the account of the angelic appearance of Dan. 10.12, or possibly the wording of *Sir.* 51.11' (*The Hymns of Luke's Infancy Narratives*, p. 170, nt. 85). 'In short,' he concludes, 'even if Laurentin were correct in his identification of the specific Hebrew words behind our Greek text, the mere occurrence of those common words does not prove that there was intent to create etymological allusions' (*The Hymns of Luke's Infancy Narratives*, 45). For details, see below.
452. The normal phrase in Greek is 'ὄνομα καλεῖν τινα' (call someone X) or 'ὀνομάζειν τινα τι' (name someone X) (Liddell and Scott, p. 1232–33; cf. Brown, *The Birth of the Messiah*, p. 130). See also Lagrange, who notes that the expression καὶ καλέσεις τὸ ὄνομα αὐτοῦ Ἰωάννην is 'tournure hebraique, (et araméenne)' (*Saint Luke*, p. 15).

3. *A Close Examination of the Greek of the Infancy Narrative*

Gen. 17.19: ἰδοὺ Σαρρα ἡ γυνή σου τέξεταί σοι υἱὸν καὶ καλέσεις τὸ ὄνομα αὐτοῦ Ἰσαακ.

Lk 1:13b καὶ ἡ γυνή σου Ἐλισάβετ γεννήσει υἱόν σοι καὶ καλέσεις τὸ ὄνομα αὐτοῦ Ἰωάννην.

a. Lk. 1.13b uses the verb γεννάω while Gen. 17.19 of the LXX contains the verb τίκτω. The advocates of the translation theory may insist that if Lk. 1.13b alludes to Gen. 17.19, the use of the verb γεννάω in the Gospel refutes the view that Luke consulted the Greek OT of Gen. 17.19 where the verb τίκτω appears. Nolland emphasizes, in fact, that 'Luke does not use the LXX word for "to bear"' (*Luke 1–9.20*, p. 29). He thus attempts to highlight the difference between the sentence in Lk. 1.13b and that in Gen. 17.19 of the LXX by pointing to the use of different verbs in these two verses.

b. Apart from the use of the verb γεννάω, Lk. 1.13b betrays two different word orders from Gen. 17.19 of the LXX: ἡ γυνή σου + name instead of name + ἡ γυνή σου; υἱόν σοι instead of σοι υἱόν.

(4) *The use of the noun* δέησις

A possible non-Lukan noun δέησις is used instead of a Lukan word προσευχή (cf. Marshall, *Luke*, p. 56). This may indicate Luke's dependence on a Greek source, which was probably translated from a Hebrew original, when the previous two factors are also taken into consideration.

(B) *Evaluation of the Suggestions*

(1) *Is there an etymological connection?*

Concerning the argument for the etymological connection in Lk. 1.13b, it is not necessary to assume that such a connection exists. Winter presupposes that a parallelism must have been there because the parallelism can be rightly understood only in Hebrew. However, why should there be an etymological allusion concerning the name 'John', which was not uncommon?[453] More importantly, is there really an explicit parallelism between the sentence 'your prayer has been heard' and the meaning of the Hebrew name 'John', i.e., 'Yahweh is gracious'? The parallelism, if it exists, is at most only an implicit one and in fact only a

---

453. Brown, *The Birth of the Messiah*, p. 261. Not only 'John', but also 'Jesus' was a common name. 'Up to the beginning of the second-century A.D the name ישוע or Ἰησοῦς was very common among the Jews' (Foester, *TDNT*, vol. 3, p. 285).

guess even on the Semitic level.⁴⁵⁴ Moreover, even if there is an etymological allusion with regard to John, this does not constitute proof that such an allusion stems from a Hebrew original; it probably existed in Greek form as in Mt. 1.21 where the etymological allusion to Jesus does not necessarily point to a Semitic original:⁴⁵⁵

> καὶ καλέσεις τὸ ὄνομα αὐτοῦ Ἰησοῦν· αὐτὸς γὰρ σώσει τὸν λαὸν αὐτοῦ ἀπὸ τῶν ἁμαρτιῶν αὐτῶν.
> and you are to name him Jesus, for he will save his people from their sins. (NRSV)

'Perhaps,' as Farris avers, 'there was similar teaching concerning other prominent figures,' including John, 'in the history of salvation' and the names were originally in Greek (*The Hymns*, p. 45).⁴⁵⁶ In sum, the etymological allusion is unlikely.

(2) *The expression '(and) you will call one's name X'*, καὶ καλέσεις⁴⁵⁷ τὸ ὄνομα + genitive + name

This locution, which does not appear at all in classical Greek, seems to be a non-Lukan expression, since it does not occur at all in the rest of the Gospel and Acts.⁴⁵⁸ It belongs to Septuagintalisms since it occurs in the

---

454. Brown refutes the view that there is an implicit etymological connection between the joy and gladness in v. 14 and John's Hebrew name by saying that 'even on the putative Semitic level the connection between "Yahweh has given grace" and "joy and gladness" is a guess' (*The Birth of the Messiah*, p. 272).

455. Farris, who argues for the Hebrew original theory of the Lukan infancy narrative, remarks that 'at Matthew 1.21 there is an undoubted etymological allusion and very few suggest that the first two chapters of Matthew were translated from a Semitic source. We may deduce from that reference that there was in the early church teaching concerning the significance of the name "Jesus"' (*The Hymns*, p. 45).

456. Commenting on Mt. 1.21, Hagner notes that 'the reader's knowledge of the meaning of Ἰησοῦς via its Hebrew meaning is assumed by the γάρ without further explanation, indicating common tradition of the Greek-speaking church' (*Matthew 1–13*, p. 19). After noting that '"Jesus" is the Greek for the Hebrew "Jeshua" (Yesua), which by popular etymology was related to the Hebrew verb "to save" (ys) and to the Hebrew noun "salvation"', W.D. Davies and D.C. Allison, Jr. assert that it is unnecessary to postulate a Hebrew source for this play on words. 'Matthew offers,' they continue, 'no clarification for his readers as he does in 1.23, and Philo (Mut nom.121) proves that the etymology of "Joshua" was recognized outside Palestine.' 'Beyond this,' they conclude, 'even Hellenistic Christianity would certainly have preserved the significance of Jesus' name.' W.D. Davies and D.C. Allison, Jr., *The Gospel According to Saint Matthew*, vol. 1. (ICC; Edinburgh: T. & T. Clark Limited, 1988), p. 209. See also Greek *Sir.* 46.1.

457. The future indicative is equivalent to an imperative as in Lk. 1.31 and Mt. 1.21 (cf. BDF 362).

458. On the basis of this observation, Jeremias regards this locution as stemming from tradition (*Die Sprache*, p. 35). We cannot absolutely confirm that the locution is non-Lukan because other expressions are not used for the meaning 'call one's name X' in chs 3–24 of

3. A Close Examination of the Greek of the Infancy Narrative 197

LXX at the annunciation of birth: Gen. 16.11; 17.19; Isa. 7.14. Gen. 17.19 to which Lk. 1.13b most probably alludes involves exactly the same locution.[459] Its presence in Lk. 1.13b thus indicates the dependence of the Lukan text on LXX style[460]; this expression is 'a non-Lukan Septuagintalism'.

(3) *The use of the different verb*

The use of the verb γεννάω in Lk. 1.13b, different from the verb τίκτω in the LXX of Gen. 17.19, is more interesting than the above suggestions. Though it is true that some words in the LXX can be altered in case of allusions, the change of the verb requires an explanation. If the verb γεννάω in Lk. 1.13b is not from the LXX but from the translation of a Hebrew text, the existence of the etymological parallelism becomes more probable.

(4) *A possible non-Lukan noun* δέησις

This possible non-Lukan word may point to the dependence of the Lukan text on a Greek source and then paves the way to the interpretation that the source was a translation of a Hebrew original. The use of a non-Lukan word itself, of course, does not constitute definite proof that the Lukan text relied on a Hebrew original. However, this non-Lukan word can be interpreted as supporting the translation theory, when considered with the above argument of a possible etymological allusion and a possible dependence of the Lukan verb γεννάω on a Hebrew original. Thus, the use of the noun δέησις also needs to be explained.

Luke and Acts. In Lk. 1.62, the passive form of the verb καλέω appears with two accusatives: τὸ τί ἂν θέλοι καλεῖσθαι αὐτό. In Acts 15.17, the compound verb ἐπικαλέω is used: ἐφ' οὓς ἐπικέκληται τὸ ὄνομά μου ἐπ' αὐτούς. The sentence in Acts is a quotation of Amos 9.12b of the LXX.

459. It is true that this Greek expression echoes a Hebrew construction, וקראת שמו in the Hebrew OT as in Gen. 16.11; 17.19; Isa. 7.14. The Hebrew construction, however, does not include the article with שמו. This does not mean, of course, that the Greek construction is absolutely independent of the Hebrew construction: a Greek genitive pronoun usually requires the article (BDF 259) whereas the Hebrew cannot use the article in such a case. However, it is also clear that the article is often omitted in the NT even when the noun governs the genitive and Semitic colurings, according to BDF, are strong in that case. This consideration makes it possible to argue that the article probably indicates that the Lukan expression does not depend on the Hebrew construction.

460. In Matthew, this expression is used three times in the infancy narrative and nowhere else: 1.21, 23, 25. Mt. 1.23 is a quotation, which probably indicates Matthew's dependence on the LXX for the locution.

(C) *Solution*

(1) *Word order and the verb* γεννάω *in the sentence* καὶ ἡ γυνή σου Ἐλισάβετ γεννήσει υἱόν σοι

Apart from the use of a different verb γεννάω, there are differences in word order in this sentence, which also require explanation.

(i)   *From the Hebrew OT?*

  a. *word order: phrase + name in apposition* – ἡ γυνή σου Ἐλισάβετ
      In Greek, when a name appears with an appositive, either the name or the appositive is placed first:[461] 'phrase + name in apposition' or 'name + phrase in apposition'.[462] In the Hebrew OT, on the contrary, the word order 'name + appositive' is almost always used when this locution is used as the subject (Gen. 17.19; 18.9–10; 25.12; 1 Kgs 20.5, etc.). The LXX follows the word order of the Hebrew text. Both in the Hebrew OT and the LXX, if a single name appears with an appositive, the name takes the first place without exception.[463] While this observation does not support the dependence of the Lukan text on the LXX, it makes unlikely the argument that the Lukan text relied on the Hebrew text of Gen. 17.19. If Luke or a composer of Luke's source had translated the Hebrew OT, he would probably have placed the name Ἐλισάβετ before the phrase ἡ γυνή σου: Ἐλισάβετ ἡ γυνή σου.

  b. *word order* – υἱόν σοι
      This word order is also different from that in Gen. 17.19 of the MT, לְךָ בֵּן, which is also reflected in the LXX, σοι υἱόν. The Lukan text does not follow the wording of the OT, either the LXX or the Hebrew text.

      With the above considerations, it has become evident that the sentence in Lk. 1.13b, ἡ γυνή σου Ἐλισάβετ γεννήσει υἱόν σοι, does not come from the translation of the Hebrew text nor from direct dependence on the LXX of Gen. 17.19.

  c. *The use of the verb* γεννάω
      The use of a different verb probably makes it difficult to argue for the

---

461. According to BDR, 'meistens steht die Appos(ition) dem Namen nach' in the NT (268.1). If the appositive is placed before the name, according to them, the appositive is emphasized. For details, see below.

462. E.g., some examples are found in Herodotus: *Selections from Herodotus* (ed. A.L. Barbour; Norman: University of Oklahoma Press, 1964), p. 57, 147, etc.

463. In Gen. 48.15, a plural noun appears ahead of names: ὁ θεός ᾧ εὐηρέστησαν οἱ πατέρες μου ἐναντίον αὐτοῦ Ἀβρααμ καὶ Ἰσαακ.

3. *A Close Examination of the Greek of the Infancy Narrative* 199

direct dependence of the Lukan text on the LXX. It does not necessarily indicate, however, that Luke depends on the Hebrew Text.

We need to seek another way to answer the problem concerning the word order and the use of a different verb.

(ii) *Possibility that Luke or the composer of the Lukan source composed the sentence in Greek, depending on his memory of the LXX*
The different word orders and the use of a different verb from the LXX are probably to be explained by pointing out that Luke or the composer of his source composed Lk. 1.13b by relying on his memory of the LXX.

a. *Why exactly does the same expression, καὶ καλέσεις τὸ ὄνομα αὐτοῦ X, appear in Lk. 1.13b as in Gen. 17.19 of the LXX?*
The expression, καὶ καλέσεις τὸ ὄνομα αὐτοῦ X (Ἰωάννην), 'call someone's name X', occurs only in the infancy story in Luke-Acts and it is exactly the same as in Gen. 17.19 of the LXX. This observation makes it possible to argue that Luke probably looked up the LXX for this construction in Lk. 1.13b. However, this locution appears in the Greek OT in a fixed form when the content relates that 'you (or somebody) will bear a son, you[464] will call his name X.' The LXX always uses exactly the same locution for the second part, 'you will call his name X', while revealing different locutions for the first part in the verses where a birth annunciation is recorded (Gen. 16.11; 17.19; Isa. 7.14). In addition, the same Greek expression is used for the meaning 'to call one's name X' in other OT Greek verses: Isa. 8.3; Hos. 1.4, 9 (cf. Mt. 1.21, 23 where the same locution is found). In other words, καλεῖν τὸ ὄνομα αὐτοῦ τι is a stereotyped expression in the LXX. The wording in Lk. 1.13b is exactly duplicated also in Lk. 1.31 where the first part is different from that in Gen. 16.11 to which Lk. 1.31 alludes.[465] These considerations make it possible to claim that Luke did not directly depend on the LXX, but on his memory of the LXX for the expression καλέσεις τὸ ὄνομα αὐτοῦ Ἰωάννην.[466]

---

464. Interestingly, the second singular subject is used in the LXX of Isa. 7.14, while the Hebrew text of this verse shows the third person singular.

465. For the detailed argument about Lk. 1.31, see the section 'Allusions'.

466. Concerning the use of the future active form of the verb καλέω in Lk. 1.13, it is noteworthy that other Hellenistic authors make use of its future middle forms. We find the future middle form of a compound verb μετακαλέσομαι, in Acts 24.25. Mealand interprets this as follows: 'in a more Graeco-Roman context in Acts he (Luke) uses the future middle forms (of the verb καλέω and its compounds) that we can also document in Dionysius, Lucian and Cassius Dio' ('Luke-Acts and the Verbs', p.75). While Mealand's argument is not strong as there is only one example for the use of the future middle form of the verb καλέω and its compounds in Acts (24.25), it is accepted that the active verb form in Lk. 1.13b derived most

b. *The word order* ἡ γυνή σου Ἐλισάβετ
The writer probably used the word order noun + name in apposition to emphasize the function of Elizabeth, i.e, 'your wife' who will bear a son.[467] In Gen. 17.19, the name, Sarah, is in focus, since God commanded Abraham to change the name of his wife from Sarai to Sarah in Gen. 17.15. Her name needs to be emphasized here. On the contrary, in Lk. 1.13, no good reason is found for emphasizing Elizabeth's name.[468] The composer thus apparently intends to emphasize the function or position of Elizabeth as Zachariah's wife.[469]

c. *The verb* γεννάω *in Lk. 1.13 and the verb* τίκτω
The use of the verb γεννάω in Lk. 1.13b instead of τίκτω of the LXX in Gen. 17.19 probably excludes the view that the Lukan text depended on the LXX. Further, it may lend support to the argument for the dependence of the Lukan text on the Hebrew OT. The following considerations, however, make this argument less probable. In the infancy narrative, τίκτω appears five times (1.31, 57; 2.6-7, 11), while γεννάω occurs three times (1.13, 35, 57).[470] Remarkably, the former is not found outside the infancy narrative of Luke, nor is it found in Acts. In contrast, the latter occurs eight times outside of the infancy story (Lk. 23.29; Acts 2.8; 7.8, 20, 29; 13.33; 22.3; 22.28). As a result, γεννάω is Lukan vocabulary for 'to bear', while τίκτω is a non-Lukan word.[471] The NT includes 17 instances for the verb τίκτω, while γεννάω is used

---

probably from the LXX where the future active form appears (see Gen. 16.11; 17.19; Isa. 7.14). This indicates that LXX style has probably influenced the use of the future active form of the verb καλέω in 1.13b instead of the future middle form.

467. For the argument for different meanings which the different position conveys, see J. Heimerdinger's article 'Word Order in Koine Greek', *Filologia Neotestamentaria*, 9 (1996), pp. 149–52.

468. Luke adopted a different word order for the same locution in 1.24: Μετὰ δὲ ταύτας τὰς ἡμέρας συνέλαβεν Ἐλισάβετ ἡ γυνὴ αὐτοῦ. The advocates of the translation theory may argue that this reflects a Hebrew original. But then how can they explain the word order in 1.13? The only possible answer would be that Luke translated with freedom. In fact, no good explanation can be given by the translation theory. Moreover, the word order in Lk. 1.24 is found in the LXX as well as in the Hebrew OT.

469. Concerning the word order, Greijdanus notes that 'ἡ γυνή σου Ἐλισάβετ; die bepaalde vrouw van u, Elizabeth. Niet eene andere vrouw, die gij zult huwen, eene tweede vrouw, doch de vrouw, die gij nu hebt, Elizabeth' (*Het Heilig Evangelie Naar de Beschrijving van Lukas*. I., p. 28).

470. In 1.57, the verb γεννάω is probably used to avoid the repetition of the verb τίκτω which appears in the same verse.

471. In the LXX, both verbs are used, but τίκτω (52 times) is used more frequently than γεννάω (30 times) in contrast to the frequency in the NT. The Hebrew word for both Greek words is the same: ילד.

3. *A Close Examination of the Greek of the Infancy Narrative* 201

about one hundred times. The verb γεννάω in the infancy narrative of Lk. chs 1–2 is Lukan and predominant in the NT. Luke probably altered the verb τίκτω in the LXX of Gen. 17.19 to γεννάω which is his own vocabulary and a more usual verb in the NT, depending on his memory of the verse in Genesis.[472]

d. *Composition procedure*
The construction of the sentence can be explained as follows: 1) Luke (or the composer of his source) depended on his memory; 2) he employed the latter part of Gen. 17.19 since it was a fixed and stereotyped expression; 3) he employed the verb γεννάω in the first part because it was a more common verb or because the verb is Luke's style.[473] At any rate, the translation theory provides the least possible explanation.[474] If someone had translated the Hebrew text, he would not have had reason to change the word order of ἡ γυνή σου Ἐλισάβετ and υἱόν σοι. In contrast, if Luke composed the sentence in Lk. 1.13b in Greek, depending on his memory of the LXX, all the factors are well explained.[475]

(2) *Is the noun* δέησις *a non-Lukanism in the sentence* εἰσηκούσθη ἡ δέησις σου?

(i) *The problem*
The noun δέησις occurs only in the infancy narrative (here and in 2.37) apart from Lk. 5.33. In contrast, another noun προσευχή occurs twelve times: Lk. 6.12; 19.46; 22.45; Acts 1.14;[476] 2.42; 3.1; 6.4;

---

472. The occurrence of the verb τίκτω in the Lukan infancy narrative probably stemmed from LXX style (1.31, 57; 2.6–7,11).

473. Luke possibly had a different LXX version before him, though this possibility is not high, since the verb τίκτω is used to announce the future birth of Jesus in Mt. 1.21, which is an allusion to Gen. 17.19: τέξεται δὲ υἱὸν, καὶ καλέσεις τὸ ὄνομα αὐτοῦ Ἰησοῦν.

474. It is impossible again to completely rule out the possibility that somebody translated the Hebrew text. The translation theory possibly provides an appropriate answer about the occurrence of the verb γεννάω; the translator employed his favourite or common word while translating a Hebrew source. However, it does not give a sufficient answer to the question of why Luke used the word order ἡ γυνή σου Ἐλισάβετ and υἱόν σοι. These factors make it difficult to accept the translation theory.

475. Ringgren interprets the deviation of Lukan OT quotations which are unique to Luke as stemming from Luke's faulty memory ('Luke's Use of the Old Testament', *HTR*, 79 [1986], pp. 227–36). Concerning Lukan quotations from the Pentateuch, Holtz claims that Luke appears not to have had a copy of the Pentateuch and that the quotations from the Pentateuch must have been from the collections of traditional testimony (*Zitate bei Lukas*, pp. 129–130).

476. In some variants, καὶ τῇ δεήσει is added after τῇ προσευχῇ.

10.4, 31; 12.5; 16.13, 16.[477] The noun δέησις seems to be a non-Lukanism stemming from the pre-Lukan source. This speculation is strengthened by the use of the noun προσευχή in Acts 10.31 where a similar expression is used (εἰσηκούσθη σου ἡ προσευχή).[478] Acts 10.31 contains προσευχή for 'prayer' while δέησις appears in Lk. 1.13.[479]

(ii) *An explanation on the basis of the distinction between* προσευχή *and* δέησις

Some scholars attempt to explain the use of the word δέησις by pointing out that the meaning of the term δέησις is distinguishable from that of the term προσευχή.[480] The first one is primarily used for a specific petition in a concrete situation while the second noun is used for general prayer.[481] A number of scholars believe such distinction exists.[482]

The problem, however, lies in the fact that it is hardly possible to distinguish between these two words. For example, both a verb form of δέησις and the noun προσευχή, are used in the same context in Acts 10.2 and 10.4.[483] In 10.2, Luke uses the verb δέομαι while employing the noun προσευχαί in v. 4. It is hard to decide whether there is the

---

477. This noun appears four times in the other Gospels (Mt. 21.13; 21.22; Mk 9.29), and two of them are in quotations from the LXX (Mt. 21.13 and its parallel Mk 11.17 [a quotation from Isa. 56.7]). In contrast, the noun δέησις does not appear in other Gospels at all.

478. The verb εἰσακούω occurs five times in the NT (Mt. 6.7; Lk. 1.13; Acts 10.31; 1 Cor. 14.21; Heb. 5.7) but 'prayer' is the subject only in the examples in Luke-Acts.

479. In Acts 10.4, where the same message of the angel is recorded as in Acts 10.31, the same noun προσευχή is used, though Luke could have avoided the repetition of the same noun by changing it to δέησις.

480. Bock notes that 'the term δέησις (*deesis*, prayer) suggests a specific petition' (*Luke 1.1–9.50*, p.82). Evans calls it 'petitionary prayer' (*Saint Luke*, p.148). This indicates that Zechariah had been petitioning for the removal of childlessness.

481. *TDNT*, vol. 2, p.41, 807. Admitting that the two nouns can be used interchangeably, Greeven argues that 'there are traces of a conscious distinction in this respect'. The noun δέησις in Lk. 1.13, he continues, refers to the specific request 'implied, though not expressly stated, which Zechariah makes for a son' (*TDNT*, vol. 2, p.807).

482. Evans assumes, for example, that Zechariah had been praying for a child (*Saint Luke*, p.148). Brown details that the prayer in Lk. 1.13 does not directly point to the general prayer of the priest for Israel during his service for incense, but the implied petition for the removal of childlessness (*The Birth of the Messiah*, p.260). See also Bock, *Luke 1.1–9.50*, pp.82–83, who considers both possibilities: the past prayer for a child and the prayer for Israel in general.

483. v. 2 εὐσεβὴς καὶ φοβούμενος τὸν θεὸν σὺν παντὶ τῷ οἴκῳ αὐτοῦ, ποιῶν ἐλεημοσύνας πολλὰς τῷ λαῷ καὶ δεόμενος τοῦ θεοῦ διὰ παντός; 'He (Cornelius) was a devout man who feared God with all his household; he gave alms generously to the people and prayed constantly to God...'

v. 4 ὁ δὲ ἀτενίσας αὐτῷ καὶ ἔμφοβος γενόμενος εἶπεν, Τί ἐστιν, κύριε; εἶπεν δὲ αὐτῷ, Αἱ προσευχαί

3. *A Close Examination of the Greek of the Infancy Narrative* 203

aspect of 'petition' in these two verses. It is certain, however, that the verb δέομαι and the noun προσευχαί must refer to the same aspect in both verses.[484] The distinction between the two words is not well observed.[485] It is unlikely, therefore, that Luke uses δέησις in Lk. 1.13 because the context requires it.[486]

In view of the above considerations, the following point is clear: the Greek noun προσευχή is the typical word for 'prayer' in Luke-Acts as well as in other Gospels, and the noun δέησις may be synonym which may be a non-Lukanism.

(iii) Does δέησις in Lk. 5.33 come from Luke's hand?

It is difficult nonetheless to confirm that the noun δέησις in Lk. 1.13 did not come from Luke's hand, because it occurs once outside of the infancy narrative, in Lk. 5.33. This example needs to be closely examined.

a. *Words for prayer and fasting in Luke-Acts*

Lk. 5.33-35 records a debate between Jesus and some people[487] concerning fasting. They asked Jesus why his disciples did not fast and pray frequently as the disciples of John and the Pharisees do (v. 33):

σου καὶ αἱ ἐλεημοσύναι σου ἀνέβησαν εἰς μνημόσυνον ἔμπροσθεν τοῦ θεοῦ. 'He stared at him in terror and said, "What is it, Lord?" He answered, "Your prayers and your alms have ascended as a memorial before God."

484. It seems that Luke intends to describe the centurion's prayer as a token of general piety. The verb then, according to a strict distinction, must be 'προσεύχομαι'. Another example is found in Acts 1.14:

οὗτοι πάντες ἦσαν προσκαρτεροῦντες ὁμοθυμαδὸν τῇ προσευχῇ σὺν γυναιξὶν καὶ Μαριὰμ τῇ μητρὶ τοῦ Ἰησοῦ καὶ τοῖς ἀδελφοῖς αὐτοῦ; 'all these were devoting themselves to the prayer with one mind with women, Mary, Jesus' mother, and his brothers...'

Although the prayer here may be an expression of piety in general, the context strongly suggests that they were praying for the Holy Spirit (Acts 1.4). In this verse, Luke uses the noun προσευχή for a specific petition.

485. Greeven admits that 'δέησις can denote prayer as an expression of piety in general as well as specific petition' (*TDNT*, vol. 2, p.41).

486. Having raised the question about the possibility that the noun δέησις is used for personalized prayer, Plummer, concludes that 'to make δέησις refer to habitual supplication and not to be prayer offered with incense, seems unnatural' (*The Gospel according to St. Luke*, p. 13).

487. According to the grammatical context, it would seem that the introductory Οἱ δέ refers to the groups mentioned in the preceding passage: the Pharisees and their scribes (v. 30). The content of the question, however, excludes this interpretation, since the disciples of the Pharisees appear in the third person: 'John's disciples, like the disciples of the Pharisees, frequently fast and pray.' For the detailed discussion, see Bock, *Luke 1.1–9.50*, pp. 514–15, and Marshall, *Luke*, p. 224. cf. Robert H. Gundry, *Mark: A Commentary on His Apology for the Cross* (Grand Rapids: Eerdmans, 1992), pp. 131–32.

Lk. 5.33: Οἱ δὲ εἶπαν πρὸς αὐτόν, Οἱ μαθηταὶ Ἰωάννου νηστεύουσιν πυκνὰ καὶ δεήσεις ποιοῦνται ὁμοίως καὶ οἱ τῶν Φαρισαίων, οἱ δὲ σοὶ ἐσθίουσιν καὶ πίνουσιν.
'Then they said to him, "John's disciples frequently fast and pray as even the disciples of the Pharisees, but your disciples eat and drink."'

Whereas the question in Matthew and Mark is limited to the fasting of Jesus' disciples,[488] Luke adds a reference to prayer and employs the Greek word δέησις: νηστεύουσιν πυκνὰ καὶ δεήσεις ποιοῦνται. Luke did not adopt this term from the common source for Matthew and Luke or from Mark as it does not occur in either.

Luke appears then to have added the concept 'prayer' to the fasting. Apart from Lk. 5.33, a combination of the two concepts, fasting and prayer, occurs three times in Luke-Acts;[489] Lk. 2.37 (νηστείαις καὶ δεήσεσιν λατρεύουσα νύκτα καὶ ἡμέραν); Acts 13.3 (τότε νηστεύσαντες καὶ προσευξάμενοι καὶ ἐπιθέντες τὰς χεῖρας αὐτοῖς ἀπέλυσαν); Acts 14.23 (χειροτονήσαντες δὲ αὐτοῖς κατ' ἐκκλησίαν πρεσβυτέρους, προσευξάμενοι μετὰ νηστειῶν). The same word is used for fasting in these verses (νηστεία and its verb form) but the term for 'pray' differs; the participle of the verb προσεύχομαι in Acts (13.3; 14.23) and the noun δέησις in the Lukan infancy narrative.[490] However, the two instances in Acts include the participial form of the verb, not the noun προσευχή. It thus becomes clear that δέησις is not used in the combination of the two concepts 'prayer and fasting' in Lk. chs 3–24 and Acts except in Lk. 5.33.

b. *Why then did Lk. 5.33 include the term δέησις?*[491]
Luke probably obtained the phrase δεήσεις ποιοῦνται in 5.33 from his peculiar source. Concerning some differences in three Gospels of

---

488. The texts of Matthew and Mark read as follows:
Mt. 9.14 Τότε προσέρχονται αὐτῷ οἱ μαθηταὶ Ἰωάννου λέγοντες, Διὰ τί ἡμεῖς καὶ οἱ Φαρισαῖοι νηστεύομεν [πολλά], οἱ δὲ μαθηταί σου οὐ νηστεύουσιν; 'Then the disciples of John came to him, saying, "Why do we and the Pharisees fast often, but your disciples do not fast?"'
Mk 2.18 Καὶ ἦσαν οἱ μαθηταὶ Ἰωάννου καὶ οἱ Φαρισαῖοι νηστεύοντες. καὶ ἔρχονται καὶ λέγουσιν αὐτῷ, Διὰ τί οἱ μαθηταὶ Ἰωάννου καὶ οἱ μαθηταὶ τῶν Φαρισαίων νηστεύουσιν, οἱ δὲ σοὶ μαθηταὶ οὐ νηστεύουσιν; 'Now John's disciples and the Pharisees were fasting; and people came and said to him, "Why do John's disciples and the disciples of the Pharisees fast, but your disciples do not fast?"'
489. There are no other instances in the NT.
490. This combination, νηστείαν καὶ δέησιν, appears together only once in the LXX (Dan. 2.18), though Theodotion's translation, which is literal, does not contain this combination anywhere.
491. A possible answer would be that Luke intended to refer to a specific supplication with the noun δέησις. However, there is no clear distinction between δέησις and προσευχή, as pointed out above. Moreover, even if one insists on the distinction between the two nouns, Lk. 5.33 indicates that the prayer in general is in view rather than a specific petition. Fasting was the token of piety for the Pharisees who fasted twice a week. John's disciples also did fasting.

3. A Close Examination of the Greek of the Infancy Narrative   205

this passage, some scholars interpret them as pointing to Luke's additional material, either oral or written.[492] This indicates that Luke probably was dependent on a source for the noun δέησις in Lk. 5.33. Otherwise, Luke simply utilized a classical idiom here by using the middle voice with a verbal noun.[493] The phrase δεήσεις ποιοῦνται in Lk. 5.33 forms a periphrastic idiom meaning 'pray'.[494] For this idiom, which occurs twice in the NT outside of the infancy narrative, the noun δέησις is used with the middle verb.[495] Luke simply seems to have used the noun for an idiomatic locution. Therefore, the presence of the noun δέησιν does not indicate that Luke attempted to use the noun alone for the meaning 'prayer'. The expression was utilized idiomatically also by Hellenistic Jewish authors.[496] Luke simply composed an idiom which contains the noun δέησις or adopted it from his source(s). He does not utilize the noun δέησις alone for the meaning 'pray' while adopting the noun for the phrase δεήσεις ποιοῦνται. This interpretation is strengthened considering that another noun 'προσευχή', is always used for the meaning 'prayer' in Lk. chs 3–24 and Acts (12x).

In sum, Luke exclusively used the noun προσευχή for the meaning 'prayer'. Another term δέησις appears twice only in the infancy

---

Their fasting was usually conducted not as a specific supplication, but as a token of their piety. The prayer accompanied with this fasting, as a result, was the general prayer. Luke did not adopt the noun δέησις to indicate a specific petition.

492. For details, see Marshall, *Luke*, p. 222. See also Bock, *Luke 1.1–9.50*, p. 503–4 and T. Schramm, *Der Markus-stoff bei Lukas: Literarkirtische und redaktionsgeschichtliche Untersuchung* (SNTSMS, 14; Cambridge: Cambridge University Press, 1971), pp. 105–11.

493. Fitzmyer, *Luke I–IX*, p. 598. See also BDF, p. 310.1 and Zerwick, *Biblical Greek*, p. 227.

494. The meaning of the middle voice is different from that of the active verb; δεήσεις ποιεῖσθαι means simply 'to pray' while δεήσεις ποιεῖν means 'compose a prayer', where the object is independent of the verb (Zerwick, *Biblical Greek*, p. 227).

495. The phrase δέησις with the middle form of ποιεῖν occurs three times in the NT: Lk. 5.33; Phil. 1.4 πάντοτε ἐν πάσῃ δεήσει μου ὑπὲρ πάντων ὑμῶν, μετὰ χαρᾶς τὴν δέησιν ποιούμενος; 1 Tim. 2.1 Παρακαλῶ οὖν πρῶτον πάντων ποιεῖσθαι δεήσεις προσευχὰς ἐντεύξεις εὐχαριστίας ὑπὲρ πάντων ἀνθρώπων. Although the example in 1 Timothy has the noun προσευχή with the middle verb ποιεῖσθαι, three nouns, προσευχάς, ἐντεύξεις, εὐχαριστίας seem to be added loosely after the noun δέησις without consisting of idioms with the verb ποιεῖσθαι. The three nouns are not used at all with the verb ποιεῖν elsewhere in the NT. This indicates that the author of 1 Timothy intended to use the idiom, δέησις with the verb ποιεῖν and expanded it.

496. In the LXX, there is only one instance for this idiomatic expression: *3 Macc.* 2.1 ὁ μὲν οὖν ἀρχιερεὺς Σιμων ἐξ ἐναντίας τοῦ ναοῦ κάμψας τὰ γόνατα καὶ τὰς χεῖρας προτείνας εὐτάκτως ἐποιήσατο τὴν δέησιν τοιαύτην. The locution appears once in Josephus' work, Jewish War 7.5.2 (18.276). For the reference, see *A Complete Concordance to Flavius Josephus*. In A. 14, 258, προσευχή is used instead of δέησις with the verb ποιέω.

narrative and once in Lk. 5.33 which must be ruled out in our consideration according to the above explanation. The noun δέησις in the infancy narrative is a non-Lukanism which probably derived from Luke's special source.

(iv) *Is the noun δέησις in Lk. 1.13a from the LXX?*
What kind of special source did Luke use? The ultimate source of the noun was probably the LXX. The noun δέησις occurs about 79 times[497] and the verb εἰσακούω appears many times in the LXX. However, an expression similar to the phrase in 1.13a is found in *Sirach* and *Tobit*:[498]

Sir. 3.5 – καὶ ἐν ἡμέρᾳ προσευχῆς αὐτοῦ εἰσακουσθήσεται 'and in the day of his prayer, it (the prayer) will be heard';

Sir. 51.11 – καὶ εἰσηκούσθη ἡ δέησίς μου 'my prayer was heard';

Tob. 3.16 – καὶ εἰσηκούσθη ἡ προσευχὴ ἀμφοτέρων, 'and the prayer of both was heard';

Tob. 3.16(s) – ἐν αὐτῷ τῷ καιρῷ εἰσηκούσθη ἡ προσευχὴ ἀμφοτέρων, 'at that very time, the prayer of both was heard.'

Interestingly, the sentence in *Sir.* 51.11 is almost identical to the one in Lk. 1.13a. The Lukan text seems to be derived from this verse. Remarkably, the Hebrew text of the verse in *Sirach* has a different locution.[499] The source of the noun δέησις could be *Sir.* 51.11 the LXX. This argument is strengthened by the fact that *Sir.* 48.10 is also alluded to in 1.17 which is also part of Zechariah's prayer. Luke (or the composer of his source) may thus have been influenced by *Sir.* 51.11 of the LXX, though one cannot be sure of this.

---

497. Προσευχή occurs about 107 times.
498. There are no further examples, but see 1 Kgs 8.29 ὃν εἶπας ἔσται τὸ ὄνομά μου ἐκεῖ τοῦ εἰσακούειν τῆς προσευχῆς; Job 27.9 τὴν δέησιν αὐτοῦ εἰσακούσεται κύριος; *Sir.* 35.13 δέησιν ἠδικημένου εἰσακούσεται; 1 Kgs 8.30 εἰσακούσῃ τῆς δεήσεως τοῦ δούλου σου; 1 Kgs 8.45 εἰσακούσει ἐκ τοῦ οὐρανοῦ τῆς δεήσεως αὐτῶν. However, the active or middle form of the verb appears in these verses.
499. The Hebrew text shows a parallelism by using two different Hebrew nouns for prayer 'as objects of the verbs "hear" and "listen" respectively':
ויאזין אל פצנוני 'then the Lord heard my voice
אז שמע קולי יײ and he listened to my petition.'
For comment, see P.W. Skehan and A.A. Dilella, *The Wisdom of Ben Sira* (The Anchor Bible, vol. 39; New York: Doubleday, 1987), p. 567. 'Ben Sira employs the literary device,' they note, 'known as "breakup of a stereotyped phrase," i.e., the words "qol tahanunay", instead of being used in a single phrase... are each used separately but in parallel (as here).'

In conclusion, the etymological allusion is uncertain and the dependence of the Lukan text on the Hebrew OT is less probable. The ultimate source of the noun δέησις is probably *Sir.* 51.11 of the LXX.[500] These considerations exclude the possibility that the Lukan text is dependent on a Hebrew original. Rather, the author appears to have depended on his memory of the LXX.

Finally, phrases and words that some scholars still believe support the translation theory do not in fact originate from the direct influence of Hebrew language. Most of them derive from the LXX; some varations occur due to Luke's intervention and the influence of Luke's Greek source(s).

---

500. See Farris who suggests that the word δέησις probably originated from *Sir.* 51.11 of the LXX (*The Hymns*, p. 170).

Chapter 4

CONCLUSION

We are now ready to formulate the conclusions of this study and its contribution to the study of the Greek of the Lukan infancy narrative. The first section will summarize the results of the foregoing investigation and the second section will deal with the implication of this study for the source issue of the infancy narrative.

A. *Summary*

The primary question of this investigation has been whether the Greek of the Lukan infancy narrative indicates the direct influence of a Semitic language (i.e., Hebrew)[1] or the indirect effect of that language via the LXX. In order to find a solution, we have examined (a) quotations from the OT, (b) allusions to the OT, and (c) phraseology derived from the OT.

 a. Three criteria have been suggested to decide whether a phrase or sentence is a quotation: first, a phrase or sentence which is preceded by an introductory formula can be a quotation; second, the subject matter has to correspond closely and discernibly to a couple of particular OT passages; third, the wording must closely correspond to phrases and sentences of a couple of OT verses. Not only the instance which satisfies all three conditions, but also one which sufficiently satisfies the last two conditions is to be counted as a quotation. There are only two instances which meet these criteria in the infancy narrative, namely, Lk. 2.23, 24. These two quotations have provided an important test for the issue of the original language of the infancy narrative (see Chapter 3.A).
 b. Allusions refer to sentences and phrases which are reminiscent of the OT expressions found in one or two, or at most several fixed OT

---

1. As pointed out in Chapter 1, there is a consensus that the Semitisms in the infancy narrative of Luke are not Aramaisms but Hebraisms. For details, see Chapter 1.B.

4. Conclusion

verses, and which cannot be counted as quotations according to the criteria which were given above. Allusions occur in the infancy narrative so frequently that it is impossible and unnecessary to examine all the instances. Only some prominent instances which clearly allude to some OT verses, and which some scholars still believe support the theory of a translation from a Semitic (Hebrew) source have been investigated (1.17; 1.31, etc. in Chapter 3.B).

c. It is true, as we saw above in Chapter 3.C, that phraseology is related to allusions so closely that one can hardly separate the search for phraseology from that for allusions. However, a clear difference may be recognized between these two categories: while locutions in allusions are derived from a small number of fixed OT verses, those for the category of phraseology do not stem from fixed OT verses.[2] It is not necessary, as in the case of allusion, to investigate all the phrases which reflect the OT influence. Here again, we have only looked at the locutions which are still regarded by some scholars as supporting the translation theory. We have investigated phraseology in 1.5; 2.13, etc (Chapter 3.C).

No instance in the Magnificat (1.46-55) and the Benedictus (1.67-79) is included in this study, not on purpose but by chance. Neither contains a quotation; though they both contain allusions to Old Testament texts (or themes), no prominent examples have been suggested by scholars. This is the case also for the phraseology; there are some phrases in the Magnificat and the Benedictus which have a Semitic flavour, but such phrases are abundant even in other parts of the infancy narrative. It is impossible and unnecessary, as pointed out above, to deal with all such instances.[3] These factors may justify applying our conclusions to the whole of the Lukan infancy narrative, though they are valid mainly for the narrative parts.

---

2. For details of the distinction between allusions and phraseology, see section C of Chapter 3, 'Phraseology'.

3. In Lk. 1.46b-47, the shift of the present tense to the aorist tense appears and the shift is probably due to the influence of a Hebrew original (see R. Buth, 'Hebrew Poetic Tenses and the Magnificat', *JSNT*, 21 [1984], pp. 67–83). Few tense alternations in the New Testament have given rise to so many different explanations as the alternation of tenses in Lk. 1.46b-47. However, the tense shift in these verses falls within the scope of Greek usage. For the argument on the basis of Greek usage, see Fitzmyer, *Luke I–IX*, p. 366 (timeless aorist); Brown, *The Birth of the Messiah*, p. 336 (ingressive aorist); B.M. Fanning, *Verbal Aspect in New Testament Greek* (Oxford: Clarendon, 1990), p. 279 (dramatic aorist); Porter, *Verbal Aspect*, p. 133 (from the influence of the LXX).

The following points summarize the major findings:

1. Quotations in the infancy narrative, which appear only in Lk. 2.23 and 24, follow the LXX rather than the Hebrew OT.[4] Some differences exist between the text in the LXX and that in Luke, but they do not support the theory of dependence of the Lukan text on the Hebrew text. They simply indicate that the author altered the LXX text for some reason (for details, see Chapter 3.A).
2. The LXX is also the ultimate source for allusions in the infancy narrative. The differences from the LXX are readily explained by Luke's tendency to impose his own style on the texts to which he alludes (for details, see Chapter 3.B).
3. In the case of phraseology, many of the expressions which other scholars think indicate the influence of Hebrew fall into the category of Septuagintalisms which point to Semitized Greek expressions that appear in the LXX (for details, see Chapter 3.C).
4. 'Hard core Semitisms', i.e., Semitic but non-Septuagintal expressions, which point to the direct influence of a Semitic language (i.e., Hebrew) are not found in the infancy narrative. Instances that scholars believe are hard core Semitisms do not in reality indicate the direct effect of Hebrew; they are either from the influence of LXX style or from Luke's hand.
5. 'Non-Lukanisms,' i.e., locutions in the infancy narrative which do not occur in Lk. chs 3–24 and Acts and for which other expressions are used in Lk. chs 3–24 and Acts,[5] appear in the infancy narrative and most of them are Septuagintalisms which ultimately derive from the LXX. They do not come from Hebrew sources. None of the non-Lukanisms in the infancy story lends support to the translation theory.[6]
6. 'Non-Septuagintalisms', i.e., expressions which deviate from LXX style, occur in the infancy narrative. Such locutions, however, do not stem from the translation of an underlying Hebrew source.[7]

---

4. Concerning the quotations in Acts 1–15, Wilcox notes that Luke, though mainly depending on the LXX, appears to have depended for some quotations on '"ready made" blocks of material, whose deviation from the Septuagint he did not choose to alter' (*Semitisms of Acts*, p. 181). These 'ready made' blocks, according to him, were probably in Greek. See also Steyn, *Septuagint Quotations*, p. 232, who admits the possibility that some elements in quotations cited by Peter and Paul in Acts, though they are very few, point to 'a *Textvorlage* which seems to be somewhat closer to the Hebrew'.

5. For example, δέησις in 1.13 (προσεύχομαι is used in Lk. chs 3–24 and Acts), τίκτω in 1.57 (γεννάω is used in other parts of Luke-Acts), etc.

6. Some non-Lukanisms originate from Luke's source(s). For details, see the next section.

7. Some of these expressions are from Luke's source(s) and others from Luke's intervention. For details, see the next section.

7. A careful investigation indicates that many non-Septuagintalisms prove to be 'unsuccessful Septuagintalisms',[8] i.e., expressions which while seeking to imitate or to evoke the LXX yet deviate (sometimes on purpose) from its style.[9] Such locutions are found in allusions and phraseology. How to interpret unsuccessful Septuagintalisms is one of the key issues in deciding the original language of the infancy narrative. The presence of unsuccessful Septuagintalisms in the infancy narrative may indicate that Luke imitated LXX style without consistency, or that Luke did not in fact attempt to imitate the style of the LXX at all. The issue centres on how to explain their presence. The first question is whether or not they render a possible underlying Hebrew construction and the second question is whether a proper explanation of the use of such features can be suggested. In most instances that have been scrutinized above, the influence of the LXX has become manifest. Unsuccessful Septuagintalisms in the infancy narrative indicate the following:

(1) In the case of phrases, they point to the influence of the LXX in the sense that they are close to the locutions in the Septuagint[10] (e.g., the use of the phrase συλλαμβάνω ἐν γαστρί [1.31], στρατιᾶς οὐρανίου [2.13], προβαίνω ἐν ταῖς ἡμέραις [1.7; 1.18; 2.36]).[11]

(2) Luke sometimes utilizes unsuccessful Septuagintalisms in accordance with his own style (e.g., ἐν ταῖς ἡμέραις + genitive pronoun or adjective in the phrase προβαίνω ἐν ταῖς ἡμέραις in 1.7; 1.18; 2.36; γεννάω in 1.13; the use of the subjunctive for the future prohibition in 1.15).[12] Unsuccessful Septuagintalisms may also be attributable to other reasons as in the phrase συλλαμβάνω ἐν γαστρί in 1.31.[13]

(3) Some seemingly unsuccessful Septuagintal expressions can be explained as Luke's intentional alteration to convey a subtle difference in meaning. Those locutions were derived most

---

8. It is not easy to decide where the line must be drawn to distinguish between non-Septuagintalisms and unsuccessful Septuagintalisms. For details, see Chapter 2.A.

9. Scholars like Wilcox, O'Fearghail, and Horton admit that there are some Greek locutions in the NT which seem to imitate the style of the LXX unsuccessfully. For their argument, see Chapter 1.B.

10. The problem concerning a phrase is more complicated than that concerning a simple word; one aspect of a phrase could indicate the influence of the LXX, while another aspect of it may speak against the influence of the LXX.

11. For details, see the section B of Chapter 3, 'Allusions' (1.31) and the section C, 'Phraseology' (2.13; 1.7, etc.).

12. For details, see the section A (1.15) and C (1.7, etc; 1.13) of Chapter 3.

13. The form of the expression is probably to be attributed to Luke's source(s). For details, see the next section.

probably from Luke's intervention for the reasons suggested in the preceding chapter (e.g., παρὰ τοῦ θεοῦ [1.37]; στρατιᾶς οὐρανίου [2.13]).[14]

In short, 'unsuccessful Septuagintalisms' in the infancy narrative most probably originated from Luke's intentional intervention.

In conclusion, there is no sufficient evidence for the argument that Luke translated or used Semitic source(s). Rather, the Greek of Luke's infancy narrative most probably reflects the influence of the LXX. It is also clear that Luke actively participated in the composition of the narrative to the extent that he sometimes changed Septuagintal expressions to unsuccessful Septuagintalisms, which strictly speaking are non-Septuagintal, in accordance with his own style and for his own purpose.

B. *The Implication of This Study for the Quest of Source(s) for the Infancy Narrative*

As pointed out in the Introduction, our study is related to the quest for Luke's source(s) for the infancy narrative. In the process of this study, some features that help to clarify source(s) in the narrative have been found: 'non-Lukanisms' especially may indicate the presence of written Greek source(s). On the basis of the results outlined above, we come to the following conclusions:

1. The Greek of the infancy story appears to be heavily Septuagintalized compared with that of the remainder of Luke's writings.[15]

---

14. For details, see sections B (1.37) and C (2.13) of Chapter 3.

15. Concerning the quest for sources in the first 15 chapters of Acts, Wilcox suggests that Luke managed to obscure the form of the older material so well that it is really hard to recognize Luke's use of sources. Fortunately Luke left some 'protruding Semitisms', which reflect the sources. These 'hard core Semitisms', according to Wilcox, could give 'the impression that Luke had certain information before him' (*The Semitisms of Acts*, p. 184). 'These little "knots" of Semitic material surviving unrevised' do not, however, indicate Luke's translation of Aramaic or Hebrew sources, according to Wilcox (p. 181). The stories in Acts may have stemmed from Aramaic – or Hebrew – speaking circles, but it is certain that Luke completely rewrote them in their present form 'in his own language and style, and no doubt, also, for his own purpose'. Following Wilcox's analysis of Acts, we could conclude that since the Greek of the infancy narrative is heavily Septuagintalized compared with that of Lk. chs 3–24 and Acts, Luke in the infancy narrative seems to have *failed* to obscure the form of the older material, with the result that readers can smell the aroma of his sources. The conclusion that Luke appears to have relied on a Greek source or sources is then inevitable. The explanation based on a Semitic original is excluded from our consideration, since it has been pointed out in the preceding section that the Semitic original theory is not probable for the infancy narrative.

4. Conclusion

Luke did not write his infancy narrative in polished Greek as he did the prologue (Lk. 1.1-4) and possibly portions of Acts chs 16–28. Obvious is that the Greek of the infancy narrative is also more Septuagintalized than that of Lk. chs 3–24 and that of Acts chs 1–15. Scholars have suggested various explanations with regard to the question of why Luke Septuagintalized his Greek in the infancy narrative more than in Lk. chs 3–24 and Acts. Despite small differences in details, the thrust of the argument is almost the same: Luke intentionally imitated LXX style in order to show a close connection between the OT and the first part of the Gospel (J. Drury, O'Fearghail, Fitzmyer, Goulder,[16] Ravens, etc).[17] Most of these scholars go one step further by arguing that Luke, not having a source at his disposal, consulted the LXX to compose the infancy narrative. In their view, Luke's use of the LXX is indicated by the presence of Septuagintalisms or Septuagintal-type expressions[18] (J. Drury,[19] O'Fearghail, Goulder, Ravens).[20] This argument provides a possible solution to the question why Luke Septuagintalized his Greek more in the infancy narrative than in the remainder of his writings. However, the presence of 'non-Lukan, non-Septuagintal expressions' makes it difficult to argue that Luke depended solely on the LXX.

2. The presence of expressions which are both 'non-Lukan' and 'non-Septuagintal' makes it likely that Luke was dependent on a source (or sources) written in Greek.[21] It is hardly possible to distinguish

---

16. For the arguments of O'Fearghail, Fitzmyer, and Goulder, see Chapter 1.B.

17. D. Ravens argues that the style of the infancy narrative 'must have seemed to some of Luke's readers a powerful reminder of Israel's Scripture'. 'To begin a Christian Gospel as though it were a part of Israel's Scripture,' he continues, 'is surely of major importance in assessing Luke's overall purpose and it is difficult to escape the conclusion that the Septuagintal style and ethos are deliberate on Luke's part.' D. Ravens, *Luke and the Restoration of Israel* (JSNTSS, 119; Sheffield: JSOT Press, 1995), p. 29.

18. Fitzmyer recognizes that Luke utilized source(s) for some parts of the infancy narrative; he bases his argument on the theological aspect, not on the linguistic aspect. For details, see section B of Chapter 1, 'A Survey of Scholarly Views on the Greek of the Infancy Narrative'.

19. For his argument, see his book *Tradition and Design in Luke's Gospel* (London: Darton, Longman & Todd, 1976), pp. 46–81. 'Luke's Gospel,' he notes, 'is midrash on Matthew, Mark, and the LXX, and much of it, particularly Luke 1–2 ... consists of creative alterations and additions to Matthew and Mark with the LXX as the likely source' (p. 20).

20. In contrast to these scholars, Martin argues that Luke did not use any Greek source, including the LXX, but translated Semitic sources for the infancy narrative (*Syntax Criticism of the Synoptic Gospels*, p. 110).

21. One could take the 'hard core Semitisms' proper as a guide to clarify Luke's *Vorlage*. However, there are no hard core Semitisms in the infancy narrative. For details, see above, nt. 15.

'non-Lukanisms' in Acts chs 1–15 because of the significant length of these 15 chapters, but it is possible to define non-Lukanisms in the first two chapters of the Gospel of Luke. One may distinguish rather easily vocabulary and syntax in the infancy narrative that deviate from Luke's style in Lk. chs 3–24 and Acts. They may support the view that Luke depended on source(s) written in Greek. 'Non-Lukan, non-Septuagintalisms' probably indicate the influence of a source or sources.[22] There are non-Lukan Septuagintalisms, many of them derived from the LXX; but not all of them were from the LXX. Some of them most probably originated from Greek source(s) [see below, 4. (2)]. Also 'hard core non-Lukanisms', which do not belong to Luke's style and reflect exactly neither the Hebrew construction nor the LXX may indicate the influence of Luke's original sources more clearly than mere 'non-Lukanisms' and 'non-Lukan, non-Septuagintalisms'.

3. Although non-Lukanisms, especially those which are also non-Septuagintalisms as well as hard core non-Lukanisms, may indicate that Luke had written source(s) in hand for some parts of the infancy narrative, Luke was 'more master than slave of the elements of his text'.[23] Of course, he was influenced by the Greek of his source(s); the Greek of his source(s) was heavily Septuagintalized and Luke adopted Septuagintal expressions from the source(s) and he was partly influenced by its style. Nonetheless, he corrected some locutions in the source according to his own style in the infancy narrative as he did in the rest of his writings. Both hard core and secondary Lukanisms indicate that Luke actively participated in the composition procedure.

4. Some features which point to the possible influence of the source(s) are summarized as follows;

   (1) Non-Lukan, non-Septuagintal expressions and hard core non-Lukan locutions most probably occur due to direct or indirect influence of Luke's source(s). Such words or phrases may of course indicate the lack of the influence of the LXX. The close investigation undertaken in chapter 3, however, has shown that non-Septuagintal aspects of such locutions in the infancy

---

22. Fitzmyer speculates that one may distinguish between Luke's direct composition and Luke's dependence on his special source L (*Luke I–IX*, p. 83). He asks 'How can one be sure that such material is really derived from "L" and not freely composed by Luke?' He answers, 'We shall never know.' However, one may say that some non-Lukanisms in the infancy narrative stem from sources; otherwise they are inexplicable.

23. M. Coleridge, *The Birth of the Lukan Infancy Narrative: Narrative as Christology in Luke 1–2* (JSNTSS, 88; Sheffield; JSOT Press, 1993), p. 17.

4. Conclusion

narrative do not exclude the influence of the LXX. They simply indicate that the locutions come from Luke's source(s) as in the manner of the quotation in 2.23 and 2.24.[24] They occur due to Luke's intervention influenced by his Greek source(s) as in 1.23 (the use of the verb πίμπλημι) and in 1.31 (the use of the verb συλλαμβάνω in the phrase συλλαμβάνω ἐν γαστρί).[25]

(2) Non-Lukan Septuagintalisms are most probably from the LXX especially in the case of quotations and allusions (δέησις in 1.13 [possibly an allusion]; the phrase ἐν γαστρί in 1.31[allusion]; the verb τίκτω in 1.31 [allusion]; μήτρα in 2.23 [quotation]). Some non-Lukan Septuagintalisms are possibly from Luke's source(s) influenced by LXX style (ἐγένετο and the absence of the conjunction in 1.5; 'τὸ ὄνομα αὐτῆς' Ἐλισάβετ' in 1.5; the absence of the article with the noun καρδία in 1.17; the verb συλλαμβάνω in 1.24, 36; 2.21; the use of the verb τίκτω in 1.57; 2.6-7, 11; the phrase 'ἐν [τῷ] νόμῳ κυρίου' in 2.23-24).

(3) Lukan non-Septuagintalisms are probably from Luke's hand rather than from his source(s) (ἐπί in 1.17; γεννάω in 1.13).

(4) Lukan Septuagintalisms are derived from Luke's hand through the influence of the LXX; they hardly stem from the source(s) (ὀνόματι in 1.5; omission of the article in 1.5; the phrase, ἐν ταῖς ἡμέραις + modifying genitive, itself in the construction προβαίνω ἐν ταῖς ἡμέραις in 1.7; 1.18; and 2.36).[26]

In sum, Luke most probably used a written Greek source or sources for the infancy narrative, at least for some parts of it, and the source(s) was (were) composed in imitation of the LXX. The presence of such source(s) explains why the Greek of the infancy narrative is heavily Septuagintalized; Luke was influenced by his source(s). This does not mean, however, that Luke was merely the reviser or compiler of his source(s). He was the

---

24. The use of a phrase, instead of a full sentence, for the quotation in 2.24 is possibly non-Lukan, non-Septuagintal, though it is not certain that such usage is non-Septuagintal.

25. The verb συλλαμβάνω itself in 1.31 (which contains an allusion) is non-Septuagintal, though the phrase as a whole is an unsuccessful Septuagintalism. For details, see section B of Chapter 3.

26. For details, see section C of Chapter 3, 'Phraseology'.

author of the infancy narrative; he rewrote the source(s) employing his own style and language for his own purpose,[27] though he did not completely manage to free himself from the style and language of the source(s).

---

27. Our study has shown that investigation of the Greek text in the Lukan infancy narrative as it stands will reveal the real intention of the author and the correct meaning of some difficult sentences: e.g., the meaning of the sentence in Lk. 1.15 (see section A of Chapter 3, 'Quotations'); 1.37 (see section B of Chapter 3, 'Allusions'); the meaning of the phrase in 2.13 (πλῆθος στρατιᾶς οὐρανίου) (see section C of Chapter 3, 'Phraseology'); the meaning of the pronoun 'their' in 2.22 (see section A of Chapter 3, 'Quotations').

BIBLIOGRAPHY

Adamson, J.B., *James: The Man and his Message* (Grand Rapids: Eerdmans, 1988).
Aejmelaeus, Anneli, *Parataxis in the Septuagint* (Helsinki: Univ. of Helsinki [diss], 1982).
Aland, K., *et al.* (eds.), *Synoptic of the Four Gospels* (Stuttgart: German Bible Society, 7th edn, 1984).
—*Novum Testamentum Graece* (Stuttgart: German Bible Society, 27th edn, 1993).
—*Vollständige Konkordanz zum Griechischen Neuen Testament* (Berlin/New York: Walter de Gruyter, 1983).
Alexander, L.C.A., 'Luke's Preface in the Context of Greek Preface-Writing', *NovT*, 28 (1986), pp. 48–74.
Anderson, H., *The Gospel of Mark* (NCBC; Grand Rapids: Eerdmans, 1981).
Archer, G.L., and G.C. Chirichigno, *Old Testament Quotations in the New Testament* (Chicago: Moody, 1983).
Argyle, A.W., 'The Greek of Luke and Acts', *NTS*, ns. 20 (1974), pp. 441–45.
—'Did Jesus Speak Greek?', *ExpTim*, 67 (1955–56), pp. 92–93, 383.
—'Greek among the Jews of Palestine in NT Times', *NTS*, ns. 20 (1973–74), pp. 87–89.
Arndt, W.F., and F.W. Gingrich, *A Greek-English Lexicon of the New Testament and other Early Christian Literature* [trans. of W. Baurer's *Griechish- deutsches Wörterbuch zu den Schriften des neues Testaments und der Übrigen Urchristlichen Literatur*] (Chicago: University of Chicago Press, 1956).
Arnold, B.T., 'Luke's Characterizing Use of the Old Testament in the Book of Acts', in *History, Literature and Society in the Book of Acts* (ed. B. Witherington, III; Cambridge: University Press, 1996), pp. 300–23.
Aytoun, R.A., 'The Ten Lukan Hymns of the Nativity in Their Original Language', *JTS*, 18 (1917), pp. 274–88.
Bacon, B.W., 'More Philological Criticism of Acts', *AJT*, 22 (1918), pp. 1–23.
Barr, J., 'Which Language did Jesus Speak? – Some Remarks of a Semitist', *BJRL*, 53 (1970), pp. 9–29.
Barrett, C.K., 'Luke/Acts' in *It is Written: Scripture Citing Scripture*. Essays in Honour of Barnabas Lindars, SSF (eds. D.A. Carson and H.G.M. Williamson; Cambridge: University Press, 1988), pp. 231–244.

Bartlett, J.V., 'The Sources of St. Luke's Gospel' in *Studies in the Synoptic Problem by Members of the University of Oxford* (ed. W. Sanday; Oxford: Clarendon, 1911), pp. 313–63.

Beentjes, P.C., *The Book of Ben Sira in Hebrew* (Leiden/New York/Köln: Brill, 1997).

Benoit, P., 'L'enfance de Jean-Baptiste selon Luc I', *NTS*, ns. 3 (1956–57), pp. 169–94.

—*Exégèse et Théologie III* (Paris: Les Editions du Cerf, 1968).

Beyer, K., *Semitische Syntax im Neuen Testament* (Göttingen: Vandenhoeck & Ruprecht, 1962).

Black, M., *An Aramaic Approach to the Gospels and Acts* (Oxford: Clarendon Press; 1st edn, 1946; 2nd edn, 1954; 3rd edn, 1967).

—'The Recovery of the Language of Jesus', *NTS*, ns. 3 (1956–57), pp. 305–13.

—'Second Thoughts – IX. The Semitic Element in the NT', *ExpTim*, 77 (1965–66), pp. 20–23.

—'Aramaic Studies and the Language of Jesus', in *In Memoriam P. Kahle* (eds. M. Black and G. Fohrer; Berlin: Topelmann, 1968), pp. 17–28. Reprinted in *The Language of the New Testament: Classic Essays* (ed. S.E. Porter; Sheffield: Sheffield Academic Press, 1991).

—'The Biblical Languages', in *The Cambridge History of the Bible, vol. 1: from the Beginnings to Jerome* (eds. P.R. Ackroyd and C.F. Evans; Cambridge: University Press, 1970), pp. 1–11.

Blass, F., *Philology of the Gospels* (London: Macmillan, 1898).

Blass, F., and A. Debrunner, *A Grammatik des Neutestamentlichen Griechisch* (ed. F. Rehkopf; Göttingen: Vanderhoeck & Ruprecht, 17th edn, 1990).

Blass, F., and A. Debrunner, *A Greek Grammar of the New Testament* (trans. and ed. by Robert W. Funk. Chicago: University of Chicago Press, 1961).

Bock, D.L., *Proclamation from Prophecy and Pattern: Lukan Old Testament Christology* (JSNTSS, 12; Sheffield: JSOT, 1987).

—*Luke 1:1–9:50* (BECNT, Grand Rapids: Baker, 1994).

—'Luke, Gospel of', in *Dictionary of Jesus and the Gospels* (eds. J.B. Green, S. McKnight, and I.H. Marshall; Downers Grove, Leicester: Intervarsity, 1992), pp. 495–510.

Böhl, E., *Die alttestamentlichen Citate im neuen Testament* (Wien: Wilhelm Braumüller, 1878).

Borgen, P., K. Fuglseth, and R. Skarsten, *The Philo Index: A Complete Greek Word Index to the Writings of Philo of Alexandria* (Grand Rapids: Eerdmans; Leiden/Boston/Köln: Brill, 2000).

Bornhäuser, K., *Studien zum Sondergut des Lukas* (Gütersloh: C. Bertelsmann, 1934).

Bovon, F., *Das Evangelium nach Lukas* (EKKNT, 3; 2 vols.; Zürich: Benziger, 1989).

Brachter, G., *Old Testament Quotations in the New Testament* (London: United Bible Society, 1961).

Brock, S.P., 'The Phenomena of the Septuagint', in *The Witness of Tradition*. (ed. A.S. Van der Woude; OTS, 17; Leiden: Brill, 1972).

Brown, R.E., *The Gospel according to John I–XII.* (Anchor Bible; Garden City: Doubleday & Company, 1966).

—'Luke's Method in the Annunciation Narratives of Chapter One', in *No Famine in the Land* (eds. J.W. Flanagan and A.W. Robinson; Missoula, MT: Scholars Press, 1975), pp. 179–94.
—*The Birth of the Messiah: A Commentary on the Infancy Narratives in Matthew and Luke* (London: Geoffrey Chapman, 1977, rev. 1993).
—'Gospel Infancy Narrative Research from 1976–1986: Part II (Luke)', *CBQ*, 48 (1986), pp. 660–80.
Bruce, F.F., *The Acts of the Apostles: Greek Text with Introduction and Commentary* (London: Tyndale Press, 1951; 3rd edn, Grand Rapids: Eerdmans, 1990).
Bultmann, R., *Die Geschichte der Synoptischen Tradition* (Göttingen: Brandenböd & Ruprecht, 1957; 9th edn, 1979).
Burkitt, F.C., 'Who Spoke the Magnificat?', *JTS*, 7 (1906), pp. 220–27.
Burney, C.F., 'A Hebraic Construction in the Apocalypse', *JTS*, 22 (1920–21), pp. 371–76.
—*The Aramaic Origin of the Fourth Gospel* (Oxford: Clarendon Press, 1922).
Burrows, M., 'The Original Language of the Gospel of John', *JBL*, 49 (1930), pp. 95–139.
—'Principles for Testing the Translation Hypothesis in the Gospels', *JBL*, 53 (1934), pp. 413–30.
—'The Semitic Background of the New Testament', *BT*, 2 (1951), pp. 67–73.
Burton, E.D., *Syntax of the Mood and Tenses in New Testament Greek* (Chicago: University of Chicago Press, 1900).
Buth, R., 'Hebrew Poetic Tenses and the Magnificat', *JSNT*, 21 (1984), pp. 67–83.
Cadbury, H. J., 'The Style and Literary Method of Luke', *HTS*, 6 (1919/1920), pp. 37–72.
—'Luke-Traslator or Author?', *AJT*, 24 (1920), pp. 436–55.
—'Lexical Notes on Luke-Acts VI', *JBL*, 48 (1929), pp. 412–25.
—'Four Features of Lukan Style', in *Studies in Luke-Acts* (eds. L.E. Keck, and T.L. Martyn; Nashville: Abingdon, 1966), pp. 87–102.
—*The Making of Luke-Acts* (London: SPCK, 1958).
—*The Acts of the Apostles* (ed. F.J. Foakes Jackson; Grand Rapids: Baker, 1979).
Calvin, J., *Commentary on a Harmony of the Evangelists Matthew, Mark, Luke*, I (Edinburgh: T. & T. Clark, 1920).
Carmignac, J., 'Studies in the Hebrew Background of the Synoptic Gospels', *ASTI*, 7 (1968–69), pp. 64–93.
—'The Meaning of *Parthenos* in Luke 1.27 – A Reply to C.H. Dodd', *BibTrans*, 28 (1977), pp. 327–30.
Carson, D.A., *The Gospel According to John* (Leicester: Intervarsity; Grand Rapids: Eerdmans, 1991).
Charles, R.H (ed.), *The Apocrypha and Pseudepigrapha of the Old Testament in English* (Oxford: Clarendon, 1913; rep., 1963).
—*A Critical and Exegetical Commentary on the Revelation of St. John* (2 vols.; Edinburgh: T. & T. Clark, 1920).
Clark, A.C., *The Acts of the Apostles* (Oxford: University Press, 1933).
Clark, L., 'The Use of the Septuagint in Acts', in *The Beginning of Christianity: Part I, The Acts of the Apostles*, vol. 2 (eds. F.J. Foakes Jackson and K. Lake; London: Macmillan, 1922), pp. 66–105.

Coleridge, M., *The Birth of the Lukan Infancy Narrative: Narrative as Christology in Luke 1–2* (JSNTSS, 88; Sheffield; JSOT Press, 1993).

Collins, N.L., *The Library in Alexandria and the Bible in Greek* (Leiden/Boston/Köln: Brill, 2000).

Colwell, E.C., *The Greek of the Fourth Gospel: A Study of its Aramaisms in the Light of Hellenistic Greek* (Chicago: University of Chicago Press, 1931).

Conrad, E.W., 'Annunciation of Birth and the Birth of the Messiah', *CBQ*, 47 (1985), pp. 656–63.

Conybeare, F.C., and G. Stock, *Grammar of Septuagint Greek: with Selected Readings, Vocabulary, and Updated Indexes* (repr. of 1905 ed., Peabody: Hendrickson, 1988).

Conzelman, H., *Die Mitte der Zeit: Studien zur Theologie des Lukas* (Beiträger zur Historischen Theologie, 17; Tübingen: Mohr, 3rd edn, 1960).

—'Die Apostelgeschichte' (*Handbuch zum Neuen Testament* ed. G. Bornkamm, vol. 7; Tübingen: J.C.B. Mohr, 1963).

Costas, P.W., *An Outline of the History of the Greek Language, with Particular Emphasis on the Koine and the Subsequent Periods* (Chicago, 1936: repr. Chicago: Ares, 1979).

Cotterell, P., and M. Turner, *Linguistics and Biblical Interpretation* (London: SPCK, 1989).

Courtenay, J.J., *The Language of Palestine and Adjacent Regions* (Edinburgh: T. & T. Clark, 1920).

Creed, J.M., *The Gospel According to St. Luke: The Greek Text with Introduction, Notes and Indices* (London: Macmillan, 1930).

Dahl, N.A., 'The Purpose of Luke-Acts', in *Jesus in the Memory of the Early Church* (Minneapolis: Augsburg, 1976).

Dalman, G., *The Words of Jesus: Considered in the Light of Post-Biblical Jewish Writings and the Aramaic Language* (trans. D.M. Kay; Edinburgh: T. & T. Clark, 1902).

—*Jesus-Jeshua: Studies in the Gospels* (trans. P.P. Levertoff; London: SPCK, 1929) pp. 1–37.

Danker, F.W., *Jesus and the New Age According to St. Luke: A Commentary on the Third Gospel* (St. Louis: Clayton, 1972).

Davies, P.P., 'The Position of Adverbs in Luke Studies', in *Studies in New Testa- ment Language and Text*. Festschrift G.D. Kilpatrick (ed. J.K Elliott; Leiden: Brill, 1976), pp. 106–21.

Davies, W.D., and D.C. Allison, Jr., *The Gospel According to Saint Matthew* (ICC, vol. 1; Edinburgh: T. & T. Clark, 1988).

Davies, W.D., and L. Frankelstein (eds.), *The Cambridge History of Judaism* (Cambridge: University Press, 1989).

Dawsey, J.M., *The Lukan Voice: Confusion and Irony in the Gospel of Luke* (Macon, GA: Mercer, 1986).

Deissman, A., 'Hellenistisches Griechisch' in *Realencyklopädie für protestantische Theologie und Kirche*, vol. 7 (ed. A. Hauck; Leipzig: Hinrichs, 3rd edn 1899), pp. 627–39. Reprinted and translated, 'Hellenistic Greek with Special Consideration of the Greek Bible in the Language of the New Testament', in

The Language of the New Testament: Classic Essays (ed. S.E. Porter trans. S.E. Porter; Sheffield: Sheffield Academic Press, 1991), pp. 39-59.
—*Bibelstudien*. Marburg: Elwert, 1895. trans. *Bible Studies* (trans. A. Grieve; Edinburgh: Clark, 2nd edn, 1909).
—*Neue Bibelstudien* (Marburg: Elwert, 1897).
—*Lichte vom Osten* (Tübingen: Mohr, 1908).
—*The Philology of the Greek Bible or New Light on the NT from Records of the Graeco-Roman Period* (trans. L.R.M. Strachan; London: Hodder & Stoughton, 1908).
Delebecque, E., *Etudes grecques sur L'evangile de Luc* [CEA] (Paris, 1976).
—'John Wrote in Aramaic', *JBL*, 57 (1938), pp. 155-71.
Denis, A-M., *Concordance Grecque des Pseudépigraphes D'ancien Testament* (Louvain: Université Catholic de Louvain, 1987).
Dibelius, M., 'Style Criticism of the Book of Acts', in *Studies in The Acts of the Apostles* (ed. H. Greeven; London: SCM Press, 1956).
Dodd, C.H., 'New Testament Translation Problem I', *BibTrans*, 27 (1976), pp. 301-11.
Dover, K.J., *Greek Word Order* (Cambridge: University Press, 1960).
Dreyer, A.J.G., *An Examination of the Possible Relation between Luke's Infancy Narrative and the Qumran Hodayot* (Amsterdam: A.A.A. Rotex, 1962).
Driver, G.R., *The New Testament in Greek* (ed. The American and British Committees of the International Greek New Testament Project; Oxford: Clarendon, 1984).
Drury, J., *Tradition and Design in Luke's Gospel: A Study in Early Christian Historiography* (Atlanta: John Knox, 1977).
Easton, B.S., 'Linguistic Evidence for the Lukan Source L', *JBL*, 29 (1910), pp. 139-80.
—*The Gospel According to St. Luke: A Critical and Exegetical Commentary* (New York: Scriber, 1926).
Elliott, J.K., 'Καθώς and ὥσπερ in the New Testament', *FilNeo*, 7 (1991).
Ellis, E.E., *The Gospel of Luke* (London: Butler & Tanner, 1974).
Emerton, J.A., 'Did Jesus Speak Hebrew?', *JTS*, ns. 12 (1961), pp. 189-202.
—'The Problem of Vernacular Hebrew in the First Century AD and the Language of Jesus', *JTS*, ns. 24 (1973), pp. 1-23.
Ernst, J., *Das Evangelium nach Lukas* (Regensburger Neues Testament, Regensburg: Friedrich Pustet, 6th edn, 1993).
Evans, C.F., *Saint Luke* (TPINTC, London-Philadelphia: SCM Press and Trinity Press International, 1990).
Fanning, B.M., *Verbal Aspect in New Testament Greek* (Oxford: Clarendon, 1990).
Farmer, W.R., 'Notes on a Literary and Form-Critical Analysis of Some of the Synoptic Material Peculiar to Luke', *NTS*, ns. 8 (1961-62), pp. 301-16.
Farris, S.C., 'On Discerning Semitic Sources in Luke 1-2', in *Gospel Perspectives* II (eds. R.T. France & D. Wenham; Sheffield: JSOT Press, 1981), pp. 201-37.
—*The Hymns of Luke's Infancy Narratives: Their Origin, Meaning and Significance*. (JSNTSS, 9; Sheffield: JSOT Press, 1985).
Field, F., *Notes on the Translation of the New Testament* (Cambridge: University Press, 1899; repr. Peabody: Hendrickson, 1994).

Fitzmyer, J.A., 'The Use of Explicit Old Testament Quotations in Qumran Literature and in the New Testament', *NTS*, ns. 7 (1960–61), pp. 297–333.
—'Review of Black, *Aramaic Approach* (3rd edn, 1966)', *CBQ*, 30 (1968), p. 428.
—'The Language of Palestine in the First Century A.D.', *CBQ*, 32 (1970), pp. 501–31.
—'The Contribution of Qumran Aramaic to the Study of the New Testament', *NTS*, ns. 20 (1974), pp. 382–407.
—*Essays on the Semitic Background of the NT*. n.p. (Missoula: Scholars Press, 1974).
—'The Phases of the Aramaic Language', in *A Wandering Aramean: Collected Essays* (Missoula: Scholars Press, 1979), pp. 57–84.
—'The Study of the Aramaic Background of the NT', in *A Wandering Aramean: Collected Essays* (Missoula: Scholars Press, 1979) pp. 1–27.
—'The Aramaic Language and the Study of the NT', *JBL*, 99 (1980), pp. 5–21.
—*The Gospel According to Luke* (Anchor Bible, Garden City: Doubleday, 1981, 1990).
—*Luke the Theologian: Aspects of His Teaching* (London: Geoffrey Chapman, 1989).
Fitzmyer, J.A., and D.J. Harrington, *A Manual of Palestinian Texts* (Rome: Biblical Institute Press, 1978).
Flusser, D., 'The Magnificat, the Benedictus and the War Scroll', in *Judaism and the Origin of Christianity* (Jerusalem: Magnes Press, 1988), pp. 126–49
Frösén, J., *Prolegomena to a Study of the Greek Language in the First Century A.D.: The Problem of Koine and Atticism* (Helsinki: Univ. of Helsinki [diss.], 1974).
Gaston, L., 'The Lukan Birth Narrative in Traditional Redaction', in *Society of Biblical Literature Seminar Papers 1976* (ed. G. MacRae; Missoula, MT: Scholars Press, 1976).
Gehman, H.S., 'The Hebraic Character of Septuagint Greek', *VT*, 1 (1951), pp. 81–90.
—'Hebraisms of the Old Greek Version of Genesis', *VT*, 3 (1953), pp. 141–48.
Geldenhuys, N., *Commentary on the Gospel of Luke: The English Text with Introduction, Exposition, and Notes*. (NICNT, Grand Rapids: Eerdmans, 1951).
George, A,. 'Jean-Baptiste et Jesus en Lc 1–2', in *Mélanges Bibliques*, Festschrift B. Rigaux (eds. A. Descamps and R.P. André de Halleux; Gembloux: Duculot, 1970).
Gewiess, J., 'Die Marienfrage, Lk 1,34', *BZ*, 5 (1961), pp. 221–54.
Gignac, F., *A Grammar of the Greek Papyri of the Roman and Byzantine Periods* (2 vols.; Milano: Istituto Editoriale Cisalpino-La Goliardica, [1976], 1981).
Gilmour, M., *The Gospel According to St. Luke and St. John* (The Interpreter's Bible, vol. 8; Nashville: Abingdon, 1952).
Goodspeed, E.J., 'The Vocabulary of Luke and Acts', *JBL*, 31 (1912), pp. 92–94.
—'The Origin of Acts', *JBL*, 39 (1920), pp. 6–21.
—'The Original Language of the NT', in *New Chapters in NT Study* (New York: Macmillan, 1937), pp. 127–68.
Goodwin, W.W., *Greek Grammar* (rev. edn by C.B. Gulick; Boston: Ginn, 1958).
Goulder, M.D., *Luke: A New Paradigm* (JSNTSS, 2; 2 vols.; Sheffield: JSOT, 1989).

Goulder, M.D and M.L. Sanderson, 'St. Luke's Genesis', *JTS*, ns. 8 (1957), pp. 12–30.
Grant, M., *Greek and Latin Authors: 800 B.C–A.D. 1000* (New York: The H.W. Wilson Company, 1980).
Green, J.B., 'Internal Repetition in Luke-Acts: Contemporary Narratology and Lukan Historiography', in *History, Literature and Society in the Book of Acts* (ed. B. Witherington; III; Cambridge: University Press, 1996), pp. 283–99.
Greijdanus, S., *Het Heilig Evangelie Naar de Beschrijving van Lukan, I, Hoofdstukken 1-12* (Amsterdam: H.A. Van Bottenburg, 1940).
Grelot, P., 'Sémitismes (dans Le Nouveau Testament)', in *Supplément au Dictionnaire de La Bible* (eds. J. Briend, and É. Cothenet; Paris: Letouzey & Ane, 1992), pp. 334–424.
Grigsby, B., 'Composition Hypotheses for the Lukan "Magnificat"', *EvQ*, 56 (1984), pp. 159–72.
Grintz, M., 'Hebrew as Spoken and Written Language in the Last Days of the Second Temple', *JBL*, 79 (1960), pp. 32–47.
Guelich, R.A., *Mark 1-8:26* (WBC, 34a; Dallas: Word Books, 1989).
Gueret, A., 'Luc I-II. Analyse semiotique', *SeB*, 25 (1982), pp. 35–42.
Gundry, R.H., 'The Language Milieu of First-Century Palestine: Its Bearing on the Authenticity of the Gospel Tradition', *JBL*, 83 (1964), pp. 404–8.
—*Matthew: A Commentary on His Literary and Theological Art* (Grand Rapids: Eerdmans, 1982).
—*Mark: A Commentary on His Apology for the Cross* (Grand Rapids: Eerdmans, 1992).
Guthrie, D., *New Testament Introduction* (Downers Grove: Intervarsity, 1990).
Haenchen, E., *Die Apostelgeschichte*, vol. 3 of *kritisch-exegetischer Kommentar über das Neu Testament*, begruedet von Heinrich Augustus Wilhelm Meyer (Göttingen: Vandenhoeck & Ruprecht, 1961).
Hagner, D.A., *Matthew 1–13* (WBC, 33a; Dallas: Word Books, 1993).
—*Matthew 14–28* (WBC, 33b; Dallas: Word Books, 1995).
Handebert, P., *La meranoia des Septante a Saint Luc* (Lavie de la parole ed. Festschrift P. Grelot; Paris: Desclee, 1987).
Harnack, A. von, 'Das Magnificat der Elisabeth (Luk 1.46-55) nebst einigen Bemerkungen zu Luk 1 und 2', *Sitzungberichte der Koeniglichen Preussischen Akademie der Wissenschaften zu Berlin* 27 (1900), pp. 538–66.
Harstad, M.J., *Greek According to Luke: A First Year Grammar* (Dubuque: Kendal/Hunt Pub. Co., 1994).
Hatch, E. and H. Redpath, *A Concordance to the Septuagint* (Oxford: Clarendon, 1897).
Hawkins, J.C., *Horae Synopticae: Contribution to the Study of the Synoptic Problem* (Oxford: Clarendon, 1899).
—'Three Limitations to St. Luke's Use of St. Mark's Gospel', in *Studies in the Synoptic Problem by Members of the University of Oxford* (ed. W. Sanday; Oxford: Clarendon, 1911), pp. 27–94.
Heimerdinger, J., 'Word Order in Koine Greek: Using a Text-Critical Approach to Study Word Order Pattern in the Greek Text of Acts', *FilNeo*, 9 (1996), pp. 139–77.

Hengel, M., *Die Evangelienüberschriften* (Heidelberg: Carl Winter/Universitätsverlag, 1984).
Hengel, M. and A.M. Schwemer (eds.), *Die Septuaginta zwischen Judentum und Christentum* (WUNT, 72; Tübingen: Mohr, 1994).
Higgins, A.J.B., 'Luke 1-2 in Tatian's Diatessaron', *JBL*, 103 (1982), pp. 193-222.
Hilhorst, A., *Semitismes et latinismes dans le Pasteur d'Hermas* (Nijmegen: Dekker & Van de Vegt, 1976).
Hippocrates, *Hippocrates*, vol. 4 (ed. T.E. Page; Loeb Classical Library, repr. 1953 London: Heinemann, Cambridge, Mass.: Harvard, 1931).
Hobart, W.K., *The Medical Language of St. Luke: A Proof from Internal Evidence that 'The Gospel of according to St. Luke' and 'The Acts of the Apostles' Were Written by the Same Person, and that the Writer was a Medical Man* (Dublin: Hodges, Figgis, 1882; repr. Grand Rapids: Baker, 1954).
Hodges, Z.C. and A.L. Farstad, *The Greek New Testament: According to the Majority Text* (Nashville/Camden/New York: Thomas Nelson, 1982).
Hoffmann, E.G. and H. von Siebenthal, *Griechische Grammatik zum neuen Testament* (Riehen/Schweiz: Immanuel Verlag, 1985).
Holtz, T., *Untersuchungen über die alttestamentlichen Zitate bei Lukas* (Berlin: Akademie, 1968).
Horsley, G.H.R., 'Divergent Views on the Nature of the Greek of the Bible', *Bib*, 65 (1984), pp. 393-403.
—'The Fiction of "Jewish Greek"', in *New Documents Illustrating Early Christianity* (Linguistic Essays V; New South Ryde: Macquarie University, 1989), pp. 5-40.
Horton, F.L. Jr., 'Reflections on the Semitisms of Luke-Acts', in *Perspective on Luke-Acts* (ed. C.H. Talbert; Edinburgh: T. & T. Clark, 1978), pp. 1-23.
Howard, G., *The Gospel of Matthew According to a Primitive Hebrew Text* (Macon, GA: Mercer University Press, 1987).
Hübner, H., 'Vetus Testamentum und Vetus Testamentum in Novo receptum', *JBT*, 3 (1988), pp. 147-62.
—'New Testament, OT Quotations in the', in *The Anchor Bible Dictionary*, vol. 4 (ed. D.N. Freedman; New York: Doubleday, 1992), pp. 1096-104.
Hühn, E., *Die alttestamentlichen Citate und Reminiscenzen im neuen Testamente* (Tübingen: Mohr, 1900).
Hurst, L.D., 'The Neglected Role of Semantics in Search for the Aramaic Word of Jesus', *JSNT*, 28 (1986), pp. 63-80.
Jellicoe, S (ed.), *Studies in the Septuagint* (New York: Ktav, 1974).
Jeremias, J., *Die Sprache des Lukas Evangeliums: Redaktion und Tradition im Nicht-Markusstoff des dritten Evangeliums* (Göttingen: Vandenhoeck & Ruprecht, 1980).
Johnson, F., *The Quotations of the New Testament from the Old Considered in the Light of General Literature* (Philadelphia: American Baptist, 1896).
Johnson, L.T., *Luke* (Sacra Pagina, Collegeville: The Liturgical Press, 1991).
Johnson, S.E., 'The Biblical Quotations in Matthew', *HTR*, 36 (1943), p. 147.
Jones, A.H.M., *The Greek City: From Alexander to Justinian* (Oxford: Clarendon Press, 1940).

Judge, E.A., 'The Reaction Against Classical Education in the NT', *Evangelical Review of Theology*, 9 (1985), pp. 167–8.
Kaiser, W.C., *The Uses of the Old Testament in the New* (Chicago: Moody Bible Institute, 1986).
Kasser, R., and V. Martin (eds.), *Papyrus Bodmer XIV–XV: Evangiles de Luc et Jean* (Tome I; Cologny Geneva: Bibliotheque Bodmer, 1961).
Kilpatrick, G.D., 'The Greek Syntax of Luke 2.14', *NTS*, ns. 34 (1988), pp. 472–75.
Kimball, C.A., *Jesus' Exposition of the Old Testament in Luke's Gospel* (JSNTSS, 94; Sheffield: JSOT, 1994).
Kirchcschlaeger, W., 'Beobachtungen zur Struktur der lukanischen Vorgeschichten Lk 1–2', *Bibel und Liturgie*, 57 (1984), pp. 244–51.
Kleiner, J.R., '"Sie gaben ihm den Namen Jesus" (Lk 2,21)', *GL*, 57 (1984), pp. 456–58.
Klostermann, E., *Das Lukasevangelium* (*Handbuch zum Neuen Testament*, 5 repr. 1975, Tübingen: Mohr, 1929).
Knox, W.L., *The Sources of the Synoptic Gospels*, II (Cambridge: University Press, 1957).
Koester, H., *Einführung in das Neue Testament* (Berlin/New York: de Gruyter, 1980).
Koet, B.J., *Five Studies on Interpretation of Scripture in Luke-Acts* (Studiorum Novi Testamenti Auxilia, XIV; Leuven: University Press, 1989).
Kühn, C.G (ed.), *Claudii Galeni Opera Omnia*, Tomus XIX (Hildesheim: Georg Olms, 1968).
Kümmel, W.G., *Introduction to the New Testament* (Nashville: Abingdon, 1975).
Lachs, S.T., 'Hebrew Elements in the Gospels and Acts', *JQR*, 71 (1980–81), pp. 31–43.
Lagrange, M.-J., *Evangile selon Saint Matthieu* (Paris: Etudes Bibliques, 1920).
—*Evangile selon Saint Luc* (Paris: Gabalda, 1921).
Lane, T.J., *Luke and the Gentile Mission: Gospel Anticipates Acts* (Frankfurt am Main/Berlin/Bern/New York/Paris/Wien: Peter Lang, 1996).
Lapide, P., 'Insights from Qumran into the Language of Jesus', *RevQ*, 8 (1975), pp. 483–86.
Laurentin, R., *Structure et Théologie de Luc I–II* (Paris: Gabalda, 1957).
—'Traces d'allusions etymologiques en Luc I–II', *Bib*, 37 (1956), pp. 435–56.
—'Traces d'allusions etymologiques en Luc I–II', *Bib*, 38 (1957), pp. 1–23.
Leaney, A.R.C., *The Commentary on the Gospel According to St. Luke* (London: Adam & Charles Black, 1958).
Lee, G. M., 'Translation Greek in the NT', in *Studia Evangelica*, VII (ed. E.A. Livingstone; Berlin: Akademie Verlag, 1982) pp. 317–26.
Liddell, H.G., and R. Scott, *A Greek-English Lexicon* (rev. edn by Jones, H.S; repr. of 9th ed.; Oxford: Clarendon, 1958).
Lieberman, S., 'Greek in Jewish Palestine', in *Biblica and Other Studies* (ed. A. Altman; Cambridge, MA: Harvard University Press, 1963).
Liefield, W.L., *Matthew, Mark, and Luke* (The Expositer's Bible Commentary, vol. 8; Grand Rapids, Zondervan, 1985).

Lindars, B., 'Steven Thomson, The Apocalypse and Semitic Syntax', *JSemst*, 30 (1985), pp. 289-91.
—*The Gospel of John* (London: Marshall, Morgan and Scott, 1972).
Longenecker, R., *Biblical Exegesis in the Apostolic Period* (Grand Rapids: Eerdmans, 1975).
Machen, J.G., 'The Origin of First Two Chapters of Luke', *PTR*, 10 (1912), pp. 212-77.
—'The Hymns of the First Chapter of Luke', *PTR*, 10 (1912), pp. 1-38.
—*The Virgin Birth of Christ* (New York/London: Harper & Brothers, 1930).
McKnight. E.V., 'Is the NT Written in "Holy Ghost" Greek?', *BT*, 16 (1965), pp. 87-93.
Maddox, R., *The Purpose of Luke-Acts* (Göttingen: Vandenhoeck & Ruprecht, 1982).
Maloney, E.C., *Semitic Interference in Markan Syntax* (SBLDS, 51; Chicago: Scholars, 1981).
Maloney, G., and W. Frohn (eds.), *Concordantia in Corpus Hippocraticum*, Tome V (Hildesheim/Zürich/New York: Olms-Weidmann, 1986).
Manson, W., *The Gospel of Luke* (Moffatt's NT Commentary; London: Hodder & Stoughton, 1930).
Marshall, I.H., *The Gospel of Luke* (NIGTC; Exeter: Paternoster, 1978; repr Grand Rapids: Eerdmans, 1989).
—*The Acts of the Apostles: An Introduction and Commentary* (TynNTC; Grand Rapids: Eerdmans, 1980).
Martin, R.A., 'Some Syntactical Criteria of Translation Greek', *VT*, 10 (1960), pp. 295-310.
—'Syntactical Evidence of Aramaic Sources in Acts I-XV', *NTS*, ns. 2 (1964/65), pp. 100-09.
—*Syntactical Evidence of Aramaic Source in Greek Documents* (LXX and Cognate Studies, 3; Missoula: Scholars Press, 1974).
—*Syntax Criticism of the Synoptic Gospels* (Studies in the Bible and Early Christianity, 10; Lewiston: Edwin Mellen, 1987).
Marxsen, W., *Einleitung in das neue Testament: Einführung in ihre Probleme* (Gütersloh: Gütersloher Verlagshaus, 1978).
Mather, P.B., 'The Search for the Living Text of the Lukan Infancy Narrative', in *The Living Text* (eds. D.E. Groh and R. Jewett, Honor of E. W. Saunders; Lanham, MD; University Press of America, 1985), pp. 123-40.
McDougall, J.I., *Diodorus Siculus* (Hildesheim/Zürich/New York: Georg Olms, 1983).
Mealand, D.L., 'Hellenistic Historians and the Style of Acts', *ZNW*, 82 (1991), pp. 42-66.
—'Luke-Acts and the Verbs of Dionysius', *JSNT*, 63 (1996), p. 86.
Menken, M.J.J., *Old Testament Quotations in the Fourth Gospel: Studies in Textual Form* (Kampen: Kok Pharos, 1996).
—'Isaiah and the "Hidden Things". The Quotation from Psalm 78.2 in Matthew 13:35', in *The Use of Sacred Books in the Ancient World* (eds. L.V. Rutgers, P.W., van der Horst, H.W. Havelaar, and L. Teugels; Leuven: Peeters, 1998).

Metzger, B.M., 'The Formulas Introducing Quotations of Scripture in the NT and the Mishnah', *JBL*, 70 (1951), pp. 299–301.
—*A Textual Commentary on the Greek New Testament* (London: United Bible Societies, Corr. edn, 1975; Stuttgart: German Bible Society, 2nd edn, 1994).
Minear, P., 'Luke's Use of the Birth Stories', in *Studies in Luke-Acts* (eds. L.E. Keck and T.L. Martyn; Nashville: Abingdon, 1966), pp. 111–30.
Montgomery, J.A., *The Origin of the Gospel According to St. John* (Philadephia: J.C. Winston, 1923).
Moor, C., *The Anchor Bible Dictionary*, vol. 6 (ed. D.N. Freedman; New York: Doubleday, 1992).
Morgenthaler, R., *Statistik des neutestamentlichen Wortschatzes* (Frankfurt am M./ Zürich: Gotthelf, 1958).
Morris, L., *The Gospel According to John* (NICNT; Grand Rapids: Eerdmans, 1995).
Most, W.G., 'Did St. Luke Imitate the Septuagint?', *JSNT*, 15 (1982), pp. 30–41.
Moule, C.F.D., *The Language of the NT* (Cambridge: University Press, 1952).
—*An Idiom Book of NT Greek* (Cambridge: University Press, 2nd edn, 1959).
—'Fulfillment-Words in the New Testament: Use and Abuse', *NTS*, ns. 14 (1967–68), pp. 293–320; reprinted in *Essays in New Testament Interpretation* (ed. C.F.D. Moule, Cambridge: University Press, 1982), pp. 3–36.
Moulton, J.H., 'Characteristics of NT Greek', *The Expositor, Sixth Series*, 9 (1904).
—'A Grammar of the Septuagint', *JTS*, 11 (1910), pp. 293–300.
—'New Testament Greek in the Light of Modern Discovery', in *Essays on Some Biblical Questions of the Day: By Members of the Univ. of Cambridge* (London: Macmillan, 1909), pp. 461–505. Reprinted in *The Language of the New Testament: Classic Essays* (ed. S.E. Porter; Sheffield: Sheffield Academic Press, 1991).
—*Prolegomena*, vol. 1 of *A Grammar of NT Greek* (Edinburgh: T. & T. Clark, 3rd edn, 1908).
—'Language of the NT', in *Discovery of the Bible* (ed. J. Hastings; Edinburgh: T. & T. Clark, 1909), pp. 528–30.
—*Accidence and Word-Formation*, vol. 2 of *A Grammar of NT Greek*, with W.F. Howard (Edinburgh: T. & T. Clark, 1929).
Moyise, S (ed.), *The Old Testament in the New Testament: Essays in Honour of J.N. North* (JSNTSS, 189; Sheffield: Sheffield Academic Press, 2000).
—'Intertextuality and the Study of the Old Testament in the New Testament', in *The Old Testament in the New Testament: Essays in Honour of J.N. North* (JSNTSS, 189; Sheffield: Sheffield Academic Press, 2000), pp. 14–41.
Müller, M., *The First Bible of the Church: A Plea for the Septuagint* (JSOTSS, 206; Sheffield: Sheffield Academic Press, 1996).
Muraoka, T., *A Greek-English Lexicon of the Septuagint: Twelve Prophets* (Peeters: Louvain, 1993).
Mussies, G., *The Morphology of Koine Greek as Used in the Apocalypse of St. John: A Study in Bilingualism* (Leiden: Brill, 1971).
—'Greek in Palestine and the Diaspora', in *Compendia Rerum Judaicarum ad Novum Testamentum*, Section I: The Jewish People in the First Century, vol. 2 (eds. S. Safrai and M. Stern; Assen: Van Gorcum, 1976), pp. 1040–64.

—'The Use of Hebrew and Aramaic in the Greek NT', *NTS*, ns. 30 (1984), pp. 416–32.
—'Variation in the Book of Acts', *FilNeo*, 4 (1991), pp. 165–82.
—'Remarks on Quotation Formulas in Gospels and Acts', in *The Use of Sacred Books in the Ancient World* (eds. L.V. Rutgers, P.W. van der Horst, H.W. Havelaar, and L. Teugels; Leuven: Peeters, 1998), pp. 49–60.
Myers, J.M., *I and II Esdras* (Anchor Bible; Garden City, NY: Doubleday, 1985).
New, D.S., *Old Testament Quotations in the Synoptic Gospels, and the Two Document Hypothesis* (Septuagint and Cognate Studies, 37; Atlanta: Scholars Press, 1993).
Nolland, J., *Luke 1–9:20* (WBC, 35a; Dallas: Word Books, 1989).
Norden, E., *Die antike Kunstprosa*, II (Leipzig: Tübner, 1909), pp. 482–92.
O'Donnell, M.B., 'Linguistic Fingerprints or Style by Numbers? The Use of Statistics in the Discussion of Authorship of New Testament Documents', in *Linguistics and the New Testament: Critical Junctures* eds. S.E. Porter and D.A. Carson; (JSNTSS, 168; Sheffield: Sheffield Academic Press, 1999), pp. 206–54.
O'Fearghail, F., 'The Imitation of the Septuagint in Luke's Infancy Narrative', *Proceedings of the Irish Biblical Association*, 12 (1989), pp. 58–78.
Oliver, H.H., 'The Lukan Birth Stories and the Purpose of Luke-Acts', *NTS*, ns. 10 (1964), pp. 202–26.
Olmstead, A.T., 'Could an Aramaic Gospel be Written?', *JNES*, 1 (1942), pp. 41–75.
O'Rourke, J.J., 'The Construction with a Verb of Saying as an Indication of Sources in Luke', *NTS*, ns. 21 (1975), pp. 421–23.
Pax, E., 'Probleme des neutestamentlichen Griechisch', *Bib*, 53 (1972), pp. 560–62.
Payne, D.F., 'Semitisms in the Book of Acts', in *Apostolic History and the Gospel* (eds. W.W. Gasque and R.P. Martin; Exeter: Paternoster, 1970).
Peters, M.K.H., 'Septuagint', in *The Anchor Bible Dictionary*, vol. 5 (ed. D.N. Freedman; New York: Doubleday, 1992), pp. 1093–104.
Philo Judaeus., *Philo* ed. F.H. Colson; (Loeb Classical Library; London: Heinemann, Cambridge, Mass.; Harvard, 1941).
Plummer, A., *A Critical and Exegetical Commentary on the Gospel According to St. Luke* (ICC; Edinburgh: T. & T. Clark, 4th edn, 1953).
Plümacher, E., *Lukas als hellenistischer Schriftsteller* (Göttingen: Vandenhoeck & Ruprecht, 1972).
Porter, S.E., 'The Language of the Apocalypse in Recent Discussion', *NTS*, ns. 35 (1989), pp. 582–603.
—*Verbal Aspect in the Greek of the New Testament with Reference to Tense and Mood* (New York: Peter Lang, 1989).
—'Thucydides 1.22.1 and Speeches in Acts: Is there a Thucydidean View?', *NovT*, 32 (1990), pp. 124–27.
—'The Greek of the New Testament as a Disputed Area of Research', in *The Language of the New Testament: Classic Essays* (ed. S.E. Porter, Sheffield: Sheffield Academic Press, 1991), pp. 11–38.
—*Idioms of the Greek New Testament* (Sheffield: JSOT Press, 1992).

—'Jesus and the Use of Greek in Palestine', in *Studying the Historical Jesus: Evaluations of the State of current Research* eds. B. Chilton and C.A. Evans; (New Testament Tools and Studies, XIX; Leiden: Brill, 1994), pp. 123-54.
Prabhu, G.M.S., *The Formula Quotations in the Infancy Narrative of Matthew: An Enquiry into the Tradition History of Mt 1–2* (Rome: Biblical Institute Press, 1976).
Quecke, H., 'Lk 1,31 in den alten Übersetzungen', *Bib*, 46 (1965), pp. 333-48.
Radermacher, L., *Neutestamentliche Grammatik: Das Griechische des NT in Zusammenhang mit der Volksprache* (Tübingen: Mohr, 2nd edn, 1925).
Ramaroson, L., 'Ad Structuram Cantici "Magnificat"', *Verbum Domini*, 46 (1968), pp. 30-46.
Raven, S.D., *Luke and the Restoration of Israel* (JSNTSS, 119; Sheffield: Sheffield Academic Press, 1995).
Rehkopf, F., *Die lukanische Sonderquelle: Ihr Umfang und Sprachgebrauch* (Tübingen: Mohr, 1959).
—'Griechisch', in *Theologische Realenzyklopädie, Studienausgabe*, Teil XIV (Berlin/New York: Walter de Gruyter, 1985), pp. 228-35.
Reiling, J., 'The Use and Translation of kai egeneto, "and it happened"', in the NT', *BibTrans*, 16 (1965), pp. 153-63.
Reiling, J., and J.L. Swellengrebel, *A Translator's Handbook on the Gospel of Luke* (Leiden: Brill, 1971).
Reiser, M., *Syntax und Stil des Markusevangeliums im Licht der hellenistischen Volksliteratur* (WUNT, 2.11; Tübingen: J.C.B. Mohr [Paul Siebeck], 1983).
Rengstorf, K.H., *A Complete Concordance to Flavius Josephus* (4 vols.; Leiden: Brill, 1973).
Rese, M., *Alttestamentliche Motive in der Christologie des Lukas* (Gütersloh: Gütersloher Verlagshaus, 1963).
—'Die Funktion der alttestamentlichen Zitate und Anspielungen in den Reden der Apostelgeschichte', in *Les Actes des Apôtres: Traditions, Rédaction, Théologie* (ed. J. Kremer; Leuven: Leuven University Press, 1979).
Riddle, D.W., 'The So-called Jewish Christians', *The Anglican Theological Review*, 22 (1929), pp. 15-33.
—'The Logic of the Theory of Translation Greek', *JBL*, 51 (1932), pp. 13-30.
Ringgren, H., 'Luke's Use of the Old Testament', *HTR*, 79 (1986), pp. 227-35.
Robertson, A.T., *A Translation of Luke's Gospel with Grammatical Notes* (New York: Doran, 1923).
—*A Grammar of the Greek NT in the Light of Historical Research* (Nashville: Broadman, 4th edn, 1934).
Ros, J., *De Studie van het Bijbelgriehsch van Hugo Grotius tot Adolf Deissmann* (Nijmegen: Dekker & Van de Vegt, 1940).
Ross, J.M., 'Jesus's Knowledge of Greek', *IBS*, 12 (1990), pp. 41-47.
Rothe, R., *Zur Dogmatik* (Gotha, 1863).
Ruddick, C.T. Jr., 'Birth Narratives in Genesis and Luke', *NovT*, 12 (1970), pp. 343-48.
Ruijgh, C.J., 'Verbal Aspect in the Greek of the New Testament with Reference to Tense and Mood', *Mnemosyne*, 48 (1995), pp. 352-64.

Rydbeck, Lars., 'What happened to NT Greek Grammar after Albert Debrunner?', *NTS*, ns. 21 (1974–75), pp. 424–27.
—*Fachprosa, vermeintliche Volkssprache und NT: Zur Beurteilung der sprachlichen Niveauunterscheide im nachklassischen Griechisch* (Uppsala: n.p., 1967).
—'On the Question of Linguistic Level and the Place of the New Testament in the Contemporary Language Milieu', in *The Language of the New Testament: Classic Essays* (Sheffield: Sheffield Academic Press, 1991), pp. 191–204.
Sahlin, H., *Der Messias und das Gottesvolk: Studien zur Protolukanischen Theologie* (Uppsala: Almqvist & Wiksells, 1945).
Salazar, A.M., 'Questions about St. Luke's Sources', *NovT*, 2 (1958), pp. 316–17.
Sanders, J.A., 'Isaiah in Luke', *Int*, 36 (1982), p. 151.
Schlatter, A., *Das Evangelium des Lukas* (Stuttgart: Calwer Verlag, 2nd edn, 1960).
Schmid, W., *Der Atticismus in seinen Hauptvertretern von Dionysius von Halikarnassus bis auf den zweiten Philostratus* (4 vols.; repr. Stuttgart: Kolhammer, 1887–1897; repr. Hilsheim: Omls, 1964).
Schmidt, D.D., 'Semitisms and Septuagintalisms in the Book of Revelation', *NTS*, ns. 35 (1991), pp. 592–603.
Schrader, C., *Thucydides: Concordantia Thucydidea* (Hildesheim/Zürich/New York: Olms-Weidmann, 1998).
—*Concordantia Herodotea* (5 vols.; Hildesheim/Zürich/New York: Olms-Weidmann, 1996).
Schramm, T., *Der Markus-stoff bei Lukas: Eine literarkritische und redaktionsgeschichtliche Untersuchung* (Cambridge: University Press, 1971).
Schürmann, H., *Das Lukasevangelium: Kommentar zu Kap. 1:1-9:50*. Herders Theologischer Kommentar zum Neuen Testament (Freiburg/Basel/Wien: Herder, 1969).
Schwarz, G., *'Und Jesus Sprach'*: Untersuchungen zur aramäischen Urgestalt der Worte Jesu (Stuttgart: Kohlhammar, 2nd edn, 1987).
—'Ex ephemerias Abis? (Lukas 1,5)', *BibNot*, 53 (1990), pp. 30–31.
Schweizer, E., 'Eine hebraisierende Sonderquelle des Lukas?', *TZ*, 3 (1950), pp. 161–85.
Shutt, R.J.H., 'Letter of Aristeas', in *The Old Testament Pseudepigrapha* (ed. J.H. Charlesworth; Garden City, NY: Doubleday, 1985).
Silva, M., 'New Lexical Semitisms', *ZNW*, 69 (1978), pp. 253–57.
—'Bilingualism and the Character of Palestine Greek', *Bib*, 61 (1980), pp. 198–219.
—*Biblical Words and Their Meaning: An Introduction to Lexical Semantics* (Grand Rapids: Zondervan, 1983).
Simpson, D.C., 'The Book of Tobit', in *The Apocrypha and Pseudepigrapha of the Old Testament in English* (ed. R.H. Charles; Oxford: Clarendon, 1963).
Skehan, P.W., and A.A. Dilella, *The Wisdom of Ben Sira* (Anchor Bible, vol. 39; New York: Doubleday, 1987).
Smith, M., 'Aramaic Studies and the Study of the NT', *JBR*, 26 (1958), pp. 304–13.
Smyth, H.W., *Greek Grammar* (rev. edn by G.M. Messing; Cambridge, MA: Harvard University Press, 1956).
Sparks, H.F.D., 'The Semitisms of St. Luke's Gospel', *JTS*, 44 (1943), pp. 129–138.
—'The Semitisms of the Acts', *JTS*, ns. 1 (1950), pp. 16–28.

—'Some Observations on the Semitic Background of the NT', *Bulletin of Studio- rum Novi Testamenti Societas*, 2 (1951), pp. 33–42.
Stanton, V.H., *The Gospel as Historical Documents: Part II, the Synoptic Gospels* (Cambridge: University Press, 1909).
Stein, R.H., 'Synoptic Problem', in *Dictionary of Jesus and the Gospels* (eds. J.B. Green, S. McKnight, and I.H. Marshall: Downers Grove: Intervarsity, 1992).
Stendahl, K., *The School of St. Matthew and its Use of the OT* (Lund: C.W.K. Gleerup, 1954).
Stevenster, J.N., *Do You Know Greek? How Much Greek Could the First Jewish Christian Have Known?* (Leiden: Brill, 1968).
Steyn, J.G., *Septuagint Quotations in the Context of the Petrine and Pauline Speeches of the Acta Apostolorum* (Kampen: Pharos Publishing House, 1995).
Stock, K., 'Die Berufung Marias (Lk 1,26–38)', *Bib*, 61 (1980), pp. 484–85.
Streeter, B.H., *The Four Gospels: A Study of Origins, Treating of the Manuscript Tradition, Sources, Authorship, & Dates* (London: Macmillan, 1924).
Strobel, A., 'Der Gruss an Maria (Lc 1,28): Eine philologische Betrachtung zu seinem Sinngehalt', *ZNW*, 53 (1962), pp. 86–110.
Sturz, F.W., *Lexicon Xenophonteum* (Hildesheim: Georg Olms, 1964).
Styler, G.M., 'Idioms of the Greek New Testament', *JTS*, ns. 44 (1993), pp. 673–74.
Swete, H.B., *An Introduction to the Old Testament in Greek* (rev. edn by R.R. Ottly; Cambridge: University Press, 1914).
Talbert, C.H (ed.), *Perspectives on Luke-Acts* (Special Studies, Series 5; Danville, VA: Association of Baptist Professors of Religion; Edinburgh: T. & T. Clark, 1978).
—'Prophecies of Future Greatness: The Contribution of Greco-Roman Biographies to an Understanding of Luke 1,5–4,15', in *The Divine Helmsman* (eds. J.L. Crenshaw and S. Sandmel; New York: Ktav, 1980), pp. 129–42.
Tannehill, R.C., *The Narrative Unity of Luke-Acts: A Literary Interpretation*, vol. 1, *The Gospel According to Luke* (Foundations and Facets; Philadelphia: Fortress, 1986).
Taylor, V., *The Historical Evidence for the Virgin Birth* (Oxford: Clarendon, 1920).
Tebb, J.R. (ed.), *Concordantia Homerica* (4 vols.; Hildesheim/Zürich/New York, 1994).
Thackeray, H. St J., *A Grammar of the OT in Greek According to the Septuagint*, I (Cambridge: University Press, 1909).
Thompson, S., *The Apocalypse and Semitic Syntax* (Cambridge: University Press, 1985).
Thumb, A., *Die griechische Sprache im Zeitalter des Hellenismus: Beiträge zur Geschichte und Beurteilung der KOINH* (Strassburg: Trübner, 1901).
Torrey, C.C., 'The Translation Made from the Original Aramaic Gospels', in *Studies in the History of Religions*, Festschrift C.H. Toy (eds. D.G. Lyon and G.F. Moore; New York: Macmillan, 1912), pp. 269–317.
—*The Composition and Date of Acts* (Cambridge, MA: Harvard University Press, 1916).
—'Fact and Fancy in the Theories Concerning Acts', *AJT*, 23 (1919), pp. 61–86, 189–212.
—'The Aramaic Origin of the Gospel of John', *HTR*, 16 (1923), pp. 305–44.

—'Medina and Πόλις and Luke 1:39', *HTR*, 17 (1924), pp. 83–89.
—'The Influence of Second Isaiah in the Gospels and Acts', *JBL*, 48 (1929), p. 35f.
—*Our Translated Gospels: Some of the Evidence* (London: Hodder & Stoughton, 1936).
—'The Aramaic of the Gospel', *JBL*, 61 (1942), pp. 71–85.
—'Julius Wellhausen's Approach to the Aramaic Gospels', *Zeitschrift der Deutschen Morgenländischen Gesellschaft*, 101 (ns. 26) (1951), pp. 125–37.
—'Studies in the Aramaic of the First Century AD', *ZAW*, 65 (1953), pp. 228–47.
—*The Four Gospels: A New Translation* (London: Hodder & Stoughton, 1958).
Tov, E., 'Did the Septuagint Translators Always Understand their Hebrew Text?', in *De Septuaginta: Studies in Honour of John William Wevers on his Sixty-fifth Birthday* (eds. A. Pietersma and C. Cox; Mississauga: Benben Publication, 1984), pp. 53–70.
Turner, N., 'Were the Gospels written in Greek or Aramaic?', *EvQ*, 21 (1949), pp. 42–8.
—'The "Testament of Abraham": Problems in Biblical Greek', *NTS*, ns. 1 (1954–5), pp. 219–24.
—'The Relationship of Luke I and II to Hebraic Sources and to the Rest of Luke-Acts', *NTS*, ns. 2 (1955), pp. 100–9.
—'The Unique Character of Biblical Greek', *VT*, 5 (1955), pp. 208–13.
—'The Language of the NT', *Peak's Commentary on the Bible* (eds. M. Black and H.H. Rowley; London: Nelson, 1962), pp. 659–62.
—*Syntax*, vol. 3 of *A Grammar of NT Greek*, by T.H. Moulton (Edinburgh: T. & T. Clark, 1963).
—'Second Thoughts-VII. Papyrus Finds', *ExpTim*, 76 (1964–5), pp. 44–8.
—*Grammatical Insights into the NT* (Edinburgh: T. & T. Clark, 1965).
—*Style*, vol. 4 of *A Grammar of NT Greek*, by T.H. Moulton (Edinburgh: T. & T. Clark, 1976).
—'The Quality of the Greek of Luke-Acts', in *Studies in New Testament Language and Text*. Festschrift G.D. Kilpatrick (ed. J.K. Elliott; Leiden: Brill, 1976), pp. 387–400.
—*Christian Words* (Edinburgh: T. & T. Clark, 1980).
—'Biblical Greek – The Peculiar Language of a Peculiar People', *Studia Evangelia*, vol. 7 (ed. E.A. Livingstone; Berlin: Akademie Verlag, 1982).
—'The Language of Jesus and His Disciples', in *The Language of the New Testament: Classic Essays* (ed. S.E. Porter; Sheffield: Sheffield Academic Press, 1991).
Tyson, J.B., 'The Birth Narratives and the Beginning of Luke's Gospel', *Semeia*, 52 (1990), pp. 103–20.
van der Horst, P.W., 'Notes on the Aramaic Background of Luke II 41–51' *NT*, 7 (1980), pp. 61–66.
Voelz, J.W., 'The Language of the NT', *ANRW*, II.25.2 (ed. W. Haase; Berlin: de Gruyter, 1984), pp. 894–930.
Vogel, T., *Zur Charakteristik des Lukas nach Sprache und Stil* (Leipzig: Dürr, 2nd edn, 1899).
—*Lukas der Arzt* (Leipzig: J.C Hinrichs'sche Buchhandlung, 1906).

Vorster, W.S., 'Bilingualism and the Greek of the New Testament: Semitic Interference in the Gospel of Mark', in *Speaking of Jesus: Essays on Biblical Language, Gospel Narrative and the Historical Jesus* (ed. J.E, Botha; Leiden/Boston/Köln, 1999), pp. 21–36.

Vriezen, K.J.H., 'Inscriptions in Mosaic Pavements in Byzantine *Palestina/Arabia* Quoting Texts from the Old Testament', in *The Use of Sacred Books in the Ancient World* (eds. L.V. Rutgers, P.W. van der Horst, H.W. Havelaar, and L. Teugels; Leuven: Peeters, 1998), pp. 49–60.

Weingreen, J., *A Practical Grammar for Classical Hebrew* (Oxford: Clarendon, 2nd edn, 1972).

Weiss, B., *Die Quelle des Lukasevangeliums* (Stuttgart/Berlin: J.G. Cotta, 1907).

Wellhausen, J., *Einleitung in die drei ersten Evangelien* (Berlin: Reimer, 1905).

Westcott, B.F., and F.J.A. Hort, *The New Testament in the Original Greek: Text* (London: Macmillan, 1898).

—*The New Testament in the Original Greek: Introduction and Appendix* (London: Macmillan, 1907).

Wilcox, M., *The Semitisms of Acts* (Oxford: Clarendon, 1965).

—'Semitisms in the NT', *ANRW*, II.25.2; (ed. W. Haase; Berlin: de Gruyter, 1984), pp. 979–86.

—'The Apocalypse and Semitic Syntax by Steven Thompson', *JTS*, ns. 30 (1987), pp. 510–12.

—'Text Form', in *It is Written: Scripture Citing Scripture: Essays in Honour of Barnabas Lindars* (eds. D.A. Carson and H.G.M. Williamson; Cambridge: Cambridge University Press, 1988), pp. 193–204.

Winter, P., 'Two Notes on the Theory of Imitation Translation Greek', *ST*, 7 (1953), pp. 158–65.

—'Magnificat and Benedictus-Maccabean Psalms', *BJRL*, 37 (1954), pp. 328–43.

—'Some Observations on the Language in the Birth and Infant Stories of the Third Gospel', *NTS*, ns. 1 (1954), pp. 111–21.

—'Hoti "recitativum" in Lc 1,25.61; 2,23', *ZNW*, 46 (1955), pp. 261–63.

—'The Proto-Source of Luke 1', *NovT,* 1 (1956), pp. 184–99.

—'On Luke and Lukan Sources', *ZNW*, 4 (1956), pp. 217–42.

Wise, M.O., 'Language of Palestine,' in *Dictionary of Jesus and the Gospels* (eds. J.B. Green, S. McKnight, and I.H. Marshall; Downers Grove, Leicester: Intervarsity, 1992), pp. 437–39.

Wyttenbach, D., *Lexicon Plutarchem* (Hildesheim: Georg Olms, 1962).

Zerwick, S.J.M., *Biblical Greek* (ed. S.J. Smith; Rome: Iura Editionis et Versionis Reservantur, 1963).

Ziegler, J., *Septuaginta: Sapientia Iesu Filii Sirach* (Vetus Testamentum Graecum Auctoritate Societatis Litterarum Gottingsis Editum, vol. XII.2; Göttingen: Vandenhoeck & Ruprecht, 1965).

Zimmerman, F., *The Aramaic Origin of the Four Gospels* (New York: Ktav, 1979).

de Zwaan, J., 'The Use of the Greek Language in Acts', in *The Beginnings of Christianity*. Part I: The Acts of the Apostles, vol. 2 (eds. F.J. Foakes Jackson and K. Lake; London: Macmillan, 1922), pp. 30–65.

INDEXES

INDEX OF REFERENCES

BIBLE

Old Testament
Genesis
1.27	64, 83	21.2	124	48.15	198		
4.1	123	22.1	145	48.16	159		
4.17	123	22.18	71	48.19	165		
4.25	124	24.1	180, 183, 184	49.25	82		
6.1	145, 146	24.3	149	50.3	175		
12.1	72	24.46	25	*Exodus*			
15.13	72	25.12	198	1.15	159		
16.1	151	25.19	147	2.1	142		
16.4	124	25.21	124, 131, 132	2.2	124		
16.11	121, 122, 124–26, 130, 131, 197, 199, 200	25.24	82, 171, 175	2.14	72		
		27.28	165	2.22	124, 131		
		29.21	175	3.2	37		
		29.31	82	3.5	72		
16.4-5.11	124	29.32-35	124	3.6	72		
17.4	165	30.5	124	3.7-10	72		
17.5	35, 157–59	30.7	124	3.13	151		
17.15	35, 157–59, 200	30.10	124	6.3	159		
		30.12	124	13.2	65, 73, 78–84		
		30.17	124	13.9	76		
17.19	192–95, 197–201	30.19	124	13.12-15	78		
		30.22	82	13.12-13	82		
18.1	192	30.23	124	13.12	65, 69, 74, 78–84		
18.9-10	198	30.41	131	13.13	81		
18.11	26, 180, 184, 185, 192	32.27-28	159	13.15	79, 81, 82, 84		
		35.10	159				
		38.3-4	124	15.3	151		
18.14	27, 112–18, 120	38.18	124	18.4	159		
		38.24-25	124	20.12-16	71		
		45.9	25	21.22	124		
19.36	124	45.21	86	22.27	72		

Exodus – continued		8.3	71	Ruth	
32.1	72	10.11	117	1.1	146
32.23	72	10.20	71	1.11	82
34.8	25	10.21	154		
34.19	81, 82	14.26	94, 95	*1 Samuel*	
		18.7	154	1.1	145, 147,
Leviticus		18.15-20	67, 71		149, 158
5.7-11	91	18.15	72, 110	1.11-15	96
5.7	88, 90, 91	24.1	64	1.11	95–97,
5.11	88–91	25.5	71		100, 102
8.33	175	29.5	94, 95	1.15	95, 97
10.4	93			4.14	25
10.9	93–95, 97,	*Joshua*		4.16	25
	101, 102	1.1	139, 145	6.6	107
12.4	89, 175	8.19	25	8.2	159
12.6-8	90	13.1	180, 184	10.26	107
12.6	87, 89	22.5	71		
12.8	87–91	23.1	180, 183,	*2 Samuel*	
13.15	73		184	1.1	139, 145
14.22	88	23.2	180, 181,	2.1	24
15.14	88		184, 185	7.1	146
15.29	88			7.13	154
19.12	154	*Judges*		8.12	124
23.29	67, 71	1.1	139, 145	11.5	124
24.11	159	1.6	77	13.1	146
		1.10	159		
Numbers		1.11	159	*1 Kings*	
3.12	82	1.23	159	1.1-2	42
6.3	93–95, 97,	6.11	75	1.1	180, 184
	100–102	6.12	37, 75	1.16	165
6.5	175	13.2-3	145	2.3	70, 77
6.10	88	13.2	137, 145,	3.2	154
6.13	175		149	5.17	154
7.1	145	13.3	37, 121,	5.19	154
8.16	82		124, 126,	8.17-18	154
11.12	124		145	8.29	206
17.18	159	13.4	93–95, 97,	8.30	206
18.15	78, 81, 82		100–102	8.33	154
25.14	159	13.5	121, 124,	8.35	154
26.30	159		126	8.45	206
26.59	159	13.6	145, 159	8.47	107
28.7	94, 95	13.7	93–95, 97,	10.1	159
			100–102,	11.12	189
Deuteronomy			121, 124	11.26	159
1.1-2	147	13.14	93–95, 97,	12.24	159
1.1	146		100–102	14.21	159
1.3	147	16.17	129	14.31	159
5.16-20	71	17.1	145, 149	15.2	159
6.5	71	19.1	138, 145,	15.10	159
6.13	71, 154		149	16.28	159
6.16	71	19.11	184	16.34	189

18.16	175	25.4	76, 77	21.24	168		
18.31	159	27.1	159	24.14	159		
20.5	198	31.3	76, 77	32.15	107		
20.29	189	33.3	160–62	32.16	165		
21.1	146	33.5	160, 161	35.19	71		
22.19	160, 161, 167	34.14	76	36.11	165		
		35.19	24	63.2	165		
		35.26	76, 77	68.26	67		
2 Kings		36.2	159	70.6	129		
7.12	175	36.5	159, 189	71.7	165		
8.20	189			76.17	165		
8.26	159	Ezra		78.2	65		
10.31	76	1.1	146	79.19	159		
12.1	159	3.4	77	82.6	71		
14.2	159			89.4	190		
14.6	77	Nehemiah		108.8	67		
15.2	159	1.1	146	114.2	190		
15.19	189	8.15	77	114.4	159		
18.2	159	9.3	76	115.4	159		
20.19	189	10.35-36	77	117.1	168		
23.29	189			118.1	76		
24.1	189	Esther		138.13	129		
		1.1	146	142.2	115		
4 Kings (LXX)							
4.17	124	Job		Proverbs			
13.3	124	1.1	142, 145, 147, 149	27.16	154		
13.5	124						
13.7	124	1.6	147	Ecclesiastes			
15.16	124	1.21	129	1.18	165		
		3.16	82				
1 Chronicles		10.13	115	Songs of Solomon			
2.29	159	10.18	129	3.4	124		
4.3	159	15.10	186	8.2	124		
7.15	159	15.35	124				
7.23	124	21.10	124, 131	Isaiah			
8.29	159	27.9	206	5.11	94, 95		
9.35	159	31.15	82	5.22	94, 95		
16.40	76	31.18	129	5.24	76		
17.11	175	32.4	186	7.12	99		
22.9	189	33.19	165	7.14	121, 122, 124–26, 130–32, 197, 199, 200		
22.12	76	38.8	129				
		42.2	115				
2 Chronicles							
2.13	149	Psalms					
3.17	159	1.2	76	8.3	124, 199		
7.8	190	9.3	116	16.10	99		
12.13	159	9.38	107	17.12	166		
14.1	136	17.27	116	24.9	94, 95		
17.9	76	17.32	189	26.18	124		
20.1	146	17.37	189	28.7	94, 95		
23.18	77	21.11	82, 129	28.11	71		

Isaiah – continued		Lamentations		2.11	95
29.9	94, 95	4.18	175	Habakkuk	
29.13	107			1.5	189
39.8	189	Ezekiel			
40.3	65, 84, 145	1.1	145	Zephaniah	
		12.25	189	1.5	160, 161, 164
40.4	109	20.26	81		
40.11	124, 131	20.39	159		
43.25	99	28.15	189	Zechariah	
46.3	129	39.7	159	8.6	115
48.8	129	48.35	159	14.9	159
49.1	129			Malachi	
55.3	84	Daniel		1.1	147
56.7	202	2.18	204	1.14	159
58.6	67	4.5	159	3.1	65
61.1	63	4.16	159	3.22	104
61.2	63	4.26	168	3.23	104, 106
61.11	67	9.11	70	3.24	106
65.22	99	9.13	77		
66.22	159	10.12	194	Apocrypha	
				1 Esdras	
		Hosea		1.31	76
Jeremiah		1.4	199	5.48	77
1.2-3	137	1.9	199	8.7	76
1.2	42	4.11	95	8.8	76
1.3	138	9.14	82	8.9	76
1.5	82	12.4	82	9.39	70
7.18	160, 162	13.4	160	9.48	76
8.2	160–62	14.1	124		
8.8	76			2 Esdras	
11.19	159	Joel		19.6	160, 163, 167
13.13	95	2.28	188		
14.9	159				
16.9	189	Amos		Tobit	
18.7	152	1.1	138	1.16	136
19.13	160–62	1.3	124, 131	3.16	206
19.24	152			4.4	82
20.17	82	1.13	124	5.12	159
20.18	82	2.4	76	6.11	155
23.6	189	5.25-27	162	7.13	70
24.6	99	9.11-12	40	8.20	175
32.17	112–17	9.11	54	10.1	175
32.27	115, 117	9.12	197	12.22	37
32.34	175			15.35	124
37.14	99	Jonah			
39.17	113	1.1	145, 146	Judith	
39.40	99			1.1	136
40.8	99	1.6	140	1.16	165
41.14	175			2.5	165
46.17	99	Micah		8.15	190
49.10	99	1.1	145	8.27	107

Index of References

13.19	107	5.14	190	11.1	138		
		6.18	26, 184	11.4	64		
Wisdom of Solomon		8.8	181, 187	11.10	66		
2.4	159			11.22	188		
6.24	165	**New Testament**		11.24	188		
7.1	82	*Matthew*		12.36	188		
7.16	142	1.16	151	12.40	81, 129		
11.15	166	1.18	130, 166	13.19	107		
11.17	166	1.21	151, 157,	13.35	65		
18.15	166		196, 197,	13.53	138		
			199, 201	15.8	107		
Sirach		1.23	130, 131,	15.13	163		
1.4	82		151, 157,	15.17	81, 129		
3.5	206		196, 197,	15.31	169		
16.1	166		199	16.22	97		
23.15	190	1.25	151, 157,	16.28	142		
35.13	206		197	17.15	169		
37.1	154	1.27	157	18.2	107		
37.26	159	1.49	157	18.35	163		
39.9	159	1.59	157	19.1	138		
40.1	129	1.63	157	19.4	64, 83		
44.7	189	2.1	138, 188	19.12	81, 129		
44.14	159	2.18	64	19.16	115		
46.12	159	2.21	157	21.1	178		
46.14	76	3.11	166	21.4	64		
48.1	104	3.15	39	21.9	7		
48.4	104	4.4	66, 71	21.13	202		
48.10	104, 106,	4.7	71	21.22	202		
	206	4.10	71	22.10	174		
48.12	189, 190	4.18	151	22.31-32	86		
48.18	189	5.3	63	22.32	86		
49.7	82	5.21	66, 91	22.35	70		
50.22	82	5.27	66, 91	22.36	71		
51.11	194, 206,	5.31	64–66	22.37	71		
	207	5.33	65, 66	23.9	163		
		5.38	66	23.47	87		
Baruch		5.43	66	24.2	98		
4.20	189	5.48	163	24.19	128, 130		
		6.7	202	24.22	116		
Bel and the Dragon		6.14	163	24.29	168		
1.2	149	6.21	107	24.35	98		
		6.22	157	25.46	166		
1 Maccabees		6.26	163	26.1	138		
1.1	145	6.32	163	26.3	151		
1.51	24	7.28	138	26.14	151		
3.50	175	8.30	142	26.24	69		
		9.9	151	26.36	151		
2 Maccabees		9.10	138	26.55	123		
2.3	107	9.14	204	27.16-17	151		
4.13	142,	9.48	157	27.22	151		
	149	10.2	151	27.32	152, 155		
4.40	26, 184						

Matthew – continued		11.9	7	1.11-20	10		
27.33	151	11.17	66, 202	1.11	37, 75		
27.40	188	12.19	71	1.13	35, 75,		
27.46	53	12.26	70, 86		120, 133,		
27.48	174	12.28	71		145, 157,		
		12.29	64		162,		
Mark		13.2	98		193–95,		
1–10	29	13.14-20	177		197–203,		
1.1-4	148	13.17	128, 130		206, 210,		
1.1-3	148	13.20	116		211, 215		
1.1	148	13.31	98	1.14	196		
1.2-3	145, 148	13.36	169	1.15	35, 63, 81,		
1.2	65, 69, 73, 148	14.12	69		82, 92–96, 99–102,		
		14.32	151, 159				
1.4	140, 144, 145, 148, 149	14.48	123		129, 166, 171, 174, 178, 179, 211, 216		
		15.29	188				
		15.34	53				
1.5	175	15.36	174				
1.8	166	21.23	130	1.16-17	111, 112		
1.9	138			1.16	108, 109, 149		
1.15	171						
1.23	142	Luke		1.17-18	189		
2.18	204	1–15	213, 214	1.17	31, 63, 103, 104, 108, 109, 111, 133, 165, 206, 209, 215		
2.23	138						
3.1	142	1–8	56				
3.5	107	1–2	1, 2, 10, 21, 24, 25, 29, 30, 32, 38, 55, 172, 173, 201, 213				
4.4	138						
4.15	107						
4.22	98						
5.11	142			1.18	149, 179, 181, 183–86, 188–92, 211, 215		
5.22	151, 152, 155	1	17				
5.25	75	1.1-4	145, 213				
5.29	75	1.4-2.52	126				
6.52	107	1.5-25	37, 126	1.20	175, 176, 178, 179		
7.6	107	1.5-7	145				
7.19	81, 129	1.5	35, 42, 101, 135, 138–55, 157–59, 166, 189, 209, 215	1.23	41, 57, 170, 173, 176, 178, 179, 215		
7.21	107						
7.34	80						
8.17	107						
9.1	142						
9.13	69			1.24-25	31		
9.17-18	169	1.6-7	192	1.24	31, 123–25, 132, 200, 215		
9.18	169	1.6	40				
9.29	202	1.7	26, 34, 37, 42, 133, 145, 149, 179–83, 185, 186, 188–92, 211, 215				
9.35	107			1.25	72, 138		
10.6	83			1.26-38	10, 126		
10.19	71			1.26	151		
10.27	115			1.27	122, 124, 151, 157, 158		
10.30	98						
11.1	10, 178						

Index of References

1.31	57, 121–24, 126, 130, 132, 145, 157, 178, 196, 199–201, 209, 211, 215	1.67-79 1.67 1.68 1.69 1.70 1.75 1.76-77 1.76	28, 209 171, 174 42 159 42 42, 182, 188–91 28 68		90–93, 208, 210, 215
				2.24	66, 68, 69, 74, 76, 85–88, 90–93, 208, 210, 215
1.32-35	32, 36, 49	1.77	68	2.25-45	92
1.32	32	1.78	31	2.25	143, 151
1.34	122, 124	2	17	2.26	182
1.35	31, 32, 78, 80, 124, 200	2.1-3 2.1	136 24, 139, 189	2.27 2.29 2.32	24, 74 119 165
1.36	32, 123, 125, 132, 215	2.6-7 2.6	200, 201, 215 57, 170, 171, 176	2.36	138, 143, 149, 179, 181, 183, 185, 186, 188–92, 211, 215
1.37	27, 112–17, 119, 120, 133, 212, 216	2.8 2.9-14 2.9 2.10	133 10 37, 75 75	2.37 2.39	201, 204 69, 74, 75, 177
1.38	119, 120	2.11	24, 200, 201, 215	2.40	175
1.39	23, 24, 31			2.41-52	39
1.41-42	81, 129	2.13	133, 160–70, 209, 211, 212, 216	2.41-50	37
1.41	82, 123, 130, 171, 174			2.50 2.51	119, 120 119
1.44	81, 82, 123, 129, 130	2.15 2.16 2.17	119, 139 25 119, 120	3–24	1, 2, 5, 10, 34, 38, 54, 55, 58–60, 98, 140, 171, 174, 175, 179, 184, 187–89, 196, 204, 205, 210, 212–14
1.46-55	28, 209	2.19	119		
1.46-47	42, 43, 209	2.20	168		
1.48	28	2.21	24, 57, 81, 82, 123, 125, 129, 130, 132, 170, 171, 176, 215		
1.51-53	42				
1.51	107, 108, 133				
1.57-66	37				
1.57	57, 170, 171, 200, 201, 210, 215	2.22-24 2.22	91, 102 57, 68, 70, 74, 75, 85, 87, 89, 90, 92, 170, 171, 176, 216	3.1-7 3.1-2 3.4 3.5 3.7 3.24 3.25	24, 181 136 69, 72 109 24 74 71
1.59	139				
1.61	143				
1.62	197				
1.63	37, 122, 157	2.23-24	103, 215	4.2	189
1.65	23, 119	2.23	65, 66, 68–70, 72–86,	4.4	54, 69, 71, 73
1.66	24, 107, 108			4.8	54, 69, 71

Luke – continued		8.38	170	15.11	148
4.10	54, 69, 73	8.41	151	16–28	213
4.11	54	8.43	75	16.1	142, 143, 148
4.12	54, 71	8.44	75		
4.16-30	29	8.49	119	16.19	142, 143, 148
4.18-19	54	8.51	170		
4.18	67	8.52	116	16.20	142, 151, 152, 156
4.21	175	9.1	116		
4.25	188, 189	9.18	139	17.4	112
4.28	175	9.27	98, 142, 143	17.11	139
4.33	142, 143			17.26	188, 189
4.36	137, 141	9.28	139, 141	17.28	188, 189
5.1	139	9.29	138	18.2-3	143
5.6	164	9.31	175	18.2	142, 143, 148
5.7	175	9.37	139		
5.12	138, 139	9.38-39	169	18.3	142, 143
5.17	139	9.39	169	18.7	98
5.26	175	9.47	107	18.17	98
5.27	151, 156	9.51	139, 175	18.20	71
5.33-35	203	9.58	167	18.22	116
5.33	201, 203–206	10.1	170	18.27	115, 119
		10.2	202	18.29	142
6.6	142, 143	10.4	203	18.30	98
6.10	116	10.19	98	18.31	177
6.11	175	10.21	167	18.35	139
6.12	188, 189, 201	10.26	70, 71	19.2	138, 151, 156
		10.27	70, 71		
6.15	151	10.38	151, 152, 156	19.7	119
6.17	116, 164, 165			19.9	149
		10.39	151	19.29	10, 89, 139, 151
6.37	98	11.1	139		
7.1	175	11.14	139	19.37	168
7.3	72	11.27	81, 82, 129, 139	19.38	7
7.6	72			19.39-44	29
7.11	139	11.31	138	19.46	69, 201
7.18	89	12.6	89	20.1	139
7.27	69, 72	12.13-21	29	20.9	188
7.31	72	12.20	148	20.28	71, 72
7.33	72	12.34	107	20.37	86
7.35	72	12.56	167	21.6	98
7.37	72, 138	12.59	98	21.18	98
7.40	72	13.10-17	29	21.20-24	177
8.1	139	13.11	138	21.22-24	176
8.3	148	13.14	87	21.22	175–78
8.5	167	13.16	149	21.23	128–32, 177
8.12	107	13.19	167		
8.17	98	13.35	98	21.24	41, 173, 175, 177, 178
8.22	139	14.1	139		
8.27	190	14.19	88		
8.29	190	14.23	174	21.25	167
8.32	142, 143	15.10	140	21.26	167, 168

Index of References

21.29	116	1.43	148	2.47	168		
21.32-33	98	2.11	148	3.1	201		
21.33	97, 98	2.12	190	3.2	81, 82, 119, 129, 151		
21.37	151, 188	2.19	188				
22.1	151	2.20	188				
22.3	151	3.1	144	3.8-9	168		
22.14	170	3.4	81, 129	3.10	175		
22.16	98, 175	3.15-16	166	3.12	110		
22.18	98	3.31	148	3.13-26	110		
22.37	177	4.4	166	3.18	175		
22.39	151	4.5	23	3.21-22	71		
22.45	201	4.46	144	3.21	72		
22.47	151	4.52	190	3.22-23	67, 110		
22.56	170	5.1	144	3.22	73, 109, 110		
22.67	98	5.3	165				
22.68	98	5.5	144	3.25	72		
23.5	72	7.23	70	4.8	174		
23.27	164, 165	7.38	81, 129	4.31	174		
23.29	81, 82, 129, 200	10.34	65, 71	4.34	143		
		12.1	144	4.36	187		
23.33	151	12.13	7	5.1	151, 152, 156		
23.49	168	14.9	190				
23.50	138, 151, 156	14.27	168	5.7	139, 141		
		15.25	71	5.12	166		
24.8	156	18.12	123	5.14	164		
24.13-35	29	19.7	75	5.16	160, 169		
24.13	89, 151	19.29	174	5.17	175		
24.18	151, 189	21.6	165	5.21	149		
24.31-32	80			5.34	151, 152, 156		
24.32	107	Acts					
24.38	107	1–15	17, 24, 29, 210	5.37	165, 188, 189		
24.44	70, 175, 177	1.2	166	6.4	201		
24.45	80	1.4	203	7	62		
24.46	69	1.14	201, 203	7.3	72		
24.53	168	1.15	189	7.6	72		
		1.16	175	7.8	200		
John		1.20	67, 72	7.14	189		
1.1-5	144	1.23	151	7.16	119		
1.1-2	144	2.1	175	7.20	200		
1.3-4	144	2.2	166	7.23	41, 149, 173, 175		
1.5	144	2.4	174				
1.6	137, 144, 145, 147–49	2.5	166	7.29	200		
		2.8	200	7.30	41, 173, 175		
		2.16	85				
1.9	147	2.17	188	7.32	63		
1.23	84	2.18	189	7.33	72		
1.29	147	2.28	175	7.35	168		
1.30	166	2.33	119	7.37	72, 110, 149		
1.35	148	2.42	201				

Acts – continued		12.23	37	18.2	151, 152, 156
7.40	63	12.41	188		
7.42-43	162	13.1	143	18.5	187
7.42	69, 72, 73, 162, 167	13.3	204	18.7	151, 152, 156
		13.6	151		
7.51	187	13.9	174	18.14	166
7.56	80	13.14	189	18.15	75
8.1	166	13.20	190	18.24	151, 152, 156
8.8	141	13.29	177		
8.9	151, 152, 156	13.32	166	18.25	187
		13.33	69, 72, 200	19.14	143
8.26	37	13.34	84	19.21	175
8.27	138	13.38	70, 75	19.24	151, 152, 156
9.3	169	13.40	85		
9.10-12	151	13.41	98	19.29	175
9.10	142, 143, 152, 156	13.45	175	20.9	151, 152, 156
		13.48	166		
9.11-12	156	13.52	175	20.24	119
9.14	119	14.1	164	21.10	151, 152, 156
9.15	149	14.8	81, 82, 129		
9.17	174			21.20	75
9.19	139, 141	14.15	112	21.22	164
9.22	168	14.23	204	21.24	75
9.23	41, 173, 175	15.5	70	21.36	160, 169
		15.14	165	22.3	166, 200
9.33	151, 152, 156	15.15-16	73	22.6	169
		15.15	66, 69, 72	22.28	200
9.35	112	15.16-18	54	23.5	69, 73
9.36	142, 143, 151, 156	15.16-17	40	24.14	177
		15.16	73	24.25	199, 200
9.37	189	15.17	197	24.27	41, 173, 175
9.40	112	15.19	112		
9.43	119	15.22	151	26.10	119
10.1	151, 156	15.37	151	26.19	162, 163, 166, 168
10.2	202	16–28	143, 156		
10.4	201	16.1	142, 143, 151, 156	26.20	112
10.6	119			27.1	150, 151, 156
10.12	167	16.5	187		
10.14	116	16.11	6	27.8	151
10.22	119, 120	16.13	202	27.16	151
10.31	202	16.14	80, 151, 152, 156	27.23	37
10.36	149			28.3	164
10.38	151	16.16	202	28.7	151, 156
11.6	167	16.18	122	28.12	190
11.21	112	16.20	151	28.22	119
11.28	151, 156	16.26	141	28.23	70
12.5	202	17.3	80	28.26	98
12.7	37, 75	17.4	164		
12.8	75	17.9	119	Romans	
12.13	150, 151, 156	17.26	167	1.17	66, 69
		17.34	151, 156	1.27	83

2.24	69	*Galatians*		*Hebrews*	
3.4	66, 69	1.15	81, 129	5.7	202
3.10	69	3.28	83	7.5	149
3.20	116			8.10	108
4.17	69	*Ephesians*		10.28	70
4.18	85	1.18	107	11.11	184
4.19	81	4.18	107	11.22	149
8.36	69	5.19	107		
9.13	69	6.5	107	*James*	
9.27	149			1.15	123
9.33	69	*Philippians*		3.14	107
10.15	66, 69	1.4	205	5.3	188
11.8	69	3.19	81, 129	5.20	165
11.26	69	4.3	123		
12.19	66			*1 Peter*	
15.3	69	*Colossians*		1.16	66
15.9	69	4.10	6	3.20	138, 188
15.11	168	4.14	6, 7	4.8	165
15.21	69			*2 Peter*	
16.18	81, 129	*1 Thessalonians*		2.1	140
		5.3	130		
1 Corinthians				*1 John*	
1.29	116	*2 Thessalonians*		2.18	140
1.31	69	2.16	166	3.19-20	107
2.9	69, 108				
6.9	83	*1 Timothy*		*Jude*	
6.13	81, 129	1.10	83	9	70
9.9	70	2.1	205		
10.7	66	6.9	166	*Revelation*	
14.21	71, 202			6.8	159
		2 Timothy		9.11	159
2 Corinthians		3.1	188	10.9-10	81, 129
3.7	149	4.11	6	12.2	130
3.13	149			12.5	83
3.15	107	*Titus*		12.13	83
6.11	107	1.12	130	16.18	140
7.11	187			19.5	168
8.15	69	*Philemon*		21.27	116
9.9	69	1.9	184		

OTHER ANCIENT REFERENCES

Pseudepigrapha		*4 Maccabees*		*Testament of Reuben*	
3 Maccabees		5.4	155	1.10	95
2.1	205	9.15	168		
4.2	107	11.3	168	Qumran	
6.18	168	15.28	149	*4Q246*	
6.38	190			1.7	32
				2.1	32

Philo
De ebrietate
127   95
138   95

De mutatione nominum
121   196

Josephus
Antiquities of the Jews (AJ)
11.145.2   153
18.23   145
18.63   140

Life of Josephus (Vit.)
266.4   187

The Jewish War (BJ)
1.432   153
2.118   153
2.481   153
2.585   153
4.37.1   153
4.155   153
6.186.1   153
6.201   153
7.5.2   205
18.276   205

New Testament
Pseudepigraph
Acta Joannis
3.2   153

Acta Pauli
4.2.1   154
4.26.3   154
4.27.6   154

Classical
Alexander of
Aphrodisias
#013
141.20   187
142.7   187
142.16   187

Appianus. Maced.
18.3   140

Diodorus Siculus
3.52.4   139
5.24.3   153
16.41.1   153
18.40.2   153

Diogenes Laertius
Vitae Philosophorum
10.35.7   187

Dionius Casius
68.4   187

Epiphanius
Anc.
80.2.3   192

Eusebius
Historia ecclesiastica
6.25.6   5

Galenus
3.641   187
19.693   94

Herodotus
6.056.01   166
VIII.72   144

Hippocrates
Aphorisms
5.46.2   127

The Diseases of Women
I.075.007 127
III.213.027 127

Irenaeus
Adversus haereses
3.1.1   5

Joannes Chrysostomus
#112
53.383.34 192
#137
50.809.1   176
50.809.6   176
#304
61.738.45 176
#442

58.29   176
Origen
#005
6.17.97.3 192
#017
56.3   176
#048
12.116.27 192
#72
51.233.16 192
#078
17.316.34 192
#131
50.788.18 192
#132
50.790.8   192

Palladius
#001
70.3.8   176

Plutarch
Moralia
III.202.B 153

Tertullian
Adversus Marcionem
4.2.2   5

Theodoretus
#26
81.637.89 176
81.804.10 176

Thucydides
3.36.4   155
4.39.2   155
7.42.2   155
7.49.4   155

Xenophon
Anabasis
I.iv.4   152
I.iv.11   152
I.v.10   152
Historia Graecae
I.iv.2   152
I.vi.29   152

INDEX OF AUTHORS

Adamson, J.B.   123
Allison, D.C. Jr.   196
Anderson, H.   144
Archer, G.L.   67, 69, 93, 100
Argyle, A.W.   14

Barr, J.   55
Barrett, C.K.   68
Beentjes, P.C.   104, 154
Benoit, P.   171–73, 182, 183, 188
Beyer, K.   56
Black, M.   24
Bock, D.L.   6, 32, 67, 68, 73, 78, 79, 81, 84, 88, 90, 97, 106, 113, 114, 118, 122, 125, 127, 168, 172, 178, 182, 185, 202, 203, 205
Böhl, E.   63, 64, 78
Bovon, F.   6, 101, 139, 182, 183
Bratcher, G.   78
Brown, R.E.   24, 35, 36, 68, 72, 74, 88, 91, 97, 113, 117, 119, 124, 134, 136, 137, 139, 144, 149, 150, 152, 157, 158, 160, 169, 170, 172, 182, 185, 194–96, 202, 209
Bruce, F.F.   5, 7, 54, 164, 165, 167
Bultmann, R.   91
Burkitt, F.C.   193
Burney, C.F.   31–33, 46, 48
Buth, R.   209

Cadbury, H.J.   8, 11, 12, 15
Carson, D.A.   144
Charles, R.H.   47
Chirichigno, G.C.   67, 69, 93, 100
Coleridge, M.   214
Conybeare, F.C.   11
Creed, J.M.   177

Dalman, G.   46, 56, 134

Danker, F.W.   115, 177
Davies, W.D.   196
Deissmann, A.   7–13, 15, 18–20, 22
Delling, G.   56
Dilella, A.A.   206
Dodd, C.H.   177
Drury, J.   213

Elliott, J.K.   148
Ellis, E.E.   5, 6, 122
Emerton, J.A.   14
Evans, C.F.   5, 6, 8, 32, 97, 136, 182, 202

Fanning, B.M.   209
Farris, S.   23, 27, 28, 30, 31, 33, 34, 40, 58, 194, 196, 207
Farstad, A.L.   62, 63, 68
Field, F.   114, 115, 117
Fitzmyer, J.A.   5–7, 14, 15, 24, 32, 36–38, 46, 49, 68, 72, 78, 83, 88, 90, 91, 97, 100, 106, 115, 117, 126–28, 131, 134, 136, 138, 141, 160, 161, 168, 172, 176, 177, 182, 183, 205, 209, 213, 214

Gehman, H.S.   15, 16
George, A.   151, 158
Gilmour, M.   7
Goulder, M.D.   38, 42, 213
Grant, M.   94, 187
Greijdanus, S.   168, 200
Grintz, J.M.   14
Guelich, R.A.   144, 148
Gundry, R.H.   203
Guthrie, D.   7, 32, 46, 60

Hagner, D.A.   163, 168, 196
Harnack, A. von   25, 28, 33, 38, 134
Hawkins, J.C.   58

Heimerdinger, J.   150, 170, 200
Hengel, M.   5
Hiberg, I.   7
Hobart, W.K.   6, 7
Hodges, Z.C.   62, 63, 68
Holtz, T.   64, 72, 73, 79, 81, 84, 88, 89, 201
Hort, F.J.A.   62, 63, 68, 93
Horton, F.L. Jr.   13, 14, 17, 45, 52, 53, 58, 67, 211
Howard, W.F.   47, 48, 51, 97
Hühn, E.   63

Jeremias, J.   98, 114, 116, 135, 151, 159, 162, 166, 172, 182, 188, 196
Johnson, F.   63
Johnson, L.T.   15, 78
Johnson, S.E.   71
Jung, C.W.   21

Kaiser, W.C.   64
Klostermann, E.   94, 96, 97
Knox, W.L.   78
Koester, H.   46
Koet, B.J.   174
Kümmel, W.G.   46, 59, 60

Lagrange, M.-J.   46, 139, 181, 194
Laurentin, R.   125, 131, 133, 194
Leaney, A.R.C.   6, 97
Liddell, H.G.   56, 57, 82, 87, 94, 114, 129, 139, 152, 166, 172, 184, 185, 191, 194
Liefield, W.L.   122
Lindars, B.   145
Longenecker, R.   62

Machen, G.   124, 150, 152, 162
Maddox, R.   6
Maloney, E.C.   13, 46, 48, 51, 58
Manson, W.   177
Marshall, I.H.   6, 24, 32, 46, 54, 68, 80, 84, 88, 90, 92, 96, 97, 109, 111, 115, 116, 118, 126–28, 137, 138, 141, 150, 151, 160–64, 167, 168, 177, 182, 185, 188, 195, 203, 205
Martin, R.A.   28–31, 213
Marxsen, W.   60
Mealand, D.L.   21, 22, 56, 199
Menken, M.J.J.   66, 84
Metzger, B.M.   66, 71
Moor, C.   155
Morris, L.   144

Most, W.G.   18
Moulton, J.H.   11, 12, 16, 18, 19, 46–48, 51, 52, 97, 134, 141
Moyise, S.   103
Müller, M.   8, 54
Mussies, G.   14, 69, 71, 74, 152
Myers, J.M.   163

New, D.S.   65, 68, 109
Nolland, J.   5, 6, 32, 46, 54, 77, 78, 80, 86, 97, 100, 106, 113–15, 122, 125–27, 133, 137, 138, 149, 150, 152, 157, 158, 160, 162, 163, 172, 181, 182, 195

O'Donnell, M.B.   36
O'Fearghail, F.   36, 39–42, 100, 134, 172–74, 211, 213
Oliver, H.H.   23
Olmstead, A.T.   13

Plummer, A.   5–7, 17, 95, 97, 125, 129, 136, 137, 139, 166, 170, 180, 203
Porter, S.E.   9, 13, 14, 16, 18–24, 31, 42, 43, 46, 53–56, 58, 81, 112, 209
Prabhu, G.M.S.   128

Ravens, D.   213
Rehkopf, F.   50
Reiling, J.   71, 91
Reiser, M.   144
Rese, M.   62, 63, 67
Ringgren, H.   67, 103, 201
Robertson, A.T.   92
Rothe, R.   8

Sahlin, H.   24, 25, 31, 32, 89, 112, 125, 133, 180, 181
Sanders, J.A.   67, 114
Sanderson, M.L.   38, 39
Schmidt, D.D.   51
Schrader, C.   155
Schramm, T.   205
Schürmann, H.   126–28, 131
Scott, R.   56, 57, 82, 87, 94, 114, 129, 139, 152, 166, 172, 184, 185, 191, 194
Silva, M.   16, 18, 19
Simpson, D.C.   155
Skehan, P.W.   206
Smyth, H.W.   97, 99, 184, 189, 191
Sparks, H.F.D.   7, 10, 14, 15, 46, 55
Stanton, V.H.   157

Index of Authors

Stein, R.H.   60
Stendahl, K.   62, 64, 67, 86
Steyn, J.G.   54, 63, 64, 66, 67, 84, 110, 210
Stock, G.   11
Stock, K.   112
Sturz, F.W.   152
Swellengrebel, J.L.   71, 91
Swete, H.B.   8, 63, 64, 78, 94

Taylor, V.   148
Torrey, C.C.   12, 13, 23, 24, 27, 31, 32, 46
Turner, N.   16, 17, 20, 26, 27, 34, 92, 97, 98, 106, 116–18, 134, 142, 147, 182, 183, 186, 187

Weingreen, J.   146
Westcott, B.F.   62, 63, 67, 68, 93
Wilcox, M.   46, 51–54, 64–66, 75, 115, 162, 210–12
Winter, P.   25–27, 33, 34, 72, 105, 106, 112, 113, 116, 133, 160–62, 181, 182, 195
Wise, M.O.   14
Wyttenbach, D.   152

Zerwick, S.J.M.   151, 205
Zimmerman, F.   18, 31, 32, 133